# Choreographing the Folk

# Choreographing the Folk

## *The Dance Stagings of Zora Neale Hurston*

**Anthea Kraut**

University of Minnesota Press
Minneapolis

Quotations from Zora Neale Hurston's correspondence and concert programs reprinted with the permission of the Zora Neale Hurston Trust.

Portions of the Introduction, chapter 2, and chapter 5 were previously published as "Re-scripting Origins: Zora Neale Hurston's Stagings of Black Vernacular Dance," in *Embodying Liberation: The Black Body in American Dance,* ed. Alison Goeller and Dorothea Fischer-Hornung (Hamburg: Lit-Verlag, 2001), 59–77. Portions of chapter 2 were published as "Recovering Hurston, Reconsidering the Choreographer," *Women and Performance: A Journal of Feminist Theory* 16, no. 1 (March 2006): 71–90; reproduced with the permission of Taylor and Francis, http://www.tandf.co.uk/journals. Portions of chapter 5 were previously published as "Between Primitivism and Diaspora: The Dance Performances of Josephine Baker, Zora Neale Hurston, and Katherine Dunham," *Theatre Journal* 55, no. 3 (2003): 433–50; copyright The Johns Hopkins University Press; reprinted with permission of The Johns Hopkins University Press. Portions of chapter 6 were published as "Everybody's Fire Dance: Zora Neale Hurston and American Dance History," *The Scholar and Feminist Online* 3, no. 2 (Winter 2005), http://www.barnard.edu/sfonline/hurston/kraut_01.htm.

Published by the University of Minnesota Press
111 Third Avenue South, Suite 290
Minneapolis, MN 55401-2520
http://www.upress.umn.edu

Library of Congress Cataloging-in-Publication Data

Kraut, Anthea.
    Choreographing the folk : the dance stagings of Zora Neale Hurston / Anthea Kraut.
       p.    cm.
    Includes bibliographical references and index.
    ISBN 978-0-8166-4711-8 (hc : alk. paper) — ISBN 978-0-8166-4712-5 (pb : alk. paper)
    1. African American dance—History.    2. Hurston, Zora Neale—Criticism
and interpretation.    3. Hurston, Zora Neale—Knowledge—Folklore.    4. African
Americans—Folklore.    5. African Americans in the performing arts.    6. Dance—
United States—History.    7. Jazz dance—History.    8. Choreography.    I. Title.
    GV1624.7.A34K73 2008
    792.8089'96073—dc22

                                                                2008014876

Printed in the United States of America on acid-free paper

The University of Minnesota is an equal-opportunity educator and employer.

15  14  13  12  11  10  09  08                    10  9  8  7  6  5  4  3  2  1

*To the memory of my grandmother,* **Marion Hyman,**
*who, well into her nineties,*
*continued to rave about* **Zora Neale Hurston**

# Contents

The roots of this project lie, in some respects, in the Chicago-area dance studios at which I spent much of my childhood and adolescence. Although I studied ballet and modern from an early age, jazz dance was my greatest love; something about the physicalization of rhythm always felt the most gratifying to me. While I soon noticed that different studios and teachers had different conceptions of what jazz dance entailed, the focus on articulating rhythm was a constant. The jazz classes I attended shared another feature: none provided any historical context for the form. In these predominantly white spaces, no mention was made of the African American origins of the idiom, although the recorded music that we used was more often than not composed or performed by African American artists.

It was not until my junior year at Carleton College, a small liberal arts school in Minnesota, when I took a course titled "Black Dance: A Historical Survey," that I confronted the racial dynamics that went unspoken in those suburban jazz dance classes. Using Lynn Fauley Emery's *Black Dance from 1619 to Today* as our main text, Professor Mary Easter led us through a survey of nineteenth-century blackface minstrelsy (the first I had heard of this racist and popular form of entertainment), the social history of the Lindy Hop, the pioneering concert dance efforts of Katherine Dunham and Pearl Primus, and the more recent achievements of Alvin Ailey and Bill T. Jones. Like a news flash, it became clear just how much jazz dance, that quintessentially American form, owed to African-derived traditions. Excited by this new knowledge, I realized that the same issues that interested me in my literature and history courses—the artistic and cultural implications of America's complicated and disturbing racial history—were woven into the very fabric of my extracurricular activities. At the same time, the fact that this was a revelation vexed me. Why had it been so easy to participate in and become passionate about a dance form without learning its history? How had my white body become the site for the continued erasure of black bodies from the received history of American culture?

As I continued my study of American dance history in graduate school at Northwestern University and grew increasingly committed to dance studies as an academic discipline, my interest in "invisibilized" histories, to borrow Brenda Dixon Gottschild's term for the systematic omission of the Africanist influences on American performance practices, only deepened. When, thanks to a tip from Professor Susan Manning, I learned that Zora Neale Hurston, a writer whose 1937 novel *Their Eyes Were Watching God* first propelled me into African American literature classes in college, had staged a concert with a spectacular Bahamian dance finale about which little was known, I was more than intrigued. What began as a more or less straightforward quest to piece together whatever information I could find about Hurston's theatrical revues gradually expanded and grew more complex as I uncovered connections between Hurston and a number of leading dance figures. To a great extent, the recovery project also became a case study of invisibilization—an attempt to understand the conditions that enable certain subjects and performances to be forgotten—as well as an inquiry of the implications of restoring those subjects and performances to the historical record. While the chronicle that follows could be relayed in different ways by different authors, it is important that the story get told. For, although Hurston's stage work was not a direct source for the various brands of jazz dancing currently being taught and performed, it did play a role in the composition of American dance as we know it today. And it should be all of our responsibilities to learn and transmit the histories of the forms and formations we inherit and perpetuate.

To that end, the next seven chapters aim to transmit the history of Hurston's theatrical productions and their influence on the American dance landscape in the 1930s. The Introduction lays the groundwork for the book by acquainting readers with Hurston's revues and the group of Bahamian dancers with whom she worked and assessing their significance for Hurston scholars, dance scholars, and those interested in the place of the "folk" in American culture.

Chapter 1, "Commercialization and the Folk," examines the paradoxes that undergirded Hurston's project of producing a concert of folk material "in the raw" within the commercial sphere. My focus here is equally on Hurston's discursive efforts to assert naturalness and the various market concerns that mediated her artistic decisions. An account of Hurston's early experiences in the theatre provides a context for understanding how she came to conceptualize her concert as a corrective to extant models for staging African American folk forms. Promoting a production she hoped would counteract the stereotyped, racist images of blackness being perpetuated in the theatrical marketplace, Hurston drew emphatic distinctions between the "untampered with" nature of her revue and contemporaneous stage renderings. Yet in mobilizing the rhetoric of authenticity, Hurston placed her concert squarely within a long tradition of commercialized representations of black culture. Her revues thus force one to confront the ways in which she was simultaneously critical of and complicit with the marketplace's operation and effects.

Chapter 2, "Choreography and the Folk," takes up the complicated issue of choreographic authorship with respect to Hurston's staging of black folk dance. First contemplating the ways in which the term "choreographer" has been understood historically, I then parse the relationship between Hurston and the Bahamian Fire Dance that appeared as the finale to her revue, probing the process by which she encountered, researched, learned, documented, and taught the dance to her assembled troupe of performers. Although she did not function as a choreographer in the conventional sense of composing new dances, Hurston's transformation of the Fire Dance folk cycle from its Caribbean vernacular incarnation to its American theatrical manifestation and her cultivation of an aura of folk spontaneity required her to perform choreographic labor, however unrecognized. This chapter also explores Hurston's strategic choreography of her own artistic role—the deliberate calculations she made as to how much and what kind of artistic credit to claim outwardly for her concert. An interrogation of how Hurston straddled the line between authorship and authenticity provides insight into the ways in which she negotiated this delicate terrain, even while raising more wide-reaching questions about the criteria used to assign attributions in the field of dance.

Chapter 3, "Producing *The Great Day*," elucidates the material and social relations that governed the 1932 New York debut of Hurston's folk concert. Enmeshed in a complex web of patronage, Hurston found herself constrained by some of the very same forces that enabled her to produce her concert. In particular, this chapter uncovers a series of power struggles for artistic control over *The Great Day* between Hurston, her wealthy white patron Charlotte Osgood Mason, and Alain Locke, the esteemed black intellectual who served as a liaison between Mason and Hurston. Weighing the extant correspondence between Hurston, Mason, and Locke against Hurston's autobiographical account of her concert, and against embodied actions only alluded to in the archive, I reconstruct the events leading up to and surrounding the January 1932 premiere of *The Great Day*. An examination of the production process exposes how steeped Hurston's stage venture was in contests for control over the representation of black folk expression. It also shows how Hurston took advantage of the nature of performance to maneuver around the impositions of those with power over her and to carve out a space for her own carefully planned staging of black folk expression.

Chapter 4, "Hurston's Embodied Theory of the Folk," provides an in-depth analysis of *The Great Day* to reveal what the concert tells us about the distinctive vision of black folk culture that Hurston sought to communicate to American audiences. Extant programs, script drafts, research accounts, and sound recordings make it possible to reconstruct much of the content of the revue. Arranged around a single day in the life of a railroad work camp in rural Florida, *The Great Day* exhibited the songs, rhythms, and movements that accompanied and defined the camp's activities, from the first stirring of the workers at dawn, to the physically demanding laying of the rail, to the recreational games, songs, and dances that lasted through the evening hours. Notwithstanding promotional claims that her program offered expressive forms "untouched," Hurston deliberately orchestrated the idioms collected during her research expeditions to enact her particular conception of black folk culture on and through the bodies of her performers. Although cloaked in the rhetoric of authenticity, Hurston's concert brought to view some of the very workings that such rhetoric customarily elides, exposing the economic forces, aesthetic codes, migration patterns, and social relations that mediate black folk expression.

Whereas chapters 1 through 4 focus on either the conditions of production or the content of Hurston's folk revues, chapter 5, "Interpreting the Fire Dance," foregrounds the reception of her stage material. An examination of the critical response—partially recoverable in newspaper accounts and reviews—establishes that, if *The Great Day* advanced in embodied form Hurston's theory of the folk, white spectators in particular did not always discern the nuances of her theory. Instead, reigning stereotypes about blacks as exotic, inherently primitive beings tended to overshadow the more complex relationship between Afro-Caribbean, southern rural, and northern urban black vernacular idioms that Hurston set out to delineate. The resulting tension between paradigmatic notions of black primitivism and an emerging awareness of transnational black culture points to an important conflict over the interpretation of black folk dance in the 1930s. Tracking the varied ideological discourses surrounding Hurston's concert and the Bahamian Fire Dance in specific, this chapter reveals the highly contingent nature of meaning with regard to representations of black folk culture. The polysemous qualities of the Fire Dance, I suggest, were responsible not only for its broad appeal but also for its ability to register dominant and resistant constructions of racial identity.

Chapter 6, "Black Authenticity, White Artistry," turns to the contests over artistic credit with respect to the Bahamian Fire Dance. Here I chart the involvement of six prominent white female dance artists with Hurston's folk material between 1932 and 1936: jazz dancer Mura Dehn; Neighborhood Playhouse director Irene Lewisohn; modern dancers Doris Humphrey, Ruth St. Denis, and Helen Tamiris; and the ballroom dance icon Irene Castle. Inasmuch as these interracial alliances testify to the extensive influence of Hurston's stage work within the dance world, they also illuminate the racialized dynamics that worked to obscure that influence. Scrutinizing the particularized power relations and allocation of artistic credit in each collaboration, this chapter shows how the basic differences in perception that attended white and black dancing bodies became a key agent of invisibilization. The chapter culminates in a discussion of the First National Dance Congress and Festival, held in New York in May 1936, in which both Hurston and the Bahamian dancers whom she first assembled in 1932 played a role. A concerted effort to convene and classify a cross section of dance traditions, the Congress and Festival illustrates the remarkably entwined nature of racial and artistic categories in the 1930s and the rigorous policing of the boundaries between them.

Finally, the Coda addresses the activity of Hurston and the Bahamian dancers post-1930s and takes stock of some of the more far-reaching implications of their representations of black folk dance. While the purview of this book is confined to a single decade and a set of productions that took place therein, the connections that can be traced between the concerns that materialized in Hurston's stagings and those that surfaced in subsequent American performances point to the ongoing legacy of her choreography of the folk.

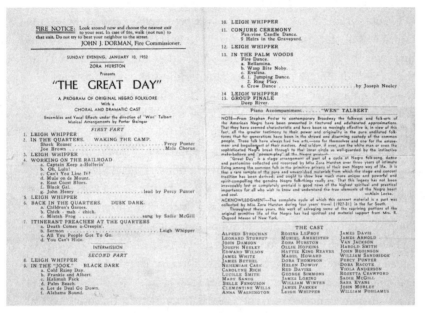

**Figure 1.** The Great Day: A Program of Original Negro Folklore, 1932. Reproduction courtesy of the Prentiss Taylor Papers, 1885–1991, Archives of American Art, Smithsonian Institution.

# Introduction: Rediscovering Hurston's Embodied Representations of the Folk

On Sunday, January 10, 1932, at the John Golden Theatre in New York, the African American artist Zora Neale Hurston premiered a concert of black folkways based on the anthropological research she had conducted in the southern United States and the Bahamas during the late 1920s. Presented under the title *The Great Day* and billed as "A Program of Original Negro Folklore," Hurston's revue traced a single day in the life of a railroad work camp in Florida, from the waking of the camp at dawn to a climactic Bahamian Fire Dance cycle at midnight.[1] In between, the concert advanced from a scene in which men performed various work songs as they spiked and lined the rails to a series of movement-oriented children's games back at the camp. An animated open-air sermon and several rousing spirituals brought the first act to a close. After a brief intermission, the second act picked up the narrative in the interior of a "jook," where the adult camp members passed the nighttime hours playing card and dice games, singing the blues, and performing social dances to piano and guitar music. Finally, camp members retreated to the woods, where in ring formation, a group of Bahamian migrant workers sang West Indian melodies and enacted the three-part Fire Dance as drummers provided dynamic rhythmic accompaniment.[2]

Representing Hurston's directorial debut, *The Great Day* was, in her words, "well received by both audience and critics."[3] New York papers such as the *Times*, the *Sun*, the *Herald Tribune*, the *Evening Post*, the *Amsterdam News*, and the *Age* all gave it favorable reviews. In addition to critics, the predominantly white audience included "many noted artists and composers," as Cora Gary Illidge reported in the *Amsterdam News*.[4] Among those present were the African American scholar Alain Locke and the African American writer Sterling Brown, both of whom traveled from Washington, D.C., to see the production;[5] the African American composer and choral director Hall Johnson; the white author, critic, and patron Carl Van Vechten, who came at Hurston's personal request;[6] white opera composer and music critic Joseph Deems Taylor; white opera singer Louise Homer; and the German-born patron of the arts Otto Kahn.[7] The attendance of such distinguished artists and intellectuals is an indication of how noteworthy an event Hurston's folk production was on the New York cultural landscape.

Although she made no money on *The Great Day*, Hurston continued to stage versions of the concert in the next few years. Using the titles *From Sun to Sun, All De Live Long Day*, and *Singing Steel*, she mounted the revue at the New School for Social Research in New York in March 1932, in a number of cities around Florida between 1933 and 1934, and in Chicago in November 1934. Archival evidence suggests that she produced variants of the folk concert as late as 1952. While Hurston consistently reworked the program—inserting and removing certain scenes, accommodating different casts, and occasionally performing a dance solo herself—the basic structure of the concert and the Bahamian folk dance finale remained constant. Besides putting on these full-length productions, Hurston presented music and dance excerpts from the revue at several venues in New York, twice at the National Folk Festival (in St. Louis in 1934 and in Washington, D.C., in 1938), and under the auspices of the Florida Federal Writers' Project in Orlando. Along the way, Hurston's folk stagings captured the attention of singer and actor Paul Robeson, NAACP leader Walter White, the Russian émigré jazz dancer Mura Dehn, theatre director Irene Lewisohn, modern dance pioneer Ruth St. Denis, and ballroom dance icon Irene Castle.

Concurrent with Hurston's series of productions, a group of Bahamian dancers whom Hurston assembled and trained for *The Great Day* went on to have a significant stage career in New York. Led by dancer-drummers known as Motor Boat and Stew Beef and fluctu-ating in size and composition, this ensemble performed throughout the 1930s, appearing on Broadway, at Lewisohn Stadium, at the First National Dance Congress and Festival, at the Cotton Club, and at the New York World's Fair. Along the way, they attracted the notice of and collaborated with such well-known white dance artists as Doris Humphrey, Helen Tamiris, and Mura Dehn, as well as with prominent African American artists like composer Hall Johnson, choreographer Leonard Reed, and the Savoy Ballroom Lindy Hoppers.

Why did performances by Hurston and the Bahamian dancers pique the interest of such an assortment of artists, and why is so little known today about these productions? What did Hurston gain by turning to the stage to present the southern black folk material that defined her life's work, and what should we make of her explicit en-gagement with dance? Where do the stagings of Bahamian folk dance fit on the broader terrain of early-twentieth-century American dance? This book sets out to answer these questions by training its eye on the string of overlooked but influential performances mounted by Hurston and the Bahamian dancers. *Choreographing the Folk* recovers the his-tory of Hurston's theatrical concerts, probes the role of dance within them, and traces the impact of her folk choreography throughout the 1930s. In doing so, I aim to illuminate both a largely forgotten chapter of Hurston's career and the often contested place of the black vernacu-lar in American culture more generally.

Although Hurston never pursued dance to the exclusion of other media, her staging of choreographed movement constituted a crucial aspect of her approach to representing the folk. A prolific author and committed folklorist, Hurston was skilled in a range of expressive modes and experimented throughout her life with various ways of ren-dering the black folk culture of the rural South. Born in Alabama in 1891, and raised in the all-black town of Eatonville, Florida, Hurston moved to New York City in 1925, where she joined the circle of art-ists and intellectuals whose collective creative output was part of the New Negro movement. The Harlem Renaissance, as the movement was later dubbed, sought to combat racism through artistic means. Over the next thirty years, in addition to directing, producing, and perform-ing in her own theatrical revues and copyrighting numerous plays, Hurston published four novels, an autobiography, two books of folk-lore, and copious short stories and essays. She also conducted research for the federal government's Work Projects Administration (originally named the Works Progress Administration) and served as a consultant for Paramount Pictures. Although Hurston fell out of the public eye toward the end of her life and died in poverty in 1960, she was rediscovered and canonized in the last quarter of the twentieth century.

Mainstream culture's recent notice of Hurston (a 2005 made-for-television movie of her 1937 novel *Their Eyes Were Watching God,* a 2003 postage stamp in her honor) comes on the heels of her growing prominence within the academy. Since the late 1970s, scholars have lavished attention on many of Hurston's literary productions, granting *Their Eyes* in particular a place in the American, black, and feminist canons. Beginning in the 1980s, critics began to consider Hurston's achievements apart from her published fiction, recovering her contributions to the fields of anthropology, folklore, and, to a lesser extent, theatre.[8] The late 1980s and early 1990s also saw several theatrical productions based on Hurston's life and work. These included George C. Wolfe's *Spunk,* an adaptation of three of her short stories; a production of *Mule Bone,* the previously unrealized play on which Hurston collaborated with Langston Hughes in 1931; and a one-woman show by Ruby Dee called *My Name Is Zora.*[9] In 1997, ten unpublished plays authored by Hurston were rediscovered at the Library of Congress, and in 2002, one of those plays, *Polk County,* premiered in Washington, D.C. The publication at the start of the twenty-first century of Valerie Boyd's *Wrapped in Rainbows,* the first new biography of Hurston since Robert Hemenway's landmark 1977 version, and of Carla Kaplan's edited volume of Hurston's collected correspondence suggests that scholarly interest in this multifaceted black woman has yet to wane.[10] Yet however "hot" Hurston has become within and beyond academia, to date, her explicit engagement with black diasporic folk dance and her participation in the field of American dance remain almost entirely unacknowledged and unexplored.

Hurston's successive stagings of black music and dance demand consideration for a number of reasons. Her revues formed an integral part of her multidisciplinary efforts to expose and elucidate black folk idioms. They were also concrete illustrations of the "*real* Negro art theatre" that she was eager to establish. In addition, Hurston's concerts advanced a unique vision of black creative expression, one that was distinct from the depictions found in her written work and from contemporaneous stage treatments of black culture. On stage,

Hurston put forth a nuanced view of the relationship between African American and Caribbean folkways and portrayed embodied practices as the site of both intraracial division and affiliation. Moreover, careful examination of Hurston's use of dancing bodies, including her own, to relay her conception of the folk casts new light on the mediated nature of her relationship to black folk culture and on the mediated nature of choreographic work itself.

The Fire Dance cycle presented by Hurston and her troupe of Bahamian dancers likewise warrants recognition for the attention it garnered in the 1930s from the host of prominent performing artists mentioned earlier. Pursued by African American and Euro-American artists alike, the dance reappeared in disparate venues throughout the decade, signaling its appeal to producers and consumers across the American dance and theatre landscapes. But as the Fire Dance continued to circulate, it took on significations different from those Hurston originally intended, creating problems for her around the issue of authorship. An exploration of Hurston's choreographic practice therefore offers key insights into the historical struggles for control over black diasporic folk dance and the meanings accompanying it. In effect, then, this book provides a microhistory of one set of such struggles to ask what they reveal about both Hurston and the representation of black folk dance in 1930s America.

## Accounting for Obscurity

What caused Hurston's persistent absence from the dance historical record? Although conjectural, several possible explanations exist. To start with, given that from her death in 1960 until the late 1970s, Hurston's published works were virtually unknown in higher education, it is not surprising that her far more ephemeral choreographic endeavors also escaped widespread notice.[11] As scholar Barbara Speisman has pointed out with respect to Hurston's theatrical career in general, the fact that so few of her play manuscripts are available in published form is "perhaps one of the chief reasons her plays have not received the attention they deserve."[12] Similarly, it is worth recalling that Hurston's chapter "Concert," which details her stage efforts, was not accessible to the public until 1995, when Cheryl Wall and the Library of America published the restored text of Hurston's 1942 autobiography *Dust Tracks on*

*a Road* in *Zora Neale Hurston: Folklore, Memoirs, and Other Writings.*[13]
To echo scholar Lynda Hill, the availability of this kind of documentation is "essential . . . to be able to write a thorough historical account"
of Hurston's theatrical productions—and thus of her choreography as
well.[14] Still, considering that Robert Hemenway's 1977 biography contains information about *The Great Day,* as well as a photograph of cast
members performing a section of the Fire Dance, it seems likely that
other forces were at play.

A confluence of historical factors no doubt worked to impede
greater recognition of Hurston's dance work. To shed light on these
conditions, it is helpful to situate Hurston in relation to the Harlem
Renaissance. Although she is customarily identified with the flourishing of African American cultural production in the 1920s, her relationship to many Renaissance figures was uneasy at best. As Hemenway
notes, Hurston's autobiography contains only passing mention of the
New Negro movement, and many of the Harlem literati mistook her
interest in performance as a lack of serious intellectual commitment.[15]
Given its problematic lineage in the nineteenth-century blackface
minstrel show, the realm of theatre raised anxieties for some African
Americans trying to shed images of the past.

The standing of dance in the New Negro movement was especially
vexed. While it may have seemed as if "all Harlem was dancing" in the
1920s, for most Harlem Renaissance artists, "dance served primarily
as a symbol of the times."[16] The figure of the dancing black female in
particular was a recurrent referent in the period's discourses of primitivism, cropping up repeatedly in the writing of men like Langston
Hughes, Jean Toomer, and Claude McKay.[17] Yet for the Harlem intelli-
gentsia, the popular black dance styles that dominated the rent parties,
nightclubs, cabarets, and musical theatre stages were too disreputable
to count as legitimate artistic expression. With ambivalence about
dance's usefulness to the New Negro—about the ability of the supposedly "primitive" form to overturn racist assumptions and thus to effect
social change—it is conceivable that Hurston's Harlem Renaissance
contemporaries were hesitant to tout her dance achievements publicly.
The apprehension of one black critic that *The Great Day* was "not . . . of
great benefit to the Negro" may have reflected the skepticism of many
of Harlem's artistic and intellectual elite.[18] Hurston, for her part, recognized that her stage endeavors went against the predominant view
that "if we don't do something highbrow we haven't accomplished any-

thing."[19] Her determination to represent the folk in the medium of performance, and to embrace black folk dance even if it carried primitivist connotations, placed her along the fault lines between vernacular dance and the New Negro movement.[20]

As John Perpener has shown, there were African American dance artists in the 1920s and 1930s, like Hemsley Winfield and Edna Guy, who shared the sentiments of the Harlem literati. Seeking to differentiate their work from the "neo-minstrel" stereotypes of vaudeville and musical theatre, they inscribed distinctions between art and entertainment dance genres.[21] In large part, such divisions were based on rhetoric and performance locale, for these choreographers unmistakably drew on black folk idioms. Like their literary counterparts, however, they perceived these forms as "raw material" that could be recast into more acceptable modes only on the high art concert stage. While Hurston also made a point of distinguishing her concerts from popular Broadway productions, she explicitly opposed the efforts of other African American performers to elevate the folk in the creation of an elite art. Her pointed critique of the "neo-spiritual" style of celebrated concert artists such as Paul Robeson and Roland Hayes, disseminated in essays and interviews, may have indirectly served to disassociate her work from the black concert dance tradition that was emerging in the 1930s.[22]

The fact that Hurston's concerts defied easy categorization surely aided in their disappearance from official chronicles of American dance. *The Great Day* and its sequels featured dance alongside a range of expressive art forms, including work songs, spirituals, children's games, and skits, and were reviewed mainly by music and theatre critics. The *New York Times*'s dance critic took note only when the Bahamian Fire Dance appeared under the auspices of a more established white dance artist. Framed in anthropological terms as the product of field research, Hurston's stagings fell between the generic boundaries that divided theatre, music, and dance, and between the lines of demarcation that separated high art from low and art from research. By a similar token, the fact that so many of Hurston's productions occurred outside the theatre dance hub of New York City allowed them to slip beneath the radar of most annotators of American dance.[23]

In the end, the question of how Hurston's contributions to the field of dance got obscured haunts this book at nearly every turn, for the process of revisibilizing her choreographic work entails a corollary consideration of the dynamics that "invisibilized" it in the first place. In this regard, I continue on the path pioneered by Brenda Dixon Gottschild, who coined the neologism "invisibilization" to call attention to the ways we have actively miscredited and miscategorized the achievements of African American artists. As her body of work consistently illustrates, "the contact zones between Africans and Europeans ... in the Americas have been unequal meeting places, with one side of the equation submerged by strategies of invisibilization, misnaming, and/ or erasure."[24] In demonstrating the need to excavate the Africanist influences on American performance that have been hidden behind "the wall of segregation and discrimination" and "tucked away in [the] interstice[s] of history," her scholarship has made possible my own investigation into how Hurston's dance stagings became buried in the cracks of the historical record.[25] Tracking down the causes of invisibilization underlines how many factors complicated the issue of choreographic credit for Hurston. They extended from the intricate system of patronage that both constrained and enabled her earliest concert efforts, to the pervasive discourse of authenticity that Hurston herself propagated, to entrenched assumptions about black dancing bodies, to the politics of interracial collaboration and notions of white originality, to the formation of artistic hierarchies. Far more than a matter of how history gets written after the fact, Hurston's erasure from the dance record was, to a remarkable degree, woven into and inextricable from the very conditions of production and reception of her stagings.

## Rewriting Hurston into the (Inter)Disciplines

This book, then, is essentially a recovery project, but one that seeks to rethink standard narratives as it re(dis)covers what lay lurking in the archive.[26] Just as Hurston's theatrical stagings confound generic demarcations between theatre, dance, music, and anthropology, so too the implications of the history recovered here extend beyond any single disciplinary field. While an array of theoretical and historical concerns circulate around Hurston's concerts, *Choreographing the Folk* exists at the intersection of literary studies, dance studies, African American studies, and American studies. More specifically, the book brings together literary criticism on Hurston, accounts of American dance and performance history, and critical treatments of the black vernacular. Long overdue for sustained academic inquiry, Hurston's stage enactments of African American and Caribbean folk dance idioms hold decided value for each of these fields.

First and fundamentally, this book offers the reclamation of a significant and neglected aspect of Hurston's career and a revisionary investigation of her approach to representing the folk. Such a reevaluation is relevant given how intensively the canonization of Hurston has centered on her engagement of black oral traditions. Propelled by Alice Walker's 1975 *Ms.* magazine article, which chronicled the novelist's search for and marking of Hurston's gravesite, and by the search for what Barbara Smith called an "identifiable literary tradition" of books by and about African American women, black feminist critics claimed a sanctioned space for Hurston as they reintroduced her into an overwhelmingly white and male American literary canon.[27] With her unassailable gift for transforming southern black folk tales and vernacular language into literary form and her ostensible proximity to a rural folk past, Hurston comfortably filled the role of foremother to subsequent black women novelists like Walker, Paule Marshall, Gloria Naylor, and Toni Morrison.[28]

In the 1990s, several scholars began to question this celebratory trend and the politics underlying it. In 1990, Michelle Wallace pointed to the potential risks of "the current unceremonious exhuming of the Hurston corpse," and in 1993, Ann duCille coined the term "Hurstonism" to describe the lionization and consumption of Hurston as the quintessential signifier of the folk.[29] Along with Madhu Dubey, duCille cautioned against the effects of a "matrilineal model of tradition" that elevated Hurston to the position of pure origin.[30] Perhaps most influentially, Hazel Carby raised concerns about the implicit parallels between the profitable academic industry that has grown up around African American women writers like Hurston and white America's fascination with black culture in the 1920s. Carby raised consequential questions about how and why the black vernacular gets invoked at certain historical moments and who profits financially from different treatments of the vernacular.[31] Together, these scholars demonstrate how quickly casting Hurston as foremother can work to naturalize and decontextualize her artistic production, and how privileging her representation of black folk heritage as "authentic" can facilitate the exclusion of other African American experiences and histories. Turning from Hurston's literary to her choreographic output, this book seeks neither to venerate nor to critique Hurston for her commitment to a

rural, black, and southern folk tradition, but rather to further scruti-
nize how she depicted that tradition.[32]

What in particular can a dance studies approach bring to an
understanding of Hurston's folk representations? Significantly (if unsurprisingly), a dance focus forces attention to the various embodied
dimensions of Hurston's treatment of the folk. Such a focus makes it
possible, for example, to recognize the important role that movement
plays in much of her written work. Hurston's first novel, *Jonah's Gourd
Vine* (1934), contains a lengthy representation of an unnamed dance
of African origin, in which a group of Alabama workers clap hands
and stomp feet, improvising rhythms around a fire as part of a hog
roast celebration.[33] The Bahamian Fire Dance itself appears in *Their
Eyes Were Watching God* (1937). Shortly after relocating to the muck
in the Florida Everglades, Janie is drawn to the "subtle but compelling rhythms of the Bahaman drummers" she encounters there, and
along with Tea Cake and their American friends, she learns to jump
at the late-night dances.[34] Other black vernacular dance idioms, including the pas-me-la and cakewalk, figure prominently in Hurston's
short stories and plays.[35] Such dance scenes allowed Hurston to underscore the kinesthetic aspects of black folk culture and to gesture at
the African roots of African American folkways. Hurston also turned
to dance in her pivotal essay "Characteristics of Negro Expression" to
exemplify such defining black aesthetic principles as angularity, asymmetry, and the "restrained," "dynamic suggestion" that she argued distinguished "Negro dancing" from white.[36] While much more could be
written about Hurston's translation of bodily motion and gesture into
print, it is clear that she maintained a serious interest in movement as
a way of knowing in both her fiction and nonfiction.

More important for my purposes here, attention to the embodied
representations that Hurston created for the stage casts new light on
her conceptualization of the folk. As I will show, the theory of the folk
that Hurston advanced in her concerts was distinct from that conveyed
in her textual productions. The narrative sequence in which she presented expressive practices over the course of her revue, as well as the
way she distributed separate but related movement styles throughout,
enabled her to introduce a nuanced representation of the black diaspora,
a "bodily writing" of what Paul Gilroy has termed the Black Atlantic.[37]
At the same time, the multivocality of dance—its ability to countenance
multiple interpretations at once—made it possible for Hurston simul-

taneously to challenge and conform to spectators' expectations about black folk performance. Consideration of the choreographic process by which Hurston transformed the Bahamian Fire Dance for the stage, meanwhile, provides key insight into her mediation of the folk. In particular, it exposes the myriad interpolations involved in the transmission of movement from Bahamian bodies to her own body to those of her cast members. Examination of Hurston's dance stagings also contributes a new perspective on her struggles to claim authorship, an operation that was not only rhetorical and textual but material and corporeal as well. Recognition of the value Hurston placed on the moving body and her reliance on embodiment as a representational strategy is thus crucial to understanding the nature of what she produced and her methods of production.

Equally vital, *Choreographing the Folk* rectifies Hurston's near-complete erasure from the dance historical record and adds to the growing body of revisionary scholarship on early-twentieth-century American dance. Although Richard Long makes brief mention of *The Great Day* concert in his 1989 *The Black Tradition in American Dance,* neither Lynn Fauley Emery's 1972 *Black Dance* (which does refer to Hurston's written analysis of dance) nor John Perpener's 2001 *African-American Concert Dance* includes any account of her theatrical productions.[38] These and other histories of African American concert dance attend to a number of Hurston's dance contemporaries: Hemsley Winfield, Edna Guy, Asadata Dafora, Alison Burroughs, Charles Williams, and, most prominently, Katherine Dunham and Pearl Primus, "the two true pioneers of Black concert dance."[39] While recent scholarship has helped elucidate the inherent problems and pitfalls of designating a separate "black dance" tradition,[40] there is little question that the formation of this tradition on the concert stage—originally termed "Negro dance"—was propelled in the 1930s by theatrical presentations of the African roots of African American dance.[41] First produced a full two years prior to Dafora's celebrated *Kykunkor* and five years prior to the momentous "Negro Dance Evening," two dance events that assume conspicuous positions in existing historical chronicles, Hurston's 1932 folk revue and its Bahamian dance finale certainly qualify for inclusion in genealogies of black concert dance.[42]

Yet even as I hope to reveal Hurston's dance productions to be important precursors to the more celebrated stagings of Dunham and Primus, I want to resist the impulse to assign Hurston foremother or "firstness" status in African American concert dance, a move that re-produces her elevation to the position of pure origin in literary stud-ies. Although as Hurston maintained, her revues gave impetus to the-atrical presentations of Afro-Caribbean dance in the United States,[43] there were others before her who incorporated African diasporic dance into their stage productions, some of whom history has doubtlessly also forgotten.[44] This book does not claim that Hurston was a choreo-graphic genius who paved the way for all ensuing African American dance producers. What I do claim is that her staging of the Bahamian Fire Dance, as well as the vision of a black diasporic folk she con-structed around it, constitute important contributions to African American and American dance. Hurston, *The Great Day*, and the se-ries of performances her concert set in motion all deserve a place in official dance records.

Rather than reifying her as an "authentic" source for future black artistic production, in writing Hurston back into dance history, this book seeks to contextualize her revues and the emergence of black concert dance. Careful contextualization demonstrates that the work of establishing the Africanist roots of African American stage dance—of constructing an Afrocentric foundation for a black concert dance tradition in the United States—was neither seamless nor inevitable. As customary as theatrical presentations of black diasporic origins became with the success of Katherine Dunham's concert tours in the 1940s and 1950s, the overpowering influence in the 1930s of primitiv-ist notions about black dancing bodies often obscured the legibility of staged African retentions. This initially made the project of staging the black diaspora through dance a precarious one.

Concurrently, the book unfixes boundaries that have been drawn between various dance genres, exposing the pivotal role that black diasporic folk dance played in the formation of multiple American dance traditions in the period between the two world wars. As I trace the diverse theatrical life of the Fire Dance subsequent to its appear-ance in Hurston's 1932 *The Great Day*, it becomes clear that black diasporic folk dance in the 1930s quite simply refused to be subsumed by neat classifications—racial, artistic, or otherwise. Instead, it served an array of at times contradictory purposes, carrying manifold va-lences and values for different artists and audiences. Precisely because the decade was one in which the categories that would come to define the U.S. dance terrain for the remainder of the twentieth century—black concert dance, (white) modern dance, jazz dance—had yet to take firm hold, it proves fertile ground for investigating the operation by which such taxonomies are instituted as well as the racialized assumptions on which they rest.

This book thus contributes to what Susan Manning has termed the "new intercultural historiography of American dance," a correction to the long-standing tendency in dance studies to segregate dance traditions according to race and genre.[45] In this sense, *Choreographing the Folk* should be seen as in dialogue with recent works by Manning, Brenda Dixon Gottschild, Julia Foulkes, John Perpener, and Mark Franko, all of whom help expose the racial hybridity of American dance and the mutually constitutive nature of various dance genres in the first half of the twentieth century.[46] At the same time, because Hurston's own role as a dance artist does not fit easily into existing attribution schemas, I hope to unearth new questions about the racial politics of how the discipline understands and grants credit for the work of staging dance. On the most basic of levels, then, the recovery of Hurston's dance practice provides an opportunity to query the terms we use to talk about dance as a mode of artistic production and to interrogate our very categories of art.

Finally, *Choreographing the Folk* sheds fresh light on the fundamentally important and highly charged relationship between black folk forms and American culture. The book's relevance thus extends beyond dance and literary studies to African American studies and American studies as well. At one and the same time, black vernacular practices have served as thriving repositories for African survivals and transformations and have been subject to continuous appropriation by the white mainstream. As such, the black vernacular has been integral to both African American and European American artistic production. Yet because of its multifarious uses, representations of the vernacular routinely give rise to pointed tensions around questions of ownership and theft, originality and imitation, purity and heterogeneity. These same tensions played out vividly in the stage history of the Bahamian Fire Dance, making it a valuable case study for teasing out the convoluted dynamics surrounding the commodification of black folk expression.

## Recovering Embodied Practices from the Archive

In a handwritten letter dated December 31, 1931, and housed in the Moorland Spingarn Research Center at Howard University, the black intellectual Alain Locke reports to the white benefactress Charlotte Osgood Mason the outcome of a meeting he held with Hurston the previous day. Worried about the program order that Hurston was planning to implement for her pending *Great Day* concert, Locke explains that he spent part of the meeting outlining for Hurston an alternative narrative sequence for the revue, one that Mason had apparently endorsed:

> As a final upshot, she saw the sanity of the program order as I
> presented it to you and agreed to take it exactly. I wrote it out
> freshly on her kitchen table—she leaning over me as I did it,—
> and with the explanations, she saw its logic and I believe adopted
> it from within as if she herself was clearing it up. In this way it
> will be more effective and will seem part of her own imagination.
> So I think and believe all is again on the right path toward the
> goal of our hopes and plans.[47]

Chapter 3 will examine this letter in more detail, focusing on what it reveals about the contests for authority that dogged the production of *The Great Day*. Here I want to take Locke's letter as an illustration of what the project of recovering embodied practices from the archive entails from a methodological standpoint. In particular, I want to flag how the document positions the historian and what it does and does not make knowable.

On one hand, the letter stands as an example of the kind of trace performances like Hurston's leave on the archive. A lasting and tangible remnant of the process leading up to the live event, the letter provides concrete evidence of the way Locke mediated between Hurston and her patron and of how actively Locke and Mason strove to exert influence over Hurston's stage undertaking. On the other hand, the letter fails to divulge anything specific about the program order, the very subject of so much concern. Significantly, although Locke expresses unqualified confidence that Hurston "adopted" his revisions "from within," subsequent exchanges suggest that she may have feigned acquiescence and continued to tinker with her program up until *The Great Day's* premiere. What cannot be ascertained is precisely what Locke delineated for Hurston at that late December meeting—and consequently, whether the program she presented on January 10 coincided with or departed from his recommended outline. On such critical questions as the authorship of *The Great Day*'s narrative structure and Hurston's defiance of or submission to those with power over her, then, the archive is frustratingly inconclusive.

Yet even as the letter exemplifies the limits of the archival record, it points to the possibility it holds for historians willing to read against the grain and engage in judicious speculation. As Saidiya Hartman has stated, "The effort to reconstruct the history of the dominated is not discontinuous with dominant accounts or official history but, rather, is a struggle within and against the constraints and silences imposed by the nature of the archive."[48] For the dance historian, whose object of inquiry is intrinsically transitory and leaves behind only vestiges of its existence, grappling with these silences and constraints is all the more vital. One way of doing so is to heed theatre scholar Sandra Richards's advice to literary critics to pay attention to the "absent potential" in dramatic scripts: those gaps and intertexts that reside between the written word on the page and material bodies in performance.[49] Correspondingly, rather than simply taking Locke's text at its word, the historian must attend, however conjecturally, to the intertext between what is "there" on the page of his letter and the embodied actions that exceed the written document. Those actions include Hurston's behavior apart from Locke's watchful eye, as well as the live version of the program she put before the New York public. Consideration of the "absent potential" in extant documents is especially imperative here given the way Hurston, precisely because of the exigencies of patronage, perfected an art of elusiveness. To fail to contend with the absences in the archive would be to miss the full complexity of the relations between Hurston, Mason, and Locke and to neglect the prospect that Hurston was able to resist the interventions of the latter two.

Without denying that the archive offers only one avenue for the writing of history and that other methodological approaches may render complementary, even competing accounts, this book proceeds from the premise that embodied practices, even those of the marginalized, can be partly reconstructed from the archive. Although long overlooked and unavoidably fragmentary, the story of Hurston's and the Bahamian dancers' folk stagings in the 1930s survives in the "disparate residual traces" that each production generated, from programs, press releases, and newspaper reviews, to photographs, film footage, and sound recordings, to written correspondence, published and unpublished research, and autobiographical accounts.[50] *Choreographing the Folk* carefully pieces together this archival evidence, submits it to close reading, and hypothesizes about how lacunae in the archive might have been filled.

The book also bears in mind that because dance is "an embodied social practice and highly visual aesthetic form," to quote Jane Desmond, it "powerfully melds considerations of materiality and representation together."[51] Accordingly, the performance reconstruction method I employ attends both to conditions of production (what enabled a given performance to take place and what the relations between producers, performers, and spectators were) and to matters of content (what occurred in performance and how it was interpreted). The project of doing dance history thus demands and models the kind of approach advocated by scholars in other humanities disciplines, such as African American studies, American studies, and cultural studies. As Tricia Rose advised in a 1992 article:

> When we speak about the production of Black popular culture,
> we need to keep at least two kinds of questions in the foreground:
> the first has to do with Black aesthetics, style, and articulation,
> and hybridization of Black practices; and the second involves the
> historical context for the creation, dissemination, and reception
> of Black popular forms.[52]

Weighing the aesthetic and the sociohistorical, the discursive and the material, text and context, this book tries to re-member the bodies around whom these dualities converged, in this case, those of Hurston, the Bahamian dancers, and the numerous individuals who played supporting roles in their stage productions.

As challenging as recovering these bodies from the archive may be, it is worth emphasizing that written documents do directly relay some corporeal information. Returning once more to Locke's letter, one discovers that the text contains a distinct visual image of Locke seated at Hurston's kitchen table, engaged in the act of writing, while Hurston, presumably standing in back of him, peers over his shoulder. What strikes me about this image is how it implicitly positions the historian behind Hurston, attempting to read over her shoulder as she reads over Locke's. With a photocopy of Locke's original handwritten letter placed before me, I find it hard not to lean over a bit further, strain a bit more, as if I just might be able to make out the contents of

Locke's "freshly" written-out program order—and thereby solve one of the remaining mysteries about Hurston's staging of the folk—if only I could get close enough. A reminder that "the production of history is a physical endeavor,"[53] this encounter with the evidence also recalls historian James Wilkinson's assessment that "the past is there, tantalizing, and yet at best it appears as through a glass, darkly. Only the smallest part of it will ever yield to the historian's efforts and become history."[54] This book, then, (re)constructs a history that is destined to be partial and incomplete. The telling I offer is based on the archival traces that only fractionally capture the movements and meanings of a group of bodies who wrestled with how to represent black folk dance in the 1930s. Reading and interpreting the presence of these bodies despite and through the archive's absences, I hope to demonstrate that what is discernible through the dark glass of history is unquestionably worth knowing.

## Theorizing the Folk

At the core of this study of Hurston's stage practice lies the complicated and convoluted question of the "folk," a category notoriously difficult to define yet of immense importance to Hurston. Variously invoked to refer to a demographic group, an aesthetic, an ideology, a way of life, and a mode of expression, the term "folk" and its close relative "vernacular" surface again and again with respect to Hurston, and with respect to African American cultural production in general. Despite its remarkable lack of precision, the salience of this terminology and its centrality to Hurston's theatrical endeavors compel us to ask what kind of work it has performed and what kind of values and pitfalls inhere in its usage. While discourse on the folk turns up in a wide range of disciplines, a brief consideration of how it has functioned in the late twentieth and early twenty-first centuries across the fields of literary and dance studies is particularly relevant for my purposes here.

In the 1980s, the folk assumed prominence in the field of literary studies as the basis for an intellectual project known as vernacular criticism. Promulgated in landmark works by Houston Baker and Henry Louis Gates Jr., this discourse embraces the vernacular as the idiom in which black folk express themselves.[55] Casting the vernacular as the driving stylistic force behind a distinctive African American literary tradition, these critics sought to recover the creativity of black oral cultures as it had been transformed into the more permanent form of print. Whereas Baker celebrates the blues impulses of black writing—the "brilliant expressive strategies" that mediate an "economics of slavery"—Gates identifies signifyin(g), the process of repetition and revision, as the dominant technique in African American literature. For Baker and Gates, a blues or "speakerly" sensibility represents the defining feature of black textual production; the vernacular, in other words, serves as the preeminent site and source of black difference. As a critical enterprise committed to letting African American textual production speak for itself, vernacular criticism contested the equation of literary theory with whiteness and helped rectify the neglect of black authors in Western literary canons. Indeed, it was the development and widespread acceptance of this mode of criticism that catapulted Hurston, hailed for her ability to adapt nonliterate folk traditions to literary forms, into her position of acclaim in the field.

But while delineations of the vernacular as the font of a unique black aesthetic presence in African American texts serve to recognize and value a tradition apart from the white bourgeois mainstream, they concomitantly tend to reify the folk as the "authentic" black experience. Recent critiques of vernacular criticism in literary studies, put forth in works by Diana Fuss, Barbara Johnson, Kenneth Warren, Ann duCille, Hazel Carby, Madhu Dubey, David Nicholls, and J. Martin Favor, help clarify the dangers of theoretical paradigms that privilege the folk.[56] Such paradigms, these scholars argue, have resulted in a monolithic master narrative that erases the complexities of African American historical experiences in favor of a singular, transhistorical notion of cultural authenticity. By creating a "critical discourse of blackness that places the 'folk'—southern, rural, and poor—at its forefront," vernacular criticism inevitably excludes other black perspectives, particularly those that do not derive from the allegedly "pure" oral culture of the rural South.[57] Similarly, as Ann duCille has noted, the emphasis on poverty and working-class culture in formulations of the folk has meant that the term "middle-class" itself, when placed on either African American artists or their subjects, "becomes pejorative, a sign of having mortgaged one's black aesthetic to the alien conventions of the dominant culture."[58] To the extent that vernacular criticism "posits an essentialist origin, . . . reifies tradition, and . . . can operate to suppress dissent," it therefore poses serious liabilities for the study of African American culture.[59]

Although not elevated to the level of a theoretical discourse, the concept of the folk has proven equally critical to the study of African American dance. In 1964, Marshall and Jean Stearns published *Jazz Dance: The Story of American Vernacular Dance,* which documented the influence of African American social dances on America's "native and homegrown" dance tradition: jazz. For the Stearnses, this influence was explained by the fact that the "Negro folk" effectively functioned as the nation's peasant class.[60] While the Stearnses characterized jazz dance as a fusion of African and European forms, they explicitly aligned rhythmic propulsion—one of jazz dance's defining qualities—with African imperatives. Some thirty years later, Jacqui Malone's *Steppin' on the Blues: The Visible Rhythms of African American Dance* took up the Stearnses' formulation, stressing that African American vernacular dance is an intricately choreographed movement system that derives from public dance settings, as well as a system of values and a means of survival for black Americans. Significantly, both the Stearnses and Malone trace the evolution of American vernacular forms from Africa to the American rural South to the urban North, a narrative that does not claim direct survivals but, rather, locates the source of the vernacular's creativity within these African influences.[61] To the extent that a focus on the vernacular illuminates the presence and tenacity of a transmissible tradition of African American dance production apart from codified Eurocentric movement systems, then, the category has been useful and enabling.

Much as in literary studies, however, a tacit correspondence between the vernacular and African American performers has proved problematic, creating dilemmas in particular for the meaning of "black dance." As dancer and choreographer Donald McKayle has pointed out, for many years black dancers were almost wholly limited to the vernacular forms of jazz and tap, as a double standard took root: while white critics adamantly opposed the use of African Americans in non-race-specific roles, white dancers were applauded for performing the roles of diverse racial groups.[62] With African American dancers pigeonholed either as "authentic" representations of vernacular styles or as part of a segregated black concert tradition, the question of what constitutes "black dance," when it is not seen reductively as synonymous with black dancers, remains open to contestation.[63] On the one hand, then, the category of vernacular dance calls attention to a vital but marginalized tradition of African American performance; on the other, it has served to confine and contain the range of acceptable black artistic practices in the United States.

Of course the folk is by no means a recent invention, and work done in other fields provides further context for understanding its historic connotations, uses, and problems. It is perhaps somewhat ironic, given its primacy in African American studies, that "folkness is Eurocentric in its origins and applications."[64] First employed as a way to describe European peasants and closely tied to emerging nationalisms, "folk" was originally a category distinct from "primitive," a term applied to more spatially distant (from a European standpoint) Others. This division blurred when Americans adopted the European discourse in the late nineteenth and early twentieth centuries and merged it with their fascination for "exotic" cultures on their own soil.[65]

Consensus among scholars also holds that "the vernacular" and "the folk," whatever their referents, are fully constructed categories.[66] In a 1992 article, historian Robin D. G. Kelley argues that the "boundaries erected around 'folk' culture are as socially constructed and contingent and permeable as the dividing line between high and low and black and white."[67] Observing that "the 'folk' are rarely such to themselves," cultural historian Robert Cantwell likewise maintains that the folk are "a social, political, and aesthetic fiction," the product of a "particular way of framing" certain social processes.[68] As folklorists like John W. Roberts and Henry Glassie point out, this framing of the folk necessarily hinges on an oppositional concept of the "nonfolk."[69] Although the expression "nonfolk" is rarely explicitly invoked, the term "folk" implicitly calls it into being. It is, moreover, the nonfolk—professionals who tend to speak *about* the black vernacular but rarely . . . *in* it"—who generally possess the power to represent folk forms.[70] Certainly this has been one of the accusations launched at academic theorists who have turned to the folk to serve their own intellectual projects.

However invented, contingent, relational, and elusive a concept, constructions of the folk are almost invariably premised on a rather consistent set of stereotypes. Predictably, these notions depend upon and enable a converse set of beliefs about the nonfolk and tend to serve the latter's interests, whether directly or indirectly. Among the most dominant images of the folk is that of an anonymous, communal mass of spontaneous cultural producers, or as Regina Bendix puts it, the "idea of a 'singing dancing throng' collectively composing."[71] This notion of unindividuated, impulsive expression facilitates the counter-vailing idea that nonfolk art is produced, or rather authored, by the solitary creative genius. It also liberates nonfolk artists to "borrow" or draw on folk forms without the burden of crediting (or compensating) their creators. In addition, the folk are typically figured as belonging to a fading or bygone era, a view that permanently consigns them to a prior, often mythic temporal moment and thus denies them coevalness.[72] This particular aspect of the folk exposes the constructedness of the entire category, for it inevitably emerges out of and in response to modern-izing forces and broader historical changes. Modernist nostalgia, in other words, gives rise to the concept of a premodern folk.[73]

In much the same vein, the domain of the folk is considered to be "immune to the dynamics of commercialization."[74] With the capitalist marketplace generally seen as a corrupting influence, or, in anthropolo-gist Steven Feld's formulation, with "lack of circulation, like lack of roy-alties . . . inextricably linked to claims for authenticity," the folk repre-sent a zone of purity.[75] It is precisely this presumed untaintedness that renders folk forms desirable as "raw material" for consumption by the commercial mainstream. Finally, and fully in line with the set of other assumptions, the folk are imagined to be a homogeneous group who speak in unified voice—a stark contrast to the hybridity, complexity, and cacophony that characterize "modern" culture.[76] Again, this vision of an undifferentiated, harmonized collective contributes to the per-ceived simplicity and authenticity of the folk and, not coincidentally, makes their expressive forms appear so accessible to the nonfolk.[77]

Broadly speaking, then, the folk can be understood as an ideologi-cal construct that mobilizes a series of interrelated notions about a purportedly cohesive group of cultural producers outside the main-stream even while serving the mainstream in various ways. Histori-cally, this construct has benefited parties with a range of agendas, and it served Hurston's purposes as well. Although she did not use the word "vernacular," "folk" appears repeatedly in her work, as well as in that of many of her Harlem Renaissance contemporaries. Hurston generally employed the term to refer to the unlettered class of African Americans residing in the rural South, as well as to the same class of West Indian peoples with whom her anthropological research put her in touch. Yet she also believed deeply that the artistic principles that distinguished the expressive practices of these populations were integral to compre-hending black culture at large—and its relationship to dominant white norms. At times, she delineated the folk more generally, as in an essay she wrote for the Federal Writers' Project, in which she defined folklore as "the boiled-down juice of human living. It does not belong to any special time, place, nor people."[78] Still, when it came to her concerts, Hurston's use of the term "folk" clearly referred to the black migrant workers of Florida and the Bahamas whose performative acts she represented on stage. There is little question that Hurston's "Program of Original Negro Folklore" depended on the currency of notions about the folk outlined earlier or that it reinforced some of these perceptions. Her revue, after all, featured a discrete community in the rural South whose entire day was full of collective expressive displays. Most prominently, Hurston promoted the idea that the folk idioms enacted in her concert were free from the taint of commercialization.

At the same time, this book argues, Hurston's stage revues complicated and disturbed commonplace views about the folk. Beneath the rhetoric of anticommercialism, *The Great Day* and its successors revealed the intricate entanglement of the commercial and the folk. In addition, though Hurston was not immune to the salvage ethos that drove anthropologists to stockpile folk samples before they were changed forever by modernization and urbanization, she was also confident that "Negro folklore is not a thing of the past. It is still in the making."[79] Her concerts pointed to the effects of modernity on the material and cultural production of an ostensibly isolated railroad work camp. Furthermore, while Hurston unquestionably sought to showcase the collectivity and collaboration that underwrote folk creativity, her revue simultaneously illustrated how individual innovation was prized within folk communities; her inclusion of solo performances in certain sections suggests as much.

Perhaps most significantly, her theatrical productions refused to portray the folk as a homogeneous monolith. For Hurston, who maintained an abiding interest in the "blended and contending" cultures of areas like south Florida, the question of intragroup difference was of the utmost importance.[80] Reflecting this interest, her concerts explored the various social alignments and conflicts that affected the creation and transmission of black folk practices, although she struggled with how best to represent these frictions. Hurston's stagings thus demonstrate that, however warranted the concerns of detractors of vernacular criticism, all invocations of the folk do not necessarily act to contain intraracial divisions. Rather, in cases like Hurston's concerts, treatments of the folk may bring to light the very tensions that conventional folk discourse tends to gloss over: tensions between communality and individuality, tradition and innovation, the commercial and the noncommercial, hybridity and unity, sameness and difference.

I will use the term "folk," then, to describe the black expressive practices that Hurston strove to portray and illuminate on stage and throughout her career, practices that emanated from a particular demographic group and a particular region—the black working classes of the rural South—but were not confined to them. To be clear, my focus is not on the existence and characteristics of the folk as such but on a particular cluster of performances that claimed to represent them; it is, after all, "as a representation" that we most often confront the folk.[81] Throughout, I also hope to preserve a sense of the folk as an inherently contested and contestable category, one whose definition and province are almost continuously in dispute. The number of individuals and institutions that developed an interest in Hurston's staging of the folk and the variety of uses to which her folk material was put suggest just how lively the contest over even a single folk representation could be.

Hurston's theatrical productions were far from the only site of such contests over the folk in the 1930s.[82] Writers like Carl Sandburg, Constance Rourke, Langston Hughes, and Sterling Brown; music collectors like John and Alan Lomax; musicians like Woody Guthrie, Huddie (Leadbelly) Ledbetter, and Paul Robeson; playwrights like Dorothy and DuBose Heyward, Frederick Koch, Marc Connelly, and Paul Green; and choreographers like Doris Humphrey, Ruth Page, Agnes DeMille, Helen Tamiris, Sophie Maslow, and Katherine Dunham all championed or sought inspiration from the folk in the period between the two world wars, as efforts to locate and build a distinctively American expressive tradition intensified.[83] If, for many of these artists, as well as for the public at large, the folk represented a bulwark against modernity and a way to build national unity during the economic recession, the specific functions and valences of the folk in this era were anything but unified.[84] While artists on the political left, many allied with what Michael Denning has termed the Cultural Front, embraced American folk themes to signal their solidarity with "the people," other folk promoters were motivated by regional conservatism.[85] And just as a number of community and little theatres turned to "folk drama" in their attempt to build noncommercial theatrical traditions rooted in native customs, so too folk idioms figured prominently on Broadway, where the profit motive was paramount.[86] Within and across artistic fields and racial affiliations, adaptations and invocations of the folk thus served "varying and sometimes contradictory cultural agendas."[87] Cultural producers of all backgrounds who tapped the folk necessarily if implicitly entered into a larger debate over who constituted the folk, who was authorized to represent them, and what particular meanings their expressive forms made salient.

With interest in the folk so extensive in the 1930s, this book's tracking of the successive commodification of a single black diasporic dance form provides a valuable window onto the distinct shape such debate could take and of precisely what was at stake. What close inspection of the stagings mounted by Hurston and the Bahamian dancers reveals about contests over the folk—and black folk dance in specific—in this decade is instructive on several counts. First, the extent to which folk expression functioned as a kind of symbolic capital for those who tried to associate themselves with it becomes evident. Given the allure of the folk's presumed distance from modern forces of urbanization and commercialization and resultant "primitiveness," cultural producers, black and white, claimed affiliation with the folk as a way to heighten the appeal of their own work and bolster their artistic reputations. Second, to represent the folk meant to exercise some (though never total) control over their ideological resonances, to possess the ability to steer interpretations of the folk in certain directions. Because of these features, black folk dance became a lightning rod not only for the negotiation of power relations between cultural producers but also for competing constructions of race, as well as class, ethnicity, and nation. Those seeking to represent black diasporic folk dance in the 1930s vied simultaneously for recognition and clout and for control over the significations of blackness.

Well aware that she was not alone in making the folk the basis of a theatrical enterprise, Zora Neale Hurston both capitalized on the period's widespread interest in the folk and strove to set her work apart from other undertakings. At every stage of production, she fought to set the terms of representation for the folk and to assert her own authority to do so. Each of the next six chapters addresses some facet of Hurston's efforts to stage her folk material and the struggles that sprang up around it.

# 1 Commercialization and the Folk

For the majority of those who have championed the folk, its primary value has been its perceived untaintedness by the "corrupting" forces of modernization, urbanization, and commercialization, generally figured as its "authenticity." But just as the meanings and uses of the folk have been hotly contested, so too have the meanings and uses of authenticity. Those who claim to represent the folk tend to stress their own authenticity, often by painting competing representations as inauthentic. Hurston's stagings were no exception. To talk about her theatrical enactments of black folk life without referencing the discourse of authenticity would be a virtual impossibility. From the beginning, Hurston relied on this discourse to frame her stage aspirations. As she excitedly wrote her friend and colleague Langston Hughes in a 1928 letter, "Did I tell you before I left about the new, the *real* Negro art theatre I plan?"[1] Early on, she referred to *The Great Day* as her "concert in the raw," and she later spoke of her desire to give "a series of concerts of untampered-with Negro folk material."[2] With critics likewise praising her presentation of "the real thing," *The Great Day* and its successors were thoroughly ensconced in the rhetoric of the natural and the genuine.[3]

In the wake of poststructuralism, assertions of real representations, stable subjects, and pure identities have become largely outmoded. As theatre historian Rena Fraden notes, the very idea of authenticity today is "almost entirely discredited by some intellectuals who believe it is a constructed category, not a universal given."[4] Certainly, the constructedness and "fallibility" of authenticity have been productively examined in a number of disciplines.[5] Yet to grant that authenticity is an illusory and problematic concept is not to deny its "formative power," especially during certain historical periods.[6] In the early decades of the twentieth century, the legacy of blackface minstrelsy and white appropriations of black expressive material made authenticity a potent issue with respect to representations of black folk culture like *The Great Day*. For Hurston, an African American woman working in the white- and male-dominated theatrical arena, authenticity was more than an expedient tool; it was the very ground on which she operated. As this chapter argues, the notion of authenticity equipped her with a powerful means to critique the workings of the theatrical marketplace, as well as a crucial way to participate in it. To be clear, I am not claiming that the concept of authenticity that was so central to Hurston's folk concerts was anything other than constructed. It is precisely how she constructed and manipulated it to draw attention to her revue in a crowded theatrical field that interests me. But in demonstrating how and why authenticity mattered to Hurston's stage endeavors, I also mean to suggest that there is continued value in asking what kind of ideological and political-economic work authenticity carries out at particular historical junctures.

Hurston's 1934 essays "Characteristics of Negro Expression" and "Spirituals and Neo-Spirituals" contain her best-known articulations of the distinctions between "genuine" black folk culture and the modified renderings working their way into the mainstream. Citing these essays and the critiques launched therein, a number of Hurston scholars have underscored her opposition to the commercialization of black culture. Perhaps most prominently, Hazel Carby has asserted that Hurston's very notion of a rural folk was "measured . . . against an urban, mass culture."[7] Hurston indeed hoped her concert would counteract the stereotyped and often racist images of blackness she saw being perpetuated in the cultural marketplace of the urban North. To paint the relationship between Hurston's artistic production and the commercial sphere as strictly antagonistic, however, would be to misconstrue it. As Brian Carr and Tova Cooper argue, idealized separations between art and commerce were generally untenable for black artists in Hurston's situation, who were "acutely aware of the inevitable cooptation of their self-representations within a system of capitalist exchange and racial patronage."[8] Yet Hurston's imbrication in this system did not prevent her from claiming that her stage enactment of black folk culture offered an authentic alternative to commodified versions.[9] Simultaneously critical of and complicit with the market's operation and effects, Hurston neither totally repudiated the commercial marketplace nor abandoned designs for authenticity within it.

Hurston's revues were not commercial in the sense that generating a profit was their chief aim. Without question, she hoped her concert would earn her some money, and she deliberately chose a Broadway theatre for its debut. But she also staged her material in a number of not-for-profit venues, like the New School for Social Research in New York and an experimental theatre associated with Rollins College in Winter Park, Florida. Neither did Hurston rely on traditional sources of capital: the bulk of the funds for *The Great Day* came from her white patron Charlotte Osgood Mason. When I speak of Hurston's complicity with the commercial marketplace, then, I mean to suggest that her concerts bore an undeniable relationship to commercial theatre, especially Broadway, and that her transformation of her research on black folk idioms into a stage production designed for public consumption amounted to a fundamental act of commerce.

While an analysis of how notions of authenticity informed Hurston's productions will inevitably bleed into other chapters, my concern in this chapter is the entanglement between the trope of authenticity and forces of commercialization; though opposed in discourse, the two could hardly be separated in practice. I argue that Hurston's invocation of authenticity depended on her knowledge of and dissatisfaction with the conventions and conditions of the commercial theatre. Equally, her ability to compete in the theatrical arena with her own commodified rendering of black folk culture depended on her ability to invoke authenticity. Needless to say, the project of mounting a show in the theatrical marketplace on the grounds of authenticity entailed certain paradoxes that could not have been lost on Hurston. To illuminate these paradoxes, I track Hurston's firsthand involvement with the commercial stage prior to *The Great Day* to reveal how this experience influenced her conceptions of authenticity. I then consider the particular construction of authenticity she fashioned to market her concert to theatregoers in New York and in other locales around the country. Finally, I explore the commercial exigencies that shaped her creative decisions, including several modifications she made to her revue over the course of its stage life. What I hope to show is that Hurston's "authentic" folk concert—in its conception, production, promotion, and reception—was always mediated by market concerns.

## Historicizing Authenticity

Before examining how Hurston engaged the discourse of authenticity in a theatrical setting, it is useful to contextualize the concept briefly. As ongoing debates about the authenticity (or lack thereof) of various hip-hop artists suggest, the allure of the "real" is by no means unique to a particular era. Neither have black expressive practices been the exclusive locus of concerns about authenticity.[10] Still, the long and complicated history of white consumption of black cultural products in the United States has made the issue particularly charged with respect to African American expression.[11] From slavery onward, white domination and surveillance of African Americans meant that the question of what constituted genuine black performance was always already vexed.[12] The institution of blackface minstrelsy is a notable and historically influential example of both white desire for "real" representations of blackness and the convoluted nature of authenticity discourse. In this, the most popular entertainment form in nineteenth-century America, European Americans, many of them Irish, applied burnt cork to their faces and performed highly stereotyped impersonations of black speech patterns, songs, and dances. As Robert Toll, Eric Lott, and Brenda Dixon Gottschild have elucidated, the expressive styles disseminated through the minstrel show both were and were not rooted in African American practices—and therefore produced great controversy over whether the performances were counterfeit or authentic.[13] What is clear is that white minstrels promoted themselves as authentic "delineators" of black culture and that some portion of the audience (mis)took their representations as the genuine article.

The consequences for black performers were profound. An 1845 playbill for an appearance by the African American dancer William Henry Lane, known as Master Juba, offers a vivid case in point:

> The entertainment to conclude with the Imitation Dance, by Mast. Juba, in which he will give correct Imitation Dances of all the principal Ethiopian Dancers in the United States. After which he will give an imitation of himself—and then you will see the vast

difference between those that have heretofore attempted dancing
and this WONDERFUL YOUNG MAN.[14]

Implicitly here, authenticity is located in the "vast difference" between
a black man's imitation of white impersonators and an "imitation
of himself": this was the morass that the complex racial dynamics of
minstrelsy wrought. Forced to darken their already brown skin and
to replicate the stereotypes propagated by their white predecessors,
African American performers, who gained access to and increasingly
dominated the minstrel stage in the last quarter of the nineteenth
century, relied on the discourse of authenticity to attract audiences in
search of verifiable blackness. So it was that Bert Williams and George
Walker, two of the most famous black performers to emerge out of
minstrelsy, billed themselves as "Two Real Coons." Although blackface
minstrelsy's popularity eventually declined, making way for the rise of
vaudeville and the musical in the early twentieth century, the form did
not die out completely, and the precedent it set for subsequent stage
representations of black culture can hardly be overstated.[15] Its influence was patently evident in the Broadway musical on which Hurston
worked prior to *The Great Day*, as well as in certain responses to her
own production.

If authenticity emerged as a critical trope in nineteenth-century
black performance, the transformations of the 1910s and 1920s gave
the issue new urgency. The mass migration of African Americans
from the rural South to the urban North; technological developments
in phonograph recordings, radio, and film; the rise of commercial en-
terprises like the Theatre Owners Booking Association, Tin Pan Alley,
and record companies; and mainstream white Americans' growing
fascination with black culture: these developments meant corresponding changes in the production, dissemination, and reception of black
expressive forms.[16] As music and dance styles and accompanying
images of African American life reached broader audiences, they increasingly crossed racial lines, raising new questions about who had
the authority to represent black culture and which versions best—or
most authentically—represented the race. For many whites, African
American idioms symbolized the country's most distinctive and readily available folk culture, and in their ostensible "primitiveness" and
"naturalness," seemed to offer the perfect antidote to the stultifying
effects of modernization. For many in African American intellectual

and artistic circles, the upheavals of modernization helped fuel a desire to reconstruct black identity, to replace old and racist stereotypes
by projecting images of a New Negro. To them, as theatre scholars
David Krasner and Rena Fraden have articulated, authenticity was a
politically empowering term, a chance to "cleanse the stain of minstrelsy" and "rally around a new type."[17] African American folk culture seemed to present an untapped repository in this quest for more
authentic representations of the race, and the mining of folk roots
became one of the defining strategies of the New Negro movement,
later known as the Harlem Renaissance.[18] By the time Hurston began
promoting her "concert in the raw" in the early 1930s, authenticity was
well established with respect to black performance as a valuable good,
a rallying cry, and a matter of often contentious debate.

## Conceptualizing a *"Real* Negro Art Theatre":
## Hurston, Commercial Theatre, and (In)Authenticity

Although the January 1932 premiere of *The Great Day* represented
Hurston's debut as a director and producer, it was not her first foray
into the world of commercial theatre. As Barbara Speisman has
pointed out, Hurston's first exposure to professional theatre dated back
to 1915, when she found work as a maid for a Gilbert and Sullivan traveling troupe.[19] Recounting this experience in her 1942 autobiography
*Dust Tracks on a Road,* Hurston describes the immediate appeal her
performative speaking style—the "simile and invective" on which she
was raised as a Southerner—held for company members.[20] The affec-
tion of these professional performers for Hurston was mutual, and she
continued to seek out opportunities in the theatre. During her years
at Howard University, which she attended from 1919 to 1924, she studied drama with Thomas Montgomery Gregory, whose Howard Players
staged plays about African American life. In addition to formal study,
Hurston made a point of attending the theatre as often as she could.
In 1926, after relocating to New York, she told a friend, "You know how
interested I am in the theatre, and I am just running wild in every direction, trying to see everything at once."[21]

　　By this point, Hurston had also begun writing—and copyrighting—
plays of her own. In 1925, at the age of thirty-four, she won second prize
for *Color Struck* and honorable mention for *Spears* in the literary con-

test held by *Opportunity,* the National Urban League's monthly magazine. That same year, she sought a copyright for a musical play called
*Meet the Mamma,* written in 1924. In 1927, she published *The First One*
in Charles S. Johnson's *Ebony and Topaz* and in 1930, she copyrighted
another of her musical revues, *Cold Keener,* along with *De Turkey and
De Law,* a three-act comedy closely related to the unfinished and contentious *Mule Bone,* on which she collaborated with Langston Hughes
in the spring of that year.[22] Although these plays and musicals were far
from Broadway-bound (none was evidently staged during Hurston's
lifetime), they do attest to her interest in engaging with images and figures derived from popular theatre.[23] Both *Spears* and *Meet the Mamma,*
for example, contain transparently "primitive" African dance numbers, complete with loincloths, bone jewelry, fervent drum beats, and
jungle settings, and bearing the influence, as Speisman maintains, of
"the Tarzan craze . . . sweeping the country at the time."[24] The rain
dance in *Spears,* in fact, is performed by a medicine man and witch
woman who immediately call to mind Eugene O'Neill's famous 1920
play, *Emperor Jones,* in which a witch doctor enacts a ritual dance that
sends Jones reeling back into his primitive past.[25] The leading character of one of the skits in *Cold Keener* is none other than Emperor
Jones himself, dressed "in all his glory" and, in Hurston's version, setting sail with his "conquering black legions" to reclaim Africa from
Great Britain, France, and Belgium.[26] Significantly, the Emperor Jones
caricature doubles as a pretext for the introduction of the Bahamian
Fire Dance, the same dance Hurston had recently encountered during
her research trip to Florida and the Caribbean and that would become
the celebrated finale to *The Great Day.* While Hurston continued to
author plays that "signified" on contemporaneous stage representations of blackness, the anthropological research she conducted in the
late 1920s allowed her to replace hackneyed depictions of primitive
dance with enactments of specific diasporic folk dances.[27] This strategy of playing with and slightly deviating from commercial theatre
norms continued to define Hurston's approach to the stage. Notably,
it was the latter half of the equation—diverging from convention by
introducing unfamiliar (at least to mainstream audiences) folk idioms
drawn from her research—that became the basis of her claims about
*The Great Day*'s authenticity.

Hurston's folklore-collecting expedition was indeed central to her
budding vision of a more authentic kind of theatre. It was during her

tour through the South that she first touted "the new, the *real* Negro art theatre" she hoped to establish.[28] Hurston had studied anthropology under Franz Boas at Barnard College, which she entered on a scholarship shortly after arriving in New York in 1925. Between 1927 and 1930, with the "spy-glass of Anthropology" and the financing of her white patron Charlotte Mason, Hurston amassed an array of folktales, songs, and dances as she traveled around the South and to the Bahamas.[29] These became the explicit material out of which she fashioned her theatrical revues. Yet the concert she presented at the John Golden Theatre in early 1932 was as much a product of her dissatisfaction with existing models for representing black folk culture as it was a product of her anthropological work. From the beginning, Hurston conceptualized her *"real* Negro art theatre" as a sorely needed corrective to two established performance genres: the concert spiritual and black musical theatre.

### The "Mediocre White Sounds" of Neo-Spirituals

No sooner had Hurston returned to New York from the South in 1930 than she began to contemplate how best to present the assorted folk idioms she had collected. While she wrote up some of this material for academic publication,[30] she became increasingly convinced that the various musical forms—work songs, blues, and spirituals—demanded a performative exposition. Her conviction that contemporaneous renderings of these folk forms fell far short of their potential fueled her inclination to pursue a theatrical treatment. As she explained in a 1934 letter to Thomas Jones, the president of Fisk University in Nashville, Tennessee,

> I had heard all of the Negro concert Artists, both soloists and groups and was depressed by the fact that while they were often great artists in the white manner, they fell so far below the folk-art level of Negroes. I thought that it was because the material was lacking. But later I found that to be true, but in addition it was thought that no negro vocalist was an artist unless he or she could take good negro music and turn it into mediocre white sounds.[31]

Hurston reiterated these sentiments many times as a rationale for her concert work. As she later affirmed in her autobiography, "I did the concert because I knew that nowhere had the general public ever heard music as done by Negroes." She maintained that she had always been conscious of this deficiency, but her research expedition "accented this situation inside of me and troubled me."[32] Although *The Great Day* would confound Eurocentric generic boundaries that tend to divide music, dance, and theatre from one another, it is clear that Hurston saw her work in relation to the genre of the concert spiritual.

The genre had its origins in the late-nineteenth-century tours of the Fisk Jubilee Singers, who performed arranged versions of traditional African American spirituals throughout the United States and Europe to raise money for Fisk University. Other black colleges, including Hampton and Tuskegee institutes, soon followed with similar groups. In the first decades of the twentieth century, Harry T. Burleigh, a prominent black musician and composer who had studied with the Czech composer Antonín Dvořák, arranged spirituals for solo presentation, and Roland Hayes and Paul Robeson gained acclaim from black and white audiences alike for their concert hall renditions.[33] Although based on the melodies of African American slave spirituals, themselves reinterpretations of Christianity "through an African cultural lens," these concert presentations of spirituals adopted the compositional techniques, erect bodily comportment, and ideals of timbre more typical of European aesthetic values.[34] Like other forms of African American stage performance in the late nineteenth and early twentieth centuries, the concert spiritual must be understood in the context of minstrelsy. As Paul Gilroy has noted, the Fisk Jubilee Singers had to compete with the distorted representations of blackness circulating on the minstrel stage, and the "aura of seriousness" they projected enabled them to distance themselves from "the racial codes of minstrelsy."[35] By the 1920s, the concert spiritual—a syncretic melding of African and European musical traditions—had become a "privileged signifier" of blackness and was embraced by many in the New Negro movement seeking to reconstruct the image of the race.[36]

It was precisely this representative status that drove Hurston's indictments of the concert spiritual. As she wrote in "Characteristics of Negro Expression," which appeared in Nancy Cunard's 1934 volume *Negro: An Anthology,* the "Glee Club style has gone on so long and become so fixed among concert singers that it is considered quite authentic."[37] She elaborated on this claim in her essay "Spirituals and Neo-Spirituals," published in the same 1934 volume. Here she inscribed a firm distinction between "genuine Negro Spirituals," on the one hand,

and the "concert artists and glee clubs," on the other, whose performances were just "based on the spirituals."[38] Although Hurston conceded that this latter group, in which she placed Burleigh, Rosamond
Johnson, Lawrence Brown, Nathaniel Dett, Hall Johnson, and John
Work, produced music that was "good work and beautiful," she insisted
that it was inauthentic.[39] In their attempt to extract and elevate vernacular forms in the creation of a so-called serious art, she contended,
they lost their genuineness.[40]

As her published and unpublished statements make plain, Hurston's
critique of concert spirituals was shot through with racial politics. To
challenge the perceived authenticity of the neo-spiritual, she hoped
to demonstrate that its musicians "put on their tuxedos, bow prettily
to the audience, get the pitch and burst into magnificent song—but
not *Negro* song."[41] Part of her purpose, as her comments to Thomas
Jones suggest, was to expose the racial biases behind mainstream notions of artistry. Comparing "the folk-art level of Negroes" to art "in
the white manner," she inverts the customary hierarchy in which they
are ordered, positioning black folk music well above "mediocre white
sounds." Despite this inversion, she preserves the racialized distinctions between the "Negro" folk artist and the concert artist "in the
white manner." The evaluative criteria she developed for concert versions of black spirituals thus equated "Negro" and "folk," on the one
hand, "white" and "impure," on the other.

The racial binaries on which Hurston's logic rests may well strike us
as problematic. Faulting black vocalists for adhering to "white" artistic
standards, Hurston seems to police the boundaries between European-
and African-derived musical traditions and thus to illustrate the ways
in which authenticity, as E. Patrick Johnson has written, "carries with
it the dangers of foreclosing the possibilities of cultural exchange and
understanding."[42] Her stance leaves little room for the possibility that
the concert spiritual's interracial blending of aesthetic styles was indeed
representative of modern African American culture. But it is important to remember that Hurston was staking out a position in a largely
class-inflected intraracial debate among Harlem Renaissance figures
about the uses of black folk idioms. Like Langston Hughes, whose 1926
essay "The Negro Artist and the Racial Mountain" criticized the black
middle class's assimilation to white bourgeois norms, Hurston pro-
tested against the branch of the New Negro movement that valued folk
forms only when they were transformed into elite high art.[43]

More to the point here, Hurston's judgments must be understood in the context of her own theatrical treatment of spirituals. The written critiques she offered were not made in a vacuum but during the same period in which she was preparing for and working to produce her folk revue. More was at stake, in other words, than winning points in a rhetorical debate. By attacking the efforts of her contemporaries with accusations of inauthenticity, Hurston sought to clear a space in the marketplace for her own stage representation.

### The "Bleached Chorus" of the Black Musical

The other major performance genre against which Hurston's idea of an authentic folk concert took shape was black musical theatre. The institution developed in the 1890s out of what David Krasner has identified as the twin forces of "white producers interested in cashing in on new forms of racial representation" and "blacks who sought to challenge that very representation."[44] With varying degrees of racist minstrel imagery, productions by both groups featured African American performers (often still in blackface), thin plots, and plentiful music and dancing that helped popularize the syncopated rhythms of ragtime. Although the black musical disappeared from Broadway for a period in the 1910s, it returned with renewed vitality with Noble Sissle and Eubie Blake's *Shuffle Along,* which opened in 1921 and ran for a total of 504 performances, spawning a series of imitators, including *Put and Take* (1921), *Strut Miss Lizzie, Plantation Revue,* and *Liza* (1922); *Runnin' Wild* (1923); and *The Chocolate Dandies* and *Dixie to Broadway* (1924).[45] Energetic dancing was a fundamental component of the formula established by *Shuffle Along* and emulated by its successors. That musical included a range of popular dances, but "the most impressive innovation of *Shuffle Along,*" Marshall and Jean Stearns explain, "was the dancing of the sixteen-girl chorus line."[46] Their intricate and rhythmic steps, executed with precision, inaugurated a new trend in Broadway musicals, and by 1926, African American theatre critic Theophilus Lewis pronounced that "the main attraction of the colored stage is its dancing."[47] The result, however, was that audiences grew to expect fast, rhythmic dancing from African American performers and accordingly condemned anything that strayed from this norm. Widespread failure to appreciate the technical skill behind black vernacular dance, furthermore, meant that the stereotype of

blacks as "natural" dancers—an assumption sanctioned by the institution of minstrelsy—became more deeply entrenched.

As far as Hurston was concerned, black musical theatre was as de-
serving of criticism as the "neo-spirituals" that prevailed in the 1920s.
Here, too, she articulated her critique in racialized terms. Especially
troubling to her were the effects musicals were having on white per-
ceptions of the black dancing body. In an unpublished article titled
"You Don't Know Us Negroes," Hurston contended that shows like
*Shuffle Along* "made a greater impression than is generally admitted."
The power of this impression, she explained, lay in the fact that

> most white people have seen our shows but not our lives. If they
> have not seen a Negro show they have seen a minstrel or at least
> a black-face comedian and that is considered enough. They know
> all about us. We say, "Am it?" And go into a dance. By way of
> catching breath we laugh and say, "Is you is, or is you ain't" and
> grab our banjo and work ourselves into a sound sleep. First thing
> on waking we laugh or skeer ourselves into another buck and
> wing, and so life goes.[48]

Again Hurston displays her concern that the white mainstream mis-
construed stage depictions of blackness as authentic representations
of African American life. The perpetuation of the minstrel stereotype of blacks as carefree and impulsive dancers became one of the
key misconceptions that her concert sought to contest.

Equally distressing to Hurston was how quickly the profitability
of black musicals had led white producers to take control of the form.
The result, she lamented in "Characteristics of Negro Expression," was
that "shows like 'Dixie to Broadway' are only Negro in cast, and could
just as well have come from pre-Soviet Russia."[49] Certainly, as Allen
Woll has demonstrated, Lew Leslie's *Dixie to Broadway* ushered in a
trend in which the term "black musical" pertained almost exclusively
to the onstage talent.[50] Yet even the casts, Hurston maintained, bore
the marks of whites' behind-the-scenes influence. "Negro shows before being tampered with," she wrote, "did not specialize in octoroon
girls." The growing preponderance of light-skinned women in the
chorus line—the "bleached chorus"—was thus "the result of a white
demand and not the Negro's."[51] As Hurston's 1925 play *Color Struck* illustrates, this privileging of light complexions could have devastating

consequences for black communities far removed from Broadway.[52] Set in rural black Florida in the early twentieth century, the play depicts the psychological deterioration of a dark-skinned African American woman racked by jealousy of light-skinned women. The racialized political economy of the black musical in the early twentieth century, Hurston recognized, had real repercussions for material bodies, both in terms of which performers got hired and what images of blackness and beauty got disseminated.

Hurston also contended that individual black vernacular dance steps were undergoing a kind of "bleaching" process as white performers took them up. Noting the "use of Negro material" by performers like vaudeville star Mae West, composer George Gershwin, and dancer Ann Pennington, she wryly remarked, "it is astonishing that so many are trying it, and I have never seen one yet entirely realistic."[53] To Hurston, this trend was more than a source of amusement, for, as Broadway publicized considerably revised versions of black folk dance forms to a wide audience, it concomitantly masked their provenance. While it is all but impossible to determine the exact source of any dance move, it is undeniable that white producers and performers frequently "borrowed" steps they learned from black performers and then took credit for the choreography.[54] Hurston, intensely interested in the genealogy of popular black dance forms, believed that they could and should be traced back to their roots in the rural South. It was not that Hurston believed black folk forms should adhere to an unchanging mold; her insistence that the spirituals "do not remain long in their original form" but are continually altered by each congregation who enacts them demonstrates her alertness to the dynamic fluidity of the vernacular.[55] Rather, she objected to the way the mainstream versions overshadowed and concealed the idioms' black folk roots.

At heart, then, Hurston's grievances with both concert spirituals and (largely white-produced) black musicals lay in the ways they submitted to what she perceived as "bleaching" forces while claiming to represent black culture. These forces manifested themselves in discrete yet related ways: through elitist attempts to elevate black folk material in accordance with Eurocentric standards of high art; through capitulation to the white mainstream's appetite for minstrel-like depictions of black culture; through the predominance of light-skinned performers and "whitened" versions of black vernacular dances; and through the masking of the black rural sources of those dances. All were the result of a white hegemony that Hurston sought to protest, often by making racially essentialist claims. And all stoked her ambition to offer a theatrical rendering that would represent black folk idioms without "bleach."

### Fast and Furious: *Hurston's First Broadway Experience*

In the summer of 1931, before going forward with her plans to stage her own folk concert, Hurston gave her time over to a pair of Broadway revues: *Jungle Scandals*, which never saw production, and *Fast and Furious*, on which she served as writer and performer. Her personal involvement with these commercial ventures is worth examining because of the direct impact it had on her attitudes toward Broadway, her construction of authenticity, and her actual theatrical practice. Significantly, her experiences only heightened her frustration with the conventions of the concert spiritual and the black musical, both of which were on display in *Fast and Furious.*

Hurston nevertheless approached these ventures as opportunities for financial gain and occasions to garner a greater foothold in the New York theatre world. Writing to her patron Charlotte Mason in July to report on both developments, Hurston was clearly pleased with the artistic charge she had been granted. She announced that she was "doing the book" for *Jungle Scandals,* and of *Fast and Furious,* wrote, "I have the greater number of the skits in it. I am so happy to be able to tell you this."[56] Although *Jungle Scandals* folded before opening, and only three of her skits found their way into *Fast and Furious,* Hurston continued to portray these undertakings as worthwhile, especially insofar as they increased her familiarity with the workings of commercial theatre and thus laid the foundation for later stage success.[57] As she told Mason, "I do not consider either of the revues as great work, but they are making the public know me and come to me, and that is important." In fact, she openly discussed her plans to follow these stints with a staging of her own conceiving, remarking, "I like the idea of going from the light and trivial to something better. . . . The public will see growth rather than decline, you see."[58] Notwithstanding her vociferous critiques of Broadway, Hurston did not consider these commercial productions at odds with her "real Negro art theatre" project.[59]

Produced and directed by Forbes Randolph, *Fast and Furious* opened on August 27, 1931, at the Boulevard Theatre in Jackson Heights, Long

Island, moved briefly to the Flatbush Theatre in Brooklyn, and finally made its Broadway debut at the New Yorker Theatre on September 15.[60] Claiming to be "the biggest colored show that ever came to town," the revue utilized a ninety-member company, a twenty-four-piece orchestra, and a band.[61] Despite drawing apparently steady crowds, the production received mixed reviews and closed only a week after arriving on Broadway. As Richard Lockridge wrote in the *New York Sun,* "No amount of scurrying and slapping of hips did more than offer to the town a show called 'Fast and Furious,' after its only significant characteristics. Nor could all the tap dancing and blackface sketches in thirty-seven scenes make the offering one to bother about."[62] According to critics, the musical departed little from entrenched models for representing blackness on the theatre stage. *Fast and Furious* reopened on Saturday, October 3, at the Lafayette Theatre in Harlem, where it played for another two weeks.[63]

Although the August 28 contract that Hurston signed with Forbes Randolph stipulated that she would provide four sketches to the revue, the *Fast and Furious* program credited Hurston for only two: "The Court Room" and "Football Game." Both were comical skits that Hurston had copyrighted several months earlier under the respective titles "Lawing and Jawing" and "Forty Yards." In the former, a judge (played in *Fast and Furious* by the popular comic actor Tim Moore) orders a prisoner to wear a muzzle in a watermelon patch for nine years; in the latter, which Hurston presented as "a Negro football game with the popular concept of Negro life," spectators exuberantly cheer on their teams at a football match between Howard and Lincoln schools.[64] Hurston and comedian Jackie (soon to be "Moms") Mabley performed as cheerleaders in the "Football Game" sketch, the plot of which was merely a backdrop for spirited chanting and dancing. Although not attributed to her on the program, Hurston was also responsible for "At Home in Georgia," which featured two folk songs that later became fixtures in her own concerts: "East Coast Blues" and "John Henry." Hurston had copyrighted a version of "At Home in Georgia" in July of 1931, under the title "Woofing." The surviving eleven-page typescript for this sketch depicts a "Negro Street in Waycross, Ga.," in which men play checkers and exchange ribbings while a woman irons white folks' clothes in the background.[65]

Hurston's participation in this Broadway undertaking exposed her directly to the power dynamics and politics intrinsic to commercial stage productions, and her initial excitement quickly gave way to frustration. Following an apparent disagreement with Randolph over the material she had contributed to *Fast and Furious,* Hurston complained to Mason that "they take all the life and soul out of everything and make it fit what their idea of Broadway should be like. Its sickening at times."[66] The show's early closing apparently came as no surprise to her. As she explained to Mason on September 25, "the man at the head of things was stupid and trite and squeezed all Negro-ness out of everything and substituted what he thought *ought* to be Negro humor." Hurston thus came to frame her disappointment in terms of Broadway's antagonism toward authentic "Negro-ness." Resigning herself to the production's banality, she told Mason that she had "decided to take whatever monies came out of the thing and wait for another chance."[67]

*Fast and Furious* brought Hurston into contact with a number of important African American artists, for Forbes Randolph had assembled a broad range of black talent for the large-scale musical revue.[68] Her relationship with these other artists was not entirely harmonious, in large part because her views on how to represent black cultural forms did not coincide with theirs. Most notable was her association with the musician and composer J. Rosamond Johnson, who wrote several musical numbers for the production in addition to training the choir.[69] Although Hurston initially noted Johnson's involvement with approbation,[70] she later blamed him for the musical's failure. "Mr. Randolph," she explained to Mason,

> trusted a good deal to Mr. Johnson's age and experience in selecting both cast and material, and he steered him too often off the highway to success. He more than once used his influence with Randolph to palm off friends of his, as good performers. People of no ability and doomed to failure and he discouraged anything that spoke the real Negro.[71]

While it is not clear which performers Hurston found objectionable, she may have been responding to Johnson's handling of her own work. The *Fast and Furious* program reveals that the Rosamond Johnson Quartet appeared in her "At Home in Georgia" sketch, helping to perform "John Henry." Considering that one critic praised the "sweet and melodious sounds" of the choral groups in this number, it seems likely that Hurston took exception to Johnson's concert treatment of her folk material.[72] As a woman who lacked Johnson's experience or authority as a musician, however, Hurston had little power to affect the overall shape of the revue. Instead, she got an up-close view of the "bleaching" forces that, to her mind, sapped black expressive practices of their authenticity.

Although the archive contains no direct evidence of Hurston's opinion of the dancing in *Fast and Furious,* she may have held similar concerns about its manifest allegiance to the "real Negro." Forbes Randolph hired Al Richard to stage the show's dances, an office he had previously performed for the annual all-black revue *Blackbirds.*[73] To the extent that *Fast and Furious* featured the kind of popular dancing that was de rigueur for black musicals on Broadway—including tap, the "violently agitating syncopation of sounds and swiftness of movements," and a chorus line of seventeen "Dancing Girls"—Hurston may have found much to bemoan.[74]

If contact with the various players involved in *Fast and Furious* thus deepened Hurston's dissatisfaction with existing artistic models for representing black expressive practices, she nevertheless chalked up her experience as efficacious. In a late September letter to Charlotte Mason, she summed up the situation: "Well, I have learned a lot about the mechanics of the stage, which will do me good in playwriting. I have received a good deal of publicity which is helpful *and* I did earn a little money."[75] In fact, her involvement in *Fast and Furious* paid off in more concrete ways, for Hurston recruited some of the show's cast and crew to work on her own concert in the making. The African American composer Porter Grainger, who contributed several of *Fast and Furious*'s musical numbers, signed on to do the musical arrangements for *The Great Day,* and two members of Forbes Randolph's Choir, Rosina Lefroy and Alexander Moody, joined her cast, though Moody withdrew before Hurston's revue opened. Carolyne Rich, one of *Fast and Furious*'s "Dancing Girls," became a lead performer in *The Great Day*'s all-important Fire Dance. Notwithstanding Hurston's criticisms of so much of Forbes Randolph's production, the musical provided a pool of talent from which she readily drew for her own all-black revue. In the most literal sense, then, Hurston's folk concert bore the traces of black musical theatre, one of the very traditions she so sharply denounced.

This overlap in casts is suggestive of the deeper entanglement between *The Great Day* and the commercial theatre. However much Hurston conceptualized her revue in opposition to existing theatrical representations of black folk culture, those representations informed her stage practice in meaningful ways. Indeed, Hurston's first direct reference to the concert that would become *The Great Day* should be read in light of her Broadway experiences. In her September 25 letter to Mason, she reports that she is "planning a Negro concert of the most intensely black type."[76] Significantly, this declaration comes in the same letter as her complaint that Forbes Randolph was "squeez[ing] all Negro-ness out of everything." With its blackface skits and frenzied chorus line dancing, on the one hand, and the choral refinements of composer Rosamond Johnson, on the other, *Fast and Furious* came to typify for Hurston the kind of commodified rendering of black culture that was captive to white demand. If this brand of theatre distorted what she believed to be the integrity of the folk, her "intensely black" folk concert would act as a corrective. The very conception of authentic blackness that undergirded Hurston's *The Great Day* thus emerged as a deliberate response to and critique of contemporaneous stage renderings in which she herself was implicated.

## Authenticity as Marketing Vehicle for *The Great Day*

For all intents and purposes, the trope of authenticity served as a powerful marketing tool for Hurston, who hoped her concert would reach a broad audience and generate some much needed income. Billed as "A Program of Original Negro Folklore," *The Great Day* enticed theatregoers with its promise of genuineness. Yet the manner in which Hurston used the rhetoric of authenticity—not only to justify her theatrical goals privately to her patron but also to promote her revue to the public at large—placed her squarely within the tradition of commercialized representations of black culture that she sought to contest. I turn now to her various public efforts to assert the naturalness of her own production, which included making anticommercial and social scientific claims.

Virtually all of the publicity material for Hurston's concert emphatically distinguished her production from other commercial stage fare. An announcement sent out in advance of the January 10 premiere of *The Great Day*, for example, spelled out:

> This program is offered with the particular wish that lovers of
> true Negro music may come to realize that the generally well
> known and highly concertized spirituals are only a small part
> of an enormous source of original and unusual songs as yet
> untouched.
>
> The spirituals used in "Great Day" are fresh and without the
> artificial polish of re-arrangement. The dances have not been
> influenced by Harlem or Broadway.[77]

As in her essays and letters, Hurston sets up a division between the
"untouched" and "fresh" "true Negro" and the "artificially polished"
versions of black culture depicted on the stages of the urban North.
Differentiating her presentation of the folk from high-art renderings
of black spirituals and from the Harlem night clubs and Broadway
shows that played to mainstream white audiences, Hurston promised
to deliver a theatrical performance purportedly free of the "taint" of
commodification.

This distinction was reinforced by a program note penned by Alain
Locke, the prominent black intellectual who was chief architect of the
New Negro movement.[78] His statement, worth quoting at length, cast
Hurston's presentation as no less than the raw material on which con-
temporaneous commercial versions were based:

> From Stephen Foster to contemporary Broadway the folkways
> and folk-arts of the American Negro have been presented in tinc-
> tured and adulterated approximations. That they have seemed
> characteristic and have been so movingly effective is, in view of
> this fact, all the greater testimony to their power and originality
> in the pure undiluted folk-forms that for generations have been in
> the shrewd and disarming custody of the common people. These
> folk have always had two arts,—one for themselves and one for
> the amusement and beguilement of their masters. And seldom,
> if ever, can the white man or even the sophisticated Negro break
> through to that inner circle so well-guarded by the instinctive
> make-believe and "possum play" of the Negro peasant.[79]

Coupling Broadway and minstrelsy through the figure of Stephen Foster,
the white composer of minstrel songs, Locke not only discriminates
here between black folk arts and their commercial incarnations. He

further differentiates between what James Scott has termed the "pub-lic" and the "hidden transcript"—the hegemonic public conduct and its counterpart, the backstage discourse that cannot be spoken in the face of power.[80] In Locke's figuration, the folk arts of American Negroes exist on two levels simultaneously: expression designed for other black folk and expression designed for whites and middle-class blacks.

Having drawn a line between the commercial and the noncom-mercial, the folk and the nonfolk, Locke proceeded to situate *The Great Day* in the most unadulterated "inner circle." The concert, his program note went on to state,

> is . . . a rare sample of the pure and unvarnished materials from which the stage and concert tradition has been derived; and ought to show how much more unique and powerful and spirit-compelling the genuine Negro folk-things really are. That this legacy has not been irrevocably lost or completely overlaid is good news of the highest spiritual and practical importance for all who wish to know and understand the true elements of the Negro heart and soul.

Such discourse of rarity and purity lent considerable weight to Hurston's own claims of authenticity. For New York theatregoers attending *The Great Day*, no doubt familiar with the "stage and concert tradition" limned here as derivative, the $1 to $2.50 ticket price offered admission to a representation all but guaranteed to be the real thing.[81]

Hurston continued to rely on this strategy of equating authenticity and anticommercialism when promoting her revue in locales far from New York. Advance publicity for her 1934 Chicago production of *Singing Steel* trumpeted the concert as "an original piece of artistry with ryth-mic [sic] music quite different from the ordinary arrangements" and a vital contribution toward "debunking the current mammy-song Jolson conception of the Southern Negro."[82] In an interview with the *Chicago Daily News*, which ran the week before the performance under the head-line "Campaigns Here for Negro Art in Natural State," Hurston touted her "musical sketch of Negro songs 'unretouched'" with language bear-ing a strong resemblance to her "Spirituals and Neo-Spirituals" essay published the same year. She declared that while the "Negro song as sung on the concert stage is a song with its face lifted," her own pro-gram offered "songs sung as the unlettered Negroes sing them."[83]

To play up the differences between her production and popular commercial entertainment, Hurston also found ways to capitalize on her distance from New York. In a lecture given at Rollins College in advance of her January 1933 staging of *From Sun to Sun* in Winter Park, Florida, Hurston announced her intention to "work up a production of enduring value" using a "cast of the true negro type rather than that of the New York-ized negro."[84] Read in relation to her running critique of the white-dominated conventions governing black theatre in New York, Hurston's comments once again signal her rhetorical repudiation of the commercial influence of Harlem and Broadway. Her new location enabled her to peddle an "untainted" cast of Southerners. She even went so far as to discredit aspects of her own earlier productions— she later asserted that "Harlem negroes would fail miserably in a true portrayal of simple negro life"—in order to boost the ostensibly unmediated "naturalness" of her current endeavor.[85]

Hurston's alignment of her folk revue with the "uncommercialized and therefore undiluted" was in fact a common maneuver with respect to black cultural production.[86] Writing about the relationship between African American and popular music traditions, Andrew Ross has cited the frequency with which "a discourse about color ('whitened' music) is spliced with a discourse about commercialization ('alienated' music)."[87] Ross offers a convincing critique of the tendency to assume a binary opposition between the commercial and the authentic and to demonize all forces of commercialization. But his point about the prevalence of this discourse also serves as a reminder that in the field of black performance, a "regime of value" rendered authenticity a prime currency.[88] Under such a regime, Hurston's pains to distinguish her work from the commercial mainstream constituted an effective sales policy.

Inasmuch as Hurston promoted the authenticity of her concert by claiming distance from the commercial, so too she emphasized the social scientific basis of her production. The program announcement for *The Great Day* stated at the outset, "Miss Hurston spent over three years in the South collecting the material used in 'Great Day,' in an effort to assemble an authentic Negro folk-cycle of representative folk songs, dances, tales and conjure rituals."[89] Locke's program note similarly declared that the folk cycle was "collected and recorded by Miss Hurston over three years of intimate living among the common folk in the primitive privacy of their own Negro way of life."[90] By stressing that she had traveled to the southern United States and the Bahamas and witnessed the folk customs being reenacted onstage, Hurston asserted a research-based authority that lent credibility to her theatrical enterprise. As her reputation as an author and scholar grew in subsequent years, conspicuous references to her academic credentials supplemented this focus on ethnographic research. A notice for her Chicago production described her as "one of the foremost living authorities on the subject" of Negro folklore and cited her membership in the American Ethnological Society, the American Folk-Lore Society, the American Anthropological Society, and the American Association for the Advancement of Science.[91] Part and parcel of her rhetorical bid for authenticity, such attention to Hurston's scholastic qualifications helped further differentiate her concert from contemporaneous representations of black culture. In the crowded field of all-black revues, Hurston's anthropological training and research were assets she could hardly afford not to exploit.

Yet in many ways, these social science trappings once again aligned Hurston's folk concert with the very tradition of popular black theatre she sought to oppose. Alleging authenticity on the grounds of first-hand collecting had long been a convention employed by purveyors of African American culture. In the nineteenth century, blackface minstrel performers promoted their enactments as more authentic than other stage shows by making claims not unlike Hurston's. As historian Robert Toll has established, early blackface entertainers frequently traveled around the country, drawing from the black folk idioms they encountered and advertising their travels as "field work" among southern Negroes.[92] More broadly speaking, according to Roger Abrahams, "a brush with slaves at play and an absorption of elements of their lore from direct observation became a way of establishing one's credentials as a vernacular artist, whether on the minstrel stage, the lecturer's platform, or the written page."[93] Once African American performers entered the minstrel field in the post–Civil War years, they reinforced their status as authentic representatives of black culture by stressing their links to the South.[94] In the twentieth century, similar claims could be found accompanying such prominent productions as *Porgy and Bess*, the 1935 "folk opera" by George Gershwin, who journeyed to an island off the coast of South Carolina and soaked up elements of Gullah culture in preparation; a reporter from the *New York Herald Tribune* documented and publicized his "fieldwork."[95] Methodological issues aside, the duration of Hurston's time in the field greatly surpassed the scope of any "research" done by these other artists. Still, the parallels in discourse demonstrate the extent to which authenticity and its attendant acts of authentication were established modes of self-promotion in commercial black performance. What Hurston and a long line of producers of black theatre shared was an understanding of the market value of authenticity and the rhetorical means to assert it.[96]

## Commercial Pressures: Resistance and Accommodation

If the very act of claiming authenticity was a savvy commercial calculation on Hurston's part, it was not the only market consideration she took into account in the course of staging her folk concert. Aside from matters of promotion and publicity, certain decisions Hurston made about the composition of her program were direct products of her enmeshment in the commercial arena. The interlocutor figure she employed in *The Great Day* is perhaps the most salient example of the conundrum she faced in simultaneously resisting and accommodating commercial forces.

Rather than moving seamlessly from one section to the next, Hurston broke up the narrative of *The Great Day* with brief interludes during which the actor Leigh Whipper, an established figure on the African American theatre scene who also played the role of the itinerant preacher, appeared in front of the curtain and spoke directly to the audience.[97] As the *New York Age* reported, Whipper prefaced each section "with a brief explanation to the large audience of whites, with a few Negroes here and there, as to the peculiar meaning or significance of the presentation which followed."[98] The explanations Whipper furnished, a kind of live enactment of program notes, were clearly designed to help bridge the knowledge gap between the predominantly white audience and the black folk material depicted onstage. Equally important, by periodically interjecting this contextual material into the narrative of her revue, Hurston signaled her departure from musical theatre, where such pedagogical devices were rarely in evidence.

Hurston's use of an actor to convey this material in *The Great Day* had the paradoxical effect of conjuring the specter of minstrelsy, the commercial institution whose legacy she was so intent on repudiating. In general, New York critics seemed to struggle to find the appropriate designation for Whipper's intermittent appearances, alternately describing him as an "oral program annotator," "before-the-curtain speaker," and "master of ceremonies."[99] Yet two separate reviews of the concert, one from the *New York Amsterdam News*, the other from the *New York Times*, characterized Whipper as the "interlocutor between scenes."[100] On the surface, this label may appear no different from the terms cited earlier; all fit the *American Heritage Dictionary* definition of "interlocutor" as one "who takes part in a conversation, often formally or officially."[101] Historically, though, the term "interlocutor" referred specifically to a key figure in blackface minstrelsy. According to Robert Toll, the interlocutor emerged as a fixture in the minstrel show during the 1850s, when a standard three-part format took hold. Characterized by his dignity and grandiloquence, the interlocutor typically sat at center stage, where he played the high-minded straight man to the raucous comedy of the two end men. Toll describes the interlocutor as the "master of ceremony," an "onstage director" who facilitated the first part of the show to meet the audience's tastes.[102] In this sense, then, the label "interlocutor" dovetails with the other terminology employed by the newspaper critics.

That some reviewers perceived Whipper's performance in terms of the nineteenth-century minstrel show speaks to that institution's continuing grip on the imagination of American theatregoers. Even the reviewer who one minute emphatically distinguished Hurston's folk concert from other stage representations by insisting that *The Great Day* "offered something . . . entirely different from that which we, in this part of the country, are familiar," in the next minute drew on the indelible imagery of minstrelsy to explain Whipper's role to her readers.[103] As a recognizable actor, Whipper made a logical choice to serve as emcee in *The Great Day*. Yet regardless of Hurston's intentions, to at least a portion of her audience the appearance of a black male mediating figure in a revue of black vernacular music and dance aligned her folk concert with a tradition of white expropriation and commodification of African American culture.[104]

Hurston may well have recognized the irony in the fact that her attempt to offset the audience's lack of knowledge about the folk had the inadvertent effect of allying her concert with the very tradition from which she sought to break. Leigh Whipper did not perform in *From Sun to Sun*, presented two-and-a-half months after *The Great Day* at the New School for Social Research, and surviving programs indicate that no figure even resembling an interlocutor appeared in this or any later stagings of the revue. Instead, Hurston relied on textual program notes to relay contextual information about the folk forms featured in her concert. Although there is no way of knowing definitively why she abandoned the master of ceremonies figure, the decision is at least suggestive of her dissatisfaction with the way it was construed by *The Great Day* audience and her desire to disassociate her work from the legacy of the minstrel show, the preeminent source of misrepresentations of blackness on the commercial stage.

At the same time, Hurston made other changes to her program that served to align her concert with the conventions of popular black entertainment. *From Sun to Sun* contained one number that did not appear in *The Great Day,* a one-act play called "The Fiery Chariot," which ran just before the finale Fire Dance.[105] Hurston had copyrighted the "Original Negro Folk Tale" in 1931, but it was based on a popular folk tale she had collected during her research expedition in the South.[106] Suspending the revue's chronological tracking of present-day life in a Florida railroad work camp, the skit introduced a new set of characters—a slave named Ike, his wife, Dinah, their young son, and Ole Massa—and transported the audience to an antebellum southern plantation.[107] In the play, Ike's devout Christianity is put to the test when Ole Massa dons a white sheet and pretends he is the Lord come to take Ike to heaven. Terrified at the sight of the white figure standing outside his door, Ike tries to con his way out of his predicament and ultimately succeeds when he convinces "God" to step back from the door so he has enough room to make a clean break.

While the skit worked on multiple levels simultaneously, both poking fun at Ike's religiosity and celebrating his survivalist tactics, perhaps its most striking feature within the framework of Hurston's program was its disruption of the concert's narrative structure. Two factors may well have eased this apparently radical disjunction. For those familiar with the body of stories about the ongoing struggle between John and Ole Massa, "The Fiery Chariot" would surely have seemed part and parcel of the daily life of the concert's black folk community.[108] For those unfamiliar with such folktales, the inclusion of a short, self-contained skit in the middle of a program of songs, dances, and pantomime resembled the revue format of many Broadway productions, which, like *Fast and Furious,* typically featured a hodgepodge of loosely connected acts rather than a straightforward, coherent plot line. Hurston had always sought to represent a broad range of African American vernacular forms, and the skit provided a vehicle for her to bring storytelling, an essential component of African American folk life, directly to the stage.[109] But she also may have calculated that the closer her program seemed on the surface to the standard format governing black musical revues, the greater her chances were for getting the concert picked up by a producer. In this case, then, Hurston may have found a way to assert her own agenda while adhering to extant theatrical conventions for black musical revues. She was evidently satisfied with this format, for she continued to include a dramatized folk tale in all subsequent stagings of her folk concert.[110]

Later changes Hurston made to her concert further increased its superficial similarities to the commercial fare she claimed to oppose. Her 1934 production of *All De Live Long Day* in Florida, for example, featured a string of spirituals, most of which had not appeared in her earlier revues. Unlike the spirituals performed in *The Great Day* that followed on the heels of a preacher's rousing sermon, these songs apparently served no narrative purpose but were presented merely for their own sake, sung alternately by a soloist and an ensemble. Given Hurston's insistence that "Negro spirituals are not solo or quartette material," her use of a soloist in a revue originally designed to challenge the prevalence of "neo-spirituals" seems incongruous.[111] Her decision was no doubt influenced by her recruitment of an able tenor-baritone and her desire to feature local talent in her revue: the soloist, A. B. Hicks, was "reported to possess a voice of wide range and unusual quality."[112] Still, the contradictions between her written critiques and her stage practice in this instance highlight the paradoxes inherent in Hurston's project and the ways she simultaneously contested and embraced existing theatrical conventions.

By a similar token, when Hurston staged *Singing Steel* in Chicago in the fall of 1934, she inserted a "Shim sham shimmy and break away" dance section into the Jook scene.[113] The section featured both the Buck and Wing, "a combination of clogs and jigs and song and dance" that was a staple of late minstrelsy and a forerunner of twentieth-century tap dancing, and the Shim Sham, a standard routine in show business created for the stage in the 1920s that involved a "slightly more complicated combination of tap and body movements."[114] Although Hurston had avowed that the dances in her concert "have not been influenced by Harlem or Broadway," she did not shy away in later years from staging idioms that actually derived from the popular theatre.[115] While she continued to strive to demonstrate the black southern roots of popular American dances, her program also evidenced the mutual influence of the folk and the commercial.

Taken together, these examples attest to the inevitable discrepancies between the rhetoric of authenticity and the practice of producing theatre in the commercial marketplace, the gaps between the discourse of anticommercialism, and the unavoidability of market mediation. Surely Hurston was aware of these contradictions, and her persistent reliance on the trope of authenticity suggests (at least) two key things about her relationship to it: first, that she considered the trope indispensable to compete in the theatrical arena; and second, that she did not believe that capitulating to certain commercial pressures negated the possibility of finding alternative ways to represent black folk expression on stage. At some level, Hurston's determination to promote the unmediated naturalness of her concert even while making commercially driven concessions is reminiscent of the "lies," or tall tales, she collected during her folklore expeditions.[116] As Ronald Radano has written, Hurston recognized the value of such "creative expressions of poetic license" and "ironic twists" as means for maximizing the black vernacular's "potential influence in the public sphere."[117] That is not to say that Hurston was lying when she professed authenticity. Rather, she refused to let the contradictions involved in making such claims outweigh her belief in their efficacy and validity. There were distinct differences between her concert and other stagings of black culture, and the language of authenticity gave her a way to frame those differences.[118] Lacking other sources of capital, she used the discourse of genuineness to participate in and critique the market for black cultural products.

Ultimately, Hurston's reliance on authenticity as an organizing trope for *The Great Day* and its successors also had distinct ramifications for her concert's reception, essentially setting the terms of the revue's appraisal. That, almost without exception, critics applauded the authenticity of her stagings indicates how effective Hurston's efforts in this arena were. As Arthur Ruhl of the *Herald Tribune* raved, "The difference between [*The Great Day*'s] various 'turns' and the thing usually seen in Negro plays and musical comedies was that this was the real thing; unadulterated, and not fixed and fussed up for purposes of commerce."[119] Critics of later iterations of the concert likewise praised the production for its "direct unvarnished manner" and "untainted" qualities.[120] Yet such testimonials to the concert's authenticity were far from unproblematic. As much as it proved a powerful marketing device, authenticity also carried distinct liabilities for Hurston. In commending her revues' naturalness and unaffectedness, critics concomitantly cast the productions as effortless, unpremeditated, and unmediated, thereby jeopardizing recognition of her artistry.

# 2
## Choreography and the Folk

Inasmuch as issues of authenticity hover over Hurston's representation of the folk, so too do issues of authorship. Given this book's focus on Hurston's production of black folk dance, questions about the authorship of stage movement are particularly pressing. Precisely what was the nature of Hurston's relationship to the dancing she incorporated into her folk revue, and what is the most fitting way to limn this relationship? To pose the question more bluntly, to what extent should Hurston be considered a choreographer? On first blush, the term may appear thoroughly inappropriate, for Hurston did not function as a choreographer in the conventional sense of inventing or orchestrating new dance moves. The dances that appeared in her concert—both the incidental dances featured in the Jook scene and the Bahamian Fire Dance finale—were preexistent, communally created and sustained folk forms. The archive provides no evidence that Hurston ever referred to herself as a choreographer, nor did she ever use the related term choreography to describe her dance work. It is worth bearing in mind, however, that in the 1920s and 1930s, terminology like "arranged," "staged," and "directed" was much more commonly used to recognize dance artists working on the theatrical stage. And in fact, the program for a 1939 exclusive presentation of the Fire Dance listed Hurston as "Dance Director" (Figure 2).[1] Whereas she employed a musical arranger and a chorus director to help train her singers for the New York debut of her concert, Hurston never sought any professional assistance with the movement numbers. Instead, she

National Exhibition of Skills
New Auditorium, Orlando, Florida
January 16 - February  6, 1939

—————————

THE FIRE DANCE
January 25, 1939 - 8 P.M.

The Federal Writers in Florida invite you to attend this program
that is being presented in connection with the new national folklore studies of the Federal Writers' Project, Works Progress Administration.

Dance Director:  Zora Neale Hurston

The Players:  Florida troupe of Negro singers and dancers

The Fire Dance, a celebration honoring the arrival of spring, is a
folk dance that originated in Africa.  It was brought to Florida by
immigrant Negro workers from the Bahama Islands.  The dance has three
parts:  The Jumping Dance; Ring Play; The Crow Dance.

Jumping Dance:  When a certain tree puts out new leaf, the priest,
or houngan, called the tribe to a celebration.  Dancing about a fire-
heated drum of goat-hide, each dancer "moves" according to the drum
rhythm and tone, which is extremely varied.  The dance keeps up until
the drum grows cold.

Ring Play:  This is African rhythm with European borrowings.  One
dancer in center begins to sing and circle the ring seeking a partner
as the verse is being sung.  This keeps up until the dancers exhaust
their repertoire of steps and verses.

Crow Dance:  This is a rhythmic imitation of a buzzard (African crow)
flying and seeking food.  The dancers are costumed to represent human beings, birds, animals and trees.  In short, it is symbolic of
all nature taking part in the procreation of life that comes with
spring.

Concerning the dance and its director:  Zora Neale Hurston is a
native of Florida.  An authority on the folklore of Southern Negroes,
she is currently editing a volume on the Florida Negro for the
Federal Writers' Project of Florida.  The dance has been presented
at the John Golden Theatre, New York, the 1934 National Folklore
Festival, St. Louis, and before audiences in Chicago, Winter Park,
Daytona Beach, Sanford, and Lake Wales.

**Figure 2.** The Fire Dance Program, 1939. Image provided courtesy of the
Zora Neale Hurston Manuscript Collection, Department of Special and
Area Studies Collections, George A. Smathers Libraries, University
of Florida.

alone took on the responsibility of transforming the Fire Dance folk
cycle from its Caribbean vernacular incarnation to its American theatrical manifestation. The question thus remains: does Hurston merit
the label choreographer for her staging of black diasporic folk dance?

As I have worked on this project over the past several years, other scholars first learning of Hurston's involvement with dance have responded with both surprise and delight. Yet my contention that Hurston "choreographed"—as opposed to "staged" or "arranged"—the black folk dances that appeared in her revues has occasionally met with skepticism. This reluctance to grant that the nature of Hurston's dance work constituted a kind of choreography, I believe, indicates that there is much at stake in how and to whom we earmark the designation "choreographer." Evidently, we dance scholars have invested a great deal in the term—but what kind of investment and for what reasons?

Recognizing the controversy that attributions can engender, this chapter aims to give thoughtful consideration to the advantages and potential pitfalls of applying the label "choreographer" to Hurston. To query her relationship to dance, I probe the process by which she encountered, researched, learned, documented, and taught the Bahamian Fire Dance to her assembled troupe of performers. Concomitantly, I examine how Hurston negotiated the seemingly conflicting poles of authenticity and authorship. An African American woman working with black folk dance in the 1930s, Hurston faced a distinct if not singular dilemma: calling attention to her methodical orchestration of her stage material and her active training of cast members compromised the perceived naturalness of her revue, yet downplaying her own artistic agency meant forgoing credit for the creativity and labor that underwrote her concert. Her response to this predicament was to calculate carefully how much and what kind of credit she claimed publicly for her concert. In attending to Hurston's choreographic practice and the strategic staging of her own artistic role, this chapter thus further exposes the complicated labor that lay behind the veil of authenticity. At the same time, it raises new questions about the exercise of power involved in the ways we acknowledge and categorize that labor.

## What Is a Choreographer?

The recovery of Hurston's dance practice, then, provides an opportunity not only to take a fresh look at her career and the American dance landscape in the 1930s, but also to reassess the very terms we use to talk about dance as a mode of cultural production, especially the term "choreographer." What kind of work has the term historically performed?

Who has been entitled to wear the mantle of choreographer, and who has been excluded from the category? What are the consequences of drawing lines between those who can and cannot claim the appellation, and what should be the parameters of what counts as choreography? While an in-depth investigation of the history of the term "choreographer" is beyond the scope of this project, a brief consideration of how the term has traditionally been used helps lay the ground for scrutinizing its relevance for Hurston.

In its most common usage, "choreography" refers to the art of making dances, and "choreographer" designates the artist responsible for a dance's creation and arrangement. What exactly this means, however, is far from settled and a matter of significant historical contingency. With its etymological roots in the Greek *choreia* for dance and the French *graphie* for writing, the word choreography referred literally in the seventeenth and eighteenth centuries to the written notation of dances. The nineteenth and twentieth centuries saw a shift in the meaning of the term as the emphasis came to center on the "actual invention and sequencing of movements."[2] But because the choreographic tradition was a European ballet-based one, it took some time for white American modern dance artists, who deliberately distanced themselves from ballet, to appropriate the appellation "choreographer" for themselves.[3] Although modern dance began as a solo form, it legitimized itself in the 1920s and 1930s in part by adopting the elite art model of the separation between the author and the aesthetic object. Under this model, "the individual choreographer was conceived of as the creative source of the work executed by the dancers, as the person who shaped and set the work of art until it was ready to be presented before an audience."[4]

Today the label is considerably less restricted, claimed by those working in concert dance, Broadway, and music videos alike, but it is clear that "choreographer" has historically been a term of privilege and power, functioning to authorize and to exclude. Accompanying the separation the term marks between the artist/creator and the dancers/performers has been a division between choreography and improvisation, with the former perceived as premeditated and intentional and the latter seen as impromptu and haphazard. While recent scholarship, such as Susan Foster's *Dances That Describe Themselves* and David Gere and Ann Cooper Albright's edited volume *Taken by Surprise,* has helped complicate the accepted dichotomy between choreography and improvisation, this binary has not been without its utility for certain parties.[5] In the early twentieth century, the constructed opposition between the choreographed and the improvised served to elevate white creative artistry, which implicitly—and often explicitly—defined itself against the putatively "natural" expressive behavior of black performers. Hurston's Bahamian Fire Dance in fact played a role in supporting the emerging bifurcation between black folk dance as improvisation and white modern dance as choreography (see chapter 6). In the history of American dance, meanwhile, examples of white artists receiving choreographic credit for moves developed by black artists and treated as "raw material" abound.[6]

For a number of reasons, the attribution "choreographer" was therefore not available to Hurston at the time she staged the Bahamian Fire Dance. Chief among these was the perception that the dancing that appeared in her revue was unrehearsed, spontaneous expression—in other words, the opposite of choreographed. The critic Arthur Ruhl's testimonial that *The Great Day* embodied the ideal of "natural and unpremeditated art" epitomizes this view.[7] However much Hurston actively cultivated the impression of naturalness and used the semblance of spontaneity to her advantage, this discourse played into entrenched racist stereotypes about instinctive black performativity—stereotypes that left little if any room for the recognition of methodical black artistry. As a black woman working with "low art" black vernacular forms during a time when dance was struggling to establish itself as a respectable field, Hurston faced a convergence of racial and artistic hierarchies that made it unthinkable for her to identify herself as a choreographer. If my employment of the term to describe Hurston is thus anachronistic, it is my hope that this usage will further trouble the binaries between choreography and improvisation, the individual and the communal, and the modern and the folk.

Still, it would no doubt be possible to problematize these dichotomies and interrogate Hurston's dance stagings without relying on the word "choreographer." As it happens, there are some rather sound reasons not to apply the term to Hurston. By no stretch of the imagination did she create the Bahamian Fire Dance. Transported to the Caribbean by African slaves, the dance commingled with European practices before finding its way to Florida, where Hurston stumbled upon it. Although I do not subscribe to the belief that such collective folk forms are "authorless," it could certainly be argued that the Western idea of the individual choreographer is an inadequate way of characterizing the kind of collaborative artistic production that is responsible for generating and sustaining dances like the Fire Dance.[8] Unlike her contemporary Katherine Dunham, moreover, Hurston's transposition of folk dance to the theatrical stage did not involve fusing the Caribbean movements with other recognizable stylistic techniques like ballet. Quite the opposite, Hurston sought to represent as "naturally" as possible the same dances she had encountered in Florida and studied in the Bahamas, despite the contradictions that entailed.

Even in taking the position, as I do, that there are judicious reasons for treating Hurston as a choreographer despite her failure to fit conventional understandings of the category, it is important to be alert to the perils involved in limning Hurston's contributions in this way. Much as it has in literary studies, making Hurston a "foremother" and "originary" source for subsequent stagings of Afro-Caribbean folk dance would once again threaten to reify her by obscuring the entire matrix of influences and historical forces that shaped her own artistic practice. For Hurston, the most immediate sources of influence were the native Bahamians whose performance of the Fire Dance first captured her interest and from whom she learned to dance it herself. More broadly speaking, describing Hurston as a choreographer risks glossing over the contributions of the innumerable folk artists who created and sustained the Fire Dance for years before and years after she incorporated it into her concert. Yet calling Hurston a choreographer need not necessarily elide or undermine the contributions of these Bahamian artists. Their authorship of the Fire Dance in its vernacular form is incontrovertible, even if their individual identities cannot be known. There is room, I would argue, for both Hurston and her Bahamian sources to be understood as choreographers.

Even so, one might wonder whether approaching Hurston as a choreographer overstates her dance accomplishments. In her autobiography *Dust Tracks on a Road*, Hurston maintains that she was "seeking no reputation" in the field of dance and denies being "a singer, a dancer, [or] . . . a musician," despite the fact that she de facto served in each of those roles in her capacities as director and performer. (She also insists that she brings up her concert work "not because it means so much to me, but because it did mean something to others.")[9] While her self-deprecation is of a piece with the evasiveness and "diversionary tactics" that typify her autobiographical writing and cannot be taken at face value,[10] dance was undeniably only one part of the "*real* Negro art theatre" she worked to realize. There is also evidence that Hurston did not always excel as the director of a dance ensemble, leaving some of her *Great Day* dancers disgruntled.[11] Whatever her leadership skills— and it should surprise no one that a black woman lacking ample funds and without experience overseeing large groups of performers encountered challenges to her leadership—applying the term choreographer to Hurston does not require proclaiming her a genius as such. Nor does it require leveling the distinctions between her and those who devoted their lives to dance. In making the case that Hurston should be considered a choreographer, I do not mean to suggest that her choreographic achievements were on a par with those of Katherine Dunham or Pearl Primus, her more celebrated contemporaries, whose dance training was extensive and formal.[12] Arguing that Hurston's accomplishments included choreography should in no way devalue the artistry of those who have already been recognized in the dance field.

In spite of the various hazards, I believe that there are compelling grounds for treating Hurston as a choreographer and that the values of doing so ultimately outweigh the risks. To better understand these grounds, it is helpful to return to the label "choreographer" and probe beneath its casual associations. Rather than hammer out a new definition of the term, I want to focus on its "author-function"—what Michel Foucault has articulated as the operation and effects of the figure of the author in discourse. In his 1969 essay "What Is an Author?," Foucault examines the "singular relationship that holds between an author and a text, the manner in which a text apparently points to this figure who is outside and precedes it."[13] The presence of an author's name, he argues, "is functional in that it serves as a means of classification." Yet this function is neither uniform across discourses, cultures, and times nor does it take shape in any simple or spontaneous manner.[14] While the meanings and effects of the designation "choreographer" likewise fluctuate in accordance with the contexts in which it is invoked, I want to flag two levels at which the term performs a fundamental kind of ideological work that are essential to recognizing its significance for Hurston.

First and most obviously, calling someone a "choreographer" assigns credit to that individual for a given dance production; the term thereby serves as an assertion of authorship. Notwithstanding poststructuralist proclamations about the death of the author, "Our investment in [the] institution [of authorship]," as scholars like Peggy Kamuf have contended, "is massive. All sorts of values are exchanged within its construction."[15] Indeed, authorship continues to hold a good deal of economic, legal, and political—as well as aesthetic and cultural—capital. Granting that authorship is a figure of discourse, then, should by no means eclipse its quite material effects. Following the insights of Foucault as well as those who have contested the death of the author, it behooves us to recognize that assertions of authorship—like those that the term "choreographer" enacts—are discursively constructed and have real repercussions.

Second and perhaps more tacitly, the designation "choreographer" acknowledges a history of labor: the use of the word simultaneously assumes and establishes that an executed dance has been worked out in advance. It is here that the distinctions between choreography and improvisation tend to get inscribed. While the term choreography marks dance as predetermined, improvisation is used to describe dance that is composed on the spot. Yet as scholarship on African American expressive forms like jazz and tap has demonstrated, improvisation depends equally on a history of labor.[16] A more accurate account of where the two modes of production diverge, I believe, would center on their different objectives, including the different ratios in each between what Susan Foster has characterized as the "known"—that "set of behavioral conventions," "structural guidelines," and individual predilections that condition and delimit an improvising body's choices— and the "unknown"—"that which was previously unimaginable."[17]

Both implications of the term "choreographer" were of consequence to Hurston. Her investment in authorship was ardent and unflagging and will be addressed in greater detail later. Her interest in invoking a history of labor, on the other hand, was more equivocal. With artlessness and simplicity at the cornerstone of her marketing efforts, affirming too much labor threatened to undermine the perceived naturalness, and therefore diminish the value, of her folk concerts. When Hurston referred to the estimation of a critic who "said that he did not believe that the concert was rehearsed, it looked so natural," she did so not deploringly but as proof of her project's success.[18]

The term choreographer has typically carried another ideological sense closely related to the denotation of authorship: that of originality. This is where the case for Hurston as choreographer becomes most tenuous, for the Bahamian Fire Dance that appeared in her revue was anything but newly invented. Yet if originality is often considered a prerequisite of authorship, the assumption that what choreographers produce must be novel deserves serious rethinking. As the art theorist Rosalind Krauss has asserted, the notion of the "originality of the avant-garde" is a "modernist myth."[19] Scholars in a number of disci-

plines have likewise demonstrated that the Western doctrine that
"*genuine* authorship is *originary* in the sense that it results not in a
variation, an imitation, or an adaptation . . . but in an utterly new,
unique . . . work" is a fairly recent formulation, the product of changes
in writing and production practices that led to the emergence of the
Romantic notion of artist as genius.[20] Hurston herself provided an
explicit challenge to orthodox views of originality in her 1934 essay
"Characteristics of Negro Expression":

> It is obvious that to get back to original sources is much too dif-
> ficult for any group to claim very much as a certainty. What we
> really mean by originality is the modification of ideas. The most
> ardent admirer of the great Shakespeare cannot claim first source
> even for him. It is his treatment of the borrowed material.[21]

Hurston's definition of originality as the reinterpretation of existing
idioms resonates with Krauss's argument about the complementarity
and inextricability of the original and the copy in an "aesthetic economy" that nonetheless valorizes the former and discredits the latter.[22]

More to the point, Hurston's remarks provide a rationale—perhaps
unwittingly—for appraising her treatment of folk dance and the question of choreography on different grounds. By and large, the emphasis
on novelty as a criterion for authorship has yet to be adequately de-
stabilized in dance studies. After all, modern dance, still the focus of
so much dance scholarship, is a tradition premised on the idea that
each generation of artists must break from the past. And as Doris
Humphrey stated in her posthumously published 1959 book *The Art
of Making Dances,* in the face of commonplace definitions of choreography as "the arranging of steps in all directions," there is a need to
"set about the problem [of choreography] in a different way and from a
different direction, which will lead to composing and not arranging."[23]
More recently, however, dance scholar Randy Martin has posited that
"a choreographer cannot initiate a particular dance by originating, in
any absolute sense, the movement of which it is composed," principally
because "the creation of all dances must begin in the middle—that is,
in the midst of those capacities for movement which the dancers embody."[24] While Martin's concern is with how the interrelationship of
structure and agency in the two constituent parts of dance, choreography and technique, is relevant for cultural studies and political theory,
I would like to approach Hurston's case as a chance to take seriously

his suggestion that choreography is not necessarily the invention of new moves but a "metatechnique" that generates and organizes "means of movement" for knowledgeable bodies.[25] Such a position is crucial for leveling the distinctions between so-called art dance and social or vernacular dance. From this perspective, creativity in ballet and folk dance alike involves the mobilization of existing movement codes.

Inasmuch as approaching Hurston's dance work as an instance of choreography (rather than simply direction or arrangement) may be a valuable way of unsettling dominant views of the choreographer as the lone genius originator, it also serves an important historiographical function. Granting Hurston a status she was not afforded in her own time, that is to say, is a deliberate tactic, designed to bring to light certain aspects of her stage practice that have gone underappreciated or altogether ignored. Regardless of how we conceptualize the term "choreographer" today, the fact remains that the designation was not attainable for her during the period she was working. While her authorial standing in relation to her concert in general and the Bahamian Fire Dance in particular was a highly contested matter, her reliance on the rhetoric of spontaneity—at a time when black performance was judged primarily if not wholly on the basis of its perceived authenticity—almost completely masked her artistic labor. Ironically, the one aspect of the term "choreographer" that Hurston could and did overtly claim was "originality": not only did she publicly announce her intent to present southern black folk material "in its most original form," but she billed her concert as "A Program of Original Negro Folklore."[26] In this instance, however, "original" meant neither newly invented nor reinterpreted but rare and "untampered with." In other words, the term here was part and parcel of Hurston's authenticity campaign, which required downplaying her own mediating role. Despite the fact that Hurston could not, this chapter strategically enlists the label "choreographer" both to help revisibilize a long-invisibilized history and to loosen the term's equation with notions of solitary invention.

## The Stakes of Authorship

While Hurston's relationship to the folk was a complicated one, her desire to be recognized as the author of her folk representations was unambiguous. The fact that she sought copyright for a number of her plays stands as a reminder of her serious interest in authorship. So too does the entreaty she made in 1925 to the writer Annie Nathan Meyer to attend an upcoming production of one of her early plays: "Do come and like a good Zora rooter Yell 'Author, author'!!"[27] If Hurston embraced the role of theatrical author at the start of her career, her longing for artistic credit only intensified in the ensuing years, particularly as she began to experience competition regarding representations of black folk culture. This rivalry was directly related to the growing circulation and popularization of black vernacular styles and, specifically, to the acclaim other, more powerful individuals were receiving for what Hurston perceived as misrepresentations of black folk material.

In point of fact, a discernible sense of vying for credit in the arena of black folk art runs through much of Hurston's correspondence in the late twenties and early thirties, particularly as she was gathering the songs, dances, and tales of southern blacks that she would later publicize in print and on stage. In 1928, for example, after receiving a copy of the 1926 volume *Negro Workaday Songs* by Howard Odom and Guy Johnson, two renowned white collectors of African American folk material, Hurston confessed to Harlem Renaissance intellectual Alain Locke, "I was almost afraid to read it, fearful lest they had beat m̶ us to it in the matter of songs."[28] As her writing here suggests, on top of the anxiety that others would disseminate the black folk idioms she was collecting before she got a chance to present them, Hurston also had to negotiate her subordinate position with respect to Locke, who carried great influence with their mutual white patron, Charlotte Osgood Mason. Replacing "m"—presumably "me"—with the collective "us," Hurston revealed her reluctance to claim sole credit for her work lest she offend her backers. She went on to say that fortunately, the work of Odom and Johnson left plenty of room for improvement, her relief a testament to the distinction she sought for herself in the field of black folk arts.

Racial politics unquestionably informed and underlay Hurston's concern over artistic credit. As she complained in a 1928 letter to her friend and fellow writer Langston Hughes, "It makes me sick to see how these cheap white folks are grabbing our stuff and ruining it. I am almost sick—my one consolation being that they never do it right and so there is still a chance for us."[29] The increasing use of black material by white authors and producers, whose greater resources and access to mass audiences put them in a better position to profit from it, thus

fueled her compulsion to stake out her own position among the prolif-
erating representations of black vernacular culture.

By far the best known of Hurston's contests, however, was her
"battle for artistic authority" with Hughes over their 1931 play *Mule
Bone*. The battle culminated in outright accusations of theft and the
demise of both play and friendship.[30] In her 1999 account of Hurston
and Hughes's alliance and subsequent rift, Rachel Rosenberg revises
earlier tellings that construed the controversy primarily in terms of
personality conflicts and jealously. Shifting the terms of the debate,
Rosenberg focuses instead on ideological differences over "definitions
and representations of authorship, artistry, and authority" that came to
the fore when Hurston objected to Hughes's efforts to depict the play's
leading black female character as a sexual temptress.[31] In particular,
Rosenberg's analysis emphasizes the centrality of performance to the
team's creative process, explaining that Hurston's manner of acting
out the various parts as the two brainstormed in the spring of 1930 not
only served "to bridge the gap between group vernacular folk performances and solitary writing" but also furnished Hurston with a sense
of ownership over the dramatic material.[32] According to Rosenberg,
however, the dominance of literary models of authorship in the New
York community in the 1930s ultimately undermined Hurston's demands for artistic control and authorial credit.

While I agree with Rosenberg's assertion that a performance-
centered vernacular approach to creativity played an important role
in shaping Hurston's conception of artistry, I would also suggest that
Hurston's understanding of authorship was more complicated than
this. For reliance on the vernacular to account for Hurston's actions
imposes a strict binary between communal-oral and singular-literary
modes of production and consigns Hurston to the realm of the oral.
As much as communal methods of expression may have informed
Hurston's approach to creativity, they by no means isolated her from
individualized conceptions of artistry. To the contrary, the premium
placed on improvisation and the resultant competitive component of
many black vernacular formations demanded individual innovation on
the part of their practitioners, as Hurston was well aware. Her account
of the Jumping Dance, one of the three sections that comprised the
Bahamian Fire Dance, provides a vivid example. One by one, Hurston
explains, the dancers take turns in the center of the ring:

Each dancer develops some particular "move" of his own. Naturally
some are more talented than others and invent marvelous steps.
These are recognized as the definite property of the inventor, and
fights frequently break out at the theft of another's steps.[33]

The communal dynamic of folk idioms like the Fire Dance thus existed alongside and even fostered individual investment in the products of creative expression. This insight compels a rethinking of the
binary between individuality and communality that is typically invoked to differentiate vernacular from other "single-author" modes of
production. Without question, creativity in folk forms is cooperative
in nature, relying heavily on the participation of an "aesthetic community" of other performer-spectators.[34] Yet it is equally evident that
the manner in which invention unfolds in vernacular arenas gives rise
to an atmosphere in which practitioners try to outdo one another and
continually vie for personal acclaim. Once we relinquish the notion
that the concept of ownership was anathema to the folk, Hurston's own
negotiation of authorship becomes a more complicated affair, one that
necessarily involved more than a dualistic straddling of single and collective, literary and vernacular models of creation. Experiences like the
*Mule Bone* controversy, in which Hurston's own contributions were
disputed and her actions dismissed as feminine jealousy, only served
to heighten her need for authorial credit.[35]

Hurston's desire for recognition was no less pronounced when it
came to her dance work. Here, too, Hurston found herself competing
for credit with friends and colleagues. Perhaps felt most keenly was the
"theft" of her Bahamian dancers and dance material by the musician and
choir director Hall Johnson, her one-time collaborator (see chapters 5 and
6). Significantly, Hurston's autobiography also provides evidence of the
rivalry she felt with the choreographer Katherine Dunham. Dunham's
name surfaces in the "Concert" chapter of Hurston's *Dust Tracks on a
Road*, as she recalls staging her folk concert in Chicago in 1934:

Katherine Dunham loaned us her studio for rehearsal twice,
which was kind of her. Anyway, West Indian dancing had gone
west and created interest just as it had done in the east. When
I got to Jamaica on my first Guggenheim fellowship in 1936, I
found that Katherine Dunham had been there a few months
before collecting dances, and had gone on to Haiti.[36]

That Dunham appears in Hurston's chronicle, given Hurston's presence in the city where Dunham began her dance career, is not surprising in and of itself. Rather, it is the order of Hurston's remarks that seems somewhat curious. First Hurston brings her folk material, including the Bahamian dance number, to Chicago, where Dunham lends her rehearsal space; then the public's fascination with Caribbean dance broadens; then Dunham beats Hurston to Jamaica. What is left out in this telling—what was no doubt common knowledge by the time Hurston wrote this account and therefore did not need to be spelled out—is how prominent a role Dunham played in creating interest in Caribbean dance. By 1941, Dunham had staged *Tropics and Le Jazz Hot,* which featured a range of black diasporic dance forms, and performed in the Broadway hit *Cabin in the Sky,* winning acclaim for herself and helping secure acceptance for representations of Afro-Caribbean dance idioms on the American theatrical stage. What is ever so slightly implicit in Hurston's remarks, I want to suggest, is a sense of divestiture, of being outstripped by Dunham, who took up the work that Hurston had begun years earlier and who, in the early 1940s, was starting to receive the kind of recognition that Hurston never obtained in the field of dance. In her autobiography, Hurston insists on her satisfaction "in knowing I established a trend" toward Caribbean dance through her folk revues. She also emphatically maintains (perhaps a bit too much so) that she is "not upset by the fact that others have made something out of the things I pointed out," even while her own name is "never mentioned."[37] But there is no denying that Hurston was writing at a time when the diasporic narrative she struggled to introduce through her folk concerts had finally become legible, even while her contributions to this effort were becoming increasingly invisible.

If in spite of themselves, Hurston's remarks convey a sense of regret at the lack of public recognition she received for her own dance productions, she had specific reason to feel outdone by Dunham. In late 1934, Hurston applied for and received a fellowship from the Julius Rosenwald Fund to pursue a PhD in anthropology and folklore and conduct research in the Caribbean. Although the fund initially made her a $3,000 offer over a two-year period, with the possibility of extension for a third year, the Rosenwald board soon reneged, reducing her award to $700, limited to a seven-month period. A year and a half later, Hurston won a Guggenheim Fellowship, which allowed her to carry out the Caribbean fieldwork that she had originally proposed to the Rosenwald Fund. It was while she was in the Jamaican Maroons, an isolated community of descendants of fugitive slaves, that Hurston discovered Dunham's prior presence. Writing from Accompongtown in July 1936 to the anthropologist Melville Herskovits, with whom she had once worked, Hurston expressed a more specific frustration than appears in her autobiography:

> I found your name up here in the visitors book and Col. Rowe told
> me that you had spent the night here two years ago. Also found
> that Catherine Dunham had been here last year carrying out the
> program that I had mapped out for the Rosenwald gang. I can af-
> ford to laugh at them, of course, but their littleness is astounding.[38]

Hurston's reference to the Rosenwald Fund's "littleness" in regard to Dunham's presence in Jamaica was not capricious, for Dunham received a fellowship from the fund to conduct research in the Caribbean in the same year that Hurston had hers revoked.[39] And although Herskovits attempted to reassure Hurston that Dunham's visit to the Maroons was purely coincidental, it seems likely that the retraction of Hurston's grant was directly tied to the bestowal of Dunham's, the amount of which almost exactly matched that which had been rescinded from Hurston.[40]

While Hurston professed to Herskovits that she had "nothing against [Dunham] and could in no way be jealous of her work," her repeated disparagements of Dunham cast some doubt on this claim.[41] In both her written correspondence with Herskovits and in her literary publications, Hurston subtly but repeatedly critiqued Dunham's anthropological methods. In the same letter to Herskovits quoted from earlier, for example, Hurston obliquely indicates that Dunham's fieldwork was perhaps less than scrupulous, calling it "a wonder" that Dunham did not stay in Jamaica long enough to witness an important Maroon ceremony.[42] A more biting though less direct criticism appears in *Tell My Horse*, Hurston's 1938 account of her Jamaican and Haitian findings. Describing her interaction with Colonel Rowe, the leader of the Maroons, Hurston writes:

> He told me how Dr. Herskovits had been there and passed a night
> with him; how some one else had spent three weeks to study their
> dances and how much money they had spent in doing this. . . . He

offered to stage a dance for me also. I thanked him, but declined.
I did not tell him that I was too old a hand at collecting to fall for
staged-dance affairs. If I do not see a dance or a ceremony in its
natural setting and sequence, I do not bother. Self-experience has
taught me that those staged affairs are never the same as the real
thing.[43]

That "some one else" was unmistakably Dunham, and Hurston again
depicts herself as the savvier, more experienced collector, more at-
tuned to the dangers of divorcing "culture and art expressions" from
their original contexts.[44] Nine years later, Hurston took a final dig at
Dunham in a review for the *New York Herald Tribune Book Report*
of Dunham's own account of her visit to the Maroon settlement in
Jamaica, *Journey to Accompong*. This time Hurston couched her re-
proach in superficial praise, commending Dunham for her ability to
"sustain the thin material to the end":

> After all, thirty days in a locality is not much in research and hardly
> affords time enough for the field-worker to scratch the surface.
> Therefore it is to the tremendous credit of the author that she has
> achieved such an entertaining book.[45]

Her dignity inevitably shaken by the Rosenwald debacle, Hurston's
repeated condescensions were no doubt an attempt to redeem her
authority as a serious ethnographic researcher.

Yet I would suggest that Hurston's sense of rivalry with Dunham
derived not solely from the Rosenwald incident but also from the fact
that, notwithstanding Herskovits's insistence that the two women
"were after entirely different things," their interests did significantly
overlap.[46] In assuring Hurston that "since Katherine Dunham is primarily interested in the study of the dance, I do not think that you
will find her material conflicts with yours," Herskovits failed to grasp
the full extent of Hurston's engagement with dance.[47] Hurston, in
contrast, perceived a direct connection between her own staging of
black diasporic dance and Dunham's interest in the Caribbean. As
Hurston once told Henry Allen Moe, the president of the Guggenheim
Foundation, "From someone in Chicago I hear that after I had given
the concert at the Chicago Civic Opera with the West Indian dancers that cause[d] very favorable comment all over [Dunham] thought
all she needed to do was to come [to the Caribbean]."[48] The accuracy

of the rumor aside, Hurston clearly believed that she and Dunham were pursuing similar material, even if she questioned the integrity of Dunham's methods.

The two women also followed analogous processes in their anthropological work: both acted as participant-observers in the field at a time when that mode of research was suspect by many, and both employed what VéVé Clark has termed a "research-to-performance" method that brought to the concert stage the cultures they studied as part of their ethnographic work.[49] Failing to perceive these connections, Herskovits effectively categorized Hurston and Dunham according to narrow disciplinary demarcations, in much the same way as recent scholars have conceptualized Hurston primarily as a novelist and Dunham primarily as a choreographer. In addition to demonstrating the pernicious effects of the Rosenwald Fund's treatment of her, Hurston's antagonism toward Dunham suggests how much was at stake for Hurston in receiving—or, more precisely, not receiving—proper credit for her study and staging of black diasporic dance forms. This chapter seeks to illuminate that which Herskovits and others since failed to discern: although she never pursued dance to the exclusion of other fields, and although her dance training and choreographic experience did not come close to Dunham's, Hurston's concert project required her to function in a choreographic capacity.

## Hurston's Choreographic Labor

By all indications, when Hurston presented the Bahamian Fire Dance as the finale to her stage revue, questions of choreographic labor—the time and effort spent training and directing a group of bodies to perform a set of movements in a certain way—were far from spectators' minds. Like her concert as a whole, the Bahamian dance cycle seemed to exemplify notions of "natural" black abandon for audience members. In the words of one critic:

> The dancers, at first wary, as if feeling their ground, gradually became more and more heated, until one expected and hoped for an orgy. The rhythm pressing harder and harder into one's very being, the seductive movements of the gayly-clad bodies, the shining eyes in their dark faces, brought thunderous applause and continuous demands for more.[50]

Such appraisals of the Fire Dancers' surrender to "primitive" instincts were buttressed by reports that the number was "performed by a group from the Bahama Islands" for whom the ritual dance was presumptively part of their native tradition.[51] Even as this overdetermined discourse of naturalness served to heighten the value of Hurston's concert in a marketplace that judged black performance primarily on the basis of its authenticity, it simultaneously worked to mask the labor that made the stage dancing possible. A closer look at the various levels of preparation that Hurston carried out to mount the Caribbean dance cycle on the theatrical stage casts light on the premeditation and mediation that underwrote her apparently spontaneous Fire Dance. It also opens up possibilities for how we might begin to reconceptualize the role of the choreographer.

### Learning the Fire Dance

Hurston's first encounter with Caribbean folk dance and music, as mentioned earlier, occurred in the late 1920s during her anthropological expedition to southern Florida. The dancing of a group of Bahamian migrant workers she witnessed there struck her as "so stirring and magnificent, that I had to admit to myself that we had nothing in America to equal it."[52] Her interest piqued, Hurston traveled to Nassau in October 1929 to find out more about Bahamian music and dance. There she not only took three reels of film footage of the dancing, she also "took pains" to learn the movements of the Fire Dance herself, as she later reported in her autobiography.[53] The footage, which Hurston sent on to her patron Charlotte Mason, who had financed much of her fieldwork and lent her the camera, has unfortunately been lost.[54]

Despite this lack of visual evidence, Hurston's written accounts of the Fire Dance provide some details about the dancing. These accounts are not always consistent, no doubt a result of the intrinsic variability of the folk forms themselves, Hurston's changing knowledge of them, and the adjustments she made in staging the dance cycle over time. Even as she steadfastly emphasized the African derivation of the Fire Dance, for example, her explanations of its nature and function within the Caribbean did not always accord. At times she described the dance as a nightly or weekly ritual; at others she claimed the dance was "part of the celebration of New Year's from West Africa," or "a celebration honoring the arrival of spring."[55] In a typescript draft of her concert,

Hurston's stage directions indicate that "John Canoe songs" were to be performed just prior to the Fire Dance, suggesting a link between the Bahamian cycle and the traditional Caribbean street festival associated with Christmas, also known as Jonkonnu.[56] Though no other typescript of the concert mentions "John Canoe," the connection was on clear display when her concert debuted in New York. As captured in the sole surviving photograph of *The Great Day*, one of her Fire Dance performers wore an elaborate houselike headdress characteristic of Jonkonnu (Figure 3).[57] The precise components of the Fire Dance also fluctuate in different portrayals. While Hurston's 1930 article "Dance Songs and Tales from the Bahamas" reports that there are two kinds of Fire Dance, she more frequently claimed it to have three parts: the Jumping Dance, Ring Play, and Crow Dance.[58]

The variety of and similarities between Caribbean dances either called the Fire Dance or associated with it help explain Hurston's indeterminacy. According to the Bahamian scholar Nicolette Bethel, the "continual presence of the fire" and a similar sequence of actions are common to the three kinds of Bahamian ring games, which she cites

**Figure 3.** Hurston (far right) rehearsing the Fire Dance with her *Great Day* cast members. Photo originally appeared in *Theatre Arts Monthly* in April 1932. Image provided courtesy of the Zora Neale Hurston Manuscript Collection, Department of Special and Area Studies Collections, George A. Smathers Libraries, University of Florida.

as the fire dance, jumping dance, and ring play.[59] All of these called for a steadily burning fire to heat and reheat the drum that established the rhythm for the dancing. In all three forms, dancers took turns performing moves inside a circle of players. In what Bethel terms the fire dance proper, however, dancers actually leapt over the fire, which here occupied the center of the ring. Generally danced with minimal clothing and supported by vocal chanting, this form of the dance was outlawed by British colonial authorities and, by the early twentieth century, was primarily a feature of stage performances. It seems likely, therefore, that the dances that Hurston observed, researched, and incorporated into her concert were versions of the jumping dance and ring play, and that she used the umbrella term "Fire Dance" to encompass the assortment of Bahamian dances she encountered.[60]

Although Hurston did not always stage the same arrangement of dances in her folk revues, the Jumping Dance–Ring Play–Crow Dance sequence prevailed. Variations notwithstanding, Hurston's written depictions make it possible to reconstruct the basic contours of each of these sections. A 1939 program for an exclusive performance of the Fire Dance describes the Jumping Dance as follows:

> There is a grand flourish of the drum—the circle forms, the drummer tears into a tune, and somebody starts to sing. The whole ring sings, claps hands, and some begin to "cut pork"— that is, make the introductory movements of the dance. Some bold person cuts pork and leaps out into the ring, does his or her "moves" (steps), chooses a partner, and retires. The rhythm is terrific![61]

Typically, the dancer performed introductory movements on the first line of the song, moved on to more intricate steps on the second line, and chose a replacement on the third line, before rejoining the circle. Hurston illustrated this pattern in her rendering of a "Full-Time Jump Song":

> *(Cutting pork)*
> Bimi gal is a rock and a roller, never got a licking till you
>     go down to Bimini
>     *(Leaps into the ring)*
> Eh! Let me go down to Bimini!
> Never get a licking till you go down to Bimini.[62]

While the Jumping Dance may have appeared simple on the surface, Hurston explained that its difficulty lay in the fact that the performer was required to coordinate his or her movements with the shifting rhythmic patterns of the drum. Specifically, the dancer had to "begin and finish each 'move' according to the subtleties of the drum rhythm and tone, which is extremely varied. The dance has no point otherwise."[63] The Jumping Dance also demanded innovation on the part of its performers, which in turn infused the form with variety and dynamism. As Hurston reported, the choreography of the Jumping Dance continued to the same rhythmic tune until the drum grew cold. Upon its reheating, a new song was chosen and a new round of dancing began.

The Ring Play, which Hurston characterized as "African rhythm with European borrowings," used the same ring configuration as the Jumping Dance but involved duets rather than solos:

> One dancer in center begins to sing and circle ring seeking a partner as the verse is being sung. At the very first beat of the refrain, the partner must join the seeker in the center and they do a duet rather than the solo dance of the "Jump." The hand-clapping is marvelous stop-time rhythm and the better the dancers the wilder the enthusiasm.[64]

Once again, Hurston broke down the stages of the dance as they corresponded to the lyrics of a typical Ring Play song:

> *(Solo dancer circling the inside of the ring seeking partner)*
> Mama I saw a sailboat
> A-sailing in the harbor
> I saw a yeller gal aboard it
> And I took her to be my lover.
> *(Chosen one dances out in ring to meet other dancer)*
> Down the road, baby!
> Two shillings in the cooker!
> It's killing, mama!
> It's killing, mama!
> Killing mama! Killing mama!
> *(This keeps up until the dancers exhaust their repertoire of steps. The one who was chosen stays in the ring and the other retires. Begin all over the same routine.)*

Peas and rice, throw it on the road,
Stand one side, make it three quarts,
Roll it, Roland, gimme some,
Roll it, Roland, gimme some! Etc.[65]

Given the European origins of duet dancing, Hurston may have considered the partnering elements to be "European borrowings," although it is equally possible that the dance's songs were more melodic and European in style.[66] According to another of Hurston's accounts, the dancing performed by the center couple was "a sensuous duet," which lasted for a "full minute or so" until the retiring dancer was "swung to his place."[67]

Unlike the first two dances, the culminating Crow Dance was essentially a solo. Signaled by a "change of drum tone and rhythm," a solitary performer took his or her place in the center of the ring and enacted "a perfect rhythmic imitation of a buzzard flying and seeking food. He enters, finds food, takes some in his beak, and flies off."[68] While the soloist danced, the rest of the players provided the following accompaniment:

SOLOIST: Oh! Ma-ma-ma come see dat crow!
CHORUS: See how he fly!
SOLOIST: Oh! Ma-ma-ma come see dat crow
CHORUS: See how he fly!
SOLOIST: Dis crow, dis crow going to fly tonight!
CHORUS: See how he fly!
SOLOIST: Dis crow, dis crow going to fly tonight!
CHORUS: See how he fly!
SOLOIST: Oh, Ma-ma-ma come see dat crow, etc.
    *(Until crow makes his screaming exit)*[69]

Singing the song for a Work Projects Administration recording in 1939, Hurston illustrated the screaming exit with a high-pitched "Caaaaawwwwh!"[70] According to her, the supporting performers also "formed the background," transforming themselves into various representatives of the natural world—"birds, animals, and even trees"—in a celebration of spring and the "procreation of life."[71] Hurston demonstrated the Crow Dance in a series of photographs taken by Prentiss Taylor in New York (Figure 4). In them, she bends her elbows and

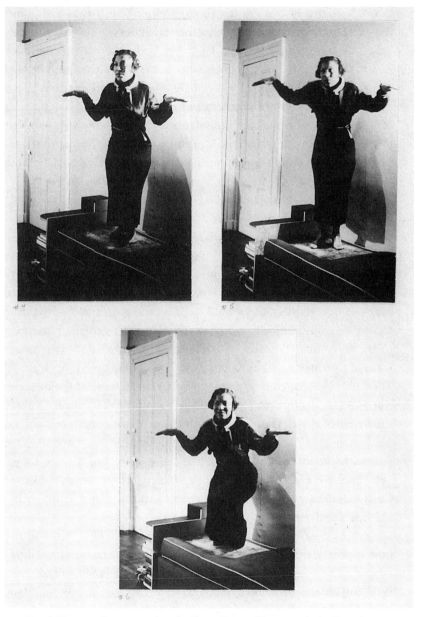

**Figure 4.** Hurston demonstrating the Crow Dance. Photographs by Prentiss Taylor. Reproduction courtesy of the Yale Collection of American Literature, Beinecke Rare Book and Manuscript Library, Yale University. Permission courtesy of R. Quiroz, Executor, Prentiss Taylor Estate.

draws her arms in close to her torso, dropping her wrists and pointing her hands outward just below her shoulders. As she alternately
draws her arms into and away from her body, she extends her neck
forward and bends and straightens her knees. Requiring both its lead
and supporting performers to simulate a bird and other animals, the
Crow Dance exemplified mimicry, one of the primary "Characteristics
of Negro Expression" as Hurston defined them. As she wrote in that
essay, the dances of black folk "are full of imitations of various animals. The buzzard lope, walking the dog, the pig's hind legs, holding
the mule, elephant squat, pigeon's wing, . . . and the like."[72]

To what extent, then, was the Fire Dance cycle a "choreographed"
dance? Clearly, each of its sections involved both a specific and relatively stable structure and a high degree of improvisation. Performing
the dance, particularly the Jumping Dance and Ring Play, required a
thorough knowledge of the dance's rules and sequencing, the ability
to perform solo as well as with a partner and a group, the capacity to
make up new steps and adapt old steps on the spot, and the rhythmic
facility to coordinate all these movements to the variable pulsations
of the accompanying drum. As Hurston explained in a 1943 interview, to execute these Bahamian dances, "you must read the drum."[73]
The drummers, of course, also registered the actions of the dancers.
But Hurston's comment attests to the need for each dancer to assay
the dynamic rhythms of the drum in the moment of performance, an
imperative that demanded a combination of experience and alacrity,
familiarity and flexibility. Thus, while those aspects of the Fire Dance
cycle that were set in advance were collectively choreographed over
time, individual participants rechoreographed the dance in unpredictable ways each time they performed it.

Before she could even think about staging the Fire Dance in her
own concert, Hurston first had to master all of the facets of its choreography. The process of taking "pains" to learn the dancing herself was
no doubt similar to that she followed to assimilate the folk songs she
collected during her research expeditions. Asked by an interviewer
how she gained knowledge of these songs, Hurston explained:

> I just get in the crowd with the people and if they sing it and I
> listen as best I can and then I start to joining in with a phrase or
> two and then finally I get so I can sing a verse and then I keep on
> til I learn all the verses and then I sing them back to the people

until they tell me that I can sing them just like them and then
I take part and I try it out on different people who already know
the song until they are quite satisfied that I know it and then
I carry it in my memory.[74]

Acquired through comparable methods of immersion, trial and error, and embodiment, the Fire Dance also became lodged in Hurston's muscle memory—that realm of corporeal knowledge that, through repetition, enables a body to recall specific postures, gestures, movements, and rhythms—where she could "carry it" around with her. Knowledge of the general contours and conditions of the Fire Dance thus remained with Hurston when she grew ready to transform it for the proscenium stage.

### *Transmitting the Fire Dance*

Back in New York in the fall of 1931, as she fine-tuned the script for the production that was to be "a dramatization of a working day on a Florida railroad camp with the Fire Dance for a climax," Hurston took the initial step of assembling a "troup of sixteen Bahamans who could dance," as she explained in her autobiography.[75] One member, Carolyne Rich, had appeared as a "Dancing Girl" in the Broadway musical *Fast and Furious,* on which Hurston worked in September of that year. Another, Leonard Sturrup (or Stirrup), who went by the name "Motor Boat," was reportedly a "colored tap dancer out of work."[76] Aside from these scant details, information about precisely who these dancers were, where Hurston encountered them, and what their dance backgrounds were is extremely sketchy.[77] In addition to Rich and Sturrup, original members of the troupe included Alfred Strochan, John Dawson, Joseph Neeley (or Neely or Nealy), William Polhamus, Reginald Alday, Bruce (Mabel) Howard, and Lias Strawn.[78] Although there was a large Caribbean immigrant population in New York in the early twentieth century, it is virtually certain that, contrary to Hurston's claim, not all sixteen of her Fire Dancers were actually Bahamian natives.[79] According to a 1947 *Crisis* article, for example, Howard was from New Rochelle, New York, not the West Indies.[80]

Whatever her dancers' credentials, by mid-October, Hurston had begun conducting rehearsals in her apartment on West Sixty-sixth Street and wherever she could find space. As she did so, she found that the research footage she had taken and sent to her patron could be put to a perhaps unanticipated use. In a letter to Charlotte Mason dated October 15, she provided a general update on her recent work and made a specific plea:

> Godmother, may I show Mr. Colledge the fire-dance films from the Bahamas? I'd see to it that no one saw them outside the Judson offices, and I'd see that they were handled carefully and returned immediately. It would save time if I could. He wants to see first a sample of all the materials and while I am training the group it takes so long for the preliminary showing and that holds back definite arrangements. Then too, seeing the films would refresh *my* memory on details. Please, may I?[81]

Preparing to audition her concert material for a producer at the Steinway Theatre, Hurston gingerly requests permission to borrow back her own film footage. Her explanation of how she plans to use the films—as a concrete representation of what she intended to present on stage and as a visual reminder to herself of the folk dances—vividly demonstrates the interconnections between her anthropological and theatrical work. Yet crucially, Hurston's allusion to the "training" of her performers suggests how mediated the translation of her recorded anthropological findings into a live stage presentation was. While several of her cast members may have been familiar with the Fire Dance, clearly not all of them were. If the entire troupe of allegedly native Bahamians had already mastered the form, which was, according to Hurston, "universal" on the island, "the educated Negroes excepted," why the need for the film cue and the training?[82]

The Fire Dance that eventually appeared in *The Great Day* thus followed a circuitous path from Bahamian bodies to Hurston's body to film, back to Hurston's body, and finally to the sixteen bodies of her ensemble. There is no way to ascertain whether Hurston exhibited her footage for her performers or merely viewed it independently and then demonstrated the moves for them. But however little is known about the dance experience of Hurston's performers, their own stylistic predispositions would necessarily have shaped their rendering of the Bahamian dances. A tap dancer like Motor Boat and a Broadway dancer like Carolyne Rich, for example, surely brought their American dance habitudes to bear on the Fire Dance choreography.

As for Hurston, dance had been part of the fabric of her early life in Eatonville, Florida, and her 1924 autobiographically based short story "Isis" (or "Drenched in Light") suggests that she was a skilled practitioner of black vernacular dances like the "pas me la."[83] As an adult, too, she observed and participated in the dance activity that took place in southern jooks and northern rent parties, such as the Black Bottom and the Slow Drag.[84] Hurston's proficiency in popular African American dance styles surely inflected how she performed the more recently acquired Bahamian steps; this in turn may have affected the way her troupe learned them.[85] At the very least, attention to this sequence of interpolations seriously complicates claims of spontaneity with respect to the staged Fire Dance, attesting to the work that underpinned the appearance of authenticity. At the same time, these interpolations, involving the body-to-body transmission of movement material, must be recognized as vital components of Hurston's choreographic practice.[86] Treating Hurston as a choreographer is a way of granting her credit for the initiative and leadership she assumed in transferring the Bahamian dance cycle to her assembled cast and of acknowledging the labor involved in this act.

## Staging Authenticity

Although most of the details of Hurston's choreographic process and rehearsal methods are lost to history, certain choreographic decisions were obligatory. Students of staged folk dance routinely point out that the process of transforming participatory dance forms for presentation on the proscenium stage involves any number of artistic choices. These encompass the selection of movement material, decisions about how much improvisation to allow on stage, and considerations of "time, space, and spectacle," all of which are constrained in certain ways by Western theatrical conventions.[87] As Amalia Hernández, the founder and artistic director of Ballet Folklórico de México, has put it, "There is no way to move village dancers directly onto a professional stage. Everything must be adapted for modern eyes."[88] Hurston faced this same set of issues in preparing the Fire Dance for her revue. The dancing she encountered in the field, she once explained, "kept up all night. Maybe two or three days."[89] After settling on which portions of the Fire Dance to stage and in what order, compressing and plotting their duration within her own concert must have been one of her foremost decisions. While it is impossible to determine how much improvisational freedom Hurston allowed her dancers and drummers, certain concessions to the proscenium stage were conspicuous. In addition to forgoing the presence of a live fire, Hurston arranged her dancers in a semicircle rather than a closed ring, which would have obstructed the audience's view of the soloists. For each section of the Fire Dance cycle, she may well also have coached her dancers on their precise spacing, degree of virtuosity, and movement scale.

At the same time, it is clear that much of Hurston's choreographic work involved masking the various capitulations she made to the theatrical stage. On various occasions, in both private letters and public remarks, Hurston made reference to her training goals and strategies for *The Great Day* and its successors. These archival traces point to another set of artistic decisions Hurston necessarily made in transforming the folk for theatrical presentation. Although they speak to her directorial labor at large, they have important implications for her choreographic treatment of the Fire Dance, which cannot be divorced from her overall representational approach to the folk. The evidence suggests that Hurston's project of cultivating an aura of folk spontaneity required a careful balancing act between countering and adhering to the conventions of the commercial stage.

Determined to present black expressive practices in a way that bore a closer resemblance to the folk from whom she had collected her material than to the black artists and entertainers who populated the New York stage, Hurston purposely sought out cast members who did not fit the Broadway mold. This included darker-skinned performers, as well as those with less experience in the professional theatre. In the same letter in which she requested use of her film footage, Hurston described to Charlotte Mason the "black" and "dark brown" singers she had assembled, concluding, "No mulattoes at all."[90] For Hurston, procuring darker-complected performers was a way of visually signaling her opposition to New York theatre customs, which increasingly "specialize[d] in octoroon girls."[91] Hurston also touted to Mason the "gawky" and "naïve" singer she had enlisted for *The Great Day*.[92] The fact that, according to Hurston, her concert was the first public performance for some of her Fire Dancers suggests she took a similar tack in recruiting dance performers.[93] Such casting decisions were integral to her project of producing a "Negro concert of the most intensely black type" and undergirded her contention that its dances had "not been influenced by Harlem or Broadway."[94]

But by no means did Hurston bar theatre professionals from her cast. Carolyne Rich, a featured dance performer in *The Great Day,* had immediate prior experience on Broadway. So too did the actor Leigh Whipper, who played the part of the itinerant preacher and served as moderator between scenes. Whipper made his Broadway debut in the role of Crabman in the 1927 hit *Porgy* by Dorothy and Dubose Heyward and quickly became a prominent figure on the African American theatre landscape. Hurston enlisted another former *Porgy* cast member, Georgette Harvey, to work on *From Sun to Sun,* the New York follow-up to *The Great Day.* A veteran actress, singer, and Broadway performer who had also toured Europe, Harvey both directed the vocal ensembles for Hurston's revue and appeared in a brief comedic skit. Hurston's logic, no doubt, was that a few seasoned stage professionals would benefit her project and perhaps help draw an audience.

Crucially, Hurston also adopted performance conventions that diverged from the polished norms of the mainstream theatre. The best example of this can be found in the personal response of the president of Rollins College to a 1933 staging of *From Sun to Sun.* In a memo to a faculty member after Hurston's concert played at Rollins's Recreation Hall in Winter Park, Florida, Hamilton Holt offered his recommendations for improvement. The production, he explained, was

> so good and so fine that it ought to be a little better. They need
> one or two strong women's voices. They need to keep their eyes
> much more to the audience, especially the preacher and actors in
> the play, and they need to do their swinging more in unison. Some
> did it from the right side and some from the left side. If you would
> give them some training in that respect, it would be great.[95]

Oblivious to Hurston's aim to dispense with the codes of professional musical theatre, Holt faults her performers for their unprofessionalism. But in complaining that Hurston's cast failed to focus their gaze on the audience and failed to swing their dancing in unison, Holt points to the very ways in which Hurston eschewed the refined, presentational style she critiqued in essays like "Spirituals and Neo-Spirituals." In place of Western standards of urbane precision, Hurston strove to replicate the asymmetry and lack of self-consciousness that were a closer approximation of the black folk aesthetic she embraced.[96]

Hurston did not reject mainstream theatrical principles outright, however, and she had her own ideas about what kind of polishing her performers needed. In early 1933, as she readied *From Sun to Sun* for performance with a newly assembled cast of amateurs, Hurston entered into negotiations with a New York theatre manager who was interested in both her folk revue and the play *Mule Bone*, her failed collaboration with Langston Hughes. "We are offered a Town Hall recital in March," she reported to Charlotte Mason. Apparently giving serious consideration to revisiting *Mule Bone*, Hurston revealed her plan to "try it out here in our laboratory and work out mistakes. *Then* New York."[97] The "laboratory" to which Hurston refers was likely a newly launched experimental community theatre called the Museum in Fern Park, Florida, a town that neighbored Winter Park. Run by several Rollins faculty, the Museum mounted *From Sun to Sun* as its inaugural performance in late January 1933. In a more general sense, though, Hurston treated the South at large as a sort of laboratory—as both training ground and prelude to a New York return. On the heels of *From Sun to Sun*'s Florida premiere, Hurston wrote to Rollins faculty member Edwin Grover to request his help in lining up additional performances in the region, explaining, "I'd like to take my group to a few places in the state to further polish them before New York."[98] Just as large-scale theatrical productions played in out-of-town cities to finalize their material before opening on Broadway, Hurston saw southern venues as a trial run leading up to an appearance in the northern metropole. Her remark to Grover concedes the need to adhere to certain professional standards and train her "cast of the true negro type" so that they were presentable for New York audiences.[99]

Hurston never did return to New York with her newly trained group, nor did she mount another version of her folk concert there. But she did continue to produce her revue outside New York throughout the 1930s, working with various groups of nonprofessionals. In the winter of 1934, she assembled and trained a cast of students at Bethune-Cookman College, an all-black school in Daytona Beach, Florida, where she presented her program in a two-thousand-seat, previously segregated theatre.[100] In the fall of that year, she drew her cast of performers from the dramatic classes at the South Parkway branch of the Young Women's Christian Association on the South Side of Chicago. The rehearsal process for this production, titled *Singing Steel*, was particularly rushed, but the concert was well received nonetheless.[101] Indeed, one Chicago critic judged that Hurston's cast, performing "with something of the high-school commencement technique in acting," managed to achieve "an earnestness that made their show more authentic than professionals could have made it."[102] For this reviewer, unlike for Hamilton Holt, lack of theatrical sophistication enhanced rather than diminished Hurston's representation of the folk. When she staged an exclusive production of the Bahamian Fire Dance in Orlando for the Florida Federal Writers' Project four years later, Hurston once again recruited and trained a group of amateur singers and dancers from around the state, including the Eatonville area, where she was then living.[103] At the same time, much as she had done in New York, Hurston occasionally recruited locally renowned entertainers to appear alongside her stage novices. In Chicago, for example, she enlisted a well-known radio personality, Dr. Andrew Dobson, to appear in a number of featured roles. Given prominent billing on the concert program, Dobson was no doubt recruited in part to attract area theatregoers.[104]

Hurston's choreography of the folk, then, was neither a straightforward nor an unmediated operation. Rather, the cultivation of a performance aesthetic located somewhere between professionalism and amateurism demanded that Hurston make a series of careful calibrations in everything from casting to training to staging. Although the techniques she used to train and direct her dancers in specific are not recoverable, the transfer of the Fire Dance from its vernacular incarnation to the proscenium stage required an equally strategic string of adjustments. Differentiating her enactment from mainstream commercial fare without foregoing commercial appeal, finding a middle ground between theatrical finesse and theatrical awkwardness: these were among the constitutive components of Hurston's choreographic practice. Although a racialized discourse of spontaneity obscured the extent of her authorship and prevented her from acquiring choreographer status at the time, conceding the term to her today helps redress a historical blind spot by granting her credit for the labor that underwrote her danced representations.

## Staging Authorship

As I have tried to show, authorial standing remained important and desirable to Hurston, the attainability of the title "choreographer" notwithstanding. Calling attention to her purposeful orchestration of folk material and her active training of cast members, however, threatened to detract from the perceived artlessness of her revue. Eager to claim both authenticity and artistic credit, Hurston strategically calibrated her performance of authorship, framing her artistic role with the utmost care. A closer look at several instances in which Hurston straddled the line between asserting authorship and cultivating an aura of authenticity provides insight into how she negotiated this precarious terrain.

Vacillation over the most appropriate way to limn her relationship to the folk material in her concert is evident in the earliest printed matter that accompanied Hurston's revue. While an early announcement for *The Great Day* billed the concert as "A Program of Original Negro Folklore Compiled by Miss Zora Hurston," the actual program for the New York premiere read, "Zora Hurston presents 'THE GREAT DAY,' A Program of Original Negro Folklore."[105] The latter version transforms Hurston from compiler to presenter, a subtle but significant amplification of her role. Subsequent programs continued to tinker with the placement of her name and description of her office. The program for *From Sun to Sun,* the immediate follow-up to *The Great Day,* cited the New School for Social Research as the concert's presenter and Hurston as its producer.[106] Later printed programs for revues staged outside of New York tended to portray Hurston as the primary feature of the show rather than the presenter or producer. In such cases, her name appeared in bold letters above the title, as in "Rollins College Dramatic Art Department presents ZORA HURSTON in her all-Negro production of Afro-American folklore 'All De Live Long Day.'"[107] Still, the fundamental and unresolved question remained how to reconcile Hurston's artistic contributions with the "originality" of the folklore that comprised her concert.

This tension was on open display on January 10, 1932, the night *The Great Day* premiered. In the middle of her concert, Hurston came out on stage to speak directly to the audience. She had already appeared on stage as a member of the ensemble in some of the revue's early scenes. But when the curtain closed on the first half, she stepped back onstage to explain her motivation for the concert. Two reviewers made mention of her address. The *New York Amsterdam News* noted that "in a short talk she said that her purpose for the presentation was to show Negro folklore in its most original form."[108] Arthur Ruhl of the *New York Herald Tribune* supplied a lengthier description:

Dragged out to say a few words, Miss Hurston—herself, up to that time, simply one of the crowd of Negro peasants on the stage—responded in a broad and ingratiating dialect that said what should have been said in just the right way. If there is such a thing as natural and unpremeditated art, here it seemed exemplified by every one concerned.[109]

In Ruhl's depiction, Hurston is the reluctant yet charming author, the content of her remarks less important than the manner in which she made them: spontaneously, in dialect, and with no detectable audacity.

Hurston's autobiography *Dust Tracks on a Road* provides a similar account of the stage address. Like Ruhl, it characterizes her remarks as reluctantly made and completely unrehearsed. As the first half of the revue came to an end, she writes:

> I was standing there in the wings still shivering [from nervousness], when Lee Whipper, who had played the part of the itinerant preacher in a beautiful manner, gave me a shove and I found myself out on the stage. A tremendous burst of applause met me, and so I had to say something.

The statement she proceeded to make was an attempt to elucidate her reasons for bringing this folk material to the stage and, not surprisingly, relied on the rhetoric of authenticity: "I explained why I had done it. That music without motion was unnatural with Negroes, and what I had tried to do was to present Negro singing in a natural way—with action. I don't know what else I said, but the audience was kind and I walked off to an applauding house."[110]

In delivering these remarks, Hurston simultaneously highlighted and blunted her position as artist. By stepping onstage to address the audience directly, and thereby breaking the narrative frame of her drama, she effected an unequivocal declaration of authorship. Standing before the curtain, she physically marked her authorial relationship to the production behind her, much as an artist might pose before a new composition or a writer might appear at a book signing. The hearty applause she received was a show of appreciation for her work in precisely this capacity. Yet the content of Hurston's address was wholly concerned with naturalness. In other words, Hurston's emphasis on art*less*ness occurred squarely within an acknowledgment of her own role as artistic producer. Speaking as author but disavowing artistry, Hurston physically embodied the tension between authorship and authenticity that lay at the root of her theatrical project.

Hurston's stage appearance also deserves scrutiny for what it reveals about her position as a black female artist in a white- and male-dominated field. Ruhl's description of her comments here becomes key, for in his account, Hurston delivered her speech in "ingratiating" dialect. This characterization of Hurston coincides with the way many of her male contemporaries portrayed her.[111] As Hurston scholars like Susan Meisenhelder have suggested, this demeanor is best understood as a strategic performance on Hurston's part, a way of appeasing whites in order to obtain the support that was necessary to get her work produced.[112] It is within this context that her address to the largely white audience on the night of January 10 must be seen. Even as the act of standing alone to accept the crowd's plaudits automatically signified her authorial status and her difference from the folk represented within the revue, her spoken dialect and unassuming manner allowed audience members like Ruhl to continue to cast her in the same terms as the folk—quaint, unaffected, and, above all, nonthreatening. This discrete strategy of authorship allowed Hurston to assert her role as director and producer without sacrificing her deferential demeanor. The fact that she made a similar stage address during the *From Sun to Sun* production just two months after *The Great Day*, this time appearing before the revue got underway and making additional announcements to promote an upcoming event of hers, suggests how effective she found the device to be.[113]

Hurston asserted her choreographic authority by augmenting her own dancing role in later concerts. In contrast to her New York productions, in which she appeared as a supporting member of the ensemble, in the *From Sun to Sun* concerts she mounted in the South, Hurston played the female lead in a dramatized skit and performed the solo Crow Dance—the section of the Fire Dance that had starred the "native" Bahamian Joseph Neely in the New York versions.[114] While her motives for appearing in the Crow Dance, despite having recruited a new group of Bahamian dancers,[115] are impossible to know definitively, one plausible reason can be found in the *Sanford Herald*'s review for a version of the concert she staged in 1934. "Zora Hurston," the paper reported, "as the author and producer of the show received considerable applause for her various appearances particularly in the

African Fire Dance which came as a climax to the performance."[116] Here Hurston is cited as creator, director, and credible performer of Africanness, all in the same breath. However casually made, this statement from the *Herald* suggests that she had much to gain by executing the Crow Dance herself. By taking over an entire section of the climactic finale, Hurston guaranteed that her personal involvement with the Bahamian dance remained immediately apparent. Making her own body the repository and conveyor of the African-derived dance, Hurston staked her claim on the material without having to spell out her choreographic role. As with her onstage address in New York, embodiment served as an effectual mode of authorship, a way of taking credit for her work without expressly declaring it.

In her autobiography, Hurston found other ways to shore up her authority as producer, director, and choreographer of the folk material in her revue. In particular, her report of the dissolution of her Bahamian dance troupe demonstrates her determination to claim credit for her artistic labor when she considered it her due. Explaining her decision to leave New York after the success of her revues, Hurston cites the toll production work had taken on her:

> I was worn out with back stage arguments, eternal demands
> for money, a disturbance in my dance group because one of the
> men, who was incidentally the poorest dancer of all, preached
> that I was an American exploiting them and they ought to go
> ahead under his guidance. Stew-Beef, Lias Strawn and Motor-
> Boat pointed out to him that they had never dreamed of dancing
> in public until I had picked them up. I had rehearsed them for
> months, fed them and routined them into something. Why had
> *he* never thought of it before I did. He had discouraged the others
> from joining me until it began to look successful.[117]

On stark display here are fundamental questions about Hurston's position vis-à-vis the Bahamian performers. The incident contains the intimation that she capitalized on the expressive talents of the folk for her own gain. Instead of countering this claim herself, Hurston ventriloquizes the defense of her lead dancers. Not only do they verify that it was her idea in the first place to stage the Caribbean material, they also emphasize the choreographic labor she undertook to discipline, finesse, and "routine" all the dancers "into something" worthy of the public theatre.

It is also worth observing how Hurston used her position as anthropologist and ethnographic researcher to navigate the competing claims of authenticity and authorship. In the 1990s, scholars working to reclaim Hurston's contributions to the field of anthropology have demonstrated how, in publications like *Mules and Men,* she simultaneously advanced and undermined the authority of the ethnographic text by blurring the lines between objectivity and subjectivity, scholarly research and aesthetic invention.[118] What has gone unremarked is how Hurston mobilized her status as ethnographer to serve her stage productions. As discussed in the preceding chapter, the fact that her concerts were products of her firsthand anthropological research conferred credibility on Hurston and her "original" folk program. A notice for her 1934 production of *Singing Steel* designated her "one of the foremost living authorities on the subject" of Negro folklore.[119] By intermingling her anthropological and theatrical roles, Hurston could advance claims about the authenticity of her folk material without eliding her agency in bringing that material to the stage.[120]

Yet Hurston did not embrace the conventions of the emerging discipline of anthropology wholesale, nor did the discipline fully embrace her. While her preference for a "methodology of ethnographic subjectivity" foreshadowed later developments in the field, it was far from accepted practice in the 1930s.[121] As Deborah Gordon has written:

> Race relations, and the increasing professional disciplinization
> of fieldwork, never allowed Hurston the status of "anthropologist."
> What those relations did allow for was a form of ethnographic
> authority that was polyvocal and conflictual, and thus, on the
> margins of professional ethnography.[122]

If Hurston's straddling of anthropology and theatre helped her mediate between the seemingly conflicting poles of authorship and authenticity, the terms "ethnographer" and "anthropologist" by no means resolved the problem of attribution for her.

In the not-yet-fully professionalized world of American concert dance, meanwhile, racial and artistic politics prevented Hurston from registering fully even on its margins. Perhaps somewhat ironically, while audiences and critics in the 1930s regarded Hurston as too close to the folk to be treated as a choreographer, today it is the perceived distance between Hurston and dance that has in part kept her from earning that status. That is, whereas Hurston's contemporaries may have appreciated dance as a vital component of her project, they failed to acknowledge the artistry and labor that underpinned her staging of movement. And whereas present-day scholars are more inclined to approach performances of the folk as mediated representations, they have thus far failed to discern the depth of Hurston's involvement with dance. Against both of these positions, adding choreography to the list of her accomplishments enables us to see the effort behind the appearance of folk spontaneity and to grasp how much of this work involved the direct bodily transmission of movement material.

Admittedly, calling Hurston a choreographer is still not a fully precise way of describing her relationship to the staged Bahamian Fire Dance. Placing so much emphasis on Hurston the individual runs the risk of detracting from the contributions of her assembled troupe of performers and the countless creators and practitioners who forged the dance out of the African and European cultural traditions that commingled and collided in the Caribbean. Yet I am by no means trying to assert that Hurston choreographed the Fire Dance. Instead, I maintain, she should be recognized as the choreographer of the version of the Fire Dance that appeared in her revues. Rather than abandoning the term "choreographer," it should be possible to preserve its ability to allocate artistic credit, especially for those who have historically been denied the privileges of authorship, without losing sight of the complex, collaborative networks in which all choreographers are situated. In the end, classifying Hurston as a choreographer—or at the least, co-choreographer—is a move that forces us to attend to her calculated and labor-intensive orchestration of dancing bodies in time and space. At the same time, it should compel us to confront the structures and relations of power that have long inhered in the designation "choreographer." If it is also a move that ultimately raises as many questions as it answers, the generation of new questions—both about the term "choreographer" and about Hurston as an artist—seems a fitting outcome to a recovery project such as this.

# 3
## Producing *The Great Day*

A full consideration of authorship with respect to Hurston's folk stagings would not be complete without addressing the complicated conditions of production that governed the creation of her concert. As Janet Wolff argued in her 1981 book *The Social Production of Art*, traditional notions of the individual artist as creator obscure the located nature of artistic work, discounting both "the numerous other people involved in the production of any work, and . . . the various social constituting and determining processes involved."[1] In Hurston's case, the influence of social and economic relations on the realization of *The Great Day* is undeniable. Just as she worked within and against the general conventions of the theatrical marketplace, so too she grappled with a more particular set of exigencies: the complex web of patronage in which she was enmeshed as she embarked on her concert venture. Although the formal arrangement between Hurston and Charlotte Osgood Mason, the elderly and wealthy white woman who financed much of Hurston's research expedition to the southern United States and Bahamas, ended in March 1931, Mason continued to support Hurston on an irregular basis throughout that year, and Hurston eventually had to request a loan from Mason to finance her revue.[2] The fact that Mason kept possession of the Fire Dance film footage Hurston had taken in the Bahamas, which Hurston borrowed back as she began rehearsing her dancers in October 1931, epitomizes the entanglement between the two women and the collection of black folk material that became the basis of Hurston's stage production.[3] Indeed, the physical location of the research films foreshadows Mason's nominal ownership of the majority of *The Great Day*'s contents, later secured by way of a legal contract.

This chapter mines Hurston's autobiography and the surviving correspondence between Hurston, Mason, and Alain Locke, the prominent black scholar who frequently served as a liaison between Mason and Hurston, to reconstruct the events leading up to and surrounding the January 1932 premiere of *The Great Day* in New York. First, I address some of the theoretical and methodological implications of tracking performance in and through the archival record of Hurston's relationship to her patron. I then chronicle the advances and setbacks that comprised the production process, from aborted collaborations to clashes over program matters to the triumphant concert debut to the tense aftermath. The chapter thus provides a window onto the material and social relations that simultaneously enabled and encumbered the debut of Hurston's folk revue. It also illustrates how Hurston capitalized on the interstices of performance to maintain some control over her theatrical representation of black folk expression.

## Patronage, Power, and Performance

When Hurston first met her white patron in the fall of 1927, she was thirty-six and Mason was in her early seventies. Born Charlotte van der Veer Quick, Mason had inherited much of her wealth from her late husband, Dr. Rufus Osgood Mason, a prominent New York surgeon. In her younger years, Mason had been something of an amateur anthropologist, spending time among the Great Plains Indians and funding research for a book on Native Americans.[4] By the mid-1920s, coinciding with the vogue for all things Negro, her interests and investments shifted to America's black population, and she became a patron to a number of Harlem Renaissance artists, including writers Langston Hughes and Claude McKay, visual artists Aaron Douglas, Richmond Barthe, and Miguel Covarrubias, and the musician and composer Hall Johnson. According to the estimates of Hurston biographer Robert Hemenway, Mason contributed somewhere between $50,000 and $75,000 to black writers and artists in the late 1920s and early 1930s.[5] But her philanthropic largesse gave her tremendous power over her beneficiaries and often proved burdensome.[6]

Mason's hostility to the theatre posed one such burden for Hurston. Years before she began work on *The Great Day*, Hurston mentioned her performance aspirations to Mason and was promptly prohibited from pursuing them. In late 1928, she told Alain Locke that Mason, or "Godmother," as Hurston called her,

> was very anxious that I should say to you that the plans—rather the hazy dreams [of] the theatre that I talked to you about should never be mentioned again. She trusts her three children to never let those words pass their lips again until the gods decree that they shall materialize. Nobody knows but us anyway so it is safe.[7]

Far from abandoning her commitment to the stage in light of Mason's objections, Hurston became discreet, sharing her intentions only with fellow beneficiaries Locke and Langston Hughes (who, along with Hurston, Mason counted as her "children") until her concert was already under way.

Mason's strictures, and more to the point, the dissembling tactics that Hurston adopted in their face, have important ramifications for the historian. Divulging to Locke information that she withheld from Mason, Hurston's 1928 letter seems to exemplify a two-tiered system of public and hidden transcription governing her personal correspondence. As James Scott asserts in his 1990 book *Domination and the Arts of Resistance,* "Every subordinate group creates, out of its ordeal, a 'hidden transcript' that represents a critique of power spoken behind the back of the dominant."[8] In relying on the body of letters between Hurston and Mason as a key source of information about the staging of *The Great Day,* then, we must take into account Hurston's expressed strategy of concealment. Despite the appearance of candor between Hurston and Locke, moreover, his authority over Hurston and his close relationship to Mason prohibit treating their correspondence as transparent truth. As later letters show, Mason and Locke often colluded behind Hurston's back. All of Hurston's written communication must therefore be read through the lens of the shifting and particularized power dynamics encompassing each of her relationships.

Differently stated, as Carla Kaplan reminds us in her edited collection of Hurston's correspondence, "Every letter is a performance."[9] Because Hurston was "*such* a versatile performer," moreover, "her letters offer more valuable insights into the self-fashioning divergent audiences demand than they offer definitive answers to the vexing questions of her life or times."[10] Treating Hurston's correspondence as textual performances that surrounded and documented—but cannot always offer clear-cut answers about—her concert underscores the way performance can double as both the lens and object of analysis.[11] A performance studies approach, in other words, is essential to accessing the theatrical production, *The Great Day,* that is the object of analysis here. Such an approach involves more than heeding the constructed nature of Hurston's letters. In order to decipher these missives, we must also weigh how the "repertoire" of embodied actions and practices may have complemented, shaded, and even contradicted that which got recorded on the page.[12] This process requires reading between the lines and against the grain and recognizing that gaps and silences in the archive are filled with meaning, even if that meaning is not always knowable.

If consideration of the embodied activity that exceeded the public transcript entails accepting some degree of uncertainty and discrepancy, these same features are key to understanding Mason's opposition to performance and, by the same token, Hurston's embrace of it—as a textual strategy and as a medium in which to present her folk material. For Mason, who repeatedly warned Hurston that she "should not rob [her] books, which must stand as a lasting monument, in order to further a commercial venture," Hurston's stagings always teetered on the brink of crass entertainment and represented a direct threat to her literary work.[13] Like some of Hurston's contemporaries in the Harlem Renaissance, Mason inscribed high art/low art divisions that ranked performance well below literature. Yet Mason's antitheatrical bias was also related, I want to suggest, to her need to maintain tight control over the "primitive" samples she commissioned.[14] In textual form, black expression was permanently fixed and safely confined between book covers. In live, public performance, in contrast, black bodies, and black dancing bodies in particular, had the capacity to signify—and titillate—in any number of unpredictable ways. The space of the theatre, as this chapter will show, complicated issues of propriety, proprietorship, and meaning, and thereby created anxiety for the domineering Mason. For Hurston, performance's very open-endedness and potential for contradictions generated opportunities to circumvent Mason's policing. Pouring her efforts into the production of a transient visual, aural, and kinesthetic event that, unlike a "lasting monument," defied containment, Hurston found wiggle room for herself.[15]

Both Hurston and Mason thus recognized and responded to what scholars of dance, theater, and performance have contended: that because bodies are "inherently unstable" and have the "tendency to spill over [their] appropriate boundaries," performance possesses a fundamental "undecidability" and "multivocality."[16] On the one hand, Hurston's experience mounting *The Great Day* reaffirms that performance's ephemerality can offer a source of resistance, especially for raced and gendered subjects like Hurston whose agency in other channels was so often constricted.[17] On the other hand, as this chapter should make clear, performance, though fleeting, neither totally disappears nor operates outside of regulatory systems.[18] Inasmuch as *The Great Day* left its mark on both the archive and the repertoire, so too did Mason's patronage leave its mark on the revue.[19] At the same time, Hurston's autobiographical account of her concert serves as a reminder that the public, written record is not exclusively a tool of the powerful, for Hurston undeniably used prose to her advantage, strategically narrating the victories and defeats that characterized the production process.[20] The following reconstruction of the steps and side steps Hurston took as she readied her folk revue for its New York debut demonstrates some of the specific ways power and performance, and the archive and the repertoire, mediate one another.

## Hall Johnson and Collaborative Setbacks

In the fall of 1931, with the close of *Fast and Furious* and the collapse of *Jungle Scandals*, Hurston devoted herself to producing a stage version of the material she had collected in the southern United States and Bahamas. By mid-October, she was fast at work, spending her mornings typing and her afternoons in rehearsal with her assembled troupe of dancers and singers. Yet no sooner had rehearsals commenced than a variety of snares began to materialize. At some point between October 15 and 26, Hurston approached the African American musician and choir director Hall Johnson, another of Mason's "godchildren," to inquire about the possibility of collaborating on the staging of her folk material. Hurston had offered her collection of folk songs to Johnson the previous year when she became convinced of their performance potential. At that time, Johnson turned her down, believing that the public only wanted to hear "well arranged" spirituals, and Hurston had since set out to prove him wrong. But while she felt comfortable overseeing and arranging the choreography for her concert, she feared she "did not know enough" to assume sole responsibility for the musical numbers, as she later explained in her autobiography. She consequently "went back to Hall Johnson with the proposition that we combine his singers with my dancers for a dramatic concert." This time, she got an affirmative answer: "Hall Johnson looked [the script] over and agreed to the thing."[21]

Although Hurston does not mention it in her autobiography, it is highly plausible that Mason lay behind the renewed interaction between the pair. Throughout the fall, the subject of Johnson's involvement in Hurston's concert receives considerable attention in the correspondence between Hurston, Mason, and Alain Locke. On October 26, Hurston reports to Mason the outcome of a conference with Johnson:

> He was *very* glad to get a message from you. He is happy to do anything that pleases you. He is very eager to help on the concert. In fact he feels that it is a privilege. He thinks it is a great idea. He is going to do the casting.[22]

Given his previous lack of interest in Hurston's folk material, Johnson's newfound enthusiasm about her project seems largely attributable to Mason's influence. Similarly, given Hurston's eagerness to differentiate her work from the kind of concert spirituals for which Johnson was known, her renewed attempt to recruit Johnson may well have been the result of Mason's provocation.

The unanimity between Hurston and Johnson, however, was decidedly short-lived, and Mason apparently also had a hand in ending their collaboration. In a somewhat cryptic letter written to Mason on November 18, Alain Locke states that he has relayed Mason's message "and reaction to the situation" to Hurston "without loss of force or blurring of the simple lines." Hurston, he reports,

> was heartened in her bewilderment, and has gone ahead to follow our advice to make swift counter-moves and retrieve the situation as far as possible. She took up my broken trail and was to see Hall before evening, if she camped on the doorstep of the stage entrance to do it. To reenforce her strength, I gave her my message to him, saying I was writing him immediately but that since there was no time to lose, I was reaching him through her.[23]

Locke's letter portrays Hurston as naively attempting to collaborate with an unresponsive Johnson until Mason, through Locke, instructs her to abandon the pursuit. The mention of "counter-moves" intimates some betrayal on Johnson's part and the necessity of redress. On

November 24, Hurston wrote to Mason that she believed "any further urging of Hall would be a waste of time" and was therefore "counting the three weeks I lost as experience bought and going on my way."[24] As a replacement for Johnson, Hurston secured the services of another musician, Wen Talbert.[25]

What transpired between Hurston and Johnson that caused their collaboration to fall apart so quickly? Hurston's autobiography reveals a frustrating series of attempts to conduct rehearsals with Johnson and his group of singers. "I took my dancers up to his studio four times," she writes, "but the rehearsals never came off. Twice he was not even there. Once he said he had a rehearsal of his own group which could not be put off, and once there was no explanation."[26] But she also cites two separate issues that contributed to the split. The first concerns an intraracial conflict between Johnson's African American singers and Hurston's Bahamian dancers. As she reveals in *Dust Tracks on a Road*, the "unfortunate" event occurred before a scheduled rehearsal. "While my dancers sat around me and waited," she writes, "two or three of the singers talked in stage whispers about 'monkey chasers dancing.' They ridiculed the whole idea. Who wanted to be mixed up with anything like that?"[27] By way of clarification, Hurston adds that "the American Negroes have the unfortunate habit of speaking of West Indians as 'monkey chasers,' pretending to believe that the West Indians catch monkeys and stew them with rice." Once she realized that her group had overheard the comments of Johnson's singers and "began to show hurt in their faces," Hurston immediately retreated. "I could not," she explains, "let [the dancers] feel that I shared the foolish prejudice, which I do not, so I had to make a move. I showed my resentment, gathered my folks, and we all went down to my place in 66th Street." In her account, she—not Mason or Locke—took the initiative to walk away from the collaboration in a gesture of protest against the cultural bias of Johnson's performers.

Significantly, the issue of difference between black Americans and black West Indians played a prominent role in *The Great Day* itself. Hurston explicitly thematized it in at least one scripted version of the drama and invoked it more implicitly in her staging of the relationship between black diasporic forms.[28] The incident between her dancers and Johnson's singers, then, represented to Hurston a much weightier question about black intradiasporic relations. While she may have been powerless to prevent Johnson's rehearsal cancellations, by presenting the slight to her dancers—and her refusal to countenance ethnic chauvinism—as the breaking point in the artistic collaboration, Hurston reclaimed a degree of control over the failed endeavor.

But Hurston was also cognizant of a second, behind-the-scenes cause for the alliance's disintegration. Feeling "licked" following Johnson's evasiveness and the verbal assault on her dancers, she paid a visit to an agent at Steinway Hall, intending to call off the entire production. This agent, according to Hurston, divulged the hidden reason for Johnson's failure to cooperate:

> [The agent] said I ought to go ahead. It sounded fine to him. But go ahead on my own. He happened to know that Gaston, Hall Johnson's manager, wanted me headed off. He saw in my idea a threat to Hall Johnson's group. "You are being strung along on this rehearsal gag to throw you off. Go ahead on your own."[29]

In this portrayal, Johnson's noncompliance was part of a larger attempt orchestrated by his manager to undermine Hurston. Though Johnson had previously rejected her folk material as too unrefined, it now represented a direct threat to his concert spirituals. In her November 24 letter to Mason, Hurston placed the blame for the collaboration's demise squarely on Johnson's white manager: "I know [Hall's] heart is in the right place, but that jew man who manages him wont let him do what he promised."[30] Citing Gaston's ethnicity, Hurston calls up a history of uneasy Jewish-black relations in show business, in which Jewish producers frequently profited off black performers.[31] Given Mason's aversion to other white patrons of black art, it is little wonder that Hurston chose in her personal correspondence to highlight an interracial conflict over and above an intraracial one. In doing so, she also avoided having to accuse Johnson in Mason's presence. Pushed and pulled by Mason's attempted orchestrations, caught between the racial politics of the theatre world and those of her own patronage situation, Hurston found some agency in deciding how to narrate the stumbling blocks in her production process.

## Alain Locke as Intermediary

Not to be discouraged, Hurston followed the Steinway Hall agent's advice to proceed with the production on her own. As she writes in *Dust*

*Tracks*, "We rehearsed at my house, here and there, and anywhere. The secretary to John Golden liked the idea after seeing a rehearsal and got me the theater. She undertook to handle the press for me, so I just turned over the money to her and she did well by me."[32] While her autobiography makes the move from Steinway Hall to the John Golden Theatre in the span of a single paragraph, the shift from one venue to the other was not quite so simple. Hurston's correspondence contains allusions to three auditions: the first, in which Hurston showed her Bahamian dance film footage to George Colledge, the concert manager at Steinway Hall, was held in late October; the second, involving live performers, took place on November 18, also at the Steinway and, according to Hurston, "went over all right"; and the third apparently occurred sometime in December and resulted in the booking at the John Golden Theatre.[33]

Although it goes unmentioned in *Dust Tracks*, Alain Locke also played a part in securing the John Golden Theatre. On December 16, he wrote Mason, "When I left New York [Hurston] was trying for January 10th—and the secretary of The Golden Theatre management promised in my presence to let her know Monday."[34] As his statement insinuates, Locke considered his attendance advantageous to Hurston's cause. Certainly, his renown as a leading black intellectual lent weight to her bid for the theatre. Still, on the whole, his participation in Hurston's production must be seen in a more equivocal light. Like Mason's, Locke's role amounted to a constant alternation between solicited assistance and unsolicited meddling.

A graduate of Harvard and Oxford and a leading academic authority on black literature and art, Alain Leroy Locke was one of the primary architects of the New Negro movement, later dubbed the Harlem Renaissance. His 1925 volume *The New Negro* heralded the arrival of this cultural movement, which sought to combat racist stereotypes and effect social change in the United States through African American artistic production. The relationship Locke maintained with Hurston was a highly complicated one. She studied under him at Howard University in the early 1920s and, in a sign of her respect for him, continued to seek his approval as she developed her own literary career. The two shared an interest in the African American folk, but their approaches were markedly different. Unlike Locke, whose "sense of the folk was mainly theoretical," Hurston regarded the folk as more than the mere producers of raw material in need of artistic refinement.[35] Indeed, Hurston grew increasingly frustrated with Locke over the years. In 1938, his negative review of her novel *Their Eyes Were Watching God* prompted her to write a piece called "The Chick with One Hen," in which she scathingly declared that "Dr. Locke is abstifically a fraud, both as a leader and as a critic. He knows less about Negro life than anyone in America."[36] In the early 1930s, however, Hurston deferred to Locke more often than not, a prudent stance given his favor with Mason. Yet his own relationship to Mason was far from unproblematic. The two met in 1926, and Locke effectively became Mason's adviser with respect to the black writers and artists she patronized. For thirteen years she in turn financed Locke's annual trips to Europe. While Locke remained loyal to Mason to her death, as David Levering Lewis has written, "He walked a tightrope between obsequious accommodation to the old lady and nervous fidelity to his own beliefs, dissembling masterfully and taking the cash."[37]

While Locke, like Mason, initially opposed Hurston's concert plans, once "won over," he left no small imprint on the revue.[38] His direct involvement with the concert can be traced back to at least early November 1931. A letter from Locke to Mason that month indicates that Hurston had requested his presence in New York and that he planned to spend two days with her there. Hurston's own letter to him, enclosed with Locke's letter to Mason, explains that she has just resumed rehearsals after recovering from an illness and implores him to "PLEASE come as there is so much to be done and talked over." Although Hurston appealed to Locke not to worry Mason about her poor health, he forwarded Hurston's letter to Mason to let her "see accurately what sweet motives [Hurston] had for not letting you know she was ill."[39] From the outset, then, Locke's role in Hurston's concert was, at least in part, that of monitor and informant, "a theatrical spy of sorts" who surveilled and relayed information about the status of Hurston's production back to Mason.[40]

Throughout November and December, Locke made periodic trips to New York from his post at Howard University in Washington, D.C., to consult with Hurston, attend rehearsals, oversee logistical matters, and keep Mason abreast of all that came to pass. Mason's notes and letters to Locke indicate how heavily she relied upon him to bring her up to date on the state of Hurston's affairs. On November 22, for example, she proclaims, "I have no word from Zora as to how the play is going and I suppose she is struggling with it."[41] Seven days later, she begins her notes wondering "where Zora is in this affair."[42] In these same November 29 jottings, Mason goes on to inquire whether a date and locale have been definitively established yet, adding that she cannot begin to recruit audience members until these details are settled. Her next words are telling: "Don't say anything to Zora now. You know how I do these things. She doesn't." Instructing Locke to withhold her apprehensions about the concert from Hurston, Mason reveals how the two worked behind Hurston's back to control how much she knew as she prepared her stage revue.

The prevailing tone of Mason and Locke's discourse on Hurston's theatrical undertaking was condescension. Even while they rooted for her success, they displayed a pronounced lack of faith in her ability to manage her production dealings. In a letter written to Mason on the heels of the Hall Johnson fiasco, Locke remarks, "The great effort and expense you have put into this must not be wasted,—even if the child did fall down the well."[43] Although there is no reason to believe that Hurston was at fault for Hall Johnson's desertion, Locke clearly implies that she has foundered. This mistrust of Hurston—and concern about her "possible fall-down"—reappears in another letter between Locke and Mason written almost a month later.[44] Hurston did lack experience as a producer-director and at times struggled to keep control of her large cast.[45] But her patrons' belittling portrayal of her as stumbling child illustrates the barriers she faced as a black woman artist striving to present her work on the Broadway stage.

## Escalating Investments

At the time of Locke's November reference to the "great effort and expense" Mason had invested in Hurston's stage endeavor, Mason had not allocated any funds specifically for the concert. She did provide access to Hurston's research films and played a role in promoting and then halting the collaboration with Hall Johnson. Although Hurston repeatedly invited Mason to attend a rehearsal, she never did. At the end of November, Mason mentioned her intent to recruit audience members once a date was set for the concert. But until the middle of December, there is no direct evidence that Hurston sought any substantial production assistance from Mason. In a later recounting, in fact, Mason claims that she had no involvement in the revue until the very end. Her dictated notes of January 17, 1932, declare that she "told Zora from the beginning that she would be in NO way responsible for the show."[46] Nevertheless, Mason's steady surveillance of Hurston through Locke throughout the fall months suggests that, far from disassociating herself from the preparation stages of the revue, Mason exerted considerable "effort and expense" to superintend Hurston's theatrical project.

In a letter dated December 16, Hurston did expressly call on Mason for monetary assistance. After mentioning some preliminary details about the concert, Hurston plunges into the real subject of her two-page missive—"the business side of it." She tells Mason to expect a letter from the publicist, Miss Dalrymple, who "waits at all times for your approval in publicity matters." With this requisite nod to Mason's authority, Hurston discloses the financial specifics:

> She told me that she must have $200.00 right away for the printing of the announcements and for the papers, and there must be some photographing done. Not a great deal, but certainly a little. Now I feel that it is highly probable that I shall be able to borrow enough cash on prospects to do the thing, but the publicity simply cannot wait. It must begin immediately. And the photography cannot be done until the dancers have their costumes, and the publicity, that is, the folders wait on the pictures. So I need to provide costumes at once. It costs three to five dollars to costume each of the sixteen dancers. So that you can see that I need 250.00 at once. I disposed of my car and put up the deposit on the theatre, and my radio brought in 16.00 which I have used to pay carfares for my group. 52 persons are a great responsibility I have found.[47] But now I have nothing more to sell. I am on the brink [of] putting the thing over and it will break my heart to fall down now. Especially since no question of merit is involved, merely getting my advertising done on time. That is in time to do the concert any good. Will you be generous yet some more and loan me that amount? I will turn over the entire box receipts to you to guarrantee [sic] the loan. I have worked harder on this than I have anything else except collecting it, and now that you have deniedn [sic] yourself that it might be collected, now that I have gone thru the rigors of it, and worked so hard to get it into shape, I am willing to make *any* sacrifice, meet any terms to give it a

chance of success. The easiest part of it all is now before us. Most any producer down town would take it over.[48]

Having pawned her car and radio, Hurston needed immediate cash to continue mounting the production. She astutely makes her appeal on the grounds that the concert represents the culmination of the years of research funded by Mason. Hurston even depicts herself as "on the brink" of success yet in danger of "falling down" without the requisite funds; whether strategically or coincidentally, she manages to co-opt the patronizing rhetoric of Mason and Locke to serve her own cause.

In this same letter Hurston also emphasizes the need to secure her performers' allegiance, in what may have been a subtle play on Mason's proprietary anxieties. Pointing to the implications of producing her concert as a one-time affair, Hurston writes:

> The singers are only looking forward to one night's pay and so my hold on the[m] would be lost at once if there are indefinite delays. I say this because I am almost certain that I shall be able to borrow money to finish the thing, but it wont be available tomorrow. If it were a regular show and they could look forward to steady employment they would be more patient, but to rehearse for weeks and weeks for one night's pay is a great deal to ask, especially, when they see nothing happening. The Negro singers and actors have been deceived and exploited so often that they are always on the defensive. I have whole hearted co-operation now and I want to keep them at white heat, and pull off the thing while everybody has heart in it. A week is a long time to them and now that I have set back the date, if I dont begin the publicity, they will conclude that they are being trifled with. I say all this to explain and in a manner, excuse my seeming rashness in asking the loan. If ever I needed you Godmother, I need you now. You and you only understand all that I have wrapped up in that sentence.[49]

However self-conscious she felt about making such an out-and-out plea to her patron, Hurston's carefully worded overture for funds paid off. With Mason's assistance, *The Great Day* went forward. But this mid-December request also marked something of a turning point in the degree of her involvement in the concert. In addition to amplifying Mason's dominion over the revue, it eventually led to escalating tensions between Hurston and her patron. By late January, Hurston found herself in the position of needing not only Mason's monetary support but her permission to use the concert material at all.

## The Battle over *The Great Day* Program

Locke's direct influence over Hurston's concert likewise increased as the folk revue neared production. Midway through December, having helped secure a venue and attended some rehearsals, he took on a more discrete role, agreeing "to arrange and write the program notes."[50] Although it is impossible to establish whose idea it was for Locke to perform this task, the appearance of his name on Hurston's concert program served as a powerful endorsement.

Less conspicuous but no less consequential was the imprint Locke left on the title and program order of Hurston's concert. While the precise facts of his involvement in these areas are rather murky, a December 31 letter from Locke to Mason provides valuable insight. Its contents are worth quoting at length:

> It seems most appropriate to be writing you this last day of an eventful year—and to give you a report of progress after the dark situation of yesterday which seemed to threaten our "last hope."
>
> After leaving you I saw Miss Dalrymple with Zora, and insisted firmly but curtly on the change of title—even though the plates and tickets had to be reprinted. That was done, and the announcements re-written. It will take today to reprint them, and I suppose it will be Saturday before Zora can get any of them to you.
>
> I then went home with Z. and gave her your message straight but informally. It was as effective as an electric shock—and it was a joy to see her come to—as a drunken man sobers up suddenly and with self-amazement.
>
> As a final upshot, she saw the sanity of the program order as I presented it to you and agreed to take it exactly. I wrote it out freshly on her kitchen table—she leaning over me as I did it,—and with the explanations, she saw its logic and I believe adopted it from within as if she herself was clearing it up. In this way it will be more effective and will seem part of her own imagination.
>
> So I think and believe all is again on the right path toward the goal of our hopes and plans. May we all have the joy and

satisfaction of seeing it realized January 10th. Surely it will be the best possible gift the early New Year can afford you, and I pray for the joy of seeing it come to pass.[51]

In essence, the "progress" on which Locke reports here is the success of his efforts to persuade Hurston to make two relatively radical changes to her program, some eleven days before its premiere. As Locke spells out, he "insisted firmly but curtly" that Hurston alter the title, despite the resultant need to reprint programs and rewrite announcements. Which title Hurston had chosen before Locke stepped in is not clear, but early typescripts indicate that she had been considering such possibilities as "In the Beginning," "From Sun to Sun," "All Day Long," "Suwanee," and "The Passing of a Day."[52] She apparently adopted "The Great Day" at Locke's behest.[53]

The issue of program order is somewhat more difficult to parse. Although several early drafts of Hurston's concert survive, none is dated. There is no way of knowing definitively, therefore, what the relationship was between the narrative sequence that Locke mapped out and the versions that Hurston devised on her own. Still, some information about the evolution of the concert's narrative is recoverable. It is evident, for example, that in the months leading up to *The Great Day*'s January premiere, Hurston experimented with the placement of the Bahamian Fire Dance in the program. While the folk dance cycle served as the finale in most of the extant typescripts, the same position it held in *The Great Day* and all subsequent productions, in one draft Hurston moved the dance to the end of the first act. In this version, the sermon delivered by an itinerant preacher appeared at the close of the second act. The archive also establishes that it was this version that Locke witnessed in rehearsal two weeks before instructing Hurston to revamp the concert's structure. In a December 16 letter to Mason, Locke reports that "Z's sermon and setting are blood-stirring and put the shoddy imitations out of commission in a few seconds. So also with her Bahama Crow-dance—I never have seen such convincing pantomime—these are the two climaxes, the Crow-dance of Part I and the sermon of Part II of the program."[54] Although Locke does not explicitly endorse the placement of these two numbers, his enthusiasm suggests as much.

Finally, it is clear that, in the days between the rehearsal Locke attended and his imposed modifications, Hurston continued to tinker with the structure of her revue. In a December 21 letter concerning Locke's agreement to write program notes for the concert, Hurston apprised Mason that she "shall send Alain the program material as soon as I get it definitely lined up. I dont want to send it until it has some shape that he can depend upon as rather permanent. I have changed it about a great deal in the last few days. But by the end of the week h[e] shall have it all."[55] Continuing to search for the most suitable "shape" for her revue, Hurston may well have moved the Fire Dance once again to the finale position before Locke insisted on his own revisions.

If Locke's description of remapping Hurston's program order leaves unanswered questions about precisely which structure he objected to and what he suggested in its place, his portrayal of how she responded to his proposed changes is more straightforwardly instructive. In his account, Hurston immediately recognized the "sanity" and "logic" of his schema and "agreed to take it exactly." In other words, as he saw it, Hurston fully appreciated the superiority of his outline and embraced it as her own. Figured as a drunk shocked into sobriety, Hurston is once again enlightened by knowledge delivered by Locke, acting as Mason's liaison. Assuming credit for the basic structure of Hurston's concert, Locke effectively paints himself as the true author of *The Great Day*, for it is he who executes the writing as Hurston peers over his shoulder.[56]

Despite Locke's aplomb, however, the matter of program order was far from settled. Hurston did not immediately comply with Locke's counsel and did not gladly incorporate his ideas as her own. Instead, she continued to rearrange her concert in ways that may well have deviated from his prescribed schema. The issue remained unresolved and controversial up to the day of *The Great Day*'s premiere.

The first indications of Hurston's defiance emerge from another piece of correspondence between Locke and Mason. In a January 5 letter to Mason, Locke reports that he has yet to see a final copy of Hurston's revised narrative structure. Requiring a definitive version in order to compose his program notes for the concert, he expresses to Mason his frustration and concern at Hurston's delay. "You will see the point here," he writes, "because it really gave my confidence a bad shock to realize that she couldn't recognize instantly an unnatural order as just as bad as doctored material. Even yet I have no final copy." Maintaining confidence in his influence nonetheless, Locke tells Mason that he is "taking it for granted that the order I outlined to you and that I copied for her has been followed."[57]

The fact that Hurston had not provided Locke with a final version of her concert program just five days prior to its premiere is telling. On

December 21, she promised Mason that Locke would have these materials in hand by the end of the week; two weeks later he still had not received them. There are several possible reasons for her hesitation. It is certainly conceivable that Hurston had yet to arrive at a conclusive version herself and continued to tweak the narrative order, even with the performance just around the corner. It is equally plausible that Hurston was holding out precisely because she did not intend to adopt Locke's plan. If she had decided against it, refusing to turn over an outline was no doubt preferable to a bold announcement of her noncompliance. Either way, Hurston's withholding of a final program can be read as a subtle yet decisive means of resistance against the onslaught of Locke's (and Mason's) editorial intrusions.

Mason's response to Locke's January 5 letter lends support to the view that Hurston's evasiveness was a tactical form of insubordination. In a telegram sent to Locke two days before *The Great Day* premiere, Mason counseled, "You realize with me how strained Zora is therefore let us accept what comes in program changes."[58] Chalking up Hurston's waywardness to preproduction distraction and stress, Mason concedes the futility of trying to pin Hurston down. Encapsulated in this one small statement—"let us accept what comes"—lies a momentous victory for Hurston. At least on the issue of program order, she succeeded in thwarting Mason's and Locke's attempts to regulate her performance work. In retrospect, it seems less likely that Hurston was stunned into enlightened acceptance by the proposal that Locke sat and outlined for her, as his account to Mason would have it, and more likely that Locke was duped by her outward acquiescence. The incident, that is to say, was an example of Hurston's mastery of the kind of "feather-bed resistance" that she identified as a form of tactical defiance among black folk.[59] By appearing to embrace Locke's changes, Hurston succeeded in securing a modicum of autonomy for herself. Her dissimulation gained her time to continue to craft her own narrative structure without outside meddling.

In the end, Mason and Locke were not fully apprised of the final program order until the evening *The Great Day* debuted. Somewhere around 4:30 p.m. on January 10, Locke finally got his hands on a copy of the program and swiftly relayed one to Mason with the following note: "I am sending you up two programs which I just received twenty minutes ago at the theatre."[60] This last-minute action suggests how desperate he and Mason were to stay abreast of the concert details, how unwilling they were to wait and simply watch the performance unfold. Mason, in fact, had explicitly instructed Locke to obtain this program for her. Claiming that Hurston had promised her a copy the day before, she sent a message to Locke early on the tenth, saying, "If you can get a program to me would be glad to have it before tonight."[61] And so, at long last, Locke and Mason had the program order laid out in writing before them. As if to accentuate this point, Locke refers specifically to "the revival scene, which is in part one," thus clarifying the placement of the climactic sermon, which, along with the Fire Dance, had formerly been a subject of debate. Although his missive conveys neither dismay nor delight with this outcome, Hurston, at least, was satisfied with it. All future stagings of the concert adhered to this same narrative structure.

Hurston was less successful in battling imposed revisions on another program issue. At the last minute, in a decision due partly to pressure from Mason, she excised an entire section of her concert. The official printed program for *The Great Day* listed a "Conjure Ceremony" between the Jook scene and Palm Woods finale, but it was never performed. Composed of two numbers, the "Pea-vine Candle Dance" and "9 Hairs in the Graveyard," a conjure section appeared in two out of three of Hurston's drafts for the concert and was heavily promoted in the show's publicity announcement.[62] The claim that "the conjure-ritual shown has never before been publicly performed" only augmented its allure.

Hurston had spent many months in New Orleans apprenticing herself to various hoodoo doctors, and her letters from the field reveal her interest in exposing some of the conjure rituals she collected to a broader public.[63] Mason, however, expressed grave concerns about Hurston's inclusion of this material in her concert program. On the day of *The Great Day*'s premiere, Mason wrote in her notes to Locke, "Very worried about her having Conjure in program as she gave her word to people down South she would not do this. May ruin her career. I have never broken a primitive law: they are mine to obey."[64] Hurston was well aware of the secrecy that surrounded hoodoo to protect it from skeptics and persecutors, but there is no surviving evidence to corroborate Mason's contention that Hurston promised her subjects she would not perform these rituals. Although it was Hurston who had become a conjure initiate, Mason claimed "primitive" law as her own. Her insistence on keeping the conjure material shielded from public consumption must be seen as a reflection of the proprietary nature of

her involvement in Hurston's project and her distaste for the theatrical arena. Mason undoubtedly communicated her worry not only to
Locke but to Hurston as well.

While Hurston's last-minute removal of the conjure section was
thus partly a product of Mason's coercion, the *New York Herald
Tribune* pointed to an altogether different reason for the omission. In
a review of *The Great Day* for the *New York Herald Tribune*, the critic
Arthur Ruhl commented on the resemblances between Hurston's production and *Savage Rhythm*, a "Negro" play running concurrently at
the John Golden Theatre. A comparison of the two shows, Ruhl relates,
"became inevitable when one of the numbers on Miss Hurston's program, the 'conjure ceremony' was omitted because, as it was explained,
it could not hope to compete with the same ceremony as presented in
'Savage Rhythm.'"[65] This explanation, which Hurston may have offered
during her onstage audience address, allowed her to blame commercial competition for the program change, rather than the demands of
her patron. Hurston's actual reasons for making the change may have
fallen somewhere between the two.

Hurston's elimination of the conjure scene, however, did not fully
appease Mason. A week after *The Great Day* premiere, she wrote to
admonish Hurston: "Remember your solemn promises made when
getting Conjure. Perfectly willing to have you write it but not put it on
the stage."[66] Again Mason refers to a promise from Hurston. But the
imprecise language of her notes makes it difficult to discern whether it
was Hurston's southern informants or Mason herself who imposed the
distinction between page and stage. A subsequent edict from Mason,
specifically prohibiting Hurston from any future use of conjure-related
material, left little ambiguity about whose laws held sway.[67] In this case,
Mason's directives appear to have won the day, resulting in the permanent removal of the conjure scene from Hurston's folk program.[68]

## Upstaging Authority on Opening Night

The January 10 unveiling of *The Great Day* proved to be yet another
front in the battle between Hurston, Mason, and Locke for creative
control over the folk concert. As the last-minute flurry of exchanges between Mason and Locke over program order suggests, for them as well
as for Hurston, opening night signified more than a Broadway premiere.
It was also the culmination of months-long grappling for control over

the representation of the black folk idioms that Hurston had collected. All had something riding on the inaugural theatrical presentation of this material. For Hurston, about to make her stage debut as an author, producer, director, and choreographer, January 10 was her longed-for chance to distinguish herself in the fields of black music, dance, and theatre and to counter contemporary representations of black folk culture. For Mason, who had put up funds for the concert and considered herself the proprietor of Hurston's material, as well as for Locke, who had lent both time and his name to the production, January 10 was the occasion to behold the results of their investments—and to learn how successful their attempts to manage Hurston had been.

Unsurprisingly, issues of control and ownership assumed prominence for Mason as the premiere approached. Among her other concerns, Mason became preoccupied with the possibility of artistic theft. Her notes to Locke on January 10 are full of cautionary measures designed to protect *The Great Day*'s cultural offerings. She instructs him: "Keep your eye on back stage performance. Her people being green may balk Zora. Have told Zora to keep people out from going back stage." Apprehensive about the relative inexperience of *The Great Day* performers, Mason evidently suspected that they might be lured away by other producers. She goes on to state, "If it is at all good there will be lots of people [who] want to make money out of it. Friends of performers must keep out till it is over."[69] But Mason perceived not only the backstage area but the audience at large as the site of potential threats. Later in her message to Locke, she imparts, "Do try to protect the material from being exploited and stolen. Keep your eyes open over the audience. Warn actors not to promise to do these things for any other producer. Get their heads turned." Mason's intention, it would seem, was for Locke to survey the audience throughout the performance to detect who might be plotting to plunder Hurston's folk material. However improbable, this mandate drives home the gravity of the threat of appropriation for Mason. Her catalog of precautions extended even to onstage activity. As she further implored Locke, "Enough on program for two concerts now. Must have *No repeating no encores.*" The implication here—that repetition of any of the concert's numbers would make them more vulnerable to theft—exposes Mason's profound distrust of the performance process. If Mason's apprehension turned out not to be unfounded, it nonetheless betrays the proprietary logic that undergirded and drove her almost paranoid concern for the material in Hurston's concert.[70]

What transpired onstage on the evening of January 10, 1932, proved to be a source of unrest in more ways than one. When Hurston stepped out in front of the curtain in the middle of *The Great Day* and spoke directly to the audience about her production, she sparked further friction between her, Mason, and Locke. While critics like the *Herald Tribune*'s Arthur Ruhl found Hurston's speech charmingly "natural" and "ingratiating," Mason and Locke were less than pleased with her remarks, to put it mildly.[71] Not only did they believe that Hurston had calculated ahead of time to make her announcement, but they interpreted her address as an outright affront to their own contributions to the project.

The fact that Hurston devoted almost a full page to this incident and the controversy it provoked in the autobiography she wrote nearly ten years later testifies to its contentiousness. In her telling, it was only at the actor Leigh Whipper's prompting that she set foot onstage at all, and only at the audience's urging that she felt obliged to make a statement.[72] Although unable to recall the precise language of her speech, she insists on "set[ting] . . . straight" one point:

> Godmother had meant for me to call Dr. Locke to the stage to make any explanations, but she had not told me. Neither had Locke told me. I was stupid. When he told me where he would be sitting, he evidently thought that would be enough. But I had not thought of any speech in all my troubles of rehearsals, making costumes and keeping things going. It just had not occurred to me. I would not have been out there myself if Lee Whipper had not shoved me. I found out later that I had seemed to ignore Dr. Locke, for which I am very sorry. I would have much rather had him make a thought-out speech than my improvising. It just did not occur to me in all my excitement. It may be too late, but I ask him please to pardon me. He had been helpful and I meant him good.[73]

Evidently, the problem with Hurston's remarks for Mason and Locke was that she made them at all. They had, it seems, decided among themselves that it was more befitting for Locke to stand in (literally and figuratively) for Hurston and to clarify the meaning of the concert to the largely white audience. As a more distinguished black intellectual, Locke would bring greater prestige to the event. The underlying implication, of course, is that he also deserved much of the credit for the work that went into *The Great Day*. Hurston's self-deprecating and contrite tone—"I was stupid" and "I am very sorry"—points to her distress at having wronged her patrons.

Yet the archival evidence further complicates the matter, for a letter from Locke to Mason written just hours before the concert began on January 10 makes reference to "the announcement [Hurston] wished to make from the stage . . . just before the revival scene."[74] Clearly, Locke knew ahead of time that Hurston intended to make some sort of statement during the presentation of *The Great Day*. Mason's notes, too, indicate prior knowledge of Hurston's stage appearance. That same day, she recorded the following: "Zora said—I'm going to come out on stage and tell about the Mother of the Primitives and all she did for me."[75] Thus, while Hurston's autobiography expresses the most concern over an apparent affront to Locke, Mason's note suggests that it was she rather than Locke whom Hurston was expected to thank from the stage.

Regardless of who was more offended (and it requires no stretch of the imagination to suppose that both Mason and Locke took umbrage when they did not receive the respective credit they believed they deserved for the affair), taken jointly, Mason's notes and Locke's letter refute Hurston's claim that she had not planned to make an announcement from the stage. Why, then, did she allege that she "would not have been out there . . . if Lee Whipper had not shoved me"? What seems most likely is that Hurston retrospectively characterized her speech as impromptu in the hopes of lessening the slight she delivered to Mason and Locke. If her announcement was only reluctantly made, she could not be accused of willfully seizing credit for the performance. That the controversy existed at all speaks to the complications Hurston's system of patronage posed to her authorship. Reading her performed and literary actions together, one discerns the complex maneuvering Hurston undertook to hold on to her position as author while attempting to pacify her demanding backers.

## Legal Ownership

Issues of authorship and credit quickly came to a head in the days that followed the debut of *The Great Day*. As if in an effort to clear up any lingering ambiguities about debt and ownership, and at the same time to make Hurston feel the weight of her power, Mason had a contract drawn up establishing her lawful claim to Hurston's concert material.

The contract, drafted on January 18, 1932, and typed up two days later, was formulated as a response to an inquiry that Hurston made on January 14, in which she asked:

> Now, I wish to know your pleasure as to the future of the material in the concert. It is yours in every way, and while I know it has great commercial value, I have no right to make a move except as you direct. I want to do something in order that I might repay your loan of 530.00.[76]

Despite strong attendance, box office receipts from *The Great Day* amounted to only $261, excluding $88 that Mason spent on tickets.[77] This was not even sufficient to cover the costs of production, leaving Hurston little choice but to request extra funds from Mason to pay her performers. As she saw it, the concert had the potential to generate a profit—if Mason would allow her to present subsequent versions. Biographer Robert Hemenway suggests, in fact, that Hurston's request constituted an attempt to "liberate" her material from Mason's claws.[78] Well aware that she was beholden to the woman who had funded the research trip in which she had amassed the contents of *The Great Day*, and equally conscious of the potential value of her concert, Hurston couched her entreaty in terms of her desire to repay Mason.

Mason's response offered little that could be considered "liberating," however. The contract she devised addressed issues of both financial debt and proprietorship, with monetary matters heading up the catalog of concerns:

> From the vouchers, it appears that you still have $80.75 to pay to cover the expenses of the production, the sale of tickets to the general public not having been large enough, in addition to the other amounts received, to pay the costs. In order that your people may not go unpaid I am, therefore, making up this final amount for you at this time.
>
> You have asserted to me that it is your ambition to repay me the whole amount which I have advanced you in order to make your concert possible and I am glad, Zora, that you want to do this.[79]

Mason expressed her gladness by requiring Hurston to sign her name as a guaranty of her intention to pay back her debt. With the additional

$80.75 paid out to compensate *The Great Day* performers, the sum total of Mason's "direct payments for the expenses of the concert" came to $610.75; this was the amount Hurston was obliged to give back.[80] Unlike Mason's past support for Hurston, monetary assistance for the concert was given out grudgingly and with the expectation of full reimbursement.

With financial matters out of the way, Mason proceeded to address the fate of *The Great Day*'s contents. In the most formal of terms, she enumerated the numbers she was "willing" that Hurston "use for concert and/or theatrical purposes." The list includes:

No. 2      In the Quarters;

No. 4      Working on the Railroad;

No. 6      Back in the Quarters—Dusk dark;

No. 7      Itinerant Preacher at the Quarters;

No. 9      In the "Jook"—Black dark;

No. 13    In the Palm Woods

The numbered segments that do not appear here were, for the most part, breaks in the narrative in which the actor Leigh Whipper addressed the audience. In fact, the only substantive segments that are not included in this list are the Conjure Ceremony, to which Mason had strong objections, and the Deep River Group Finale, directed by Wen Talbert. The next provisions placed further restrictions on Hurston's treatment of *The Great Day* material:

First, that you make no use whatsoever of my name, whether in print or orally, in connection with the material in any future production, except where you bring it out in book form with the rest of your material collected in the South.

In connection with commercial use of the material, if we decide together your success warrants it, it is understood between us that you will repay from time to time amounts on account of the total advances of $610.75 above referred to. This may help you to keep accounts steady and hold in check the pressure these commercial people will put upon you.

Finally, it is understood that the other data and material which you have collected on the mission for which I sent you shall not be used for any purpose without further permission from me, particularly that dealing with the Conjure Ceremony and rituals which, though printed in the concert program of January 10, 1932, was not performed.

Mason's requests reflect the two competing but coexisting interests that drove her: her desire for the tightest of control over Hurston's undertakings and her disdain for the commercial theatre. Whereas only a week earlier, Mason intimated her resentment at not being verbally credited at the premiere of *The Great Day*, she now insists that Hurston remove her name from any future theatrical presentations. At the same time, Mason presupposes her involvement in any future theatrical ventures; "if *we* decide *together*" to pursue commercial opportunities, she writes, in what can only be read as an effort to preserve her authority to govern Hurston's stage endeavors. As if Hurston needed reminding, Mason then returns to the issue of outstanding loans, using the specter of financial debt to keep Hurston in check.

What choice did Hurston have but to sign the contract with the assurance that she had "read the foregoing letter and agree[d] to the terms thereof"? Indebted to Mason for her years of patronage, Hurston could do little now to repudiate or contest the above stipulations. Still, the fact remains: despite the steps Mason took to secure her legal ownership of *The Great Day* material, despite her objections to the theatrical use of this material, Hurston continued to rework and re-present versions of *The Great Day* on the public stage with and without Mason's endorsement.

### *The Great Day*'s Aftermath

In the months immediately following *The Great Day*, Hurston found herself in a particularly complicated position. On one hand was the fanfare stemming from the Broadway debut of her folk concert, including a flourish of congratulatory calls and notices. On the other were the disapproval and resentment of Mason and Locke, the imposition of further restrictions on her use of the concert material, pressure to return immediately to her writing, and, not least of all, the mandate to repay a six-hundred-dollar loan. Given *The Great Day*'s critical success, the concert itself represented the logical solution to Hurston's financial dilemma: if a Broadway producer offered to back the show,

surely she could make enough money to repay Mason and support herself. Despite Mason's urging that she abandon her stage project, and
despite her own later claim that she had "no intention of making concert [her] field," Hurston aggressively pursued a range of stage opportunities during the winter of 1932—largely without Mason's knowledge
or approval.[81] Not all of these materialized into production work. But
by March, preparations were under way for another evening-length
performance of Hurston's folk concert.

On Tuesday, March 29, 1932, Hurston presented *From Sun to Sun*
at the New School for Social Research. Apart from the new title, several casting changes, and the substitution of a short skit called "The
Fiery Chariot" for the Conjure Ceremony, *From Sun to Sun* was essentially a restaging of *The Great Day*. Although Hurston kept Mason and
Locke out of the loop as she made the arrangements for the second
concert, she could not conceal the production from them entirely. In
late March, in what was surely an attempt to avoid the controversy
created by her stage address in *The Great Day*, Hurston asked Locke
to deliver a brief speech during *From Sun to Sun*.[82] Poor weather in
Washington ultimately prevented him from attending, but Mason was
there, despite complaints about having to cancel other engagements.[83]

Practically speaking, Hurston's staging of *From Sun to Sun* further
strained her already tense relationship with Mason. Hurston considered
the concert an accomplishment. Although she again failed to make any
money, neither did she lose any, and she assured Mason that she "made
lots of new connections."[84] Unimpressed, Mason admonished Hurston
that "people do not run up bills for things with no prospects of pay-
ing for them."[85] The Sunday following the New School concert, Mason
sent Locke to pay Hurston a visit. An April 4 letter from Hurston
to Mason, which refers to this "long and intimate session," provides
a good sense of what the meeting entailed.[86] Written in a sober tone
that diverges markedly from her usual display of optimism, Hurston
offers a point-by-point rejoinder to the catalog of concerns delivered
by Locke on Mason's behalf. These encompassed four major topics:
Hurston's housing arrangements, her need for employment, the status
of her literary work, and her health. While Hurston's financial depen-
dence lay at the root of most of these problems, the most contentious
issue was her work. It was here that Locke seems to have dispensed his
severest criticism, leaving a dispirited Hurston nearly unable to defend
herself. She writes to Mason:

I understand that both you and Alain feel that I have lost my grip
on things. I cannot comment on that because anything I might
say could be construed as a bid for my own comfort. I shall leave
that to time. For after all you are the last word, no matter what
I do or dont. I can neither be present when you sit in judgment,
nor cry out under sentence. You cannot be wrong, for everything
that I am, I am because you made me. You can smile upon me,
and you can look off towards immensity and be equally right. You
have been gracious, but you were following no law except your
inclination.

In the plainest of terms, Hurston expresses the powerlessness of her
position, painting Mason as the ultimate arbiter of her fate. Yet in the
midst of this avowed defenselessness, Hurston makes an appeal to her
patron on the grounds of authorship. Pushing her "familiar strategy
of ingratiation"[87] to its limits, Hurston appoints Mason as the author
of all that she has become, as the reflection of Mason herself: "everything that I am, I am because you made me." In the very instance that
she concedes how little autonomy she has, Hurston manipulates her
position in an attempt to regain Mason's favor.

Hurston's letter, however, seemed only to produce more animos-
ity on Mason's part. Her dictated notes of April 8 unleash a flood of
bitterness over Hurston's turn to the theatre.[88] After commenting
that "reluctantly, I consented to your idea of the concert which you
had been trying for ever so long before you said anything about it,"
she then dismisses the concert as a failure and faults Hurston for lacking leadership as a director. At one and the same time, Mason accuses
Hurston of assuming too much authority—by planning her folk revue
behind her patron's back—and not enough—by letting herself be manipulated by cast members and people who sought to use her "as a
tool . . . to get ideas for their own work." This double-edged critique is
symptomatic of Hurston's predicament as a black woman artist working to produce her "*real* Negro art theatre" while under the thumb
of her white patron. Although Mason grudgingly provided Hurston
with an April allowance and paid off her concert debts, the fallout
from the New School concert led to a geographic break between the
two. By May, Hurston fled New York for Florida, where she set about
writing her first novel, *Jonah's Gourd Vine*, and staging new versions
of her revue.

However encumbering, Mason's patronage did make it possible for Hurston to first mount her folk concert. As this chapter has shown, it also made it necessary for Hurston to adopt a distinct strategy of dissemblance. Steadily appearing to conform to the regulations placed upon her, she all the while worked to advance her own vision of how black folk culture should be represented onstage. As a number of literary scholars have noted, this subversive masking on Hurston's part calls to mind the figure of the trickster, so prominent in African American folklore.[89] In many ways, I would argue, the performance arena afforded Hurston even greater maneuverability. While the protean nature of theatre allowed her to maintain a certain elusiveness about her *Great Day* program and thus retain final say over its narrative structure, the materiality of theatre enabled her to embody her authorship just by stepping in front of the curtain to address the audience. In contrast to the determinacy of print, which once issued, cannot be altered, Hurston's performances—and here I refer to her performative behavior and to her formal stage production—could not be pinned down in any definitive way. For ultimately, questions like how many of Locke's narrative revisions Hurston incorporated, and just how calculated or improvised her onstage remarks during the concert were, remain unanswerable. In this sense, Hurston continues to evade the order that others, including historians, seek to impose upon her. Yet rather than dwelling exclusively on Hurston's powerlessness or uncritically celebrating her defiance, we must appreciate the complexity of the conditions under which she worked, recognizing both the magnitude of the constraints placed upon her and the shrewdness of her response to the power relations in which her stage praxis was enmeshed.

# 4

## Hurston's Embodied Theory of the Folk

T hus far, we have examined the conditions of production that
formed the backdrop for and shaped Hurston's efforts to author her theatrical folk concert. Now we turn our attention to the
culmination of those efforts, the sequence of folk idioms dramatized
in *The Great Day*. In her 1942 autobiography, Hurston characterized
her concert as an attempt to "tr[y] out [her] theory" that there was
an alternative to the highly arranged, conservatory-trained model of
presenting black folk music.[1] Taking her cue, which resonates with
scholar Barbara Christian's observation that "people of color have always theorized—but in forms quite different from the Western form of
abstract logic," this chapter proceeds from the premise that *The Great
Day* represented Hurston's embodied theory of the folk.[2] Like her volume *Mules and Men* and her numerous essays, the 1932 concert not
only publicized the folk material Hurston had amassed in the course
of her anthropological research in the South and the Caribbean, it
also conveyed an interpretation of that material. Despite promotional
claims that her program offered "untouched" black expressive forms,
Hurston carefully orchestrated a handpicked group of work songs,
games, dances, and spirituals to reflect her particular conception of
African American folk culture. The choices she made were designed to
alter her audience's understanding of the nature and place of black folk
expression in American culture.

This chapter reconstructs the onstage action of *The Great Day* to
provide insight into what was distinctive about Hurston's embodied

theory. The outcome of her calculations for the stage was not synonymous with her textual representations, for her concert called upon and required a sensitivity to the dynamics of live performance. Theatre provided Hurston the means to illustrate the physicality of black folk culture and to spotlight the corporeal power of the Fire Dance. In addition, her choreography of the folk resituated African American cultural products in relation to the material conditions of labor in a southern rural community, as well as to African diasporic roots and routes. Bringing to life the rhythmic and kinesthetic dimensions of black folk aesthetics, Hurston staged the tensions and unities that, for her, defined the folk.

## The Narrative Action of *The Great Day*

Set in the "present day" in "a railroad camp in South Florida," *The Great Day* opened with a section titled "In the Quarters: Waking the Camp."[3] As the curtain rose, the voice of the shack rouser Dick Willie, played by Percy Punter, was heard from stage left:

> Wake up bullies and git on de rock,
> Taint quite day but it's five o'clock.[4]

Against a background of moss-draped trees, Dick Willie slowly made his way across the darkened stage, rapping his stick against the ground and chanting improvised rhymes, which were answered by the humming of an offstage male chorus. As the camp began to stir in response to this shouting, a gang of men congregated with their dinner pails and jumper jackets draped over their arms. Once all the men had assembled, they set off down the road toward their work site. The curtain came down as they sang a song called "Joe Brown" about "de longest train I seen" and exited the stage.[5] The curtain rose again on the second scene, "Working on the Railroad." At the prompting of their captain, the men lined up along the steel rail and began their work. A water boy, doubling as a "singing liner," walked up and down the track, "raising up" various tunes for the men to sing. While he called out the verses, the men performed the chorus in response. Alternating between spiking songs like "Oh, Lulu!" and lining songs like "Can't You Line It?" the men pantomimed the motions of pulling the rail into place and spiking it down. Each time the hammer came down on the track, the men let out a guttural "Hanh!"—a vociferous, rhythmic grunt that punctuated their singing and served to synchronize their actions. Save for one interruption, when a woman named Maimie made her way down the track singing "East Coast Blues," the men progressed through a series of six different songs, including "Captain Keep a-Hollerin'," "Mule on de Mount," "Black Gal," and "John Henry." Finally, the captain announced the workday over, and the men left the stage, jovially heading back toward the camp. A blackout signaled the end of the "Working on the Railroad" section.

The next section, "Back in the Quarters: Dusk Dark," returned to the action of camp, where a group of children had transformed the space in front of their shacks into a makeshift playground.[6] A series of spirited children's games followed, including "Chick-mah-chick," in which the youth assumed the parts of a hawk, a hen, and a brood of chicks, and chanted, marched, danced, and chased one another around the stage. The games continued until the children grew tired. At that point, Sadie McGill, playing one of the camp women who had congregated nearby, sang her son to sleep with a hillbilly lullaby called "Mistah Frog." Just as the woman and child exited, a traveling preacher, played by Leigh Whipper, wandered into view, initiating the next section, "Itinerant Preacher at the Quarters." First mistaking him for a bootlegger, the camp members grew quiet once the stranger took out a Bible. One of the preacher's two female attendants raised up the spiritual "Death Comes a-Creepin'," and everyone joined in. After the spiritual, Whipper launched into a rousing, breathy sermon titled "Behold de Rib," which recounted how God created a mate for Adam. As he delivered his recitation, the camp-turned-congregation bore him up, intoning their approval, swaying along, and breaking into song. When the thundering sermon came to a close, the cast performed one final spiritual, "You Can't Hide," and the curtain came down on act 1 of *The Great Day*.

Following a brief intermission, the plot resumed with "In the 'Jook': Black Dark." Inside the confines of the local pleasure house, the adults of the camp took to the business of amusing themselves. While small gatherings of men played lively dice and card games, couples danced the languorous Slow Drag around the floor. Others sang secular blues tunes like "Cold Rainy Day" and "Halimuh Fack," accompanied alternately by a thumping piano and guitar "fits." When the jook's bustling activity began to die down, the entire ensemble headed off for "In the Palm Woods," the penultimate section of the concert.[7]

On a dimly lit stage, the cast energetically reentered, circled around the space, and seated themselves on the ground. In contrast to the workday clothing worn in the preceding sections, some of the performers now donned colorful and elaborately patterned costumes, including feather-adorned robes and extravagant headpieces. Led by a cohort of West Indian migrant workers, the company began singing a series of Caribbean folk songs with titles like "Bellamina," "Wasp Bite Noby," and "Evalina." These songs inaugurated the climactic Fire Dance cycle. The first dance in the cycle was the Jumping Dance, which began with "a grand flourish of the drum." Assuming a ring formation, participants clapped and sang along as individuals took turns in the center, leaping and stepping to the drum. Beneath its simple and repetitious tune, the Jumping Dance was quite difficult to execute, for each soloist had to invent and perform personalized steps without straying from the accompanying drum rhythms. The dancing continued until the drum grew cold. After reheating it over an imaginary fire, the drummers selected a new rhythmic tune, which initiated a new round of dancing. In the Ring Play, the second dance in the Fire Dance cycle, participants again formed a ring and kept "marvelous stop-time rhythm" with their hands. In place of the Jumping Dance's solos, each dancer in the center now selected a partner and performed a "sensuous" or "florid" duet; the more skilled the couple, the more enthusiastic the crowd's response. A final change in drum rhythm and tone marked the transition to the Crow Dance, a solo performed in *The Great Day* by Joseph Neeley, who enacted "a perfect rhythmic imitation of a buzzard flying and seeking food."[8] This mimetic dance brought the climactic Palm Woods section, the culmination of a full day's activity, to a close. Only the Group Finale, a counterpoint choral performance, remained. Here, Wen Talbert, who provided the concert's piano accompaniment, led part of the cast in the spiritual "Deep River" on one side of the stage, while the rest of cast intoned a secular blues song on the other.[9]

## Experiencing *The Great Day*

As the preceding reconstruction suggests, *The Great Day* offered a stirring presentation of black music, song, and dance for the largely but not exclusively white audience assembled at the John Golden Theatre on January 10, 1932. From the opening curtain to the Group Finale, spectators were treated to a range of musical performances—from work songs to spirituals to blues to Caribbean melodies—and an array of kinesthetic displays—from men swinging imaginary picks to the ritualized gestures of children's play to the sensual Slow Drag to the vigorous Fire Dance. Rhythm was the thread that united this panoply of sacred and secular folk idioms. Whether in the form of syncopated blues tunes, workers' coordinated grunts, dynamic hand-clapping, the preacher's breathy exhalations, the slapping of cards onto a table, or the complex polyrhythms of the Bahamian drumming and dancing, the concert made palpable the rhythms that served as the driving force behind the daily activities of this folk community. The effect must have been exhilarating. While the rhythm was nearly continuous, each of the concert's two acts built toward a rousing climax: the preacher's fiery sermon and group spirituals in the first act, and the sensational Fire Dance spectacle in the second. Audience members erupted into enthusiastic applause after both high points.

Much of what fascinated spectators about *The Great Day* was its simultaneous resemblance to and divergence from contemporaneous stage renderings of black folk culture. Although one reviewer thought the production "differed less than might have been expected from songs amply familiar in the concert rooms under the guise of 'Spirituals'" and "sometimes veered toward Broadway," on the whole, critics agreed that *The Great Day* was a "rare" presentation of the "source material" on which "jazz-age imitations" were based.[10] Spectators, in other words, generally experienced the expressive forms in the concert as "originals." To understand how Hurston accomplished this, it is helpful to rehearse briefly how *The Great Day* departed from three established models for staging black folk idioms in the early 1930s: the black musical, the concert spiritual, and black folk drama. All three would have been on what Hans Robert Jauss termed the "horizon of expectations" of spectators attending her concert—"the background of other works of art" with which audiences would likely have been familiar.[11]

These other models all relied heavily on black folk material, but each framed this material differently. In black musical revues, which experienced something of a resurgence in the early 1930s following their heyday a decade earlier, blues singing and jazz dancing were most often contained in specialty numbers rather than integrated into a unified plot.[12] Although nostalgia for Dixieland was frequently a theme of such productions, with southern folkways serving as the vehicle for that nostalgia, these musicals tended to have a "northern and urban focus."[13] Meanwhile, in recitals like those given by the Hall Johnson Negro Choir, singing ensembles performed arranged versions of spirituals a cappella in stark concert hall settings. Presented for their own sake, as art, concert spirituals eschewed any surrounding narrative. In contrast, black folk dramas aimed to tell serious stories about African American life while incorporating music, especially spirituals, into their plot structures. The success of *The Green Pastures*, which opened in 1930, toured the country for five years, and won a Pulitzer Prize for its white author, Marc Connelly, was largely responsible for this trend. The play retold Old Testament stories from a purportedly black rural perspective and featured the Hall Johnson Choir.[14]

*The Great Day* did not quite fit into any of these existing genres. As the writer and eyewitness Sterling Brown summed up, it was "more a series of folk scenes than a play, but it contained good raw dramatic material."[15] Hurston's concert, that is, was dramatic without being a drama and musical (and dance heavy) without being a musical. Although, like a black musical revue, it featured a mélange of music, song, dance, and dialogue, *The Great Day* cohered around a single narrative through line. That through line, however, did not follow the trials and triumphs of a hero or heroine, but focused on the quotidian affairs of an entire railroad work camp community in Florida. Also, audiences encountered spirituals as part of that community's religious practices—"with action," as Hurston later put it—and not as an extracted and isolated art form.[16] Social dances were likewise woven into the daily fabric of the community. In large part, then, *The Great Day* appeared "raw" because it recontextualized black folk idioms, setting them in a southern rural milieu and dramatizing the socioeconomic conditions that gave rise to them. Differently stated, Hurston's revue gave the impression that she had placed the "the spyglass of Anthropology" between New York theatregoers and a southern black folk population.[17]

If *The Great Day*'s dawn-till-dusk structure and collection of folk scenes succeeded in giving it a novel feel relative to more conventional stagings of black music and dance, these features were also critical to Hurston's nuanced theory of black folk expression. In situating black folk idioms in the cultural context represented in *The Great Day*, Hurston constituted the folk in a particular manner, calling attention to aspects of those idioms that were especially meaningful to her. That is not to say that hers was the only theatrical treatment of black expressive practices to insinuate a theory of the folk. Whether identified as art or entertainment, all stage enactments of black folk culture could be read as embodied representations of the folk. My interest here is in excavating what was distinctive about the theory Hurston's production made manifest. An analysis of the relationship between the various folk forms featured in *The Great Day*, as well as between the forms and their dramatized environment, makes it clear that Hurston structured her concert to highlight four discrete yet related dimensions of the folk: material, aesthetic, geographic, and intraracial.

## Labor and the Folk

Hurston's decision to set *The Great Day* in a southern labor camp was neither an automatic choice nor a foregone conclusion. During her folklore-collecting journey in the late 1920s, Hurston visited not only rural Florida but New Orleans, Miami, and Nassau as well. By choosing the labor camp setting, I want to suggest, she sought to illustrate the connections between black expressive practices and the work conditions of blacks in the rural South during the early twentieth century. As Tiffany Ruby Patterson has noted, "For Hurston . . . location was a historical agent and producer of culture. In the South black culture emanated from the workers."[18] By its very design, *The Great Day* exposed this close relationship between material and cultural production. Arising out of and in response to physical toil, music and dance facilitated and served as a means of resistance to the work that structured the daily lives of the folk.

The demands of labor were in evidence from the opening minutes of the revue, when Dick Willie awakened the camp chanting "Cap'n got a new job and need a hund'ed men" and instructed the men to "make time for de straw-boss."[19] As Hurston explained in *Mules and Men,* the straw boss was "the low-paid poor white section boss on a railroad."[20] *The Great Day* thus wasted no time in introducing the class and racial dynamics of the workday; they were embedded in the verbal expression that launched both the day and the drama. By the second scene of the program, the interdependence of physical toil and cultural performance was impossible to ignore. Throughout the "Working on the Railroad" section, one of the longest in the concert, the men worked and sang simultaneously. As Hurston explained in a 1939 Work Projects Administration (WPA) interview with fellow folklorist Herbert Halpert:

> A rail weighs nine hundred pounds, and the men have to take these lining bars and get it in shape to spike it down, and while they are doing that, why they have a chant and also some songs that they use the rhythm to work it into place and then the boys holler bring them a hammer gang and they start spiking it down.[21]

In other words, work songs did more than just accompany the men's actions as they laid the track. The tunes' rhythms actually set the pace at which the men pulled the heavy rail into place and hammered it into the ground. Accordingly, their song repertory included both lining and spiking rhythms, and the men alternated between the two to carry out their task. In both cases, vociferous grunts uttered at periodic rhythmic intervals infused their singing. In "Oh, Lulu!," for example, the gang of workers sang:

> Oh Lulu!
> Hanh!
> Oh, oh, gal!
> Hanh!
> Want to see you!
> Hanh!
> So bad.
> Hanh![22]

On each "Hanh," the men pantomimed swinging their hammers down into the rail's spikes. A similar approach but different rhythm and technique characterized "Can't You Line It?":

> When Ah get in Illinois
> Ahm gointer spread de news about de Floriduh boys.
> Sho-ove it over!
> Hey, hey, can't you line it?
> Ahshack-uh-lack-uh-lack-uh-lack-uh-lack-uh-lack-
>      uh-hanh!
> Can't you move it?
> Hey, hey, can't you try?[23]

On the "Hanh," the men strained in unison at the rail, using imaginary long steel bars to shove it into place. In this way, the work songs' lyrics, in combination with the rhythmic grunts, served to galvanize the men's movements. The presence of a "singing liner" who strode alongside the track and initiated various tunes for the men to sing underscored music's officially sanctioned position on the job.

Even while the "Working on the Railroad" section demonstrated the reciprocal relationship between labor and song, Hurston also revealed how music could serve as a reprieve from strenuous labor. Twice the male crew interrupted their spiking and lining for the performance of social songs.[24] The first instance occurred when the female character named Maimie appeared onstage walking down the track and launched into a rendition of "East Coast Blues," lamenting the theft of her man.[25] One of the men picked up a guitar to accompany her while the others stood around and listened.[26] A reprimand from the captain to "put down that guitar and grab that hammer" sent them back to work, and Maimie continued on her way. Shortly thereafter, the captain accused the men of too much singing and talking and not enough working. They replied that they were doing their best, but "taint no John Henry's round here." When the captain questioned who this figure was, the men entreated Percy Punter, who had earlier served as the shack rouser, to sing "John Henry."[27] Deemed by Hurston "the king of railroad track-laying songs," the ballad relayed the story of the famous steel driver who boasted that he could beat the railroad company's new steam drill with a nine-pound hammer.[28] Despite eventually dropping dead from exhaustion, John Henry succeeded in beating the drill for a time, thus becoming a folk hero. As scholar David Nicholls has pointed out, in its "articulation of beleaguered resistance to the hard work of laying down track," and its "reminder of workers' alienation under capitalism and of the ever-present threat of replacement by machines," the popular folk song contains an implicit social protest.[29] Although "suited to the spiking rhythm," "John Henry" was apparently performed as a solo in *The Great Day* while the captain and other workers listened, thereby amplifying its resistive qualities.[30] By the time the song was completed, the captain announced that 5:30 had arrived and gave the workers permission to "knock off."[31]

Although the end of the "Working on the Railroad" section marked the completion of the workday, the recreational activities that filled the remaining hours of the day played out within the labor context established at the concert's outset. Certainly, the various amusements of the jook and the midnight dancing in the palm woods represented a much-needed release from the arduous toil required on the railroad. Seen in conjunction with the labor they succeeded, the cultural performances enacted after-hours were a chance for camp members to, in scholar Robin D. G. Kelley's words, "take back their bodies for their own pleasure rather than another's profit."[32] At the same time, underlying even these "free" expressive displays was the knowledge that another long day of work lay ahead. Although Hurston was neither the first nor the last observer of African American culture to highlight the interrelationship of material and cultural production, her concert not only vividly theatricalized this relationship but made it the basis for her entire revue.[33] Arranging her program of black folkways around the labor and leisure that comprised a day in the life of a railroad work camp, Hurston enacted on stage her belief that black folk practices could not be understood apart from the socioeconomic context in which they arose.[34]

## Aesthetics and the Folk

The stylistic and formal qualities that united the idioms featured in *The Great Day* bolstered the link between labor and recreation that Hurston signaled with her concert's work camp milieu and workday framework. Her interest in documenting and elucidating the core aesthetic attributes of black folk culture is plain in essays like her 1934 "Characteristics of Negro Expression." Much as she did in that publication, Hurston strove in her stage production to promote an appreciation of the kinds of aesthetic codes that underwrote black expressive idioms. For her, these codes diverged in important ways from the Eurocentric standards governing most of the art familiar to white Americans. Rather than enumerating and explaining these properties to an audience of readers, Hurston took advantage of the medium of theatre to reproduce them materially, making them palpable for an audience of spectators.

One of *The Great Day*'s most conspicuous aesthetic motifs bore a direct connection to the works songs. The rhythmic exhalations that were so prominent in the "Working on the Railroad" scene recurred not once but twice over the concert's duration. This distinctive "Hanh!"

first reappeared in the thundering sermon that formed the centerpiece of the "Itinerant Preacher at the Quarters" section. Following the typical African American preaching manner, the actor Leigh Whipper infused his exhortation with a vocal breathiness by intermittently uttering "hah" to separate individual lines and emphasize individual points. Toward the middle of his recitation, for example, he trumpeted, "So God put Adam into a deep sleep / And took out a bone, ah hah!"[35] Describing this familiar "breathing device" of the Negro preacher in her essay "Spirituals and Neo-Spirituals," Hurston wrote, "It is the tail end of the expulsion just before inhalation. Instead of permitting the breath to drain out, when the wind gets too low for words, the remnant is expelled violently."[36] Used for rhythmic effect, the exhalation was equally a byproduct of the physical demands of speaking. Indeed, in a glossary explanation in *Mules and Men,* Hurston characterized the breathing as a corollary to "warm[ing] up" and as a "straining" that black congregations wished to hear.[37] The preacher's straining thus paralleled the straining of the railroad workers as they spiked and lined the track. As the literary critic Eric Sundquist has written, Hurston's repeated use of the term "straining" suggests the "cognate rhythmic labor" evident in both endeavors. In effect, the "punctuations of breath" amounted to a "hidden rhythmic law" governing the work and religious practices of this folk community.[38]

Crucially, for Hurston, the preacher's pronounced exhalations were also what distinguished black vocal expression from white, effectively making it "the very antithesis of white vocal art." "European singing," she clarified in her essay, "is considered good when each syllable floats out on a column of air, seeming not to have any mechanics at all. Breathing must be hidden. Negro song ornaments both the song and the mechanics." The unabashed breathiness that characterized the preacher's sermon in *The Great Day* was not only the mark of his adherence to a set of codes dramatically different from those governing white oral forms; it was also the locus of his artistry, as he carefully selected "every syllable and every breath."[39]

The resurfacing of this expressive breathing in the jook scene proved how thoroughly these aesthetic codes permeated southern black folk culture. The same distinctive "Hah!" punctuated each line of the song "Let the Deal Go Down," which accompanied the Georgia Skin card game. Even amidst the bustle of dancing, blues singing, and piano playing, the by-now familiar utterance could not have been missed. Hurston considered these rhythmic exhalations indispensable components of the Georgia Skin game: she cited their presence in *Mules and Men* and performed them herself in an interview with Herbert Halpert.[40] As she explained, players made the exclamation in this "most favorite gambling game among the workers of the South" just as they slapped a new card down on the table.[41] The result was to insert meter and emphasis into song and game, imbuing them with a rhythmic cadence. The same breathy rhythmic code that governed this folk community's work and religious ceremonies, Hurston thus demonstrated, equally governed its leisure practices. Put another way, the grunts that first appeared to be an outgrowth of mandatory group labor turned out to be a pervasive and unifying feature of African American vernacular expression.

Although these repeated exhalations were perhaps the most pronounced instance in Hurston's concert of stylistic continuity across a range of expressive idioms, other aesthetic patterns were in evidence too. Several kinesthetic motifs emerged in both the children's games and the Bahamian dances that concluded the revue. The ring formation of "Chick-mah-chick," in which children formed a single-file line and circled around a solitary player, for example, was reprised in the Fire Dance cycle. Both also shared the alternation of solo performers in the center of a circle and the pantomiming of bird behavior. From a more general standpoint, the physical agility necessary to perform the ritualized gestures and choreographic patterns of the children's games matched and complemented the physicality exhibited throughout Hurston's concert: from the motions of the railroad workers as they lined and spiked the track, to the rhythmic swaying that accompanied the preacher's sermon, to the solo and duet dancing showcased in both the jook scene and the Caribbean dance finale. As these resonances suggest, Hurston wove what she discerned to be the essential features of southern black folk culture into a cohesive thread that united the various sections of her stage production.

This demonstration of stylistic and formal integrity had an ancillary effect that was equally vital to Hurston's formulation of the folk. Exposing her audience to the expressive patterns that permeated the daily customs of this southern rural community, Hurston implicitly contested stereotypes about blacks' "innate" physical and rhythmic agility. Paramount here is her decision to devote an entire section of her revue to the enactment of children's games, whose physical and musical exercises echoed and anticipated the activities of the older members of the camp. In effect, these ritual games showed how corporeal and rhythmic facility were socialized in this folk community from an early age. In Hurston's portrayal, play "serve[d] as training for performance."[42] By repeating certain aesthetic conventions and establishing an interdependence between child and adult pastimes, Hurston revealed rhythmic adeptness to be a systematically learned skill, not a "natural" or "instinctive" behavior.[43]

As much as Hurston's enactment of certain recognizable motifs throughout her concert pointed to the stylistic continuity of black folk culture, *The Great Day* also highlighted the mutability of that culture. For Hurston, improvisation was fundamental to black folk practices. The "great variety" of black folklore, she took pains to relate in her written work, "shows the adaptability of the black man: nothing is too old or too new, too domestic or foreign, high or low, for his use."[44] Although it was less amenable to visual representation in a scripted and rehearsed staged production, Hurston found subtle ways to indicate the improvisatory nature of the idioms performed by her cast. In the opening section of the concert, for instance, as the shack rouser ran through a series of chants and hollers to wake the camp, he tailored some of his rhymes to address individual workers or to indicate where he was headed next.[45] The variation in his lyrics was designed to show, as Hurston articulated in an interview, that "sometimes he makes them up as he goes along."[46] Later, while singing the lining rhythm "Mule on de Mount," a song Hurston marked as notable for its "diversified subject matter," the workers ad-libbed a verse about Maimie as they detected her approaching them along the railroad tracks. "Here come Maimie, walkin' down de main line Southern," they sang, exemplifying how this "most widely distributed and best known of all Negro work songs" grew incrementally by incorporating verses "about everything under the sun."[47] Taken together, these incidents demonstrated the nimble responsiveness of black folk practitioners to the situation at hand.[48]

Equally important, Hurston's concert called attention to the conditions that supported and drove the improvisatory dimensions of black folk culture. Throughout, *The Great Day* spotlighted the individual-group dynamic that simultaneously encouraged innovation and guaranteed aesthetic continuity. Hurston succinctly described this dynamic in her 1934 essay "Spirituals and Neo-Spirituals":

Beneath the seeming informality of religious worship there is a
set formality. Sermons, prayers, moans and testimonies have their
definite forms. The individual may hang as many new ornaments
upon the traditional form as he likes, but the audience would be
disagreeably surprised if the form were abandoned. Any new and
original elaboration is welcomed, however, and this brings out the
fact that all religious expression among Negroes is regarded as art,
and ability is recognized as definitely as in any other art.[49]

Precisely these interactive bonds—between embellishment and tradition, individual and audience—were on display during the itinerant preacher's sermon in *The Great Day*. Fulfilling their function as
"Greek chorus," the camp members dramatized their approbation of
the way the preacher handled the sermon form by repeatedly "bearing
him up," emphasizing his "every telling point."[50] Hurston's rendering
of this episode, prominently situated at the conclusion of her concert's
first act, thus provided a vivid illustration of what scholar Gerald Davis
has termed an "aesthetic community": "a group of people sharing the
knowledge for the development and maintenance of a particular affecting mode or 'craft' and the articulating principles to which the
affecting mode must adhere or oppose [in performance]."[51] Because
this shared knowledge ensured that the modifications made by an individual performer neither violated nor abandoned the stylistic codes
governing a given form, the aesthetic community provided a matrix—
an infrastructure of sorts—within which improvisation and stylistic
consistency could productively coexist.

This interplay between individual artistry and communal participation was discernible in a number of the expressive practices enacted
in *The Great Day*, from the call and response of the shack rouser's
chants to the singing-liner-led work songs to the children's games. It
again became salient in the Caribbean folk dance cycle at the end of
the concert's second act. The very arrangement of participants in the
Jumping Dance and Ring Play—a single performer or couple positioned
inside a ring of dancers—visually denoted the reciprocal relationship
between individual and collective. In a parallel to the congregation's
role during the preacher's sermon, the onlookers in the ring urged the
dancers on with their hand clapping, actively appraising the solos and
duets by shouting their approval of especially skilled performances.
Both the sermon and Fire Dance scenes, then, depicted the relation-

ship between performers and participatory audiences, and both dramatized the process by which those performers adorned established idioms with "glorious individualistic flights."[52] In this way, *The Great Day* demonstrated how the aesthetic community formed by the folk contributed to what Amiri Baraka has identified as the "changing same" of black cultural forms.[53]

## Geography and the Folk

As suggested earlier, situating black folk culture squarely in the rural South was central to Hurston's strategy of recontextualization. A promotional notice in the *New York Sun* declared that *The Great Day* featured "Not Harlem—But the Heart of the South."[54] As such, the concert seems to support critic Hazel Carby's claim that "the creation of a discourse of the 'folk' as a *rural* people in Hurston's work in the twenties and thirties displaces the migration of black people to cities."[55] Yet if the milieu depicted in Hurston's revue ostensibly excluded the urban North, North-South relations were by no means irrelevant to the production. To the contrary, whereas Carby maintains that "Hurston did not take seriously the possibility that African-American culture was being transformed as African-American peoples migrated from rural to urban areas," careful scrutiny of the performed cartography of *The Great Day* reveals that the program was Hurston's response to precisely those transformations.

Even as the concert's setting positioned the folk in a bounded southern locale, evidence of the broader world permeated the confines of the camp. The rail construction work in which the men were engaged yoked the folk community to the transportation system that made large-scale migration possible. And in work songs like "Can't You Line It?," the folk sang of the travel intrinsic to their migrant lifestyle. The opening lyrics of the song—"When I get to Illinois / I'm going to spread the news about the Florida boys"—actually forecast a northern move.[56] More to the point, Hurston's choice of setting enabled her to demonstrate the southern rural underpinnings of the black vernacular forms that were increasingly entering urban mainstream culture. Whereas *The Great Day* program announcement proclaimed that "the dances have not been influenced by Harlem or Broadway," her revue staged dances that served as influences *on* Harlem and Broadway.[57]

Here the presence of the jook scene in *The Great Day* assumes heightened significance. In "Characteristics of Negro Expression," Hurston spelled out the magnitude of this "Negro pleasure house," declaring it the birthplace of the black music and dance styles that "circulated over the world."[58] By making the jook and its expressive activities a centerpiece of her concert, Hurston focused her New York audience's attention on the roots of more popular incarnations of black cultural forms. As Sandra Richards has written with respect to the cakewalk enacted in Hurston's 1925 play *Color Struck*, "An ability to read the body in performance would have demonstrated . . . that in certain respects, the distance between the supposedly uncultured rural folk and urban sophisticates was minimal, and that through the language of dance as well as that of music, the former were helping to reconfigure urban culture on terms that were not entirely inimical to their value system."[59] By the same token, while the blues songs and social dances that Hurston presented in the jook scene, including the Slow Drag and the Black Bottom, were stylistically distinguishable from the commercialized versions seen on New York stages, they necessarily bore some resemblance to those versions. If Hurston insisted on locating black folk culture in a southern rural milieu, she equally sought to vivify the relationship between South and North, rural and urban, folk and commercial.

Hurston's mapping of the folk extended beyond an invocation of North–South U.S. migratory routes. As detailed earlier, Hurston placed the Bahamian Fire Dance at the end of her program, which followed the activities of a Floridian work camp from sunup to sundown. After immersing her audience in the folkways of southern black Americans, in other words, Hurston's stage production erupted into a display of a distinctly Caribbean dance form, thereby shifting the geographical terrain of the revue. Although the presence of a small group of West Indians among the migrant workers had received attention much earlier in the program, the dance enacted in the palm woods section foregrounded and intensified the Bahamian dimension just as the concert reached its conclusion.[60] *The Great Day* thus not only resituated African American culture in relation to working conditions in the rural South; it also recast black expressive practices— dance in particular—in a broader, transnational framework. Moving from the United States to the Caribbean and invoking African origins through the "primitive" Fire Dance, Hurston created a teleology that gestured toward the diasporic roots of African American culture, effectively tracing the Middle Passage in reverse. This Afrocentric narrative enabled her to point toward the origins and evolution of black vernacular dance apart from its problematic history on the American minstrel and postminstrel theatre stage.

Although the term "Afrocentricity" did not exist in the 1930s and was not a part of Hurston's rhetoric, there is no question that she was interested in tracking African survivals in the Caribbean and United States.[61] In staging the West Indian Fire Dance, whose African origins she continuously underscored, Hurston exposed the existence of these survivals on American shores. As she later wrote in an essay for the Florida WPA, "Nightly in Palm Beach, Fort Pierce, Miami, Key West, and other cities of the Florida east coast the hot drumheads throb and the African-Bahamian folk arts seep into the soil of America."[62] Up to thirty thousand Bahamians, she explained, resided in a city like Miami, their "African songs, dances, and instrumentation" transforming the place into "a pure African colony."[63] Hurston clearly understood that these African-derived expressive practices owed their presence in the United States to the waves of migration that brought West Indians to Florida. The Great Day demonstrated that forms like the Fire Dance were transported on the bodies of West Indian migrant workers in particular. Material conditions thus also underwrote these important intercultural encounters and transmissions.

Beyond her repeated written references to the Fire Dance's diasporic origins, Hurston's staging of the dance underscored its difference from the concert's American idioms. Recounting The Great Day finale in her autobiography, Hurston wrote, "As soon as the curtain went up on the Fire Dancers, their costuming got a hand."[64] The attire of the Fire Dance performers, which one reviewer described as "costumes of varied patterns in brilliant colors," sharply distinguished the piece from the workday clothing that preceded it.[65] A photograph taken by Theatre Arts Monthly captures a moment from a rehearsal of the "grotesquely costumed" dance number, as the caption limned it.[66] The photo shows Hurston and fourteen of her dancers arranged in a semi-circle, leaning in and clapping along as they intently observe a male and female dancer who perform in the center of the ring (see Figure 3). While the women all wear boldly patterned dresses, three of the men stand out for their elaborate headpieces and feather-adorned robes. The male dancer in the center wears only a snakeskin loincloth, cape, and headpiece, leaving his legs and torso completely bare. Between the striking costumes, exposed male body, "subtle but compelling" drum rhythms, vigorous leaping and dancing, and air of ceremonial ritual, the Fire Dance in performance surely fulfilled the publicity announcement's promise of a "primitive and exciting folk dance."[67] With this distinctive Caribbean cycle offered as the climax to a day in the life of a Florida work camp, Hurston's 1932 concert staged a theory of African influences well before the concept of Afrocentricity entered academic discourse.

Yet if the placement of the Fire Dance at the end of the concert traced a line of descent back toward the Caribbean, the choreography that operated within this structure betrayed a more complex and heterogeneous vision of diaspora. Categorically, the unfamiliar Fire Dance stood apart from all other forms featured in the concert. But between the recognizably American vernacular dancing of the jook scene, and the children's games, which bore decided affinities to the Bahamian dance finale, Hurston's concert played simultaneously with at least three distinct yet related dance styles: urban popular, rural folk, and (Afro-)Caribbean.[68] By dramatizing this spectrum, Hurston implicitly staged the similarities and differences between movement practices of the African diaspora, demonstrating the retentions and the transmutations that took place as such practices traveled from the Bahamas to the United States. It is also worth recalling that Hurston described the middle part of the Fire Dance not as uniformly African but as "African rhythm with European borrowings"—already modified and hybrid in its Caribbean incarnation. This variegated vision of diaspora was one that Hurston held from early on. As she explained to her friend Langston Hughes in a 1929 letter from the field, she was interested in the Bahamian material for two fundamental reasons: "(1) There are so many of them in America that their folk lore definitely influences ours in South Fla. (2) For contrast with ours."[69] For Hurston, Afrocentric survivals necessarily existed alongside revision and transformation, and the embodied cartography of her concert expressed just this multiplicity.

Seen in this light, Hurston's *The Great Day* anticipates and answers the concerns of more recent theorists of the black diaspora. In the 1990s, scholars like Paul Gilroy and James Clifford articulated provocative and influential formulations of diaspora that approached culture not as a fixed, bounded entity but rather as a category produced by movement and travel between places.[70] In particular, Gilroy's acclaimed 1993 book *The Black Atlantic* proposes that rather than perceiving identity as tied to "roots and rootedness," we should understand it "as a process of movement and mediation that is more appropriately approached via the homonym routes."[71] With its attention to cross-cultural exchange and transnational discontinuities, Hurston's concert represents an important early moment of diaspora consciousness, an enactment of the Black Atlantic that predates by decades Gilroy's coinage of the term. At the same time, her stagings complicate any a priori assumption that espousals of African roots and transatlantic routes are antithetical, showing them instead to be alternating and interlacing constituents of cultural identity.

## Intraracial Difference and the Folk

In a 2001 article, Sandra Gunning urges scholars to attend not only to "the revolutionary and subversive power" of diaspora identifications but also to "the very real impact of color, status, region, and gendered experience as sites of intra-racial difference within the context of black diaspora."[72] Having charted the relationship between Caribbean and American expressive practices in *The Great Day*, it bears asking how Hurston treated the interpersonal dimensions of that relationship. What kinds of identifications and disidentifications resulted from the intercultural encounters in the work camp, and how did intraracial difference play out more generally in the folk community depicted on stage? Put another way, how did Hurston's concerts weigh what Gunning calls "the balance between the racial unity and cultural difference that structure even the most celebratory text of black diaspora community"?[73] In *The Great Day*, both ethnicity and gender emerged as sites of difference, though to varying degrees.

Within the narrative of Hurston's concert, as indicated earlier, the Fire Dance owed its appearance to a small group of immigrant Bahamians living and working alongside the other camp members. While not immediately demarcated from their African American cohorts, the West Indians attracted notice toward the end of the "Working on the Railroad" section. In a typescript draft of the revue titled "The Passing of a Day," the spiking tune "Black Gal" leads to the following exchange between several of the workers:

**JIG WILEY:** Hey you two saws, why don't yo-all sing, whistle or dance? Tain't nothin' to you at all.
**STEW BEEF:** Don't you call me no saw—I'll mash you like a cockroach.
**JIG WILEY:** You from Nassau, ain't you?
**STEW BEEF:** Yeah, but don't you call us no saws—and another thing, we don't dance on no railroad—we got a time and a place.
**JOE WILLARD:** Where is it and when—we ain't never seen it.[74]

Although only Stew Beef speaks here, Wiley's reference to "two saws" establishes the presence of more than one Bahamian. In the script, the captain interrupts the conversation, instructing the men to get back to work, and the subject of ethnic difference is entirely dropped until the final section of the revue, when the Fire Dance is performed.

The use of a pejorative label to refer to the Bahamian workers bears a remarkable resemblance to a real-life clash between Hurston's dance group and the musician Hall Johnson's singers, detailed in Hurston's *Dust Tracks on a Road* and examined in chapter 3. Johnson's singers' denunciation was based on stereotypes of West Indians as "monkey chasers." By contrast, the Bahamians in Hurston's dramatized rendering stand out for their failure to participate in the singing, whistling, and dancing engaged in by the rest of the workers. Indeed, in complaining "Tain't nothin' to you at all," Wiley suggests that the men in the camp are judged chiefly by their display of performative idioms. Stew Beef's justification—that he and his fellow Bahamians have their own time and place for dancing—effectively disrupts the homogeneity of the folk present up to that point in the revue. His statement introduces the existence of multiple folk communities and raises the possibility of competing aesthetic codes among the folk. Although grouped together to perform the same manual labor, the Bahamian migrants maintain their cultural distinctiveness by refusing to adopt wholly the ways of African American folk.

Notably, this incident transpires differently in another surviving typescript for Hurston's revue. In the draft titled "From Sun to Sun," the issue of intraracial discrimination leads directly into the enactment of the Fire Dance. Arising a bit later on in the "Working on the Railroad" section, the exchange between workers commences in the same fashion as in the draft quoted from earlier:

**WILEY:** Hey you two 'saws! Why dont y'all sing whistle or dance? Taint nothin to you atall.

**BILL:** Dont you call me no saw! I'll mash you like a cock roach.

**WILEY:** You from Nassau aint you?

**MOTOR BOAT:** Yeah, but dont you call us no saws. We dont like it. We dont like yo' songs and we dont like your dance neither.

**BILL:** We got our own songs and dance.

**WILEY:** I aint never seen you do it.

**BILL:** We dont sing on no railroad. We go in de woods and make a fire. Thats why we call it Fire Dance.[75]

Here, too, the captain interrupts the discussion. But instead of being forced to resume their work, the men are allowed to break:

**CAP'N:** Say! Git to hittin down there! You aint gittin paid to talk yo' dance.

**BILL:** We homesick for our dance. We got to have one, [or] we dont work no more.

**CAP'N:** All right, all right, its dinner time. Knock off but be back on de job at one.

**MOTOR BOAT:** We like more time, but this will do. Come on Bill, we go get our gang.

**BILL:** *(Does a step or two)* Down de road baby, less go to de palm grove.

According to stage directions, the curtain was to close at that point and reopen on a palm grove setting, where the spectacular Fire Dance was to be performed until a one o'clock whistle called the men back to work.

The discrepancies between these two typescripts—the slightly altered dialogue and the substantially different placement of the Caribbean dance cycle—had real repercussions for Hurston's depiction of intraracial relations. Perhaps most important, the latter rendering intensifies the divisions between the Bahamian and American workers. In "The Passing of a Day" draft, Stew Beef asserts only that the Bahamians prefer not to dance along the rail. "From Sun to Sun" contains a more pronounced condemnation of the Florida workers' expressive forms, with Motor Boat declaring, "We dont like yo' songs and we dont like your dance neither." The latter scenario implies that the Bahamians object to more than just the milieu in which the Floridians perform but actually resent the form and style of their singing and dancing. In addition, in the "From Sun to Sun" draft, the Fire Dance is portrayed as a meaningful link to the Bahamas, the homeland of this group of migrant workers; Bill states explicitly, "We homesick for our dance." Only by performing the dance will they assuage their homesickness and be able to return to work. In no uncertain terms, this longing for their homeland marks the Bahamians as a distinct ethnic and national group whose expressive techniques signal their difference from black Americans. When they finally perform the Fire Dance, this difference is made manifest. Gathering together the rest of their "gang" and isolating themselves from the American members of the work community, the Bahamians enact their own form of creative expression. Here the cultural misunderstanding between several workers escalates into a kinesthetic display of a disparate folk tradition.

The placement of the Fire Dance, then, had a direct bearing on how Hurston's concert represented the relationship between African American folk and Caribbean folk. While no record of the dialogue actually used in *The Great Day* survives, Hurston's placement of the Fire Dance in the finale position is telling. If she once considered a version of the program that depicted an uneasy coexistence between Bahamians and African Americans with the dance cycle functioning as a break in the workday and a rupture between the two groups, the version she ultimately adopted presented the Fire Dance as a force that united the heterogeneous folk communities of the railroad work camp by inviting the participation of the entire cast. As "The Passing of a Day" typescript makes clear, when the Bahamians get ready to leave the jook for the palm grove in the second half of the concert, the Americans' curiosity about the dance provokes all to follow.[76] Furthermore, though earmarked over the course of the revue as the distinct province of the Bahamian workers and unfamiliar to the American-born workers (not to mention the American audience), resemblances between the Fire Dance cycle and the children's games helped wed African American and Caribbean practices. Tensions between the two communities notwithstanding, both groups shared certain kinesthetic patterns and movement qualities. In particular, the circle formation of the Jumping Dance and Ring Play, echoing the earlier ring of "Chick-mah-chick," served as an embodiment of "interethnic assimilation."[77] Situated at the close of the narrative, enlisting universal participation, the Fire Dance helped bridge national differences introduced during the workday. In the end, Hurston used her production to broach intraracial tensions without letting them become factious.[78]

Ethnicity was not the only axis of difference that factored into *The Great Day*. Hurston's concert also gestured at the gender divisions that operated within black communities in the rural South. In plain terms, *The Great Day* revealed how the segregated nature of labor in the work camp made for segregated performances. Until Maimie interrupted the gang of men on the railroad tracks with her rendition of "East Coast Blues," the concert's portrait of folk culture was exclusively male. Of course, women's roles as mothers were evident in the children's games section, and women were equal partners in the blues singing and couples dancing of the jook, as well as in the first two sections of the Fire Dance. But between the shack rouser's chants, the work songs, the preacher's sermon, and the jook's card playing, the majority of the revue's expressive displays were male dominated. In Hurston's concert, as in her written productions, it was clear that "the most highly regarded types of performance in African-American culture," as scholar Cheryl Wall has written, "are in the main the province of men."[79]

Significantly, however, the "Conjure Ceremony" that Hurston originally planned to stage in *The Great Day* would have helped balance the gender asymmetry. Consisting of two numbers, "Pea-vine Candle Dance" and "9 Hairs in the Graveyard," the conjure scene was a follow-up to Maimie's story. When she first appeared on the railroad tracks, Maimie announced her intent to seek a hoodoo doctor to retaliate against a woman who had stolen her husband. The actual ceremony, situated between the jook scene and the Fire Dance in the concert's second act, was to unfold when Maimie and the other female members of the cast paid a visit to Ant Judy to place a spell on the "tee-rolling" woman. The ensuing ritual, led by Ant Judy and her assistant Ole Man Giff, involved a danced march in a serpentine pattern around a maze of lit candles in an offering to Death. The drill ended with Ant Judy "prostrate before the Death," performing a chant in the voice of an inhabiting divinity while the female onlookers danced around the altar and echoed her incantations.[80] Several scholars have identified hoodoo as a source of female empowerment in Hurston's work, and certainly, *The Great Day*'s conjure ceremony exposed an arena within the folk community in which a woman commanded authority through her ability to resolve social conflicts.[81] Even apart from the issue of power, the episode's physical makeup was noteworthy within the schema of Hurston's stage revue. Not only would the female-dominated scene have offset the concert's earlier all-male work song section, but the conjure ceremony's stirring female performance would have paralleled the itinerant preacher's charismatic display.

The omission of the conjure ceremony from the final production, therefore, directly affected *The Great Day*'s representation of gender. Pressured to drop the scene by her white patron, Hurston ultimately presented a less even depiction of gendered participation in southern black folk culture. Although she never restored the conjure section to her program, she did tinker with the concert's overall gender balance in subsequent stagings. In her 1934 production *All De Live Long Day*, Hurston replaced the opening shack rouser number with a song called "Baby Chile," led by a female soloist and backed by a female ensemble.[82] Similarly, while Joseph Neeley performed the Crow Dance in *The Great Day*, Hurston herself danced the solo when she staged the revue in Florida. These casting and program changes suggest Hurston's commitment to calling attention to women's roles as cultural producers despite conspicuous gender divides among southern rural black folk.

Furthermore, the subject of the prominently situated sermon in *The Great Day* was gender parity. Addressing the camp, the itinerant preacher recounted how God created a mate for Adam, intoning, "God Amighty, he took de bone out of his side / So dat places de woman beside us."[83] As Cheryl Wall has pointed out, "Female equality was not, is not, a common subject in black sermons."[84] Assessing the function and placement of "Behold de Rib" within the narrative of Hurston's folklore volume *Mules and Men*, Wall convincingly argues that Hurston's selection of this particular sermon, which was not the only one she had collected, was strategic insofar as it legitimized the aggressive conduct of a powerful woman in the following scene. In *The Great Day*, however, the "Behold de Rib" sermon was succeeded by a different episode: the close of the first act and Hurston's direct address to the audience, in which she explained her reasons for staging the concert.[85] In Hurston's telling, in fact, it was the actor who played the preacher, Leigh Whipper, who nudged her onto the stage. Delivered by Whipper, the preacher's message of gender equality may thus have tacitly prepared audience members to accept Hurston as author and director of the onstage events they were witnessing. As it played out in the course of the performance, in other words, the sermon discreetly allowed Hurston to mobilize the wisdom of the folk to sanction her own female authority.[86] With her embodied representation of the folk encumbered by external pressures that forced her to forgo the woman-centered conjure ceremony, Hurston's most pronounced engagement with gender difference, it would seem, occurred in her ongoing struggle to carve out a space for herself as an artistic authority in the theatrical arena.

Although Hurston cloaked her concert in the rhetoric of authenticity, the theory of the folk she enacted in *The Great Day* gave the lie to notions of the folk as timeless, artless, or homogeneous. In exposing the economic structures, aesthetic codes, migration patterns, and social relations that underwrote black folk expression, the revue brought to view some of the very forces that the discourse of authenticity customarily elides. Instead of spelling out her claims about the attributes and conditions of black folk idioms, Hurston posited them in, on, and around the bodies of her cast members, allowing them to take live shape as each episode in her narrative unfolded.

Performed rather than written, Hurston's embodied theory of the folk was both subtler and more assertive than the formulations she advanced in her literary works. Perhaps most important, the medium of theatre permitted her to insinuate significations that were not easily conveyable in print or that she may have deemed too bold—and therefore politically imprudent—to commit to writing. In performance, Hurston was able to draw upon the kinesthetic knowledge of her audience to intimate a relationship between popular mainstream, southern black rural, and Afro-Caribbean dance styles. Her insistence on the correlations between labor and cultural production, so evident in the setting and structure of her revue, moreover, does not receive nearly the same focus in her novels. And while her written articulations of the "Characteristics of Negro Expression" at times seem an endorsement of notions of innate black talent, her staging of children's games emphasized the socialized nature of those characteristics.

By a similar token, Hurston's delineation of diaspora played a more forceful role in her stage concert than in her literature. Certainly, Hurston continued to explore the relations between Caribbean and African American practices in other media, and Africanist dance scenes appear in both *Jonah's Gourd Vine* and *Their Eyes Were Watching God*. Yet the prominence of the Bahamian dance cycle in *The Great Day*—its position as the climactic finale of the production and its sheer intensity in live performance—undeniably amplified its import to Hurston's presentation of the folk. In fact, I would argue, Hurston took advantage of the theatrical arena to put forward a complex vision of harmonious heterogeneity among the folk without having to enunciate it explicitly. By representing the Fire Dance as a unifying force, capable of healing the cross-cultural discord introduced earlier in the concert, Hurston held up to her audience a model of black diasporic solidarity. This was not necessarily a solidarity that Hurston encountered offstage. In the space of performance, however, Hurston demonstrated the possibility of a folk collectivity forged in and through dance.[87] For the African American workers, the initial "cultural strangeness" of the Bahamians, to borrow Kimberly Jaye Banks's term, was "only made familiar through embodiment."[88] Even as *The Great Day* entertained theatregoers with its lively display of black music, dance, and pantomime, Hurston pointed to the southern rural work camp as a site where disparate black folk communities converge, contend, and coalesce, and, in the process, generate cultural forms that influence American culture at large.

Admittedly, it is impossible to ascertain the extent to which contemporary spectators recognized the implications of Hurston's choreography, some of which may have become apparent only in retrospect.[89] If certain aspects of Hurston's folk ideology were more salient in embodied form, the inherently indeterminate and polyvalent nature of performance also meant that her representations were subject to multiple, even contradictory readings.

# 5
## Interpreting the Fire Dance

As the previous chapter argued, Hurston's dramatization of a day in the life of a railroad work camp in rural Florida enacted a nuanced vision of diaspora. While the culmination in the Bahamian Fire Dance asserted the presence of African retentions and evoked the Middle Passage in reverse, the concert also pointed to the variations and tensions between movement practices and black folk communities of the African diaspora. Still, the question of how audiences responded to Hurston's treatment of black folk culture remains. To what extent was her theatrical portrait of black expression as the product of specific material conditions and of diasporic roots and routes legible to American spectators in the 1930s? An examination of the reception of Hurston's concerts reveals the formidable hurdle that reigning stereotypes about blacks as exotic, primitive beings posed to recognition of her delineation of a black diaspora. The resulting contest between diaspora and primitivism produced yet another conflict for Hurston to negotiate.

Although as Marianna Torgovnick maintains, the trope of the primitive is "infinitely docile and malleable," primitivism customarily assumes a hierarchical and evolutionary relationship between Western civilization and savage, racialized others.[1] Closely allied with colonial discourse, primitivist thought works to position the other as both fundamentally different and interminably distant from the Western self, whether temporally, spatially, or both.[2] In the early decades of the twentieth century, a confluence of forces—the rise of Freudianism and a belief in the primitive unconscious, the brutal destruction of World War I, European painters' newfound interest in African art—coalesced to give the idea of the primitive new currency.[3] Even as these trends valorized blackness as a vital, unfettered alternative to the alienation of modernity allegedly afflicting whites, the fantasy of the primitive only furthered racist assumptions that peoples of African origin were somehow outside of history, permanently suspended in a prior temporal moment.

Anthropologists working in the 1920s, '30s, and '40s offered a challenge to this view. Influenced by the cultural relativism of Franz Boas, the German émigré and father of American anthropology, social scientists like Melville Herskovits, with whom Hurston worked for a time, documented the survival of African cultural traditions in the New World. The assertion of African retentions and transformations in turn facilitated theorizations of a black "diaspora," which, as Brent Hayes Edwards explains, became the "term of choice" in the second half of the twentieth century "to express the links and commonalities among groups of African descent throughout the world."[4] The work of Paul Gilroy in particular advanced a transnational approach to black identity, one that focuses not only on African roots and cultural continuities, but also on the routes, ruptures, and cross-cultural exchanges that are equally constitutive of the black diaspora.[5] A paradigm shift from primitivism to diaspora thus had profound consequences for conceptions of blackness in the preceding century. In disclosing a transatlantic tradition of black cultural practices, the notion of diaspora not only troubles stereotypes of black people as unthinking, uncivilized exotics. It also replaces the hierarchies and dichotomies on which primitivism depends with a model of black influences and exchange not wholly dependent on any white arbiter. That is, whereas primitivism views blackness only vis-à-vis whiteness, diaspora foregrounds the relations within blackness.

If scholarship at large underwent a gradual transition from overridingly primitivist to primarily diasporic approaches to black culture over the course of the twentieth century, the reception history of the Bahamian Fire Dance that Hurston staged in *The Great Day* suggests that a comparable struggle between these two frames played out earlier in the theatrical arena. Or, to be more accurate, the stage life of the Fire Dance paints a more complicated picture of the relationship between primitivism and diaspora, problematizing any supposition that articulations of diaspora necessarily or directly succeeded in retiring the logic of primitivism. The shifting resonances of the Fire Dance in the 1930s indicate how much fluctuation, wrangling, and entanglement between various conceptions of blackness existed at a time when ideas about diaspora were only just beginning to take hold in the American public's imagination. The stage dance thus exemplifies theatre scholar Harry Elam's contention that African American theater and performance constitute "powerful sites for the creation, application, and even the subversion of notions of blackness and of concepts of African American identity."[6]

This chapter charts the varied ideological discourses surrounding Hurston's folk concert and the Bahamian Fire Dance in particular to explore the contingent and contested nature of meaning with regard to representations of blackness. First, I examine Hurston's efforts to control interpretations of her revue, exposing the struggles between artistic intent and audience reception and the kind of work that was necessary to unseat and at times accommodate ingrained primitivist beliefs. I then track how the significations of the Fire Dance shifted when the folk cycle appeared outside of Hurston's revue in productions by other artists in the 1930s. The process of elucidating these microshifts in meaning, I hope, will correspondingly reveal something about the macroshifts that transpire between emergent and residual conceptions of black dancing bodies.[7]

## Hurston's Framing of the Fire Dance

Although each component of Hurston's concert contributed to her overall vision of black folk culture, her delineation of diaspora hinged on the Bahamian Fire Dance. The rousing dance cycle was both the most palpably African number in the concert and the principal site of difference between the African American and West Indian workers in the camp. While the narrative framework of her revue played a crucial role in situating the Fire Dance vis-à-vis the other expressive forms on display, Hurston found ways to underscore the Caribbeanness of the dance apart from this framework. Her insistence on the Bahamian identity of her Fire Dance ensemble, for example, served as an effective way of highlighting the diasporic dimensions of her stage material. An advance publicity announcement for *The Great Day* declared the Crow

Dance to be a "primitive and exciting folk dance performed by a group from the Bahama Islands."[8] Not all of the Fire Dance performers were in fact Bahamian natives, but the promotional material encouraged spectators to view them as such. This assertion of national difference reinforced the distinction between U.S. and Caribbean blacks while helping to authenticate Hurston's presentation of diaspora.

Hurston's emphasis on the Caribbean identity of the Fire Dancers clearly had an impact on spectators. Writing in the black newspaper the *New York Age,* Lucien White reported that the Crow Dance was "given by 'a group from the Bahama Islands.'"[9] His use of quotation marks suggests he may have suspected the veracity of the claim. But nearly every other reviewer unhesitatingly classified the "thrilling" dance finale as Bahamian, and some were duly impressed by its parentage. The most telling example came from the *New York Herald Tribune* critic Arthur Ruhl, who remarked that the dance finale was presented "by Negroes who had either just come from the Bahamas or were transplanted blacks who had kept alive, in surprising fashion, the forms and spirit of their native rites."[10] In attributing the Fire Dance to the memory of these native performers, Ruhl registers a dawning awareness of the very meaning of diaspora—of the ability of "transplanted" peoples of African descent to preserve specific expressive idioms.

Despite the attention bestowed on the Fire Dance and its transatlantic makeup, however, critics generally ignored Hurston's balanced depiction of the continuities and discontinuities among black diasporic forms. Cora Gary Illidge from the black newspaper the *New York Amsterdam News* did offer the observation that the "presentation of this rare Negro folklore material offered something . . . entirely different from that which we, in this part of the country, are familiar."[11] But although the vast majority of newspaper accounts mentioned that Hurston spent time in both the southern United States and the Bahama Islands, none addressed the relationship between the cycle of American folk idioms that formed the bulk of the concert and the Caribbean material of the finale.

Neither does the evidence suggest that Hurston's delineation of diaspora succeeded in dislodging entrenched assumptions about black performance. The same critic who seemed newly alert to the existence of an African diaspora, for example, relied on prevailing racial notions to explain *The Great Day* to his readers. Applauding the revue for its lack of self-consciousness, Ruhl capitulated to well-worn stereotypes of blacks' instinctive performativity, characterizing the concert as "an obviously spontaneous enjoyment."[12] The comments of reviewers from other white newspapers testify to the vitality of such stereotypes: the *New York Sun* alluded to the "irrepressible pantomime of the Negro," as well as to the "great vivacity and the peculiar stage talent which all their people seem to possess."[13]

For all intents and purposes, Hurston's complex portrait of diaspora failed to prevent white audience members from seeing the Bahamian dance as merely another example of black primitivism. Lucien White, the African American critic from the *Age*, expressed precisely this concern when he concluded that because of its emphasis on "the exotic and erotic," Hurston's revue did "not appear to be a vehicle of great benefit to the Negro."[14] In voicing this grievance, White fell in line with other members of the black community who disapproved of unabashed exhibitions of black vernacular expression. These were the same "bourgeois blacks" who, as Hurston biographer Robert Hemenway explains, deemed her stage work "counterproductive in the fight against segregation."[15] Angered by such views, Hurston railed against African American elitism in articles like her 1934 "Race Cannot Become Great Until It Recognizes Its Talent."[16]

Yet the reception of Hurston's Fire Dance makes pointedly clear that primitivist notions about black culture were capable of thriving even alongside recognitions of the more complicated workings of diaspora. Perhaps the most blatant example of the ability of primitivist interpretations to withstand assertions of diaspora came in 1934, when Hurston brought the Caribbean dance cycle to St. Louis for the First National Folk Festival.[17] On this occasion, Hurston introduced the dance in person, explaining to the audience that the Fire Dance "still is done as a New Year's day dance by Negroes in Southern Florida."[18] Her express articulation of the dance's ongoing existence within the United States did not fall on deaf ears, for reviewers made a point of identifying the Fire Dance as "an American survival of an organistic African dance." But despite acknowledging an Africa diasporic presence inside national borders, reviewers continued to cast the dance as an exotic rarity. "Dressed in bizarre and rather scanty costumes," the *St. Louis Globe Democrat* noted, "the ten Negroes in Miss Hurston's group danced and yelled in primitive fashion, such as is read about in books but rarely seen in life, while a tom-tom throbbed with a jungle rhythm."[19] For such spectators, the Fire Dance was a unique physical embodiment of blackness as it typically appeared only in fantastic literary accounts; in performance, the ten black dancing bodies both shocked and conformed to white expectations for black corporeality.

It is important to keep in mind that blacks and whites alike invoked the label "primitive" in reference to the folk material in Hurston's concert. In fact, both Hurston and Alain Locke, who wrote the program notes for *The Great Day*, used the term to promote the revue.[20] The problem for Hurston, I want to suggest, was not simply the currency of the term but the extent to which the trope of black primitivism functioned as the primary lens through which Caribbean dancing was read. Given how easily her representation of diaspora could be subsumed by entrenched notions of black bodies as wild, uncivilized Others, the complex relationship between African, Caribbean, southern rural, and northern urban black vernacular idioms that Hurston set out to portray may well have remained largely invisible to spectators in the early 1930s.

Surely Hurston must have been aware of this conundrum, of the difficulty of conveying the subtleties of diasporic migrations to an audience in the habit of seeing the black dancing body in purely primitivist terms. After all, she had firsthand experience with her white patron Charlotte Osgood Mason's appetite for documented examples of "the doings of the Negro farthest down," whom she considered "utterly sincere in living."[21] It was common knowledge, furthermore, that white New Yorkers flocked to nightclubs like the Cotton Club to take in what they perceived not as carefully choreographed and rehearsed routines but as unfettered physicality. Is it possible, then, that anticipating the potency of primitivism as an interpretive framework, Hurston embedded a sort of double address within her concert? That is to say, might Hurston have designed *The Great Day* and subsequent stagings with two audiences in mind: a large white audience with certain inveterate assumptions about black performance and a smaller but nonetheless significant audience of discerning viewers who might be more responsive to the heterogeneity of black expressive styles? It is worth recalling that Hurston's most explicit statement about her dual interest in the continuities and discontinuities between Bahamian and American folk dance forms was made in a private letter to Langston Hughes, who was much more likely to appreciate the complexity of cross-cultural influences.[22] It requires no great stretch of the imagination, therefore, to speculate that Hurston intentionally framed her staging of diaspora in such a way as to make it legible to white New

Yorkers while simultaneously presenting a more complicated theory of retentions and transformations. In this sense, primitivism functioned as a screen behind which diaspora, for those ready and equipped to perceive it, could flourish.

## Weighing Diaspora and Primitivism in the South

As Hurston continued to stage her folk concert in the months and years following the New York premiere of *The Great Day* in 1932, she continued to navigate the competing and overlapping significations assigned to black folk culture. More specifically, she found ways to exploit the conventions of primitivism while insinuating alternative ideas about black culture into her production. Reliance on the cover of primitivism became even more necessary in the South, where Jim Crow segregation seriously hampered her efforts to reach a black audience. As Hurston informed Charlotte Mason as a version of her revue *From Sun to Sun* neared production in January 1933, tickets to the event on the Rollins College campus were available "to the general public— except Negroes. I tried to have a space set aside, but find that there I come up against solid rock."[23] Part and parcel of her goal of building a "*real* Negro art theatre," the presence of black spectators was key to Hurston's ability to reach an audience receptive to her embodied theory of a transnational black culture. Native black Floridians, possessing greater familiarity with southern black folk practices, would be especially equipped to appreciate the diasporic nuances of her concert. But despite her repeated attempts to arrange for black spectators, *From Sun to Sun* played to no mixed race audiences in 1933.[24]

It comes as little surprise, then, that primitive tropes pervaded the critical discourse surrounding Hurston's Florida stagings. Writing in the *Winter Park Herald* in advance of a production of *From Sun to Sun*, Will Traer encouraged audience attendance with the following entreaty:

> What the negro *[sic]* has brought to America is too vital to be
> allowed to vanish from the earth. His barbaric color adds pattern
> to the Nordic restraint around him. America needs this because
> its civilization, like Minerva, sprung full grown from the head
> of Europe, and so there is not the wealth of native folk-lore as in
> Europe, Asia, Africa and other continents where civilization had
> to grow through long ages.[25]

The notion of an essentially rich black folk culture as the requisite cure for the ailments of white civilization epitomizes primitivist thought of the time. It factored equally into the response of a reviewer for the *Rollins Sandspur*, who, in a rare recognition of the labor underwriting the expressive displays in Hurston's concert, remarked that "the children's games, back in the quarters, the stories, the scene in the jook or pleasure-house—the songs and colorful oratory of the minister and the dancing couples . . . all show careful and effective planning by the director." When it came time to assess the Fire Dance finale, the writer lapsed into utterly primitivist rhetoric:

> The dancers, at first wary, as if feeling their ground, gradually
> became more and more heated, until one expected and hoped
> for an orgy. The rhythm pressing harder and harder into one's
> very being, the seductive movements of the gayly-clad bodies, the
> shining eyes in their dark faces, brought thunderous applause
> and continuous demands for more.[26]

The unmistakable kinesthesia described here—the visceral rhythms traversing the performer-spectator divide—speaks to the power of the dance. But the reviewer seems unable to render the scene in any other than stereotypically racial terms, relying on hegemonic formulations of black dancing bodies as dark, sexualized Others.

Some of the modifications Hurston made to her concert in the South may well have facilitated a primitivist reading. On January 5, 1934, Hurston presented *All De Live Long Day,* a follow-up to *From Sun to Sun,* at Rollins College's Recreation Hall. Announced as "a return engagement with a new program and a new cast," the concert adhered to the same narrative structure as *The Great Day* and *From Sun to Sun,* moving through the various phases of daily life in a southern work camp, from daybreak to dusk.[27] But while *All De Live Long Day's* finale was nearly identical to the conclusions of these earlier concerts, featuring three West Indian songs plus the three-part Fire Dance, Hurston changed the title of the closing Bahamian dance scene to "On the Niger." The names of earlier finales—"In the Palm Woods" for *The Great Day,* "Way in the Midnight" for *From Sun to Sun*—either marked the natural temporal progression of the day or indicated a secluded spatial location. In contrast, "On the Niger" implied that the dancing transported participants and observers alike from a Florida milieu to a distant African setting. In case audience members did not pick up on this clue, Hurston inserted another geographical indicator into the program, listing the Fire Dance musician George Nichols as an "African drummer." The effect of this reference was immediately clear in the review that ran in the *Rollins Sandspur*. "[M]ost unique," the paper reported, "were the dances. Colorful, primitive, intense— dark girls and men danced to the beat of an African drum, a chant and the pounding of naked heels."[28] Hurston's decision to play up the African dimensions of her folk material is confirmed in her pro- motion of *All De Live Long Day* as "an authentic program of *African folk life*."[29] However minor these adjustments, such direct assertions of Africanness replaced the more subtle delineation of patterns of diasporic diffusion that characterized Hurston's previous productions. Her decision to play up the exotic nature of the Fire Dance may well have been a response to the near-totalizing whiteness of her Florida audiences.

At the same time, Hurston continued to use her concert to tell a more complicated story about the relationship between expressive forms of the African diaspora and to problematize homogenizing views of black culture. Most notably, in the jook section of *All De Live Long Day*, retitled "Funnin' Around," Hurston inserted several popular Ameri- can dances, including a number devoted exclusively to "Buck and Wing Specialties." One of the featured dancers in this section was Alphonso Johnson, whose "tap and buck and wing work" were singled out for mention in an advance press release.[30] By juxtaposing these more rec- ognizable black American dance styles with the imported, less familiar African-derived dance, Hurston invited her audiences to discern both the differences and the correlations between black diasporic vernacu- lar dances. Her satisfaction with this expanded range of dance styles is evidenced by the fact that she added the Shim Sham, another popular tap routine and show business standard, to her production of *Singing Steel*, staged in Chicago some nine months after *All De Live Long Day*. In this way, Hurston's later concerts offered an increasingly complex and diversified picture of the Black Atlantic, even while remaining palatable to primitivist interpretations.

Hurston's refusal to abandon her attempt to situate the Fire Dance in a diasporic—and not solely a primitivist—context was on prominent display when she mounted an exclusive production of the Bahamian number in Orlando in 1939. Her presentation of *The Fire Dance*, the

first and only time the folk dance cycle stood alone on a program, was
a product of her work for Florida's Federal Writers' Project (FWP), a
branch of the Works Progress Administration (WPA), which Hurston
joined in 1938.[31] During her year-and-a-half tenure with the FWP,
Hurston collected and edited material for *The Florida Negro*, a state
guidebook, and organized a recording expedition for the WPA's Joint
Committee on Folk Art. In January 1939, however, as Congress threatened to eliminate the WPA's arts divisions, it was Hurston's theatrical
expertise that was mobilized to help generate grassroots support for
Florida's arts programs. When asked by her boss, Carita Doggett Corse,
to stage a presentation of Florida folklore for an Orlando audience,
Hurston settled on the Fire Dance as the most fitting material. While
the archive offers no insight into why she selected the Bahamian folk
dance over some of the other idioms from her past concerts—idioms
that were indigenous to Florida—her choice allowed her to revisit the
dance in a forum that underscored its importance to Florida culture.

Presented on January 25, 1939, amidst a several-week-long National
Exhibition of Skills of the Unemployed, the performance featured a
cast of twenty whom Hurston had assembled and trained from around
the region. State-sponsored and free of charge to the public, the production attracted a large audience.[32] Strikingly, the press gave the most
attention to the geographical contours of the Fire Dance. Reporting
on the performance both before and after its occurrence, the *Orlando
Morning Sentinel* noted that "the dance originated in Africa and was
brought to Florida by emigrant workers from the Bahama Islands."[33]
This articulation of the idiom's roots and migratory routes was an almost word-for-word recapitulation of the notes that appeared on the
official Fire Dance program, surely authored by Hurston.[34] Not only
did the program supply contextual information, but a narrator supplemented the live enactment of the dance with descriptions of the nature and function of the Jumping Dance, Ring Play, and Crow Dance.[35]
The narration opened with the declaration, "There are thousands of
Bahamians in south Florida, and nightly in the Everglades around
the bean fields and sugar mills can be heard the pulsing of the dance
drums."[36] In no uncertain terms, Hurston sought to impart the relevance of the Caribbean idioms to Florida folk life and to elucidate exactly how African-derived dances came to reside on American soil.
State patronage undoubtedly drove Hurston's explicit delineation of
the dance's local bearing, which in turn shaped newspaper coverage.
Still, her emphasis on the Floridian dimensions of the Fire Dance and

the role of Bahamian immigrants in its circulation clearly paid off. Although accounts continued to limn the dance as "barbaric," Hurston succeeded in representing the Bahamian cycle as *both* an African survival and a local phenomenon.[37]

However tenuous, this balance between primitivism and diaspora, and between the continuities and discontinuities of black diasporic forms, proved more difficult to maintain when Hurston wielded less control over stage productions of the Fire Dance. Although she could never dictate how her West Indian material was perceived, the narrative context she employed in *The Great Day* and *From Sun to Sun* at least located it securely within a Floridian milieu. And when Hurston presented the Fire Dance outside of her full-scale concert, as she did at the National Folk Festival in St. Louis in 1934 and at the FWP Exhibition in Orlando in 1939, she used program notes, press releases, and stage announcements to call attention to the presence of Bahamian migrants and their expressive practices within U.S. borders. But as her stagings drew attention from a variety of artists, the Fire Dance became subject to other narrative frames and interpretive schemas.

## African Warrior Dance

If white spectators tended to reinscribe the familiar tropes of black primitivism even when presented with nuanced alternatives, African Americans proved equally capable of allowing primitivism to overshadow the more subtle diasporic implications of the Fire Dance. Just months after the debut of *The Great Day*, Hurston and her Bahamian material were recruited for a production of much greater magnitude. On May 31, 1932, Hurston received a letter from Walter White of the National Association for the Advancement of Colored People (NAACP). Reporting that he had "been asked to assist in the casting of what appears to me likely to be one of the very big events of next season," White went on to explain:

> Professor Warner Josten, head of the Department of Music at Smith College, has done a pantomime-opera of BATOUALA. René Maran did the libretto from his novel. Stokowski and the Philadelphia Orchestra crowd are putting this on next season. Paul Robeson will probably do the role of Batouala. There are roles for dancers. Mr. Josten came to New York last week and he,

> Paul and I had a long talk. Paul and I, of course, thought of you at
> once when he asked about dancers.[38]

An indication of Hurston's reputation as an authority on black folk
dance, White's letter also testifies to the appeal the Fire Dance held
for other producers of black theatre, or more specifically, the not-yet-
developed genre of black opera. Despite the backing it received from
Leopold Stokowski of the Philadelphia Orchestra, the opera version of
*Batouala* never saw realization. Nevertheless, the record of Hurston's
involvement in the aborted project points to the multiple resonances
that encircled the Fire Dance in the 1930s.

René Maran's novel depicted African tribal life in the Congo under
French colonial rule around the time of World War I.[39] The mere fact
that Hurston's Bahamian dance came to mind for a performance with
an explicitly African setting is significant, for it affirms the legibility of the Afrocentric claims implicit in her staging of diaspora. For
White and Robeson, Hurston's framing of the Fire Dance evoked an
Africanness they hoped to re-create on the operatic stage. Even so,
the conflation of African diasporic origins with a more stereotypical
primitivism persisted in this new context. Plans indicate that Robeson
was to play the title role in the production, with Ethel Waters as the
female lead. The cast also called for three musicians and five "robust
warrior dancers."[40] The latter were the dance roles to which White referred. What is remarkable about this characterization is its seeming
incongruence with the Fire Dance; nowhere were the movements of
the West Indian cycle figured as warrior-like. It would seem, then, that
the appeal of the Bahamian dancing here lay in its ability to stand in
for a kind of "savage" African dance.

Undeterred by these arguably primitivist intentions, Hurston was
eager to participate in this new collaboration and readily agreed to
supply a group of dancers in the specified capacity. In an undated telegram to White, she expressed her hope that he could still arrange to
include her, assuring him that she could "guarantee all dancers and
drummers."[41] Writing from Florida, she pledged to return to New
York just as soon as she was needed. In the meantime, she offered to
lend White and company the drums she had used for *The Great Day*
for whatever use they might see fit. "But," she assured him, "I am getting you one made down here from the genuine goat-hide and properly
and authentically decorated."[42] Admittedly, Hurston's motives for this
offer may not have been wholly altruistic. Both the drums and the cos-

tumes from *The Great Day* were still in the possession of one of her evidently disgruntled Bahamian troupe members, John Dawson, and Hurston may have considered White's interest as an opportunity to recover these items without having to wrangle for them herself.[43] Still, Hurston may have also seen these relics from her concert as material reminders of what she could deliver and thus a means of securing a spot for herself in the *Batouala* production. Her enthusiasm for the project even led her to volunteer herself as a cast member—"Paul's 42nd wife in the play for one night."[44] Although Hurston had critiqued Robeson just months earlier as "getting too white in his singing," she was clearly keen to take part in what looked to be a momentous New York theatrical event.[45] "Put me on the staff . . . if you can," she concluded her letter to White.[46] For Hurston, the project represented a chance to work as chief choreographer for a major black theatrical event.

For reasons that may have included lack of funding, the opera never came off, and the collaboration ended acrimoniously for Hurston and White. Almost two years after White first contacted her about the undertaking, Hurston composed an angry letter to him, demanding the return of her costumes.[47] In an equally angry response, White accused Hurston of manipulating him into obtaining and storing her belongings.[48] Surely, the dissolution of such a promising endeavor was a source of frustration for her. But Hurston's desire to regain possession of her costumes may well have been driven by an entirely different custody dispute, one involving Hall Johnson and the Bahamian dancers she originally promised to White. For Hurston, it was one thing to weigh the balance between primitivism and diaspora when she was directly involved in productions using her Caribbean dance material; it was quite another when the Fire Dance circulated outside of her control.

## Dance of the Full Moon

In the 1930s, the dissemination of the Bahamian Fire Dance progressed simultaneously on two separate tracks. Even as Hurston continued to present the number in different locales around the country, the Fire Dance maintained an active stage life in New York quite apart from her. Although the group of sixteen dancers Hurston assembled and trained for *The Great Day* disbanded following the March 1932 production at the New School for Social Research, the Bahamian dancers by no means disappeared from the dance scene. Under the leadership of Leonard Sturrup, known professionally as "Motor Boat," the "Bahama Dancers" (at times the "Bahama Negro Dancers" or the "Bahaman Dancers") continued to perform the Fire Dance in various New York venues. In 1933, several members of this troupe appeared in Hall Johnson's musical drama *Run, Little Chillun!*, which began its four-month Broadway run on March 1 at New York's Lyric Theatre.[49] Billed as a "Negro folk drama in four scenes," *Run, Little Chillun!* was authored by Johnson, produced by Robert Rockmore, and directed by Frank Merlin.[50] The first act culminated in a dance number that was strikingly similar to the climactic finale of *The Great Day*—and was in fact based on the same cycle of Bahamian dances that Hurston had collected and restaged. Officially, the white modern dance artist Doris Humphrey "arranged" the dances in *Run, Little Chillun!*; her involvement will be addressed in the following chapter. At issue here are the resonances the Fire Dance acquired as a featured number in Johnson's long-running Broadway production.

The precarious tension between conventional primitivism and emerging conceptions of an African diaspora that the Bahamian dancing in Hurston's concerts manifested seems largely to have dissolved in Johnson's drama. The very content and structure of *Run, Little Chillun!*, which told the story of religious conflict in a southern rural black community, enabled primitivist views to flourish. Whereas Hurston's narrative represented the Bahamian Fire Dance as such—an extant ritual practiced by West Indians who had migrated to southern Florida—in Johnson's narrative, the dance was made to signify the ceremonial practice of a cultlike moon-worshipping group called the New Day Pilgrims. This fictitious pagan group served as both antithesis and threat to the play's upstanding Baptist community. Although many reviewers detected parallels between the fervor of the Pilgrim ritual dance (performed by the Bahamians) and the zeal of the concluding religious revival, the opposition between the two competing creeds was apparent. In the words of a Baptist character, the Pilgrims were "a ban' of people . . . wid a lot of heathenish notions sich as holdin' meetin' in de woods, singin' unknown tongues, . . . dancin' half-naked, playin' guitars, banjers an' sich, an' doin' all sorts of things dat ain't fitten fer civilized folks to do."[51] In short, the Pagans played primitives to the civilized Baptists, and the Bahamian folk dancing that concluded act 1, renamed the "Dance of the Full Moon," functioned as the visible embodiment of their primitivism (Figure 5).[52]

A Wild Climax to "Run Little Chillun," at the Lyric

The New Pilgrims, a nature-worshiping sect, representing the African inheritance of one of the groups of Southern Negroes in "Run, Little Chillun," go completely native at the height of a ritualistic ceremony led by Brother Moses, the tall figure with outstretched arms

Figure 5. *New York Herald Tribune* cartoonist's rendering of the "Dance of the Full Moon," the first act finale to Hall Johnson's 1933 *Run, Little Chillun!*

The Bahamian material in Johnson's drama also acquired a sexual-ized and gendered dynamic that was absent from Hurston's theatricali-zations. In *Run, Little Chillun!* temptation takes the form of a female character named Sulamai, who entices the Baptist minister's son Jim to leave his wife and religious faith. Significantly, it is Sulamai who introduces Jim to the ritualistic practices of the New Day Pilgrims. Unable to resist their energetic dancing, Sulamai joins in and eventu-ally must be carried offstage by Jim. The conflict she poses for Jim is resolved in deus ex machina fashion at the end of the play, when a bolt of lightning strikes down the pregnant Sulamai in the middle of Hope Baptist Church. In positing a link between Sulamai's transgressive sexuality and the Bahamian dancing, *Run, Little Chillun!* signaled its adherence to predominant views of black primitivism as erotic as well as exotic. The effects of this coupling are evidenced in the terms crit-ics used to describe the Dance of the Full Moon scene: "mad sexual," "frenzied and lascivious," and leading to "an orgiastic climax."[53]

Nonetheless, the Bahamian dancing featured in *Run, Little Chillun!* was meant to invoke an Africanist presence. According to Johnson's stage directions, the founder of the New Day Pilgrims, Elder Tongola, is African, and the sect should be pictured as "not too directly African, but with a strong African flavor."[54] Yet Johnson also specified that the "general impression" of the Pilgrims' ceremony "should be of some-thing approaching voodoo."[55] As Rena Fraden has argued about a later Los Angeles run of *Run, Little Chillun!*, "the staging and costumes" of the play's featured dance number looked "like every other voodoo African Caribbean production the [Federal Theatre Project] put on for their Negro units. This was a theatrical tradition, not an authentic African dance."[56] To be sure, Johnson invoked the term "voodoo" as a catchall designation for unorthodox religious practices rather than in reference to a precise set of Afro-Caribbean customs and beliefs. With the ultimate goal of creating a memorable spectacle rather than delineating an existent diasporic practice, Johnson's treatment of the Caribbean dance fully conformed to prevailing stage images of black exotic otherness. Little wonder, then, that *Run, Little Chillun!* specta-tors generally failed to discern the Caribbean derivation of either the dance or some of its performers.[57] Instead, critics like the *New York Age*'s Vere E. Johns commended the show for bridging "a gulf of thou-sands of years" through its juxtaposition of the ancient (the Pilgrim dance number) and the modern (the Baptist revival).[58] As it played out in Johnson's drama, the ostensible primevalness of the Fire Dance inhibited any recognition of its contemporary geographic markers.

In equating the Bahamian dancing with "voodoo," moreover, Johnson reproduced exactly the type of depiction that Hurston set out to counter. Her unpublished 1934 article "You Don't Know Us Negroes" contains a scathing comment about the tendency of recent black productions to "drag in" a "fanatical religious scene, or a hoodoo dance."[59] This could well have been an allusion to *Run, Little Chillun!* Her remark in *Mules and Men* that "there are no moon-worshippers among the Negroes of America" almost surely was.[60] Although Hurston's concerts were by no means immune to the primitivist discourse that enveloped stage representations of blackness, she worked hard to portray the Caribbean folk cycle as a modern-day practice, not a heathen ritual. Placed in the hands of another director and choreographer, however, the Bahamian Fire Dance was facilely put to the very effects she deplored.

## "African Jumpers"

On November 26, 1934, several of the Bahamian dancers returned to Broadway. This time they performed at the Venice Theater in the short-lived musical *Africana,* written and composed by the African American musician Donald Heywood and produced by John Mason. Although they did not appear as an ensemble, the *Africana* cast list includes two performers who danced in both *Run, Little Chillun!* and *The Great Day,* Joseph Nealy (or Neeley or Neely) and Leonard Sturrup (also known as Motor Boat), as well as John Dawson, who danced in Hurston's concert alone. Described as a "Congo operetta," *Africana* chronicled the tale of an African king and his European-educated son, a take on the familiar "civilization versus savagery theme."[61] The Bahamian dancers took the roles of "African Jumpers," with Sturrup also playing one of several witch doctors. Because there is no record of the choreography, it is impossible to know whether it was based on the Fire Dance. At the very least, it is safe to say that the dancers' stage experience performing the Caribbean cycle qualified them for movement tagged as African. According to one critic, the show was rumored to be "a more or less serious work based on the author's visit to Africa, and making use of genuine African dances and rhythms."[62] Despite these claims, the critic deemed the musical to be little more than "third-class Harlem comedy," and *Africana* promptly closed three nights after premiering.[63] Regardless, as with the unrealized *Batouala* opera, the Bahamian dancers' capacity to perform a generic Africanness proved key to their ability to find work.

## The Jungle Jingle

On September 24, 1936, several members of the Bahamian ensemble performed at a more widely heralded event: the opening of the downtown Cotton Club. The program on which the "Bahama Dancers" appeared was a revue headlined by Bill Robinson and Cab Calloway and featuring an array of black performers, including "50 Sepian Stars" and "50 Copper Colored Gals."[64] As suggested by the cast description, the downtown establishment, located in the heart of Broadway's theatre district at Broadway and Forty-eighth Street, adhered to the same formula that had made the Harlem Cotton Club such a hot spot for thirteen years.[65] That formula meant light-skinned chorus girls, male soloists or partner acts, jungle decor, and a whites-only policy for patrons.[66] Counting on a hit to launch the club's lavish reopening, manager Herman Stark and producer Dan Healy assembled "first-class Negro entertainment" guaranteed to draw large crowds. The Bahamian dancers were apparently a late addition to the cast of 130.[67] Their participation in the *Cotton Club Parade,* as the revue was titled, adds another wrinkle to the story of the Fire Dance's ideological entanglement with notions of primitivism and diaspora.

According to the Cotton Club revue program, the Bahamian dancers performed in a number called "The Jungle Jingle," in which they supported a trio of nightclub regulars named Kaloah, Anne Lewis, and Henri Wessels (Figure 6).[68] Lewis's specific talent is uncertain, but Kaloah and Wessels were both popular eccentric dancers, a class of performers who, as Marshall and Jean Stearns explain, had "their own non-standard movements and [sold] themselves on their individual styles."[69] Kaloah was also an exotic dancer whose specialty was Shake dancing, a technique most commonly performed by women, which involved rhythmic undulations of the body.[70] While no definitive record of the content of their act has survived, *Variety* reported that the "Bahama Dancers are good backup for Kaloah's rippling tummy calisthenics."[71] The title "Jungle Jingle" provides further evidence of the

THE WORLD FAMOUS

# COTTON CLUB

BROADWAY & 48th ST., N. Y. C.    LAck. 4-7300

HERMAN STARK, Director

FIRE NOTICE: Look around now and choose the nearest exit to your seat. In case of fire, walk (not run) to that exit. Do not try to beat your neighbor to the street.    JOHN J. McELLIGOTT, Fire Chief and Commissioner.

Revue Starts 7:30 P.M.    -    Midnight 2:00 A.M.

THE COTTON CLUB

Presents

### DAN HEALY'S

# COTTON CLUB PARADE

27th EDITION

Book, Lyrics and Music By
BENNY DAVIS AND J. FRED COOTS

Production and Dances By
CLARENCE ROBINSON

FEATURING

## BILL ROBINSON + CAB CALLOWAY

AVIS ANDREWS        BERRY BROS.        HENRI WESSELS        KATHERINE PERRY

WHYTE'S MANIACS        TRAMP BAND        ANNE LEWIS

Dynamite Hooker        Wen Talberts Choir        Bahama Dancers        Broadway Jones

"KALOAH"

CAB CALLOWAY AND COTTON CLUB ORCHESTRA

ARTHUR DAVY AND HIS ORCHESTRA

50 Sepian Stars        50 Copper Colored Gals

Entire Room Conceived and Decorated By
JULIAN HARRISON

### THE REVUE

SALUTATION ............................................DAN HEALY        OVERTURE ............CAB CALLOWAY AND ORCHESTRA
OPENING—"CLASS"

#### CAB CALLOWAY – BILL ROBINSON

with HENRI WESSELS AND ENSEMBLE

"BLACK MAGIC" ..............................DYNAMITE HOOKER        SPECIALTY ......................................HENRI WESSELS
"THERE'S LOVE IN MY HEART" ..............AVIS ANDREWS        "I'M AT THE MERCY OF LOVE" ..........KATHERINE PERRY
"ALABAMA BARBECUE"        "COPPER COLORED GAL"
BROADWAY JONES - WEN TALBERT CHOIR
with WHYTE'S MANIACS AND ENSEMBLE

#### BILL ROBINSON – CAB CALLOWAY

and the COPPER COLORED GALS

SPECIALTY ........................................ANNE LEWIS        "DOIN' THE SUSI-Q"—(The new dance craze)
"SWINGTIME ON THE SWANEE" ..............TRAMP BAND        BILL ROBINSON AND ENSEMBLE
"COTTON BLOSSOM LANE"        SPECIALTY ....................................BERRY BROTHERS
AVIS ANDREWS - WEN TALBERT CHOIR        GRAND FINALE ..............................CAB CALLOWAY
"FRISCO FLO" ..................CAB CALLOWAY AND CHOIR        "THE WEDDIN' OF MR. & MRS. SWING" ...............
"HI-DE-HO MIRACLE MAN" ..............CAB CALLOWAY        AVIS ANDREWS—Bride
"THE JUNGLE JINGLE"        HENRI WESSELS—Groom
KALOAH - ANNE LEWIS and HENRI WESSELS        BROADWAY JONES—Deacon and
with the BAHAMA DANCERS AND ENSEMBLE        the Entire Company
SPECIALTY ....................BILL (Bojangles) ROBINSON        REPRISE ..................................ENTIRE COMPANY

Costumes Executed by VERONICA
Designed by BILLY WEAVER
Orchestrations by Will Vodery
Musical Score published by Mills Music, Inc.
Shoes by BEN & SALLY
Press Relations—HARRY SOBOL

All Art Photographic Studies by the
Viennese Photographer
JAMES J. KRIEGSMAN

**Figure 6.** Program, "Dan Healy's Cotton Club Parade," no date given, but likely from 1936. Manuscripts, Archives and Rare Books Division, Schomburg Center for Research in Black Culture, The New York Public Library, Astor, Lenox and Tilden Foundations.

temper of the piece. That the inaugural revue of the downtown Cotton Club contained a self-consciously primitive number is anything but surprising. From the artificial palm trees to Duke Ellington's "Jungle Band," primitivism had always been the venue's stock and trade. As James Haskins has argued, such trappings allowed white patrons to believe "they were witnessing firsthand the emergence of the primal African from beneath the sequined costumes and tan skins of the performers."[72] For its new location, club owners had commissioned the decorator Julian Harrison to cover the ceiling of the main room with 10,000 square feet of fresco depicting "minstrels, crows and cupids in amusing consummation of their varied tasks." The adjoining bar featured murals "of tropical and southern motif," bearing such titles as "New Orleans in 1900" and "Tropical Madness."[73]

A photo of an unidentified group that was probably the Bahamian ensemble included in the program booklet suggests that the dancers served to bring the imagery of the surrounding decor to life (see Figure 7). The still, by James J. Kriegsmann, displays four male drummers and one female dancer, all dressed in exotic garb.[74] The men's bodies, with the exception of loincloths and feathered neck pieces, are completely bare, while their faces are covered with tribalistic paint markings. Unlike some of the bare-breasted women pictured in other Cotton Club photos, the female dancer wears a tasseled top and short skirt, as well as feathered ankle- and wristbands.[75] The woman stands at center with her torso slightly angled toward the camera, arms bent, and palms flexed. Flanking here are two of the men, who stand above their drums with torsos inclined inward, hands poised midclap. The other two men crouch beside them, beating their respective drums. The reminiscence of Leonard Reed, an African American choreographer who was brought in to produce Cotton Club revues in 1937, bolsters the likelihood that the female dancer in the photo was a member of the Bahama Dancers rather than the soloist Kaloah. In a 1997 interview with Fred Strickler for the Oral History Project, Reed recalled working with a group called "Motorboat":

> They played trongos and bongos. They did the African thing that they'd written from the foreign thing. They had this African dance. The girl had the little short—did the African thing. They wanted that for [sic] the white people to understand this is how black people are—the Africans—they did the whole African thing.[76]

Figure 7. Five Bahama Dancers. Cotton Club Program. 1936. Photograph by James Kriegsmann. Copyright MichaelOchsArchives.com. Manuscripts, Archives and Rare Books Division, Schomburg Center for Research in Black Culture, The New York Public Library, Astor, Lenox and Tilden Foundations.

Beyond substantiating the presence of a female member in the company, Reed's description is instructive on several counts. His comment that the group "had this African dance" strongly suggests that, rather than learning a new dance for the Cotton Club, the Bahama Dancers based their act on the Fire Dance that they had performed many times over the course of the 1930s. Perhaps more important, Reed's repeated use of the label "African" to characterize the group's dancing posits a fundamental link between the terms "Bahama," "African," and "jungle." What the Cotton Club officially tagged as conventional jungle fare, Reed insists evinced an expressly African character. Both formulations, it should be noted, elide the Caribbean derivation of the dancing (to say nothing of its Floridian components), bypassing the Bahamian milieu for a more remote designation. The simultaneity of the descriptives "African" and "jungle," moreover, speaks to the concurrent yet discrepant resonances of so-called primitive black dancing. On the one hand, the Fire Dance supported the entrenched language that whites applied to the kind of Negro entertainment that drew them to venues like the Cotton Club and satisfied their appetite for unencumbered exoticism. On the other hand, at least to one African American onlooker, their performance came across as a genuine display of African roots. These, then, were two available ways of reading black diasporic dance in the 1930s, two meanings of the word "primitive" that overlapped and coexisted even while carrying very different implications.

The intentionality that Reed ascribes to the group he calls "Motorboat" helps elucidate the tension between these two interpretations of the Bahamian folk dance cycle. Contending that the dancers designed their repertoire with a white audience in mind, he depicts their goal as one of rectifying rather than accommodating white expectations. In declaring that "they wanted . . . the white people to understand this is how black people are—the Africans," Reed implies that the Bahamian dancers sought to amend whites' misguided beliefs about black dance and to present a more accurate picture of the race by exposing their African roots. While this reading depends on essentialized notions of racial difference that also underpinned the Cotton Club's racist policies, Reed's brand of essentialism is grounded in an understanding of Africanist retentions rather than in stereotypes of black savageness. Whether or not the club's white audiences received the Bahama Dancers' performance along the lines laid out by Reed— as an "authentic" African representation and not a typical display of primitive exoticism—is difficult to say given the dearth of spectator reports. Nonetheless, Reed's account offers valuable insight into how other Cotton Club entertainers may have perceived the Bahamian ensemble, not to mention how the group saw itself. Indeed, his remarks suggest that the dancers had inherited something of Hurston's mission in staging the Caribbean folk cycle. According to Reed, they, like her, conceived their material as a corrective to common misrepresentations of the disposition and origins of black vernacular dance.

Although the Bahama Dancers did not appear continuously in Cotton Club revues after the 1936 grand reopening, Reed's reminiscence leaves little doubt that the group returned to the nightclub to reprise their performance in subsequent years. The exposure the Bahamian ensemble—and the Fire Dance that was presumably a part of their act— received as a result of their work at this popular nightspot is incalculable. According to a Cotton Club program booklet, the premiere performance at the downtown location drew 15,000 patrons during the first week alone and 100,000 within two months of opening.[77] Like their 1933 *Run, Little Chillun!* engagement, and unlike Hurston's productions, the Cotton Club furnished the Bahamian dancers with a protracted performance run and a mass audience, not to mention a steady source of income.

But as had also been true of their Broadway run, this mass exposure entailed certain ideological concessions. As a result of their incorporation into these commercially successful theatrical productions, the Bahamian dancers and their movement material accrued certain context-specific valences that necessarily colored their reception. In the case of Hall Johnson's musical, the Fire Dance had become a sign of a fictitious pagan practice; in the plotless Cotton Club revue, the dance served as the requisite exotic number in a show—and an institution—underwritten by notions of black primitiveness. This was a far cry from the meanings Hurston tried to assign to the folk dance cycle in her own concerts, where it represented an African survival corporeally transmitted to Florida by migrant Bahamian workers. What Hurston's reaction to the Bahamian dancers' engagement at the Cotton Club might have been, presuming she caught word of it, is a matter of sheer conjecture. But it is no great stretch to assume that she would have deplored the co-optation of the Fire Dance by an institution that trafficked in precisely the type of distorted notions of blackness that drove her desire to stage the dance in the first place.

Yet Leonard Reed's retrospective remarks about the Bahamian dance seriously complicate any impulse to dismiss the Bahamian dance's tenure at the Cotton Club as a complete capitulation to racist white expectations or a total vitiation of the idiom's diasporic dimensions. First, Reed serves as reminder that, notwithstanding its whites-only customer policy, the Cotton Club did provide a mixed-race audience, for the club's aggregate of black performers must be taken into account as spectators of each other's routines. And second, Reed's reading of "Motorboat's" act provides evidence that, even in a milieu ensconced in fantastical depictions of black primitiveness, the salience of the dancing's African lineage prevailed for some. Granted, without the surrounding narrative context that Hurston crafted for her concerts, the ability of the Caribbean folk dances to gesture at transnational routes was severely limited. Still, it would be misguided to rule out the possibility that the Fire Dance's countenancing of Afrocentric roots remained legible to white and black audiences alike.

In fact, an appearance by two of the Bahamian dancers at the 1939 New York World's Fair, which came in the wake of their Cotton Club work and is the last performance of the group that I have been able to document, leaves little doubt as to their ability to register as primitive and African simultaneously. For several months in the spring and summer of that year, Motor Boat and Stew Beef (the stage name of another ensemble member) played as drummers for the Savoy Ballroom's exhibit in the fair's Amusement Area. The gig likely arose out of their engagement at the Cotton Club, where Herbert "Whitey" White's Lindy Hoppers, a professional swing dance ensemble based at the Savoy, also performed. Framed as "an anthology of the dance, from the roots of black dancing in Africa to the Lindy Hop," as participant Norma Miller recalls, the approximately twenty-minute show opened with an "African jungle scene, feathers and all," before progressing to a cakewalk demonstration and a Lindy Hop finale.[78] In a photo spread that ran in *Life* magazine on May 15, 1939, two weeks following the fair's opening, an image depicts a scantily dressed female dancer and a male dancer, wearing only a leopard-print skirt, positioned next to two other dance couples (Figure 8).[79] The caption below the photograph reads: "The Savoy Ballroom presents the evolution of Negro dance forms. At left are the savage dancers of Africa, who demonstrate primitive rhythms to the accompaniment of tom-toms. Couple in the center are

**Figure 8.** Savoy Ballroom Dancers at the New York World's Fair, 1939. Photograph by Cornell Capa; courtesy Magnum Photos.

cakewalkers of the early 1900's. At right are swing-steppers of today."[80] Here Motor Boat and Stew Beef serve at one and the same time as markers of an African lineage that continues to influence contemporary urban dance crazes, and as symbols of an imagined jungle savagery. Even Miller, who described the two drummers as "the best," explained that the female "African" dancer named Tanya was "supposed to be an authentic representation of our roots, but as far as we could see, she looked like a regular shake dancer, and we doubted she'd ever seen Africa!"[81] This doubleness performed by the Bahamian dancers—pointing to an African past and supporting fanciful white notions of black exoticism—speaks once again to the way primitivism enabled and impeded the production and reception of black diasporic dance.[82]

The Fire Dance thus functioned in multiple capacities over the course of the 1930s, acquiring different ideological resonances depending on where it appeared, how it was framed, and who was watching. Able to register both dominant and resistant constructions of racial identity, the Bahamian folk dance continued to evoke the familiar tropes of black primitivism even while the Caribbean roots and routes it referenced offered an alternative to those tropes. Seen from a broader perspective, the Fire Dance is part of a long history of stage enactments of distinctly Africanist dance forms in the United States and of shifting perceptions of those enactments. Well before Hurston first exposed audiences to the Bahamian cycle, African American artists integrated African idioms into their stage productions, both for novelty purposes and to reveal the connections between black Americans and their African past. To cite one famous example, Bert Williams and George Walker's encounter with a group of native Dahomeans at the 1894 Midwinter Fair in San Francisco inspired them to introduce African elements into their 1903 all-black musical *In Dahomey*. As Walker later related, "The departure from what was popularly known as the American 'darky' ragtime limitations to native African characteristics has helped greatly to increase the value of the black performer on the American Stage."[83] From the turn of the twentieth century, establishing links to non-U.S. sources offered black performers a way of skirting minstrel stereotypes.

But if Hurston's enactment of the Fire Dance was by no means the first use of Africanist material to refer to a transatlantic black diaspora, African and Afro-Caribbean dance became increasingly prevalent on the American stage in the years following her concert's debut. In 1937, a group of African American choreographers eager to establish "Negro Dance" as a serious artistic genre organized a concert in New York. Titled "Negro Dance Evening," the concert was divided into four sections: Africa, the West Indies, United States, and Modern Trends. As an advance publicity announcement spelled out:

> The program commences in Africa. This is to make immediately apparent to the audience the roots of the dancing in the Americas today. Then the scene goes across the ocean in slave ships to South and North America, and we see what becomes of the African in feast dances, war, religious and love dances.[84]

The Chicago-based choreographer Katherine Dunham made her New York debut in the "Negro Dance Evening," performing Caribbean dances with her group in the "West Indies" section and a solo in the "Modern Trends" section. In the years that followed, Dunham went on to gain acclaim for her work on Broadway and in film and for the full-length concerts she produced with her company, such as *Tropical Revue* in 1943, *Bal Nègre* in 1946, and *Caribbean Rhapsody* in 1950. Enacting a diaspora narrative similar to that of the "Negro Dance Evening," these productions depicted the transformations of black dance forms as they moved from the Caribbean to the United States. Along with Pearl Primus, whose African-themed choreography also captured the interest of American audiences in the 1940s and 1950s, Dunham helped standardize the staging of diasporic forms in the field of black concert dance.

Taking stock of the impact of her own presentation of Bahamian folk dance in her 1942 autobiography *Dust Tracks on a Road,* Hurston wrote, "I am satisfied that I proved my point. . . . Primitive Negro dancing has been given a tremendous impetus. . . . In that performance *[The Great Day]* I introduced West Indian songs and dances and they have come to take an important place in America."[85] These remarks suggest the extent to which Hurston considered her concert to be a turning point in the staging of black folk dance, ushering in a wave of presentations of diasporic roots. At the same time, her language serves as another reminder of the currency of the term "primitive" even while this trend was taking place. The very word that assigned blacks to a primeval and exotic state functioned for Hurston as a way to describe a coeval, dynamic practice, distinct from but related to U.S. black idioms. Ultimately, the simultaneity of these significations indicates that the principal significance of the staged Fire Dance lay not in its pivotal position along some smooth teleological progression from primitivism to diaspora but, rather, in its demonstration of the ways in which diaspora emerged out of and through primitivism. However much primitivism's hegemonic grip on American audiences tended to overshadow the nuances of a Black Atlantic, it may equally have facilitated the introduction of diaspora as an alternative mode of conceptualizing blackness.

# 6
# Black Authenticity, White Artistry

As described in chapter 3, just before the curtain was set to rise on *The Great Day* on the evening of Sunday, January 10, 1932, Charlotte Osgood Mason, Hurston's vigilant white patron, sent a communiqué to Alain Locke, the renowned black intellectual who frequently served as a liaison between Mason and Hurston. Voicing her fears about the imminent public exposure of Hurston's stage material, Mason told Locke, "If it is at all good[,] there will be lots of people [who] want to make money out of it." She promptly charged him with insulating both performance and performers from the advances of prospective profit seekers. "Do try to protect the material from being exploited and stolen," she instructed him. "Keep your eyes open over the audience. Warn actors not to promise to do these things for any other producer."[1] While chapter 3 discussed Mason's anxieties in the context of her proprietary claims over Hurston's work and her antitheatrical bias, her comments are pertinent here because they proved surprisingly prophetic. If the success of *The Great Day* is to be measured by the amount of interest it generated from outside parties, then the production must be considered a hit. Although the inaugural New York showing failed to bring about a sustained Broadway run, in the months and years that ensued, Hurston's concert material in general, and the Bahamian Fire Dance in particular, were in high demand.

Between January 1932 and May 1936, the list of artists who pursued Hurston's Fire Dance in some capacity included the white jazz dancer Mura Dehn, the white Neighborhood Playhouse director Irene

Lewisohn, the African American choral director Hall Johnson, celebrated white modern dance artists Doris Humphrey, Ruth St. Denis, and Helen Tamiris, and white ballroom dance icon Irene Castle. Their pursuits resulted in a succession of stage reproductions of the Fire Dance in a range of venues during that period, from Broadway to the concert hall to the nightclub. For the most part, these subsequent theatrical enactments were bilateral undertakings based on willful cooperation and not the kind of outright theft that Mason so dreaded. Neither, however, did these collaborative ventures transpire on equal playing fields. The fact that a dance form originally staged by Hurston circulated so widely in the 1930s, combined with the fact that to date, her contributions to the field of American dance remain almost entirely unacknowledged and unexplored despite her canonization in the field of literary studies, raises some red flags for the historian. Given the number of white artists who made use of this black diasporic folk dance, Hurston's absence from the dance record seems a classic case of "invisibilization," the term coined by scholar Brenda Dixon Gottschild to describe the systematic denial and miscrediting of the African influences on Euro-American performance practices.[2] What is striking about Hurston's erasure, to say nothing of the paucity of information about the Bahamian dancers whom she recruited for *The Great Day* and who went on to have an appreciable performing career in New York, is that it did not stem from deliberate denials or disavowals of her influence. Rather, this chapter will show, the masking of the contributions of Hurston and the Bahamian dancers to American dance history resulted from the power imbalances governing the diffusion of the Fire Dance and the racial politics of categorization and attribution. As Dixon Gottschild has documented was so often the case in European and American cultural history, the inability/refusal to recognize Hurston's and the Bahamian dancers' choreographic labor allowed credit to accrue to white dancers, who were able to construct themselves as innovative artists working with black "raw material."[3]

The collaborations between Hurston, the Bahamian Fire Dancers, and several white female artists thus provide a window onto the messy process by which aesthetic hierarchies are formed. For, even as interest in the Fire Dance crossed racial and generic boundaries, the dance played a role in fixing up those boundaries. In this regard, the circulation of the Fire Dance in the 1930s serves as an instructive illustration of sociologist Pierre Bourdieu's theory of the field of cultural production and the struggles for legitimacy between artists within a given field.[4] In the arena of dance in the 1930s, competition revolved around the question of who possessed the authority to represent what and, to a great degree, the definition of artistry itself. Keeping in mind Bourdieu's assertion that "every position, even the dominant one, depends for its very existence, and for the determinations it imposes on its occupants, on the other positions constituting the field," it is hardly surprising that the white artists striving to establish modern dance as an official genre had a stake in the positions occupied by Hurston and the Bahamian dancers, and vice versa.[5] Probing the conditions that enabled Hurston's invisibility therefore casts light on a broader contest over how the dance landscape was to be carved up for much of the twentieth century.

## White Bodies, Negro Chanters: Mura Dehn

In the wake of her January 1932 presentation of *The Great Day,* interest in Hurston's folk material only grew. In mid-March, Hurston was approached about a possible European tour for her concert, as well as a London engagement for her dance troupe.[6] A solicitation from Elizabeth Burchenal, who collected and taught folk dances to public school girls in New York City, followed.[7] Neither of these prospects panned out, but a new performance opportunity arose when the Russian émigré choreographer Mura Dehn sought out Hurston's group of singers for a ballet called *The Wise and Foolish Virgins.* This became the principal feature of a dance concert presented on April 10, 1932, at New York's Guild Theatre, during which Dehn also performed solos influenced by the Lindy Hop, "Oriental" and "Negro Primitive" themes, and Russian folk dance.[8] Best known today for her seven-part film *The Spirit Moves,* which documents an extensive range of African American social dances, Dehn began her dance career touring Europe with the Ellen Tels Moscow Art Dance Ensemble, a group that performed in the style of early American modern dancer Isadora Duncan, who took her inspiration from classical music and ancient Greek art. In 1925, Dehn witnessed the dancing of Josephine Baker in Paris and became a lifelong advocate for jazz dance. By 1930, she had relocated to New York City, reportedly to be in the "home of jazz dance," and began frequenting the Savoy Ballroom, where she studied the movement styles of African Americans.[9] The April 1932 presentation of *The Wise and Foolish Virgins* represented Dehn's American debut.

Significantly, Dehn used Hurston's name in all the advance publicity for the concert. The promotional material cited "Zora Hurston's Negro Chanters" and singled out Georgia Burke and Percy Punter for mention (see Figure 9).[10] Notwithstanding their visibility in the publicity announcements, Hurston and her performers were not visible at all during the performance. Instead, while Dehn and a group of thirteen white female dancers from various New York companies danced onstage, Hurston's "chanters" "punctuated and accented the choreography" from an offstage position.[11] This organization—white dancers accompanied by black voices—anticipated the racialized division of casting in Helen Tamiris's 1937 *How Long Brethren?*, in which a group of Euro-American women danced to spirituals sung by a group of African Americans. The cultural logic and complicated implications of this practice, along with its critical acceptance in the 1930s, have been assessed by Susan Manning, who uses the term "metaphorical minstrelsy" to describe the "convention whereby white dancers' bodies made reference to nonwhite subjects." Tamiris's casting arrangement, she maintains, meant that "while the black singers . . . lent authenticity to the voices . . . the white female dancers generalized the applicability of the lyrics beyond the experience of African-Americans."[12] In much the same vein, a *New York Herald Tribune* announcement for the 1932 *Wise and Foolish Virgins* ballet labeled (the Russian) Dehn and her dancers "American" and the chorus "Negro," casting the white performing body in universal national terms and the black performing body in strictly racial terms.[13] Although a critic from the *New York Sun* described Hurston's chorus as "invisible," no reviewer queried the placement of the singers out of sight.[14]

In the sole surviving record of Hurston's opinion of the collaboration, she registers only satisfaction. Writing to Charlotte Osgood Mason, Hurston states that the "concert (Miss Dehn) of last Sunday night went well. I think that Mura Dehn has more talent than most dancers and for that very reason she will not be so easily understood. Her African primitive number was exceedingly fine."[15] If Hurston had qualms about the casting logic, she nevertheless painted the event in a positive light. Yet her remark that Dehn was likely to be misunderstood was incisive, for there was no lack of controversy surrounding *The Wise and Foolish Virgins*. As questionable as Dehn's organization of black

*Lithograph by Adolf Dehn*

# BALLET
## "THE WISE AND FOOLISH VIRGINS"
### WITH

# Mura DEHN

Minna Kanfer
Lilyan Kanfer
Gertrude Hallenberg
Gertrude Brenner
Mildred Bright
Frances Wilensky

Sylvia Stone
Barbara Bright
Pauline J. Stein
Fanny Scher
Ida Bildner
Vivian Lee
Jane Dudley

### ZORA HURSTON'S NEGRO CHANTERS
with Georgia Burke and Percy Punter

Speaking Chorus arranged and directed by Donald B. Brayshaw

## "HARLEQUINADE IN LINDY-HOP"
## "STYLE IMPRESSIONS IN DANCE"

CONCERT MANAGEMENT ARTHUR JUDSON, Inc.
Division of Columbia Concerts Corporation of Columbia Broadcasting System, Inc.
Steinway Hall          113 West 57th Street          New York City

**Figure 9.** Program, *The Wise and Foolish Virgins*, Mura Dehn, 1932. Jerome Robbins Dance Division, The New York Public Library for the Performing Arts, Astor, Lenox and Tilden Foundations.

singers and white dancers may appear from a twenty-first-century perspective, the critical response to her concert indicates how radical her embracing of jazz and African American sources was for her time.

Although details of the choreography of *The Wise and Foolish Virgins* remain murky, several aspects of the ballet are recoverable. It contained three sections: "Prologue," "The Creed of the Foolish Virgins," and "The Virgin's Reward." A lithograph by Dehn's husband, Adolf, was the motivation for the piece, and a reproduction depicting a horde of women with twisted, contorted bodies appeared on the announcement for the recital. In performance, Dehn and her thirteen female dancers donned masks and pantomimed the two types of virgins suggested by the ballet's title. Meanwhile, Hurston's offstage chorus chanted three numbers with the peculiar titles "Halitosis," "It's Off Because It's Out," and "Eventually, Why Not Now?" According to the *New York Sun*, the sung and spoken words "bore on present-day advertisements, slogans and the like and the delicate grounds on which stand the varied types of present-day virgins." Authored by Mura Dehn, this score bore no apparent connection to Hurston's folk material; her role, it seems, was limited to supplying and directing the vocal performers.[16]

Spectators were evidently unsure precisely how to read Dehn's choreography—or how to categorize it. A reviewer from the *World Telegram* denounced the dancing as "meaningless calisthenics," and the *Sun* critic claimed that it "lacked rhythmic coordination and bordered on the interpretation of lively comedy," eliciting "much interest and laughter" from the audience. In contrast, the *New York Times*'s John Martin described the audience as "large and cordial."[17] As Mary F. Watkins conceded in the *Herald Tribune*, "It is difficult to place Mme. Dehn on such brief acquaintance. She seems to be a dancer with original and somewhat perverse ideas, with a distinct flair for cynicism and satire to the point of burlesque."[18] A week later, however, Watkins was more confident in her estimations. In an *Arts Weekly* column that surveyed recent trends in the dance world, Watkins referred to Dehn's debut concert as "that poisonous and insidious and totally offensive striving for sensation . . . which should be avoided as the plague."[19] Her scathing indictment is a reminder of the kind of resistance that met choreographers who attempted to "elevat[e] the Jazz Era to the Art World" by presenting jazz dance on the concert stage in the early decades of the twentieth century.[20] In an outraged letter of response to Watkins's critique, Adolf Dehn blamed America's puritanical streak for hindering appreciation of his wife's choreography. "Even the stiff old ladies in black satin in . . . the most reactionary and provincial city in Germany where Mrs. Dehn was a ballet mistress," he avowed, "accepted her dancing as an art form."[21]

Interestingly, the word "satire" surfaced in a number of reviews of Dehn's concert, including Watkins's. In John Martin's judgment, Dehn presented "a new note in the dance recital field by introducing a flavor of satire so strong as to be classified as caricature." One number in particular, "a jazz dance done in archaic style" by Dehn and Jane Dudley, was met with such roaring laughter that it had to be repeated.[22] Yet Adolf Dehn's defense of his wife's choreography makes no mention of satiric intent. He characterizes Dehn's concert as an earnest representation of "primitive" sources rather than deliberate caricature and implies that Mura was caught off guard by the critical response. The spectacle of white female bodies performing an amalgam of Isadora Duncan–inspired expressive dance and popular black vernacular styles, it seems, elicited no small degree of confusion for audience members.[23]

Controversy notwithstanding, Dehn apparently considered her New York debut a gainful endeavor. Or, more accurately, Dehn considered her involvement with Hurston valuable, for the collaboration assumed a prominent place on her résumé. "In 1930, upon arriving in New York," an undated version of her curriculum vitae housed at the New York Public Library reads, "Mura Dehn began a serious study and work with the Black jazz folk dancers. Her first recital at the Theatre Guild in 1932 was with Zora Neale Hurston['s] Bahama Dancers."[24] The reference to the Bahama Dancers here is peculiar; there is no evidence that members of Hurston's dance ensemble participated in *The Wise and Foolish Virgins*. The error is probably best explained by the fact that in 1936, Dehn worked with the troupe of Bahamian dancers who performed in Hurston's *The Great Day*. She may therefore have conflated the two experiences inadvertently. Nonetheless, the fact that Dehn associated Hurston with the field of "Black jazz folk dance" and cited her affiliation with Hurston among her credentials is significant. Much as Hurston turned to the backing of a black male intellectual, Alain Locke, to bolster her own authority as a producer of black folk art in promoting her concert (as discussed in chapter 3), here Hurston lent legitimacy to the project of a white immigrant female artist.[25]

The alliance between Hurston and Dehn that made *The Wise and*

*Foolish Virgins* possible demonstrates the complexity of issues surrounding interracial stagings that drew on black folk idioms. Certainly, the prominence of Hurston's name in all of Dehn's concert publicity increased Hurston's visibility in the theatrical arena, in addition, one can only assume, to providing her some measure of financial remuneration. Nevertheless, on the night of performance, Hurston and her chanters were relegated to an offstage position. As the uneven response of the critics indicates, moreover, the concurrence of white female dancing bodies and black voices, and of early modern dance movement and jazzier, black-themed material, created something of a perceptual conundrum for spectators. These same tensions over questions of recognition, categorization, and aesthetic appraisal would continue to loom over the trafficking in Hurston's folk choreography.

## "Something quite off the beaten track": Irene Lewisohn at the Vanderbilt

Just twelve days after the Dehn recital, Hurston and members of her *Great Day* cast were involved in a second theatrical production under the direction of a white female artist. This time, Hurston also contributed a sizable share of the performance content. On Friday, April 22, 1932, Irene Lewisohn presented the Bahamian music and dance idioms from Hurston's concert as part of a dinner cabaret at the Vanderbilt Hotel in New York. Billed as an evening of "authentic Latin-American, Caribbean and Negro entertainment," and described by Hurston as a "folk-dance carnival," the program was divided into two sections.[26] The first offered songs and dances from Mexico, South America, and Panama; the second exhibited African American spirituals, Harlem Lindy Hoppers, and Hurston's Bahamian material. In between the various folk numbers, a Cuban orchestra and African American band played while audience members, who had dined prior to the performance, were invited to partake in general dancing.

The event was presented as the annual spring production of the Neighborhood Playhouse, the little theatre on New York's Lower East Side established by Irene Lewisohn and her sister Alice as an extension of their work at the Henry Street Settlement. The playhouse, which was dedicated to pursuing alternatives to the commercial theatre, technically only operated from 1915 to 1927, after which it was converted into the Neighborhood Playhouse School of the Theatre. In 1928, Irene launched an annual series of what were known as "Orchestral Dramas" and continued to produce and choreograph yearly concerts into the 1930s.[27] Involving large ensembles, these productions were performed with professional symphony orchestras and staged at sites like the Manhattan Opera House and Lewisohn Stadium (named after the uncle of Irene and Alice). Alhough the Neighborhood Playhouse no longer operated as such in 1932, all of the newspaper announcements and reviews identified the Vanderbilt Hotel event with the institution, even while they saw it as a marked departure from typical playhouse fare. As the *New York Times* proclaimed, "The Neighborhood Playhouse Breaks Own Record for Doing the Unusual."[28] The radically different venue of Lewisohn's 1932 offering—the Della Robbia Room of the Vanderbilt Hotel rather than a formal concert hall—immediately signaled that this would be "something quite off the beaten track, and unusual even when judged by the Neighborhood Playhouse standards."[29]

It is not clear when or how Hurston first came into contact with Irene Lewisohn, though it is possible that Lewisohn attended the January 10 premiere of *The Great Day*. The earliest mention of Lewisohn's name in the surviving correspondence between Hurston, Charlotte Mason, and Alain Locke occurs in a March 14 letter from Locke to Mason, in which he reports having confronted Hurston about the "Lewisohn matter." Arrangements for their collaboration had evidently been under way for some time, for Locke voices concern that *The Great Day* may have lowered Lewisohn's opinion of Hurston's material. "I urged Zora to try to redeem it," he writes, "by doing it well at the School of Social Research and making sure that Miss L. was there."[30] On or around March 4, Lewisohn asked Hurston to help recruit Panamanian dancers to fill out her planned program, apparently considering Hurston to be an expert on the New York folk dance scene. Hurston promptly went in search of such a group, although it is uncertain whether she was responsible for locating the Panamanian ensemble that appeared at the Vanderbilt. On March 19, Hurston told Mason that "Miss Lewisohn is going to use us after all."[31] Hurston promoted the event at her March 29 New School production of *From Sun to Sun* and personally invited Mason to "come to the Vanderbilt to see the dancing."[32]

While Lewisohn contributed much of the choreography for her annual Orchestral Dramas, she had little direct involvement with the dancing at the Vanderbilt. Instead, in her capacity as director, Lewisohn assembled a host of authorities and "authentic" representatives to enact Latin American, Mexican, African American, and Caribbean cultural traditions. In addition to Hurston, Lewisohn enlisted Armando Zegri and his Grupe Inter-Americano of the Roerich Society for the Mexican and South American songs and dances, Elena Koris for the Panamanian dances, Hall Johnson's Negro Choir for the spirituals, and Shorty Snowden and his Lindy Hoppers.[33] This collection of "native" folk dance practitioners from all over the Americas was indeed a divergence from earlier Playhouse productions, which featured performers like Helen Tamiris, Sophie Maslow, and Anna Sokolow, all children of Russian Jewish immigrants.[34] The Vanderbilt event thus marked Lewisohn's turn from staging productions danced exclusively by Euro-Americans to mounting a program danced exclusively by blacks and Latinos.

Despite the "vastly different program" offered at the Vanderbilt, the seeds of the 1932 cabaret were present in much of Lewisohn's earlier directorial work.[35] During the twelve years that the Neighborhood Playhouse was in operation, Lewisohn developed an eclectic approach to choreography that incorporated a range of movement practices, from Delsarte and Dalcroze techniques to Duncan influences to elements of folk and classical dance.[36] Crucially, the playhouse productions regularly drew inspiration from "foreign" cultural traditions, especially Oriental ritual dance and drama.[37] Like many artists in the early twentieth century, Lewisohn saw these putative "premodern" cultures as an antidote to the perceived banality and excessive commercialization of Western theatre. Lewisohn's earlier experimentation with folk forms, however, may well have been obscured by her more recent pursuit of abstract dancing closer in style to the emergent practice of modern dance. As Melanie Blood and Linda Tomko have documented, Lewisohn's Orchestral Dramas employed the likes of modern dance choreographers Martha Graham, Doris Humphrey, and Charles Weidman. According to Blood, the dancing in these productions entailed a "dramatic and symbolic" embodiment of the melody and instrumentation in the accompanying music.[38]

For the *New York Times*'s John Martin, the novelty of the Vanderbilt production was less its performers' racial backgrounds than its abandonment of the proscenium stage. In a piece devoted to the "rapid growth in the number of folk-dance events in the concert calendar," written several weeks after the performance, Martin raised questions about the appropriateness of presenting folk dancing on the concert stage given that its value, in his estimation, lay "not in seeing it done but in doing it."[39] Conventional Western theatrical devices that privileged the spectator's point of view, he claimed, were "inimical" to what he saw as the essential properties of "strictly folk" forms, spontaneity and "group unity among the dancers."[40] As such, Martin found Irene Lewisohn's approach—what he branded "An Attempt at Informality"—refreshing and even "courageous":

> Miss Lewisohn in her recent Latin-American fiesta opened a
> new field by considering the audience to a larger extent than
> usual and making it a part of the scene. Sitting about informally
> at tables, enjoying an inviting dinner, dancing in its own fashion
> whenever so moved, it was subtly inducted into the fiesta ritual.
> When, therefore, festival dancers of other cultures entered upon
> the scene they found an atmosphere much more suitable than
> could be provided in any theatre.[41]

Despite his enthusiasm for Lewisohn's deliberate blurring of the audience-performer divide, Martin expressed disappointment with the "preconceived audience sense" of some of the performers. To his eye, this was "most strikingly exhibited by the appearance of a quartet of Negro singers attired in evening clothes, presenting a group of spirituals."[42] Martin's gripe with Hall Johnson's choir resonates with Hurston's own critique of "neo-spirituals" and the tendency of concert singers to "put on their tuxedoes, bow prettily to the audience, get the pitch and burst into magnificent song—but not *Negro* song."[43] For both Hurston and Martin, the adoption of Western theatrical standards by singing groups like Hall Johnson's resulted in adulterated versions of folk idioms. This moment of agreement between Hurston and the *Times* critic is certainly noteworthy. But though the two may have shared an interest in preserving the boundaries of black folk expression, Martin's larger purpose here was to trumpet the achievements of a white artist.

In stark contrast to Martin's approbation of Lewisohn's dinner cabaret was the reaction of Charlotte Mason, Hurston's white patron. In several mid-April exchanges, Mason grilled Alain Locke about the affair; in response, he questioned Hurston and sent Mason newspaper clippings about the production. While Locke expressed some reservation about the event, Mason decried its very premise. "Why Alain," she wrote in an April 17 letter, "I am so shocked at what it purports to be on the surface that I'd be ready to annihilate anyone who told me that Irene Lewisohn was going to do such a thing. I think it isn't possible for anything to be lower than this is. An enclosed dinner dance so that white people may have a . . . haute parisian debauch."[44] Unfortunately, Mason's (or her scribe's) handwriting in this last line is difficult to make out. It is nonetheless evident that she was outraged by Lewisohn's creation of a sanctioned space where white patrons might carouse freely with racially marked bodies.

However hypocritical given her own primitivist appetite, Mason's perspective provides a useful counterpoint to Martin's. The very cabaret format that Martin deemed a "courageous" effort to present folk dance on its own terms was offensive to Mason. Because Mason voiced no complaints about *The Great Day*'s predominantly white audience, it seems likely that the source of her indignation was the affinity between the Vanderbilt affair and the low art nightclub. As Lewis Erenberg has shown, the growth of public night life in American urban centers and the concomitant evolution of the cabaret culminated in the 1920s, when Harlem clubs in particular became meccas for white New Yorkers seeking embodied examples of black sensuality.[45] For John Martin, whose primary consideration was tracking developments in theatre dance, Lewisohn's established reputation with the legitimate theatre rendered her experimentation with the cabaret format original and bold. Heavily invested in the nascent field of modern dance, in which white artists had begun to mine folk sources in the hopes of creating an authentically American art, he aligned the Vanderbilt production with this movement. For the proprietary Mason, Lewisohn's dalliance with Hurston's folk material represented a descent into crass commercialism.

Mason also raised questions about what kind of compensation Hurston received from Lewisohn. In a May 7 letter to Locke, Mason confessed, "I think Alain (don't say this out loud) a good proportion of her pay was in flattery."[46] While there is no archival evidence to substantiate Mason's suspicion, there is also none to refute it. Still, Hurston had more than monetary payment alone to gain from an alliance with Lewisohn. Judging from her willingness to scour New York in search of Panamanian dancers, Hurston was eager to associate herself with the Neighborhood Playhouse director. If part of Hurston's overall objective was to establish a name for herself in the theatrical arena, the publicity the Vanderbilt event garnered from major newspapers (four separate notices in the *Times* alone) surely strengthened her reputation as an authority on Bahamian folk dance. By participating in what was taken to be the annual Neighborhood Playhouse offering, moreover, Hurston effectively inserted herself into the mainstream theatre dance landscape, for the amount of space that Martin devoted to the event certified its prominence on the New York dance scene.

The irony is that it was only once Hurston presented her material under the auspices of a reputable white director that her work was included in this scene. Although the *Times* covered *The Great Day*, it received nowhere near as much attention, nor was it considered a part of the dance season.[47] Paradoxically, then, the very factors that caused Hurston to be written into the official dance record simultaneously enabled her marginalization, for the racist formulations that defined black and Latino folk expression as simple, naive, and fundamentally natural meant that Irene Lewisohn, the more prominent white woman, received almost exclusive artistic credit for the creativity of the Vanderbilt production. Consequently, Hurston's choreographic efforts, not to mention those of the folk performers who provided the bulk of the labor, remained almost entirely illegible.

## "Sources . . . used and not given credit to": Doris Humphrey and *Run, Little Chillun!*

Just as Hurston garnered attention from white artists interested in her staging of the Fire Dance, so too did the group of Bahamian dancers whom she trained for *The Great Day.* In 1933, they appeared in Hall Johnson's *Run, Little Chillun!* whose dances were officially "arranged" by the white choreographer Doris Humphrey, considered one of the founders of American modern dance. Although the programs for Hurston's and Johnson's respective productions list only four cast members in common—R. Alday, L. Stirrup, J. Nealy (elsewhere listed as Neeley and Neely), and W. Polhamus—there was appreciable overlap in the material they performed for both shows.[48] Later deemed "one of most successful musical dramas in the history of the Harlem Renaissance," *Run, Little Chillun!* told the story of religious conflict

in a southern black community and contained an open-air "orgiastic" dance scene that bore an uncanny resemblance to the finale of
Hurston's concert.[49] Because *Run, Little Chillun!* ran for a full four
months on Broadway, it represents one of the most prominent show-
cases of the Bahamian Fire Dance in the 1930s. As such, the event offers key insights into the linkages between black diasporic folk dance
and white modern dance, while providing a window onto the processes
that nudged Hurston through the cracks of American dance history.

While not entirely recoverable, the story of how the Bahamian
dancers wound up in Johnson's hit show, and how Doris Humphrey
came to receive credit for its dance numbers can be partially pieced together from surviving correspondence, programs, newspaper reports,
and autobiographical accounts. Hurston's *Great Day* dancers first
crossed paths with Johnson in late 1931 when Hurston took the group
to rehearse with Johnson's singers in a failed collaboration effort. Some
of her cast members may have briefly joined up with Johnson again
during the winter of 1932.[50] It is not hard to understand why Hurston's
performers were tempted to sign on with another producer, especially given the trouble she had compensating them.[51] Johnson's motives and methods, however, appear more suspect. In the summer of
1932, just months after leaving New York for Florida, Hurston learned
that Johnson had enlisted members of her dance group. She promptly
wrote Charlotte Mason to express her ire:

> No need for me to come North. I wired Hall Johnson's manager
> and he hedged and backed water. Pretended to be so indignant
> at the very thought. But I have word from three or four quarters
> that he was messing with our stuff.
>
> Nerves burnt out but calm. I am glad that I made the frontal
> attack and forced his hand.[52]

That news of Johnson's tampering with her (or rather, her and Mason's)
"stuff" reached Hurston in Florida suggests that dubious circumstances
surrounded his engagement of the Bahamian dancers. That Hurston
considered returning to New York to confront Johnson indicates how
seriously she took the threat. Her resentment was still evident over a
year later: in a 1934 letter, she referred to "the cupidity of Hall Johnson
and those miserable wretches that he corrupted for his own ends."[53]
From Hurston's perspective, Johnson had hijacked her dancers, in whom
she had developed a discernible proprietary interest.

Somewhat curiously, preparations for *Run, Little Chillun!* were cloaked in secrecy. In late February 1933, one week before the production opened, Alain Locke sent a letter to Mason providing an update on the latest activities of Johnson and Langston Hughes, both one-time beneficiaries of Mason. Enclosed with the letter was a newspaper clipping with the headline "Mystery About Hall Johnson Musical." The report heralded the upcoming premiere of "what is expected to be a decided innovation in musical and theatrical presentation," adding:

> For months Harlem has been expecting some such announcement. Mr. Johnson has been staging great rehearsals with the utmost secrecy. First he used the auditorium in the C.M.A. building, later moving to another address. To all inquiries which the ANP addressed to him, he replied that he was not yet ready to disclose his plans.[54]

It may be a stretch to posit that Johnson went to such great measures to cover up his use of Hurston's Bahamian performers and material. Still, the possibility that his misgivings contributed to the lack of advance publicity for his show cannot be dismissed.

A later communiqué from Locke to Mason, written a month after the successful March 1 debut of *Run, Little Chillun!,* describes Johnson as contrite:

> He still feels keenly, I believe, that both you and I really know the sources he has used and not given credit to: and he tries on every occasion to placate me—which is really an attempt to apologize or explain to you. And because of that (which I sense) I have to keep him at a distance, because I cannot forgive disloyalty to you, though I could easily forget or forgive the same to me or to Zora.[55]

In this formulation, it is Mason who suffered the greatest wrong, even though the sources Johnson used and failed to credit were the product of Hurston's research and stage work. However shaded by his deference to Mason, Locke's report corroborates Hurston's view that Johnson's appropriation was less than scrupulous.

Certainly, the plundering of performers and the theft of dance routines are and have always been a regular part of show business. Nevertheless, Johnson's "borrowing" of Hurston's material seems to have been especially noteworthy and something of an open secret in the New

York theatre community. Word of the exceptional similarities between her concert and Johnson's again reached Hurston in Florida in the wake of the drama's Broadway opening. As she writes in her autobiography *Dust Tracks on a Road,* she "heard that Hall Johnson had raided my group and was using it in his 'Run Little Chillun.'" "I never saw the production," she adds, "but I was told that the religious scene was the spitting image of the one from my concert also. As I said, I never saw it so I wouldn't know."[56] Letting the rumors speak for themselves, Hurston implies that both the Bahamian dance number and the Baptist revival scene, the two high points of Johnson's drama, were indebted to her. Indeed, the scattered references to her interactions with Johnson throughout the "Concert" chapter of her autobiography—including her remark about how "fine of Hall" it was to congratulate her following the premiere of *The Great Day*—seem strategically positioned to cast aspersions on his actions without accusing him directly.

Even Doris Humphrey was aware of Hurston's prior involvement with the Bahamian dancers. In a handwritten manuscript titled "Bahama Fire Dance," Humphrey explains that the Bahamian troupe's "first appearance on any stage was at the John Golden Theater with Miss Zora Neal *[sic]* Hurston, Jan. 10, 1932 and at the New School of Research, March 29, 1932."[57] Although the document is undated, it is likely that Humphrey wrote the piece as a preliminary draft for her 1933 article in the journal *American Dancer,* which recounted her work with the Bahamian dancers for *Run, Little Chillun!*[58] In the published version, however, Humphrey omitted any reference to Hurston, thus aiding the erasure of the latter's contributions to American theatre dance from the public record.

Humphrey got her professional dance start with Ruth St. Denis and Ted Shawn's Denishawn company, the most prominent touring American dance ensemble in the early twentieth century. She left the company in 1933, teaming up with fellow Denishawn veteran Charles Weidman to present concerts that they hoped would help establish a dance tradition based on contemporary national experience rather than on foreign sources.[59] Scarce financial resources made Humphrey inclined to accept Hall Johnson's invitation to stage the dances for his musical when he contacted her out of the blue. She related the development in a letter to her parents:

> Hall Johnson just called up—you must have heard his choir
> on the radio—and wants me to help with a voodoo scene in a

musical play he has written. I don't care much for the play, but
he has a group of dancers that is very interesting indeed. They
do traditional dances that have a real native look. These people,
or their ancestors were brought from Africa to the Bahamas or
some isolated place down there and have kept up the ritual of
the dances pretty much untouched ever since. The fact that they
now do them to English or American tunes hasn't changed the
savage character of the movement in the least. There is one called
the Jim Crow dance in which one imitates a bird and the others
dance their encouragement and admiration—obviously a relic
of animal worship. Then there is a courting dance—as erotic as
anything I've ever seen. The job is to cut and rearrange these
rather wandering rituals to fit the play and also to conform to the
one-view stage which of course ritual never needed to think of.[60]

Humphrey's interest in the "traditional dances" with "a real native look"
may have been cultivated by a vacation cruise to the West Indies she
took in the summer of 1931.[61] At any rate, she took it for granted that
the troupe of Bahamians had been practicing these ritualistic dances
for years and years rather than having been trained by Hurston. Yet
her description of the dances in the Bahamians' repertory corresponds
exactly to the sections that comprised Hurston's staging of the Fire
Dance. While the "Jim Crow" dance was unquestionably the solo Crow
Dance (an interesting if ingenuous slip), the erotic courting dance was
clearly the Ring Play, a number whose European influences were indis-
cernible to Humphrey (recall that Hurston identified this section as
"African rhythm with European borrowings").[62] Humphrey's *American
Dancer* article also describes a dance in which the Bahamians leapt
over an imaginary fire—unmistakably the Jumping Dance. The mate-
rial that Humphrey was hired to "cut and rearrange" was the same Fire
Dance cycle that Hurston presented in *The Great Day.*

Even John Martin's review of *Run, Little Chillun!,* which he no
doubt covered because of Humphrey's involvement, registered the
correlation between Hurston's dance material and Johnson's drama.
"Those who recall with pleasure the native dances presented a season
or two ago by Zora Hurston and her company," he wrote, "will regret
that the material selected for 'Run Little Chillun' is not up to the same
standard." He speculated that this disparity was "probably dictated
somewhat by a regard for the proprieties, for Miss Hurston's research
uncovered folk material that might not be as acceptable to a Broadway

dramatic audience as it is to a dance audience."[63] Despite favoring Hurston's version, Martin went on to heap praise on Humphrey, declaring her undertaking "a thoroughly workmanlike job, but one for which she is likely to get less credit than is her due." His concern that Humphrey's achievement would not be properly appreciated is certainly ironic given the way history played out. The assumptions that underpin his differential treatment of two women's staging of the same cycle of folk dances deserve careful scrutiny.

First commending Humphrey for creating the "solemn processional and dance" that led up to the Bahamian dance sequence, Martin goes on to admire her setting of this movement on black performers:

> Having inexperienced dancers to work with she has wisely confined
> herself to the simplest of movements and be it said to the credit
> of the young women under her direction that they have absorbed
> the spirit of ritual dignity and give an impressive reverence to
> their processional. It is a triumph of simplicity over choreographic
> invention.[64]

The barely concealed inference here is that Humphrey's great feat lay in taming the supposedly untamed black dancers enough to make them appear poised and dignified. Next, Martin compliments Humphrey on the rousing number that followed the procession, notwithstanding his acknowledgment that it was "built on authentic folk material from the Bahamas." The "wild revel," he explains,

> owes to Miss Humphrey the fact that it looks as if it had not been
> staged at all, which is the highest praise for any sort of folk dancing
> across a set of footlights. It has, however, been pruned extensively
> and given a rude form, without which it would presumably go on
> indefinitely until the dancers dropped from exhaustion.

Essentially, Martin lauds Humphrey for producing movement that came across as both carefully staged and entirely unstaged.

But Martin went further, crediting Humphrey with choosing the very style of dance featured in Johnson's drama. Using his reflections on *Run, Little Chillun!* to unleash a disquisition on the state of African American theatre dance, he explains his preference for seeing black dancers in numbers like the Bahamian dance:

It is in such dances as these that the Negro dancers are at their best, in Mr. Johnson's play as elsewhere. Their vitality, their boundless energy and high spirits are tremendously exciting to watch. When they attempt more sophisticated dancing, they show clearly that they have not found themselves. There are several interesting and talented Negro dancers now active, among them Hemsley Winfield, Edna Guy and Randolph Sawyer, but none of them has yet achieved a dance art that is much more than imitative when it departs from folk ways. Nor has any white choreographer supplied them with material worthy of their mettle.[65]

Martin's evaluative logic here is rooted in the double standard that haunted African American dance artists throughout the first half of the twentieth century: any dancing that departed from jazz, tap, or folk styles was deemed imitative and inferior, yet dancing that stayed within the realm of the vernacular was perceived as raw, instinctive expression rather than cultivated art. A white artist's engagement with black folk idioms, however, launched an appreciation of both her "excellence of . . . theatrical judgment" and her choreographic mastery, for Martin effectively ascribes to Humphrey all the tasks of a choreographer—even while worrying that her labor would go unrecognized.

Martin actually assigns Humphrey more credit than she took for herself. Reflecting back on her work for *Run, Little Chillun!,* Humphrey describes the adjustments she made to the preselected dance material:

In order to fit this dance into the play, a good deal of editing had to be done. A certain time limit had to be observed; otherwise the dance would overtop the drama and fail to be an integral part of it. Then the tempo and the movements had to be built to a dramatic climax at the time the heroine bursts into the circle of dancers and is subsequently carried off by her lover. Also an entrance had to be devised that would be suitable both for the dance and the stage space, and most of all, the dancers had to be taught to project. Being a non-theatrical ritual, they were all quite apt to turn upstage for the most interesting part of the movement, or to stand behind some one else.[66]

Hurston, of course, faced identical considerations, and it is worth noting that not a single review complained about lengthiness or upstaging in the Fire Dance section of her concert. Certainly, Hurston had much less experience than Humphrey working with the proscenium stage. Nevertheless, I would argue that the more substantive distinction between Humphrey's and Hurston's stagings of the Bahamian folk dance cycle was a difference in the *perception* of their labor.[67]

Martin's privileging of Humphrey's artistry over Hurston's demonstrates how heavily the perceived relationship between artist and dance material weighed on determinations of authorship. Despite her Americanness, Hurston's assumed proximity to the West Indian Fire Dance helped render her choreographic labor illegible. By contrast, Humphrey's distance from the dance—in terms of both her race and performance history—led to an inflated portrayal of her role. It would seem, then, that it was Hurston's blackness, her racial "authenticity," that made it possible for Martin to acknowledge the success of her earlier presentation while disavowing her artistry, and that in turn allowed him to let a Euro-American woman's influence on the dancing in *Run, Little Chillun!* eclipse an African American woman's. Because of Martin's own status as an authority on American theatre dance, his distorted allocation of choreographic credit ultimately became part of the received historical record.[68]

## Dancing for Ruth St. Denis

By no means, however, did the circulation of the Fire Dance amount to a zero-sum game in which Hurston invariably lost out. Even as the Bahamian folk dance continued to be disseminated without her sanction or control, Hurston continued to make a name for herself with it. Just four days after *Run, Little Chillun!* opened on Broadway, Hurston was busy pursuing a collaboration with another prominent white female artist, Ruth St. Denis, a pioneer of early modern dance in this country who was best known for her danced interpretations of "Oriental" subjects and for the Denishawn company and school she ran with Ted Shawn from 1915 to 1932. "Zora Hurston Dances For Ruth St. Denis" ran the headline of the two-paragraph-long story in the March 8 issue of the *Rollins Sandspur*, the weekly paper of Florida's Rollins College.[69] The performance was the result largely of coincidence; it was merely by chance that these two women's paths crossed in Winter Park in early March 1933. Apparently, several Rollins College officials who had just backed a production of Hurston's concert decided that her folk material would be of interest to St. Denis, in town to deliver a lecture dance recital, and hastily arranged for the performance.

While Hurston was experiencing an upsurge in her theatrical career, Ruth St. Denis was struggling to support herself at the tail end of hers. Having rejected the formalism of classical ballet, St. Denis performed theatricalized and often religiously inclined dance dramas that drew on elements of physical culture and on borrowings from "exotic" foreign cultures. Her national and international tours helped legitimize art dance as a reputable practice for white women in the early century.[70] By 1933, however, the Denishawn school faced bankruptcy, and St. Denis was forced to pursue a number of moneymaking schemes. These included joining the lecture circuit, which brought her to Winter Park. Following her talk titled "The Philosophy and Dance of the Orient," St. Denis performed a group of her most famous dances, *The White Madonna, Bas-Relief Figure from Angkor-Vat,* and *Dance of the Black and Gold Sari,* all accompanied by piano.

The showing for St. Denis, the *Rollins Sandspur* reported, was a "special half hour performance of folk songs and dances . . . by Zora Hurston and her company of negroes *[sic]*." Joining St. Denis in the audience were the directors of the local experimental theatre workshop that had produced Hurston's full-length concert and "several invited students and townspeople."[71] Fresh from a string of performances given earlier in the winter, Hurston must have swiftly assembled members of her cast and selected highlights from her revue to present. These included the Fire Dance cycle, "done in characteristic costumes and with the rhythmic beat of tom-toms."[72] Because Hurston performed the Crow Dance solo in all other stagings of her concert in 1933, it is safe to assume that she did so as well for St. Denis.

According to the *Sandspur,* "Miss St. Denis was enthusiastic about the Bahama dances"—so enthusiastic, in fact, that she was not content merely to be a spectator to the dances but decided she ought to perform alongside them.[73] "Ruth St. Denis was here and saw us," Hurston wrote in a letter to Alain Locke, "and wishes to appear with us as a soloist-dancer."[74] Evidently, an exchange took place following the performance in which St. Denis presumably praised Hurston's dance work and suggested that the two might collaborate on a future presentation. What exactly St. Denis had in mind—how a solo performance by a white modern dancer could possibly have been integrated into

Hurston's program of Floridian and Bahamian folkways—can only be a matter of speculation. Perhaps realizing the implausibility of St. Denis's proposition, Hurston nonetheless responded with undaunted pragmatism, telling Locke, "I know its novelty-publicity seeking but it will help *us* never-the-less."

With this comment, Hurston provides valuable insight into how she construed outside interest in her material, in what serves as an important counterpoint to the perspective of her patron, Charlotte Mason. Most notably, her statement demonstrates a savvy awareness of the politics of interracial collaboration and of the cultural capital that her "primitive" dance idioms afforded her. Assuring Locke that she is not naive enough to think that anything other than self-interest lay behind St. Denis's proposal, Hurston intimates that the real appeal of her material for white artists was the novelty of association with black dancing bodies, rather than the prospect of exploring the contours and nuances of black folk culture. Yet instead of bemoaning St. Denis's opportunistic motives, Hurston sees the white woman's attention as a chance to advance her own publicity-seeking cause. For, had St. Denis's proposed stage alliance actually come to pass (and the archive provides no indication of why it did not), Hurston's standing as a dance authority would certainly have been bolstered. At any rate, both St. Denis, who, by her own account, was "suffering a complete eclipse" in the field of dance, and Hurston, whose reputation was flourishing, were poised to profit from a collaborative venture.[75] Of course, the power imbalance between the two women cannot be disregarded. The fact that St. Denis was entitled to a free showing of Hurston's folk material testifies to the asymmetry of their relative positions.[76] Still, Hurston's determination to capitalize on St. Denis's solicitation refutes the notion that white trafficking in black vernacular dance was exploitative in any unidirectional sense or to the benefit of any single party. It was only, however, when Hurston could publicly retain her affiliation with the Bahamian folk idioms that she stood to gain personally from such transactions.

## The "Bahama Negro Dancers" and Helen Tamiris at Lewisohn Stadium

Not long after concluding their run in Hall Johnson's musical, the Bahamian dancers, now a sixteen-member group working under the name the "Bahama Negro Dancers," assumed a featured role in a dance program with white modern dancer Helen Tamiris. Given on August 18 and 19, 1933, at Lewisohn Stadium, the massive outdoor amphitheatre in uptown New York, the concert consisted of three solos by Tamiris, four numbers by the Bahamians, one piece danced jointly by Tamiris and the Bahamians, and two musical offerings by the Philharmonic-Symphony Orchestra. Whereas *Run, Little Chillun!* showcased an abridged version of the Fire Dance cycle, it is clear from the concert program that the songs and dances performed at the stadium were more or less identical to those Hurston presented in her folk revues.[77] What is not clear is how many of the "Bahama Negro Dancers" who performed with Tamiris were part of the troupe Hurston initially assembled, because—and this point is worth underscoring—the stadium concert program did not list the names of the black performers. Reviews did single out two solo dancers for mention: Motor Boat, who had worked with Hurston from the beginning, and Pearl of Nassau, whose name does not appear on any earlier cast lists.[78] Archival evidence indicates that the composition of the Bahamian troupe fluctuated from one engagement to the next.

In many ways, the linkage between the Fire Dance and Tamiris is less startling than the linkage to Ruth St. Denis, for unlike St. Denis, Tamiris's career was closely intertwined with "Negro dance." Born to Russian Jewish immigrants, Tamiris studied movement with Irene Lewisohn at the Henry Street Settlement, as well as ballet, but was best known for her choreographic interpretations of Negro spirituals, which she began performing in the late 1920s. While she repeatedly expressed her "conviction of kinship with the Negro dance," Tamiris also pursued a broader project of mining the rhythms of black vernacular dance in the creation of a national dance.[79] By embodying references to black spirituals and protest songs, Tamiris "performed America," as Susan Manning has argued, and thereby "render[ed] the white female body a vehicle for circulating multiple identities."[80] Tamiris's interest in African Americans extended beyond her use of source material; she taught dance classes in Harlem and was a noted social activist.[81] Nonetheless, the 1933 Lewisohn Stadium concert marked the first and possibly only time she shared the concert stage with black dancers.

The impetus for the shift in Tamiris's performance practice, from appearing either solo or with other white female dancers to performing with black bodies, evidently came from an external source. According to an August 1933 article in *Time* magazine,

> One day last month Mrs. Charles S. Guggenheimer, energetic
> chairman of Manhattan's Philharmonic-Symphony, seeking an
> added attraction for the Lewisohn Stadium concerts, telephoned
> for advice to Hall Johnson, Negro composer and choir mas-
> ter. Cautiously he mentioned the Bahama Negro dancers who
> appeared in his folk play *Run, Little Chillun!* . . . Enthusiastic,
> Mrs. Guggenheimer suggested that they present a joint program
> with Tamiris, a wiry New York white girl with a growing reputa-
> tion for dances based on Negroid themes.[82]

In turning for suggestions to Hall Johnson, whose choir had performed
at Lewisohn Stadium the previous year, Mrs. Guggenheimer was con-
ceivably engaged in some "novelty-publicity seeking" of her own, perhaps
looking for a touch of primitivism to round out the stadium offerings.[83] A
belated addition to the summer schedule, the pair of Tamiris-Bahamian
performances served as the culmination to a "highly popular succession
of dancers" presented at the stadium that year, including the Strawbridge-
Koner Ballet and the Humphrey-Weidman Ballet.[84] The "caution" with
which Johnson recommended the Bahamian dancers could be a sign of
qualms he held about the circumstances surrounding his own enlist-
ment of the troupe. For Mrs. Guggenheimer, the pairing of the Caribbean
dancers with the "wiry New York white girl" was just the "attraction"
she was looking for. Although far from the first production to unite the
Bahamian ensemble with a white female artist, the Lewisohn Stadium
concert marked the first instance in which a white woman performed
side by side with the troupe.

Overall, the stadium program cohered around interpretations of
black source material. From the orchestra's renditions of the "dusky"
"In Old Virginia" and the "thumping" "Bamboula," to Tamiris's danced
expressions of Negro suffering, to the intermittent Bahamian numbers,
virtually all of the concert's offerings were based on African diasporic
folk idioms and black-oriented themes.[85] At least in structure, the
stadium concert painted a diffuse picture of the black diaspora, approached from a variety of vantage points. As received, however, the
range of African-influenced and black-inspired numbers did not come
together to form a unified whole but instead conveyed a discordant vision that played into spectators' preconceptions about black and white
dancing bodies.

For the most part, critics were in agreement that the concert offered, in the words of one unidentified reviewer, "premeditated, interpret[ive] dancing by Tamiris; natural, unabashed dancing by the Bahama Negro Dancers."[86] In unmistakable language, this critic articulates the racialized thinking that likely informed many spectators' reactions to the concert: namely, that black vernacular dance, including the Caribbean folk dances, involved neither premeditation nor interpretation. Such reasoning effaced any and all training and choreographic preparation behind the Bahamian group's performance. Considering the ease with which reviewers made such elisions, it is no wonder that headlines such as "Tamiris Offers Dance Program at the Stadium" were typical.[87] With few exceptions, critics took Tamiris and her "deliberately" staged dancing to be the stadium concert's chief attraction. The outright omission of the Bahamians' contributions to the program in these headlines reproduced the assessment that black vernacular dance did not count as art.

Even those critics who saw the Bahamians as the concert's primary feature were of the view that the differences between Tamiris and the Bahama Negro Dancers were greater than their affinities. Both the *Amsterdam News* and the *World Telegram* reversed the bias in favor of Tamiris and cited only the Bahamian dancers in their headlines. But while the *Telegram*'s Pitts Sanborn portrayed Tamiris as ancillary to the program, he fully adhered to conventional racial classifications. "At the Stadium last evening," Sanborn enthusiastically proclaimed, "Bach, Beethoven, Berlioz, Brahms, Bruckner, Borodin, Bax and all the other busy B's of symphony music yielded the field to black Bahama bucks, and an audience of 3,000 re-echoed the tom-tom rhythm in its elated applause."[88] For this critic, only the spectacle of a group of scantily dressed black dancing bodies performing in one of New York's bastions of culture rendered the Bahamians central to the program.

A satirical sketch that ran in the weekly black newspaper the *Amsterdam News* likewise portrayed Tamiris as peripheral to the Bahama Dancers and likewise highlighted the incongruities between the two (see Figure 10). Titled "Cartoonist's Conception of Bahama Dancers at Stadium," the illustration apparently took the place of a written review of the concert.[89] The cartoon prominently depicts five silhouetted figures, two male-female couples plus a male drummer who kneels in the lower left-hand corner, engaged in part of the Fire Dance cycle. With their bent knees, crouched positions, and extended arms, the dancers' postures, if somewhat exaggerated in the cartoonist's version, bear a strong resemblance to those captured in the *Theatre Arts*

**Figure 10.** Bill Chase's rendering of the Bahama Dancers and Helen Tamiris at Lewisohn Stadium, 1933. General Research and Reference Division, Schomburg Center for Research in Black Culture, The New York Public Library, Astor, Lenox and Tilden Foundations. Permission courtesy of *New York Amsterdam News* Archives.

*Monthly* photograph of Hurston and her group over a year earlier. In the upper left-hand corner of the cartoon, directly above the kneeling drummer, is an image of Tamiris in bare legs and a black leotard, engaged in a deep lunge. Slightly smaller than the other figures, she appears against a black background that contrasts the white background behind the Bahamians. While her lunge is directed toward the other figures, her head is turned away from them, and she appears to be gazing out into space. Whereas the four Bahamian dancers are clearly interacting with one another, Tamiris seems entirely unaware of the other performers, and her solo bears no palpable relation to the dancers with whom she shared the stadium stage. Tamiris's physicality also contrasts with the other figures. Although her lunge echoes the bent knee of one of the female Bahamian dancers, her balletic turnout is the exact inverse of the other female dancer, who prominently turns in her knees and feet. Tamiris's erect torso is likewise distinct from the fluid torsos of all the other performers. While no explicit critique emerges from the drawing, it is clear that, like the overwhelming majority of reviewers, the cartoonist believed the dance styles of Tamiris and the black dancers to be incompatible, even amusingly so.[90]

Such insistence on differentiating Tamiris from the Bahamian ensemble created serious perceptual problems for reviewers when it came to evaluating "Gris-Gris Ceremonial," the one number in which the black and white dancers not only shared the same space but did so concurrently. Originally choreographed for twelve white female dancers who carried small percussive instruments and provided their own musical accompaniment, the piece had been warmly received when Tamiris premiered it in 1932.[91] But when presented at the stadium concert, where it was set on Tamiris and eight male members of the Bahamian troupe, reviewers uniformly judged "Gris-Gris" to be a failure. The *Evening Post*'s Henry Beckett, who deemed the work "so bad that it was almost good," provides the most evocative account:

> Tamaris [sic], intended to be an awe-inspiring figure planted in the center of the stage, wiggled her shoulders slightly in the way of a muscle dancer and immediately the group of Negroes went into a tantrum, leaping and shouting and gyrating in what appeared to be a combination of the jitters, the heebie-jeebies and delirium tremens.[92]

However unsuccessful the piece, Tamiris's movements are still cast as controlled and expressive, while those of the Bahamians are deemed reckless and overwrought. If the novelty of a joint recital with Tamiris and the Bahamians succeeded in grabbing theatregoers' attention, the unambiguous condemnation of "Gris-Gris Ceremonial" suggests a general aversion to seeing black and white bodies as dancing partners on the concert stage.

Even so, the theatrical alliance seemed to work to Tamiris's advantage and against the Bahamians, for most critics shared the opinion that "it was Tamiris rather than the Bahamans who scored last night's success."[93] Once again, the authoritative John Martin offered an explanation for this lopsided outcome. "The appearance of Tamiris and the Bahama Negro Dancers . . . at the Lewisohn Stadium," he wrote a week after the concert,

> proved to be in performance the reverse of what it was generally expected to be. The enormous size of the place made it seem inevitable that the solo dancer would be swallowed up while the group would capture the evening's honors. What actually took

place can be explained on two grounds: first, that Tamiris succeeded in scaling her movement to the dimensions of the space
about her and, second, that the material of the Negroes was
monotonous and aimless.[94]

With six thousand seats and room to accommodate thousands more,
Lewisohn Stadium was certainly a less than ideal setting for appreci-
ating individualized movements. But Martin positively gushed about
the augmented "natural beauty" of Tamiris's dancing and applauded
her decision to appear at such a large venue, citing the need for the de-
veloping modern dance movement to reach out to a mass audience.[95]

As Martin contended in a separate account, the Bahamians' short-
comings represented a marked departure from their prior stage appearances. "The same dances, and at least some of the same dancers,"
he maintained, "made quite a different impression some three years
ago when they were first presented here under the leadership of Zora
Hurston."[96] While the Fire Dance no doubt looked different in the
dwarfing context of Lewisohn Stadium, Martin had another explanation for the change. "With their good-natured tendency to strive
to please," he alleged, the Bahamian performers "added the popular
touches of Harlem sophistication, but . . . were apparently unable to
counterbalance this fault with a further adaptation of their material in
the interest of form."[97] Attempting to shed light on a dilemma faced
by all performers who present vernacular dances on the theatrical
stage, Martin's reasoning actually reveals a catch-22: he accuses the
Bahamian dancers of adapting their material both too much and not
enough, of appearing too artful and at the same time too artless.

A number of reviewers also invoked Harlem in their appraisals
of the stadium concert. While some concluded, like Martin, that the
group suffered under the influence of the uptown black district, other
critics found just the opposite: that the Bahamian dancers paled by
comparison with the "gaieties" of Harlem's nightlife.[98] For this latter group of spectators, the stately bare stage of Lewisohn Stadium,
with its lack of miscellaneous production elements, was an unsuitable
milieu for the spectacle of Afro-Caribbean folk dancing. As Henry
Beckett of the *Evening Post* explained, "At the Stadium, where no grass
grows and there is nothing to suggest the jungle, these dancers have
to create their atmosphere by an excess of shouting and beating of
the drums."[99] Either way, the frequency with which Harlem cropped

up in critics' assessments points to the extent to which dance styles associated with the nightclub, cabaret, and musical theatre stages of Harlem served as the standard against which all black stage dancing was judged. With critics insisting that Harlem both corrupted the purity of the folk and was the most suitable forum for black vernacular dance, success for the Bahamian dancers, at least from the point of view of the mainstream press, was a virtual impossibility.

Crucially, the reliance on Harlem as a paramount frame of reference for the Bahama Negro Dancers and the double bind it posed for them was not without its utility. In evaluating the Bahamians' performance with a fraught set of standards, that is to say, critics effectively made room for Tamiris's performance, indirectly sanctioning her white dancing body as the rightful interpreter of black vernacular material on the legitimate stage. Such sanctioning was not always indirect. John Martin asserted that Tamiris's group of Negro spirituals "assume[d] a certain new validity when seen at close proximity to actual Negro movement."[100] In this pithy remark, Martin discloses just how much privilege the white dancing body carried in 1933. Rather than casting doubt on Tamiris's entitlement to or suitability for black source material, the presence of the Bahamian dancers bestowed more legitimacy upon her. Next to the black dancing bodies who appeared both too primitive and no longer primitive enough, the white modern dancer's artistry was upheld and magnified.[101]

Once again, however, it would be wrong to conclude that validity only accrued to figures like Tamiris and only dissipated for black performers as a result of such collaborations. Aside from the always relevant financial incentives, the association with Tamiris and the sheer size of the audience at the stadium productions yielded tremendous exposure for the Bahamian dancers despite less than favorable reviews from the mainstream press. Surely it is significant that, within two years of their theatrical debut, the group had worked with several prominent choreographers, acquired an official manager, and been seen by literally thousands of New Yorkers.[102] Tamiris's interest in Caribbean dancing, moreover, evidently outlasted the August performance. "Her class in Bahama folk dancing in Harlem," an unidentified newspaper clipping from December 1933 reads, "is a tremendous thing, achieving the revival and preservation of a primitive art."[103] Whether or not Tamiris employed any of the Bahama Negro Dancers to assist in this enterprise is unknown, although the possibility certainly exists. Regardless, the class helped further promote black diasporic folk dance, and the Bahamian dancers continued to find work on the New York stage.

## Teaching Irene Castle Something New

Meanwhile, Hurston continued to present the Fire Dance in various locales around the country, and it continued to prove its drawing power for her white contemporaries in the field of dance. In the fall of 1934, at the invitation of the South Parkway Young Women's Christian Association, Hurston staged a version of her folk concert in Chicago. Retitled *Singing Steel,* the revue followed the same basic structure of *The Great Day* and retained the Bahamian folk dance finale. On or around November 22, the ballroom dance icon Irene Castle stopped by one of the final rehearsals for the concert and briefly interacted with the group of amateur Chicago dancers whom Hurston had newly assembled and trained. As reported by the *Chicago Daily News,* Irene Castle McLaughlin, who had remarried after the 1918 death of her famous dancing partner and husband, Vernon Castle, was captivated by what she saw.

"Trying to teach Mrs. Irene Castle McLaughlin something new about dance rhythm," the paper notes, "was listed in the category of things that were not to be until she dropped in on a rehearsal of the Negro folk drama, 'Singing Steel' . . . She found the 'Fire Dance,' as interpreted by this group, so original and exciting that she joined in with them."[104] This account appears below a photograph of Castle posing with four dancers, two men and two women, identified as Herman McMillan, Allen Shaeffer, Edna Bryant, and Margaret Payne (Figure 11). As the female cast members lunge in the foreground, Castle stands in back between the two male dancers and strikes a dramatic pose. Her body is turned at an angle, her fingers are outstretched, and her palms face the camera in classic jazz fashion. The cast is in costume, donning their patterned "primitive" garb; Castle wears a dark dress. The caption above the photo reads "Irene Castle Learns New Dance."

Castle's kinesthetic reaction to the Fire Dance calls to mind Ruth St. Denis's response almost two years earlier. For both women, observing the Bahamian folk dance was not enough; each felt compelled to insert her body into the dancing in some capacity. While St. Denis proposed a formal stage collaboration with Hurston and her troupe,

**Figure 11.** Ballroom dance icon Irene Castle posing with some of Hurston's *Singing Steel* cast members, *Chicago Daily News,* 1934. Reproduced from the collection of the Library of Congress.

Castle posed for a photograph while attempting to master the black dancers' moves. Yet because Castle approached the number from a very different position within the field of American dance, her appearance with Hurston's dancers conjured up its own set of associations and implications. These new implications shed light on yet another dimension of the long and tangled relationship between white dancers and black folk dance.

Whereas St. Denis established herself as a dance artist by incorporating Asian images and gestures into her work, Castle's career rested on the appropriation and adaptation of concrete black social dances. Together with Vernon Castle, Irene played a major part in the ragtime dance craze that swept the country in the first two decades of the twentieth century. In their dual capacity as performers and instructors, the Castles promoted dancing as an acceptable and healthy activity for white Americans. Emphasizing refinement, grace, and discipline, they disseminated "whitened" versions of rag steps that derived from black communities. Key to the success of the Castles' operation was their African American bandleader, James Reese Europe, who provided them with direct access to black vernacular culture and introduced them to specific dance steps like the fox-trot.[105] Although Irene retired from the dance scene in the mid-1920s, she had not faded from public memory in 1934, as the *Daily News* coverage suggests.[106]

To be sure, the portrayal of Castle's interaction with the *Singing Steel* dancers demonstrates the extent to which she was still considered an expert in the arena of vernacular dance. The ironic rhetoric of the *Daily News* caption—based on the assumed impossibility that this glamorous ballroom star would have anything to learn from the black performers—positions the white woman as the unmistakable authority on dance rhythm and casts the African American dancers as improbable teachers. The scene is presented as a humorous inversion of the norm: it should have been Castle, the newspaper implies, doing the instructing. Admittedly, Irene Castle was the retired professional here, and Hurston's cast members were acknowledged amateurs. Even so, the real irony is that the supposedly anomalous transmission of knowledge from black bodies to white was no anomaly at all. Castle's career frankly depended on black sources. In addition to her ongoing reliance on musical director James Reese Europe, Castle once sought out private dance instruction from Ethel Williams, a black dancer in New York.[107] For Castle, in short, learning new dances from African Americans was in the category of things that *were*, not "things that were not to be."

The *Daily News*'s depiction of Castle's encounter with the Fire Dance is of particular significance, therefore, because of the way it simultaneously reveals and conceals the relationship between this prominent white dancer and black folk dance. On the one hand, by publicizing her fascination with the number, the photograph and accompanying caption expose the essential link between white dancers like Castle and black practitioners of vernacular dance. On the other hand, by insisting on a hierarchy of white experts and black amateurs, and by depicting black dancers' tutelage of Castle as the exception rather than the rule, the account covers over a history of cultural borrowing, exchange, and theft—on both an individual and a national level.[108]

The other absent presence in the *Daily News* feature, of course, is Hurston herself. Although she may not have been physically present at the rehearsal, the fact that her name appears nowhere in a report that mentions her cast, her choreography, and her folk drama is nonetheless telling. Her authority was evidently of less consequence than Castle's. In addition to demonstrating the diversity of dance figures who were drawn to Hurston's Fire Dance, the episode thus illuminates how interimplicated formulations of white and black dancers were, or more precisely, how the veneration of white artists went hand in hand with—indeed rested upon—the marginalization of black artists.

## Race and Genre: The National Dance Congress and Festival

Four years after Hurston separated from her *Great Day* Bahamian troupe, the two parties once again crossed paths—or nearly did. The occasion was the First National Dance Congress and Festival, organized in New York in May 1936. Spearheaded by the New Dance League, the Dance Guild, and the Dancers' Association, all left-leaning coalitions, the congress was conceived as a means "to advance the artistic, educational and economic interests of the Dance in the United States."[109] Apparently modeled after annual festivals held in Germany before the Nazis came to power in early 1933, the Congress and Festival spanned the week of May 18–25 and consisted of performances, lectures, and discussions, all held at the Ninety-second Street Young Men's Hebrew Association's Theresa L. Kaufmann Theatre. Over the course of the week, twenty-five different speakers lectured on the themes of "Dance in a Changing World," "Dance Organization," "Economic Status of Dancers," and "Dance and Criticism." Unlike the modern-dance-oriented Bennington Festival, the National Congress and Festival sought to feature a "cross-section of all forms of the Dance in America." More than two hundred dancers appeared on six separate programs devoted to modern, ballet, folk, theatre and variety, and lecture-demonstrations.[110] Among those engaged in this ambitious undertaking were Hurston and the Bahamian dancers.

Their involvement is significant in several regards. The alliance of both parties with an organization with clear leftist ties points to their willingness to take advantage of the leftist patronage that was available to black dance artists in the 1930s.[111] This is of particular note in Hurston's case, given the attention her anticommunist politics have received.[112] As a discrete effort to convene and categorize a "cross section" of dance traditions, furthermore, the National Dance Congress and Festival provides a useful topographical index of American dance in the 1930s. Keeping in mind Pierre Bourdieu's field of cultural production, it is possible to read the assembly of players from diverse locations as an illustration of the interconnected nature of dance genres and the relational struggles to assert artistic legitimacy. Upon close inspection, the Congress and Festival enterprise also reveals the underlying if tacit racial dimensions of those classifications and struggles. While this chapter has thus far examined the distribution of power and artistic credit in individual cases of cross-racial collaboration involving the Fire Dance, the engagement of Hurston and the Bahamian dancers with the Congress and Festival presents an opportunity to reflect on how the Fire Dance—and black diasporic folk dance more generally—fit into the American dance scene at large.

The nature of the Bahamian group's participation in the festival is easy to discern: they performed on both the "Folk" and the "Theatre and Variety" programs.[113] Hurston's contributions to the event are somewhat more ambiguous. Her name crops up in several different places in the National Dance Congress records. In December 1935, she lent her name to the congress's call for action, evidently sent out to a variety of artists and dancers "to try opinion as to the desirability of the proposed congress and festival."[114] Her name also appears on an advance publicity flyer as part of a catalog of performers scheduled to appear on the various evening programs.[115] A separate unidentified newspaper clipping, dated May 9, 1936, announces that "Zora Hurston and 'Motor Boat' of the Bahaman dancers" will be among the festival's performers.[116] Whether Hurston actually planned to perform with the Bahamian dancers, or whether the announcement was based on a mistaken if reasonable assumption given their history together, it is

impossible to say. Clearly, Hurston intended to be an active participant in the festival. Having relocated to New York to find work in the
fall of 1935 following the publication of her folklore volume *Mules and
Men*, Hurston took a job with the Works Progress Administration's
Federal Theatre Project. She served as dramatic coach, assisting with
the Harlem unit's inaugural production, Frank Wilson's *Walk Together,
Chillun*, and as playwright, though the hastily written, untitled play
of hers never saw production.[117] Whatever reunion between Hurston
and Motor Boat may have been in the making was ultimately not to
be. When the Congress and Festival opened, Hurston was no longer
even in the country. In late 1935, she had applied for a Guggenheim
Fellowship to do further research in the Caribbean, and by March 18,
she received word of her acceptance. Two days later, she resigned her
WPA job, and by April she had left New York for Jamaica.[118]

The Bahaman Dancers, as they were now dubbed, did proceed with
their scheduled performances. Led by Motor Boat (Leonard Sturrup),
the group in 1936 was down to three women and six men, including a
drummer. Of these nine, Ruby Braithwith and Reginald Alday, in addition to Motor Boat and Stew Beef (whose real name remains a mystery), had been part of either the *Run, Little Chillun!* or the *Great Day*
and *From Sun to Sun* casts. On the evening of Tuesday, May 19, the
second day of the festival, the troupe appeared on a folk dance program that also featured American, Polish, English, Ukrainian, and
Swedish groups. Opening the second act of the concert, they presented
six individual numbers in succession: "The Crow Dance," "Bellemina,"
"Congo," "Coconut Oil," "Evelena," and "Jumping Dance (Fire Dance)."
This was the same series of songs and dances that Hurston had staged
as the finale to *The Great Day* and that the Bahama Negro Dancers
had presented at Lewisohn Stadium in 1933.

Restaged for the festival folk program, this series was positioned
as part of an evening of "delightful" folk traditions, an example of
several distinct national dances that thrived apart from the theatre
stage. As John Martin noted in his review of the program, the festival
demonstrated exceptional skill in presenting this genre, or, as he put
it, in "adapting to the stage an art that is not essentially theatrical."[119]
Indeed, it seems that the Bahamian dances were far more palatable
to Martin under the Congress and Festival rubric than they had been
when featured alongside Tamiris's choreography on the Lewisohn
Stadium stage. Although for the first time, Martin's review made no

reference to the Bahamians' performance history, the absence of any complaint about the group (or of any mention of Harlem's corrupting influence) suggests that he considered the folk program a more fitting milieu for the dancers. Martin's unqualified praise for the festival's exhibition of folk dances can thus be read as a decided preference for seeing the Fire Dance in relation to other national folk traditions rather than in relation to the emerging American modern dance tradition.[120] With a separate evening devoted to dancers of the modern school, the boundaries between the folk and the modern were upheld, and the "spirit and vitality" of the former were all the more enjoyable.[121]

The Bahamian dancers' participation in the theatre and variety program on Sunday, May 24, however, raises questions about the relationship between the "nontheatrical" form of folk and the theatrical form of jazz. On this second appearance, male members of the ensemble performed in a piece called *Tiger Rag* choreographed by Mura Dehn, the same Russian-born dancer who had used Hurston's "Negro Chanters" some four years earlier. By 1936, Dehn had more firmly established her commitment to African American dance, and her profile in the festival program reflected this. As it reported, her work with Bahamian dancers and Lindy Hoppers was "her first step towards creating a Negro Ballet based on various Negro technics."[122] Curiously, while the program notes for the Folk Dance Evening cited Motor Boat as the Bahamian troupe's leader, a separate "Who's Who" of festival performers listed Dehn, along with Stew Beef, as the group's directors.[123] The fact that Dehn's work with several members of the Bahamian group earned her recognition as their "director" speaks once again to the implicit but always-operative power structure that automatically conferred authority on white dancers when allied with black dancers.

Since no review commented specifically on *Tiger Rag*, it is difficult to ascertain much about its choreography, performed by Dehn and four of the Bahamian men. What is clear is that Dehn was now interested in making movement for white and black bodies. According to the festival program, *Tiger Rag* was danced to jazz music, though program notes list the Caribbean drummer Gabriel Brown as an accompanist.[124] Whether Brown's style of rhythmic drumming elicited the label "jazz" or whether it supplemented some arrangement of American recorded jazz music can only be a matter of speculation. Either way, the dance's pairing of the Bahamian Fire Dancers with a

white female jazz dancer entailed—perhaps depended on—some blurring of distinctions between folk and jazz.

The entire variety and theatre program, in fact, was a medley of
disparate dance forms. In addition to *Tiger Rag,* Dehn choreographed
and performed in a solo called *Promenade Amoureuse* and danced in
a group piece by the white jazz dancer Richard Pryor Dodge. The evening also featured the African American dancer Edna Guy, who performed two Negro spirituals, the ballroom dance team of Anita Avila
and Jack Nile, an interpretation of "Yemenite youth after hearing rab-
binical sermon," and Shorty Snowden's Lindy Hoppers. By a long shot,
this was the most racially integrated of the Congress and Festival programs. But except for Dehn's *Tiger Rag,* black and white dancers did
not perform in the same pieces.

What logic united this rather curious array of dance numbers into
a single program that was distinct from the folk, ballet, and modern
programs? While the evening was clearly intended to present a mixed
bag of dance styles, the lineup seems oriented toward dances based on
popular American social dance forms. It should not go unremarked,
however, that Guy, who had modern dance training with Ruth St. Denis,
was placed on the variety and theatre program, while one of the modern programs contained a solo called *Blues Trilogy,* described as "an
elaboration in form and theme of the American Negro Blues folksong"
and performed by the white dancer Felicia Sorel. Actually, a number of
the modern works were overt interpretations of folk material.[125] Guy's
inclusion on the variety and theatre program along with the Bahamian
performers, therefore, suggests a correlation between blackness, jazz,
and folk that underscores the circumscription of racially marked dancing bodies in the 1930s.[126]

At the same time, the Bahamian dancers' appearance on the folk
as well as the variety and theatre programs speaks to the amenability
of black diasporic dance to multiple generic frameworks. Or, perhaps
more accurately, it indicates an ambiguity about where to situate black
dancers amidst the existing and emerging dance disciplines. When
the Bahamian dancers performed on their own, they were linked up
with other self-identified national folk groups on a program that represented the least inherently "theatrical" of dance forms. Yet when they
performed under the direction of the white dancer Mura Dehn, they
were placed on a lineup of miscellaneous numbers—jazz, ballroom,
spirituals, folk—collectively deemed "theatrical."

But if Afro-Caribbean dance displayed a simultaneous pliancy and resistance to definitive categorization, it remained at all times subordinate to the disciplines of ballet and modern. Although John Martin judged the folk program the most successful of the festival's offerings, there is no question that the greater share of critical attention and appreciation of artistry was reserved for practitioners of those two "academic" idioms, the latter of which Martin helped legitimate. This partitioning and ranking of dance genres obscured the Bahamian ensemble's earlier collaborative ventures with several major modern dance figures.

The appeal the Fire Dance held for everyone from Irene Lewisohn to Ruth St. Denis to Doris Humphrey to Helen Tamiris suggests that black diasporic folk dance played a critical role in the formation of modern dance in the 1930s. With its aura of primitive authenticity, the Fire Dance complemented and served the larger artistic projects of these white choreographers. But by 1936, the proscriptive classification system governing racially marked and unmarked dancing bodies had taken firmer root. Appearing only on the separate and necessarily unequal folk and theatre and variety programs, where there was no danger of spectators confusing their danced representations with those of the white artists who made up the modern program, the Bahamian dancers were now effectively—and permanently—disentangled from that genre. While subsequent years saw other black dancers make inroads into the white-dominated field, the Bahamian group's interface with modern dance had come and gone.

Finally, then, returning to Charlotte Mason's mandate to Alain Locke at the premiere of *The Great Day* to "protect the material from being exploited and stolen," I want to suggest that the real threat to Hurston's folk material lay neither in the public display of black vernacular forms nor in white trafficking in those forms. Rather, as the patterns that emerge from the critical responses to the Fire Dance indicate, the danger lay in the underlying assumptions that attended stage enactments of black diasporic folk dance and shaped spectators' disparate perceptions of white and black dancing bodies. In effect, what invisibilized Hurston's choreographic contributions were racialized notions of artistry and authenticity, notions that insisted on essential, immutable differences between black folk performers and white "creative" artists. These same notions also worked to limit her ability to retain control over productions of the Bahamian dance and therefore her ability to assign her own meanings to the idiom. Hurston and the Bahamian dancers' stagings of the Fire Dance thus exemplify cultural critic Robin Kelley's observation that terms like "folk" and "authentic" are in actuality "socially constructed categories that have something to do with the reproduction of race, class, and gender hierarchies and the policing of the boundaries of modernism."[127] For if the extensive circulation of the Bahamian dance cycle reveals how imbricated black folk dance and white modern dance were in the 1930s, it equally demonstrates how rigorously the boundaries between racial and artistic categories were policed. Launched by Hurston's assembly and training of a dance troupe and her exhibition of Caribbean idioms on the New York theatrical stage in 1932, the extensive circulation of the Fire Dance—both with and without Hurston's personal involvement—obtained widespread exposure for the folk cycle even as it created problems for Hurston regarding questions of authorship and credit. To a remarkable extent, the proliferation of Hurston's stage version of the Fire Dance coincided with the erasure of her choreographic role in its production.

# Coda: Hurston's Choreographic Legacy

From Broadway to college campuses and experimental theatres, to the outdoor Lewisohn Stadium and the National Dance Congress and Festival, to the Cotton Club and a WPA exhibition: the Bahamian Fire Dance that Hurston first staged as the finale to *The Great Day* in January 1932 had a remarkably diverse life over the course of the 1930s. The extent of the dance's popularity and the wide assortment of institutions and individuals it brought into affiliation are a testament to the distinctive character of the dance and the decade. With its dynamic drum beats and hand clapping, complex rhythmic patterns, bold leaps, intricate footwork, and rousing kinetic energy, the Fire Dance cycle struck American audiences as both novel and familiar. Clearly, the Jumping Dance, Ring Play, and Crow Dance that comprised the Caribbean cycle diverged from the conventional jazz and tap styles typical of black musicals and nightclub acts. Yet the frenetic, polyrhythmic dancing and animal impersonation on display in the Fire Dance were still wholly in line with dominant models of black performance, making the Bahamian number seem simultaneously exceptional and palatable to artists and spectators from a range of locations.

At the same time, the widespread embracing of the Fire Dance owed much to the unique climate of the 1930s, a time of economic crisis, national introspection, heightened political activity, and artistic flux. Perhaps most significantly, the decade witnessed a struggle over the definitions and uses of the folk as well as a struggle for authority within the field of American dance. In the 1930s, in the wake of the Jazz Age when the Charleston and Black Bottom swept the country, the trope of the black primitive was neither new nor obsolete. As they had in the 1920s, African Americans continued to capitalize on and contest primitivist notions, often in debates over the relationship between black folk culture, race, and nation. This set of deliberations coincided with increasingly visible strivings by choreographers of various backgrounds to establish new dance traditions on the theatre stage, most prominently American modern dance, but also Negro dance and jazz dance. The Bahamian Fire Dance was a locus for both of these trends, a site where overlapping and competing efforts to sort through the significations of blackness and the classifications of dance genres converged.

If the transitions of the 1930s thus provided favorable conditions for the production and reception of the Fire Dance, what became of the dance and those responsible for staging it in subsequent years? Hurston, for her part, continued to pursue multiple lines of work, moving between research expeditions (including trips to Honduras and the Bahamas), publishing fiction and nonfiction, giving lectures, and writing plays.[1] Although her stage activity certainly lessened in later years, she never abandoned her concert project. In the fall of 1939, Hurston made plans to mount another folk revue at the North Carolina College for Negroes, where she was hired to organize a drama program, but eventually called it off due to inadequate preparation time. In a speech to the Carolina Dramatic Association in October of that year, Hurston proposed the formation of a production company devoted to dramatizations of black folklore, though this, too, dissolved when, frustrated by lack of support, she resigned her faculty position and left North Carolina in 1940.[2] A 1952 letter to her literary agent, Jean Parker Waterbury, however, establishes that some of Hurston's ongoing theatrical goals did see fruition. Writing from Eau Gallie, Florida, Hurston reports:

> I have done a series of five folk concerts here in the last six weeks and picked up a little money that way. I could do more but it takes from my writing time. I had no intention of doing any, but people here discovering my reputation in that respect begged me to do

it. Four concerts for white audiences and one for colored, and
now I am being asked all over to keep it up. Too much work for
too little money. I already have a national reputation that way, so
I do not need to work for one and ignore money.[3]

Although they proved a limited source of income, Hurston's folk revues still met with favor and invitations for repeat performances.
And notwithstanding the observation made in her autobiography ten
years earlier that she "is never mentioned" in conjunction with the
spread of "West Indian dancing and work songs" on American stages,
Hurston's letter expresses satisfaction with the name she has made for
herself through her stage productions.[4] Eight years before her death,
Hurston continued to disseminate her embodied theory of the folk.
Concomitantly, she continued to wrestle with the contradictions and
predicaments that this project entailed: packaging the folk for public
consumption in the pursuit of financial gain and personal acclaim; the
intensive labor required to cast, direct, choreograph, and produce live
performances; and the thorny task of negotiating a racially fractured
audience. In this, her last surviving mention of the folk concerts to
which she devoted so much energy two decades earlier, Hurston evi-
dences her commitment to the stage as a medium for representing the
folk even as she attests to the difficulties it posed.

The exploits of the Bahamian dancers following their 1936 engagement at the downtown Cotton Club, their last documented performance as an ensemble, is almost as much a mystery as their activity
before Hurston assembled them for *The Great Day* in late 1931. It is
clear that troupe members found employment individually. As discussed in chapter 5, Motor Boat and Stew Beef joined the Savoy Lindy
Hoppers at the 1939 New York World's Fair, although it is not known
what became of them in the 1940s. Scattered bits of information
hint at the endeavors of several other members of the group. Gabriel
Brown, for example, who performed with the "Bahaman Dancers" at
the First National Dance Congress and Festival in 1936, may have gone
on to play a supporting role in productions mounted by the Negro
Unit of the WPA's Federal Theatre Project, including *Turpentine* in
the summer of 1936 and *Haiti* in 1938. (Admittedly, there is no way
to verify that the Gabriel Brown whose name appears on these different programs was one and the same.)[5] The archive also reveals that
Lolita Griffith (sometimes listed as Lola Griffeth) left the troupe after

performing at the National Dance Congress and Festival to appear in Momodu Johnson's *Bassa Moona*, the "African dance drama" staged in December 1936 by the African Dance Unit of the Federal Theatre Project.[6] According to the *Afro-American Washington Final*, Griffith, who played the role of Voodoo Goddess in the production, was born in Central America and raised in the United States. "Miss Griffith," the paper went on to say, "danced with the well known Bahama Dancers for some time. She appeared as a feature dancer in the African drama, 'Almany Samory,' which was produced on Broadway and with Chief Mokity's dancing group at the World's Fair in Chicago."[7]

Besides signaling the renown of the Bahama Dancers, this description suggests that, like Hurston in Florida and other troupe members in New York, Griffith took advantage of whatever outlets she could find that provided institutional and financial backing for presentations of black diasporic folk dance. In the 1930s, broad interest in the folk multiplied the number of outlets available. But by the close of the decade, changing conditions—including the termination of the WPA's Federal Theatre Project (the entire Work Projects Administration was disbanded in 1943) and the increasing partitioning of dance genres—meant fewer such opportunities existed. World War II even helped put a halt to World's Fairs: none was held in the United States between 1940 and 1962.

Nonetheless, the influence of the stage work that Hurston and the Bahamian dancers carried out in the 1930s continued to be felt in ensuing decades. While Hurston was by no means the first to incorporate Afro-Caribbean material into a U.S. production, the years that followed the debut of *The Great Day* saw a marked increase in theatrical presentations that highlighted Caribbean idioms and themes, from Orson Welles's famed "Voodoo" *Macbeth* in 1936, to Katherine Dunham's full-length dance concerts in the 1940s and 1950s, to Sam Manning's 1947 *Caribbean Carnival*, choreographed by Pearl Primus and Claude Merchant and billed as "the first calypso musical ever presented," to Truman Capote's 1954 *House of Flowers*, which featured Pearl Bailey, Juanita Hall, Josephine Premice, and Alvin Ailey.[8] As she maintained in her autobiography, Hurston "felt the influence of [my] concert running through what has been done since," and she clearly believed she contributed to the spike in interest in Caribbean dance.[9] Given the sheer number of artists, cultural producers, and spectators who were exposed to the Fire Dance over the course of the 1930s, the role of Hurston and the Bahamian dancers in propelling this trend cannot be dismissed.

But the legacy of Hurston's folk concerts is discernible not only in the expanded prominence of the Caribbean in American performance; it also survives in the repertoire of classic African American modern dance choreographers. Choreographic echoes and continuities in approach can be traced from Hurston's program to several notable dance productions that followed in her wake. The Crow Dance section of the Fire Dance, for example, must have born a decided resemblance to Sierra Leone native Asadata Dafora's *Ostrich,* first performed in the United States in 1934, later re-created by Charles Moore, and at the turn of the twenty-first century, in the repertory of the Dayton Contemporary Dance Company.[10] Likewise, Hurston's jook scene unquestionably shared affinities with Katherine Dunham's *Barrelhouse Blues,* which was choreographed in the late 1930s and became part of her Americana compositions, as well as with Alvin Ailey's 1958 *Blues Suite.*[11] Beyond the common jook joint setting, all featured versions of black social dances like the Slow Drag and the Shimmy. The sequence of children's games that appeared in Hurston's revues, furthermore, later found resonance in Donald McKayle's 1951 *Games,* with its focus on urban schoolchildren and use of chanted rhymes. That is not to say that Hurston was the direct font for these other choreographic works. It is to suggest, rather, that her focus on the southern black and Africanist folk roots of mainstream American dance became one of the defining characteristics of black concert dance in the twentieth century. Although Hurston's particular emphasis on contextualizing rather than extracting the folk was not necessarily shared by the leaders of this choreographic tradition, there is no denying that her attention to folk sources had lasting reverberations in the concert dance field.

And what of the legacy of white investment in Hurston's folk material? Needless to say, the Fire Dance was neither the first nor the last black diasporic dance to capture the interest of Euro-Americans. While the category of the folk may not occupy the same place in the American imaginary today as it did in the 1930s, the celebrated "rawness" and exotic appeal of movement forms like break dancing and capoeira point to the enduring currency of black vernacular dances that originate outside the white mainstream. Indeed, white artists from Twyla Tharp to Madonna continue to mine black dance forms to lucrative effect in the concert hall, on Broadway, and in music videos.

Despite considerably greater awareness of the transnational circuits through which African-derived forms are transmitted and transformed, primitivist associations continue to cling to black dancing bodies. On the theatre stage, inside the dance studio, and in images that tend to grace advertisements for "ethnic" arts festivals, the black body still frequently functions as a sign of authentic Otherness.[12] Notions of "natural" black physical prowess, meanwhile, remain potent. Whereas the Fire Dance fascinated white artists and audiences in the 1930s, today the allure of the black body extends well beyond the theatre stage to permeate much of popular culture. The black body, as Brenda Dixon Gottschild notes, has "through dance, sports, fashion, and everyday lifestyle, become the last word in white desirability."[13] The contentious issues that inhered in enactments of black folk dance seventy years ago thus continue to play themselves out in American culture.

# Acknowledgments

This book came about only through the support of many people over many years. I begin by thanking two of my professors at Carleton College, Mary Easter and Kofi Owusu, whose encouragement led me to pursue American dance studies in the first place. The book started its life as a dissertation at Northwestern University, where I benefited from the direction and insight of numerous scholars and mentors. I owe the deepest debt of gratitude to Susan Manning, a truly exceptional adviser, whose continual guidance, careful readings, and across-the-board generosity over the last decade have meant more to me than I can say. The input of Sandra Richards and Adam Green likewise proved indispensable, and I am equally grateful to Madhu Dubey for believing in my project early on. Tracy Davis, Julia Stern, Billy Siegenfeld, Micaela di Leonardo, and Dwight Conquergood all shaped my thinking in crucial ways. I also wish to extend my heartfelt thanks to the members of my dissertation group, Deborah Paredez, Marta Effinger, and Hsiu-chen Lin Classon, who offered invaluable feedback and solace.

A number of grants and fellowships along the way facilitated the archival research for and writing of this book. Initial trips to various archives were made possible by an American Society for Theatre Research Dissertation Fellowship and a Northwestern University Dissertation Grant; a Dissertation Year Fellowship from Northwestern enabled me to complete the writing of the thesis. As I worked to transform the dissertation into a book, I received support from the W. E. B. Du

Bois Institute for African and African American Research at Harvard University. My genuine gratitude goes to the scholars I met there, especially to Henry Louis Gates Jr., Evelyn Brooks Higginbotham, and Karen C. C. Dalton for the warm reception they gave my work. A Woodrow Wilson Postdoctoral Fellowship in the Humanities at the University of California Humanities Research Institute afforded me time and the opportunity to interact with a remarkable community of scholars in the Global Intentions: Improvisation in the Contemporary Performing Arts resident group, convened by George Lewis, Susan Leigh Foster, and Adrienne Jenik. Academic Senate Research Awards from the University of California, Riverside allowed me to make follow-up trips to the archives, and a University of California President's Research Fellowship in the Humanities gave me precious time to complete the manuscript. The generous support of Dean Stephen Cullenberg of UC Riverside's College of Humanities, Arts, and Social Sciences helped make possible the publication of this book.

I would also like to acknowledge the following individuals and institutions for helping me navigate the archives: Kathleen Reich, head of Archives and Special Collections at Rollins College, whose extraordinary hospitality was singular; Frank Orser at the University of Florida's George A. Smathers Libraries; Patricia Willis at Yale University's Beinecke Rare Book and Manuscript Library; Anne Bailey and Wendy Hurlock Baker at the Smithsonian Institution's Archives of American Art; Robin Van Fleet at Howard University's Moorland Spingarn Research Center; Rosemary Hanes at the Motion Picture, Broadcasting and Recorded Sound Division of the Library of Congress, and Ann K. Hoog at the Library of Congress's Archive of Folk Culture; Beth Madison Howse at the Fisk University Library; Anthony L'Abbate at the George Eastman House; James Hatch at the Hatch-Billops Collection; and Marty Jacobs at the Museum of the City of New York. Many thanks also go to Robert Hemenway for opening up his personal Hurston files to me, and to Gay Clock for facilitating my visit to the University of Kansas.

I am extremely grateful to the friends, colleagues, and mentors who read and commented on portions of the manuscript. In particular, Susan Leigh Foster provided sage advice as I began revising the dissertation, and Susan Manning offered discerning feedback on a final draft of the manuscript. Special thanks go to Priya Srinivasan for her emotional and intellectual support and for the stimulating dialogue that has undeniably enriched this project, and to Eileen Hayes, whose close readings and exchanges over Thai food and e-mail propelled me forward. Deborah Paredez, Jacqueline Shea Murphy, Jayna Brown, Emory Elliott, and Susannah Quern Pratt all lent thoughtful feedback and/or general support. I also extend my profound thanks to the Hurston scholars whose work inspired my own and whose encouragement gave me confidence in the project: Cheryl Wall, Ann duCille, Valerie Boyd, Carla Kaplan, and Robert Hemenway. Chuck Kleinhans, Terry Monaghan, Nadine George-Graves, and Joel Dinerstein generously shared information about the Bahamian dancers with me. The backing of my colleagues in the Dance Department at the University of California, Riverside has been instrumental to this book's completion; my sincere thanks to all of them—Derek Burrill, Neil Greenberg, Wendy Rogers, Susan Rose, Anna Scott, Jacqueline Shea Murphy, Priya Srinivasan, Fred Strickler, and Linda Tomko—for providing me with an academic home. At the University of Minnesota Press, I have profited from the steady guidance of Richard Morrison, the always dependable assistance of Adam Brunner, and the meticulous copyediting of Mary Byers. I am particularly grateful to Carrie Mullen for her enthusiasm for this project before she left the Press. I am also indebted to the Press's superb manuscript readers, Brenda Dixon Gottschild, David Krasner, and especially Thomas DeFrantz, whose incisive commentary and willingness to discuss the book went above and beyond the call of duty. Any and all limitations of the book are wholly my own.

Finally, I can hardly find the words to express my gratitude to my parents, Susan and Richard Kraut, my sister, Naomi, and my brother, Jonah, without whose unconditional love none of this would have been possible, and to Dave Bjerk, for believing in me and giving me so much to look forward to.

# Appendix A. Chronology of Known Performances by Hurston and the Bahamian Dancers

**January 10, 1932**   Hurston presents *The Great Day* at the John Golden Theatre in New York.

**March 29, 1932**   Hurston presents *From Sun to Sun* at the New School for Social Research in New York.

**April 10, 1932**   Mura Dehn presents *The Wise and Foolish Virgins* ballet with Hurston's "Negro Chanters" at the Guild Theatre in New York.

**April 22, 1932**   Irene Lewisohn presents a dinner cabaret featuring Hurston's Bahamian dancers at the Vanderbilt Hotel in New York.

**January 20, 1933**   Hurston presents *From Sun to Sun* at the Museum, a new experimental community theatre, in Fern Park, Florida, with the backing of Rollins College.

**January 27, 1933**   Hurston gives a repeat performance of *From Sun to Sun* at the Museum.

**February 11, 1933**   Hurston presents *From Sun to Sun* at Recreation Hall on the Rollins College campus in Winter Park, Florida.

**March 1, 1933**   Hall Johnson's *Run, Little Chillun!* begins its four-month run at the Lyric Theatre in New York with dances "arranged" by Doris Humphrey. The "Dance of the Full Moon" that closes the first act is based on the same Bahamian Fire Dance cycle that served as the finale to Hurston's concerts and features several of her former dancers.

**March 5, 1933**   Hurston presents a special half-hour performance that includes the Bahamian Fire Dance for Ruth St. Denis and invited guests at the Museum theatre in Fern Park, Florida.

**April 8, 1933**   Hurston presents *From Sun to Sun* at the Orlando Municipal Auditorium in Orlando, Florida.

**August 18–19, 1933**   "Bahama Negro Dancers" perform with Helen Tamiris and the Philharmonic Symphony Orchestra at Lewisohn Stadium in New York.

**October 16, 1933**   Hurston presents excerpts from her folk concert on a mobile sound truck through the business district of Sanford, Florida.

**November 3, 1933**   Hurston presents *From Sun to Sun* at Sanford City Hall in Sanford, Florida.

**January 5, 1934**   Hurston presents *All De Live Long Day,* a revised version of her folk concert, at Recreation Hall on the Rollins College campus in Winter Park, Florida.

**April 1934**   Hurston presents a version of her folk concert with a cast of students from Bethune-Cookman College at the Daytona Beach auditorium in Daytona Beach, Florida.

**April 29–May 2, 1934**   Hurston and ten of her performers from Florida present excerpts from her concert, including the Fire Dance, at the First National Folk Festival in St. Louis.

**November 23–24, 1934**   Hurston stages *Singing Steel* at the Chicago Woman's Club Theatre in Chicago, Illinois.

**November 26, 1934**   Several Bahamian dancers (including Leonard Sturrup, John Dawson, and Joseph Nealy/Neeley/Neely) appear as "African Jumpers" in Donald Heywood's musical *Africana* at the Venice Theatre in New York. The show closes after three performances.

**May 19 and 24, 1936**   The "Bahaman Dancers" perform on the folk and theatre and variety programs of the National Dance Congress and Festival at the Ninety-second Street Young Men's Hebrew Association's Theresa L. Kaufmann Theatre in New York.

**September 24, 1936**   The "Bahama Dancers" perform in the *Cotton Club Parade* at the opening of the downtown Cotton Club in New York. They continue to appear at the Cotton Club in subsequent years.

**May 2, 1938**   Hurston presents a version of her folk concert at the Winter Park Woman's Club under the sponsorship of the Rollins College Folk Lore Group.

**May 6–8, 1938**   Hurston and a group of her Florida performers present concert excerpts at the Fifth National Folk Festival at Constitution Hall in Washington, D.C.

**January 25, 1939**   Hurston presents *The Fire Dance* at the New Auditorium in Orlando, Florida, under the auspices of the Florida Federal Writers' Project.

**Spring and summer 1939**   Two of the Bahamian dancers, Motor Boat and Stew Beef, perform as drummers at the Savoy Ballroom's exhibit at the New York World's Fair.

**February–March 1952**   Hurston presents five folk concerts around Eau Gallie, Florida.

## Appendix B. Known Members of the Bahamian Dancers between 1932 and 1936

Reginald Alday
Ruby Braithwith (or Braithwaite)
Gabriel Brown
Gwendolin Butler
James Cooper
John Dawson
Lolita Griffith (or Lola Griffeth)
Bruce Mabel Howard
Motor Boat (Leonard Sturrup or Stirrup)
Joseph Neeley (or Neely or Nealy)
John Oliver
William Polhamus
Carolyne Rich
Stew Beef (real name unknown)
Lias Strawn (real name unknown)
Alfred Strochan

# Notes

## Introduction

1. Program, *The Great Day*, 10 January 1932, John Golden Theatre, Prentiss Taylor Papers, Archives of American Art, Smithsonian Institution.

2. Although the term "West Indian" is a legacy of colonialism, Hurston used it regularly, and this book does not avoid it. Technically, the "West Indies" refers to the archipelago of islands that extend from Florida to South America and separate the Caribbean Sea from the Atlantic Ocean. The Greater Antilles, the Lesser Antilles, and the Bahamas all comprise the West Indies. I alternate between the terms "Bahamian," "West Indian," and "Caribbean."

3. Zora Neale Hurston, *Dust Tracks on a Road* (Philadelphia: J. B. Lippincott, 1942; repr., New York: HarperPerennial, 1996), 172.

4. Cora Gary Illidge, "'The Great Day' Heartily Received," *New York Amsterdam News*, 13 January 1932, 7.

5. Robert Hemenway, *Zora Neale Hurston: A Literary Biography* (Urbana: University of Illinois Press, 1977), 181. Like Locke, Brown was on the faculty at Howard University; it is possible that the two traveled to New York together. Brown praises *The Great Day* in his 1937 book *Negro Poetry and Drama*, though he misdated it to 1927. Sterling Brown, *Negro Poetry and Drama and The Negro in American Fiction* (New York: Atheneum, 1937; repr., 1969), 122.

6. "Announcing 'Great Day,'" program announcement, James Weldon Johnson Collection, Beinecke Rare Book and Manuscript Library, Yale University [hereafter Beinecke]. A handwritten note on the program announcement reads, "Dear Carl, Please let me see you in a close-up seat. Love, Zora."

7. Zora Neale Hurston to Thomas Jones, 12 October 1934, Thomas Elsa Jones Collection, Special Collections, Fisk University Library [hereafter Fisk].

A number of Hurston's letters have been published in Carla Kaplan's edited volume *Zora Neale Hurston: A Life in Letters* (New York: Anchor Books, 2003). The research for this book was conducted prior to the publication of Kaplan's volume. It is possible that Taylor, Homer, and Kahn attended *From Sun to Sun*, the second presentation of Hurston's concert, on 29 March 1932 at the New School for Social Research, rather than *The Great Day* premiere. According to the notes of Hurston biographer Robert Hemenway, the Harlem Renaissance writer Richard Bruce Nugent also attended Hurston's concert. Robert E. Hemenway Personal Files, University of Kansas, Lawrence [hereafter Hemenway Files].

8. On Hurston's theatrical endeavors, see Lynda Marion Hill, *Social Rituals and the Verbal Art of Zora Neale Hurston* (Washington, D.C.: Howard University Press, 1996); Kathy Perkins, ed., *Black Female Playwrights: An Anthology of Plays before 1950* (Bloomington: Indiana University Press, 1989); Barbara Speisman, "From 'Spears' to *The Great Day:* Zora Neale Hurston's Vision of a Real Negro Theater," *Southern Quarterly* 36, no. 3 (Spring 1998): 34–46; Sandra L. Richards, "Writing the Absent Potential: Drama, Performance, and the Canon of African-American Literature," in *Performativity and Performance,* ed. Eve Sedgwick and Andrew Parker (New York: Routledge, 1995), 64–88; Warren Carson, "Zora Neale Hurston: The Early Years, 1921–1934" (PhD diss., University of South Carolina, 1998); Rachel Rosenberg, "Looking for Zora's *Mule Bone*: The Battle for Artistic Authority in the Hurston-Hughes Collaboration," *Modernism/Modernity* 6, no. 2 (1999): 79–105; David Krasner, "Migration, Fragmentation, and Identity: Zora Neale Hurston's *Color Struck* and the Geography of the Harlem Renaissance," in *A Beautiful Pageant: African American Theatre, Drama, and Performance in the Harlem Renaissance, 1910–1927* (New York: Palgrave Macmillan, 2002), 113–30; and Elin Diamond, "Deploying/Destroying the Primitivist Body in Hurston and Brecht," in *Against Theatre: Creative Destructions on the Modernist Stage,* ed. Alan Ackerman and Martin Puchner (New York: Palgrave Macmillan, 2006), 112–32. Work that has highlighted Hurston's importance to the field of anthropology includes Gwendolyn Mikell, "The Anthropological Imagination of Zora Neale Hurston," *Western Journal of Black Studies* 7, no. 1 (1983): 27–35; John Dorst, "Rereading *Mules and Men:* Toward the Death of the Ethnographer," *Cultural Anthropology* 2, no. 3 (August 1987): 305–18; Deborah Gordon, "The Politics of Ethnographic Authority: Race and Writing in the Ethnography of Margaret Mead and Zora Neale Hurston," in *Modernist Anthropology: From Fieldwork to Text,* ed. Marc Manganaro (Princeton, N.J.: Princeton University Press, 1990), 146–62; D. A. Boxwell, "'Sis Cat' as Ethnographer: Self-Presentation and Self-Inscription in Zora Neale Hurston's *Mules and Men,*" *African American Review* 26, no. 4 (Winter 1992): 605–17; and Graciela Hernández, "Multiple Subjectivities and Strategic Positionality: Zora Neale Hurston's Experimental Ethnographies," in *Women Writing Culture,* ed. Ruth Behar and Deborah A. Gordon (Berkeley and Los Angeles: University of California Press, 1995), 148–65.

9. See Lynda Hill, "Staging Hurston's Life and Work," in *Social Rituals* (171–98) for a discussion of these productions.

10. Valerie Boyd, *Wrapped in Rainbows: The Life of Zora Neale Hurston* (New York: Scribner, 2003); Kaplan, ed., *Zora Neale Hurston: A Life in Letters*.

11. See Ann duCille, "The Mark of Zora: Reading between the Lines of Legend and Legacy" (*The Scholar and Feminist Online* 3, no. 2 [Winter 2005], http://www.barnard.edu/sfonline/hurston/ducille_02.htm), for the important insight that Hurston was "never quite as lost as legend would have it," thanks in large part to the disparate efforts of black women who took it upon themselves to circulate Hurston's written work, even when it was out of print.

12. Speisman, "From 'Spears' to *The Great Day*," 34.

13. Cheryl A. Wall, ed., *Zora Neale Hurston: Folklore, Memoirs, and Other Writings* (New York: Library of America, 1995). As Wall notes, the title page of the *Dust Tracks* manuscript contains a handwritten note that reads, "Parts of this manuscript were not used in the final composition of the book for publisher's reasons" (982).

14. Hill, *Social Rituals*, 201.

15. Hemenway, *Zora Neale Hurston*, 35. See, for example, Langston Hughes's reference to Hurston as a "perfect book of entertainment" in his autobiography, *The Big Sea* (quoted in Hemenway, *Zora Neale Hurston*, 64). Lynda Hill speculates that it was Hurston's commitment to the theatre that may have resulted in her contemporaries' emphasis on her "stagelike persona" over and above her serious intellectual pursuits (*Social Rituals*, xxiii).

16. Langston Hughes and Milton Meltzer, *Black Magic: A Pictorial History of the African-American in the Performing Arts* (Englewood Cliffs, N.J.: Prentice-Hall, 1967; repr., New York: Da Capo Press, 1990), 91; John O. Perpener III, *African-American Concert Dance: The Harlem Renaissance and Beyond* (Urbana: University of Illinois Press, 2001), 16–17. See also Wendy Perron, "Dance in the Harlem Renaissance: Sowing Seeds," in *emBODYing Liberation: The Black Body in American Dance*, ed. Dorothea Fischer-Hornung and Alison D. Goeller (Hamburg, Germany: Lit Verlag, 2001), 23–39.

17. The work of John Lowe, Nathan Huggins, and Barbara Christian all provides insight into the relationship between the image of the black female dancer and the trope of the primitive. See John Lowe, *Jump at the Sun: Zora Neale Hurston's Cosmic Comedy* (Urbana: University of Illinois Press, 1994); Nathan Huggins, *Harlem Renaissance* (London: Oxford University Press, 1971); and Barbara Christian, "The Rise and Fall of the Proper Mulatta," in *Black Women Novelists: The Development of a Tradition, 1892–1976* (Westport, Conn.: Greenwood Press, 1980), 35–61. For examples of such images, see Langston Hughes's "Jazzonia," reprinted in Alain Locke's *The New Negro* (New York: Albert & Charles Boni, 1925; repr., New York: Atheneum, 1992), 226; Jean Toomer's "Theater," in *Cane* (New York: Boni & Liveright, 1923; repr., New York: Liveright, 1975); and Claude McKay's "Harlem Dancer," *Seven Arts* 2 (1917): 741.

18. Lucien H. White, "The Great Day," *New York Age*, 16 January 1932, 7.

19. Hurston made this comment during a 1939 talk she gave at the annual fall meeting of the Carolina Dramatic Association in Chapel Hill, North Carolina, on building a "Negro Folk Theatre." Hemenway Files.

20. It is possible that Hurston's falling out with Langston Hughes over their failed collaboration on the play *Mule Bone* in 1930 also played a role in perpetuating Hurston's absence from the official dance record. Hughes's 1967 book *Black Magic*, a pictorial history of African Americans in the performing arts coauthored with Milton Meltzer, contains a chapter on "Dancers and Dancing" that references a number of Hurston's dance contemporaries, including Asadata Dafora, Katherine Dunham, Hemsley Winfield, Eugene von Grona, and Pearl Primus—but nowhere mentions Hurston. Hughes was not the first to script a history of black dance on the theatre stage (see, for example, Edith Isaacs's *The Negro in the American Theatre* [New York: Theatre Arts Books, 1947]), nor did he alone determine the course of African American dance historiography. Still, it is conceivable that he was cognizant of Hurston's folk concerts and chose not to document them.

21. Perpener, *African-American Concert Dance*, 18.

22. Zora Neale Hurston, "Spirituals and Neo-Spirituals," in *Negro: An Anthology*, ed. Nancy Cunard (London: Wishart, 1934), 359–61; repr. in *The Sanctified Church* (Berkeley, Calif.: Turtle Island, 1981), 79–84. See also Frank L. Hayes, "Campaigns Here for Negro Art in Natural State," *Chicago Daily News*, 16 November 1934, 27.

23. Thanks to Susan Manning for underscoring the relevance of this fact.

24. Brenda Dixon Gottschild, *Digging the Africanist Presence in American Performance: Dance and Other Contexts* (Westport, Conn.: Greenwood Press, 1996), 132.

25. Brenda Dixon Gottschild, *Waltzing in the Dark: African American Vaudeville and Race Politics in the Swing Era* (New York: St. Martin's Press, 2000), 4; Dixon Gottschild, *Digging the Africanist Presence*, 59.

26. See the March 2006 special issue of *Women and Performance: A Journal of Feminist Theory* (16, no. 1) on "Recall & Response: Black Women Performers & the Mapping of Memory," edited by Tavia Nyong'o and Jayna Brown, for a collection of articles that reconsider the politics of recovering black female expressive artists.

27. Alice Walker, "In Search of Zora Neale Hurston," *Ms.* 3, no. 9 (March 1975): 74+; Barbara Smith, "Toward a Black Feminist Criticism" (1977), repr. in *Within the Circle: An Anthology of African American Literary Criticism from the Harlem Renaissance to the Present*, ed. Angelyn Mitchell (Durham, N.C.: Duke University Press, 1994), 416–17.

28. For examples of the construction of Hurston as foremother in black feminist criticism, see Alice Walker, *In Search of Our Mothers' Gardens* (New York: Harcourt Brace Jovanovich, 1983); Marjorie Pryse, "Zora Neale Hurston,

Alice Walker, and the 'Ancient Power' of Black Women," in *Conjuring: Black Women, Fiction, and Literary Tradition,* ed. Marjorie Pryse and Hortense J. Spillers (Bloomington: Indiana University Press, 1985), 1–24; Dianne Sadoff, "Black Matrilineage: The Case of Alice Walker and Zora Neale Hurston," *Signs* 11, no. 1 (1985): 4–26; Michael Awkward, *Inspiriting Influences: Tradition, Revision, and Afro-American Women's Novels* (New York: Columbia University Press, 1989); and Cheryl A. Wall, *Women of the Harlem Renaissance* (Bloomington: Indiana University Press, 1985).

29. Michelle Wallace, "Who Owns Zora Neale Hurston? Critics Carve Up the Legend," in *Invisibility Blues: From Pop to Theory* (London: Verso, 1990), 175; Ann duCille, *The Coupling Convention: Sex, Text, and Tradition in Black Women's Fiction* (New York: Oxford University Press, 1993).

30. Madhu Dubey, "Gayl Jones and the Matrilineal Metaphor of Tradition," *Signs* 20, no. 2 (Winter 1995): 245. See also Daylanne K. English, "Somebody Else's Foremother: David Haynes and Zora Neale Hurston," *African American Review* 33, no. 2 (Summer 1999): 283–97.

31. Hazel Carby, "The Politics of Fiction, Anthropology, and the Folk: Zora Neale Hurston," in *History and Memory in African-American Culture,* ed. Geneviève Fabre and Robert O'Meally (New York: Oxford University Press, 1994), 28–44. See also Hazel Carby, "Ideologies of Black Folk: The Historical Novel of Slavery," in *Slavery and the Literary Imagination,* ed. Deborah E. McDowell and Arnold Rampersad (Baltimore: The Johns Hopkins University Press, 1989), 125–43.

32. This is not to say that all scholarship on Hurston falls into either the exalting or the skeptical camp. Barbara Johnson, Mary Helen Washington, Susan Willis, Eric Sundquist, Carol Boyce Davies, and Trudier Harris, to name a few, have all offered nuanced analyses of Hurston's representations of the southern rural folk. Their work portrays Hurston's evocation of southern vernacular culture as always part celebration and part critique and highlights her constant mediation and balancing of various positionalities. See Barbara Johnson, "Thresholds of Difference: Structures of Address in Zora Neale Hurston," in *"Race," Writing, and Difference,* ed. Henry Louis Gates Jr. (Chicago: University of Chicago Press, 1986), 317–28; Mary Helen Washington, *Invented Lives: Narratives of Black Women, 1860–1960* (Garden City, N.Y.: Doubleday, 1987); Susan Willis, *Specifying: Black Women Writing the American Experience* (Madison: University of Wisconsin Press, 1987); Eric Sundquist, *The Hammers of Creation: Folk Culture in Modern African-American Fiction* (Athens: University of Georgia Press, 1992); Carole Boyce Davies, *Black Women, Writing, and Identity: Migrations of the Subject* (London: Routledge, 1994); Trudier Harris, *The Power of the Porch: The Storyteller's Craft in Zora Neale Hurston, Gloria Naylor, and Randall Kenan* (Athens: University of Georgia Press, 1996). In the last few years, furthermore, several scholars have responded explicitly to Hazel Carby's 1994 essay "The Politics of Fiction, Anthropology, and the Folk: Zora Neale Hurston,"

in which she argued that Hurston's work throughout the 1920s and 1930s created "a discourse of the 'folk' as a *rural* people" that "displace[d] the migration of black people to cities" and was thus fundamentally romantic and ahistorical (31). John Trombold, David Nicholls, Leigh Ann Duck, and Tiffany Ruby Patterson have all sought to demonstrate the historically situatedness of Hurston's engagement with the folk. See John Trombold, "The Minstrel Show Goes to the Great War: Zora Neale Hurston's Mass Cultural Other," *MELUS* 24 no. 1 (Spring 1999): 85–107; David Nicholls, *Conjuring the Folk: Forms of Modernity in African America* (Ann Arbor: University of Michigan Press, 2000); Leigh Anne Duck, "'Go there tuh know there': Zora Neale Hurston and the Chronotope of the Folk," *American Literary History* 13, no. 2 (Summer 2001): 265–94; and Tiffany Ruby Patterson, *Zora Neale Hurston and a History of Southern Life* (Philadelphia: Temple University Press, 2005). Like these scholars, I seek to contest Carby's claim that Hurston turned her back on the transformations occurring to African American culture in the early twentieth century. An interrogation of her stagings of black diasporic folk dance illustrates that one of her primary concerns was to delineate the tangled relationship between mass urban culture, southern rural folk practices, and Caribbean expressive idioms.

33. Zora Neale Hurston, *Jonah's Gourd Vine* (1934; repr., London: Virago Press, 1987), 58–62.

34. See Zora Neale Hurston, *Their Eyes Were Watching God* (1937; repr., New York: Harper and Row, 1990), 133, 146, 147. Motor Boat and Stew Beef, two of the Bahamian dancers whom Hurston recruited for *The Great Day*, even appear as characters in the novel. In her article "Dance as Metaphor in Zora Neale Hurston's *Their Eyes Were Watching God*" (*Zora Neale Hurston Forum* 4, no. 2 [Spring 1990]: 18–31), Kariamu Welsh-Asante documents and examines "nine literal examples of dance" in *Their Eyes* (22).

35. For a discussion of Hurston's efforts to alter audiences' notions of black vernacular dance in *Color Struck, The First One,* and *Mule Bone,* see Anthea Kraut, "Reclaiming the Body: Representations of Black Dance in Three Plays by Zora Neale Hurston," *Theatre Studies* 43 (1998): 23–36.

36. Hurston, "Characteristics of Negro Expression," in *Negro: An Anthology,* ed. Nancy Cunard (London: Wishart, 1934); repr. in *The Sanctified Church* (Berkeley, Calif.: Turtle Island, 1981), 54, 55–56.

37. On "bodily writing," see Susan Leigh Foster, "Choreographing History," in *Choreographing History,* ed. Susan Leigh Foster (Bloomington: Indiana University Press, 1995), 3. Foster cites Roland Barthes as an inspiration for this notion. Paul Gilroy's *The Black Atlantic: Modernity and Double Consciousness* (Cambridge, Mass.: Harvard University Press, 1993) challenges dominant notions of the nation-state and racial purity by delineating a transnational tradition of intellectual and cultural exchange between Africa, the Caribbean, Britain, and the United States.

38. Richard Long, *The Black Tradition in American Dance* (New York:

Rizzoli, 1989); Lynn Fauley Emery, *Black Dance from 1619 to Today* (Palo Alto, Calif.: National Press, 1972; 2nd ed. Pennington, N.J.: Princeton Book Company, 1988). Susan Manning's *Modern Dance, Negro Dance: Race in Motion* (Minneapolis: University of Minnesota Press, 2004) also cites Hurston's staging of Bahamian folk dance (15, 76).

39. William Moore, "The Development of Black Modern Dance in America," in *The Black Tradition in American Modern Dance,* ed. Gerald Myers (Durham, N.C.: American Dance Festival, 1988), 15. See also Joe Nash, "Pioneers in Negro Concert Dance: 1931 and 1937," in Myers, *The Black Tradition in American Modern Dance,* 11–14.

40. See, for example, Brenda Dixon-Stowell [now Dixon Gottschild], "Black Dance and Dancers and the White Public: A Prolegomenon to Problems of Definition," in Myers, *The Black Tradition in American Modern Dance,* 20–21; Zita Allen, "What Is Black Dance?" in Myers, *The Black Tradition in American Modern Dance,* 22–23; and Thomas DeFrantz, "African American Dance: A Complex History," in *Dancing Many Drums: Excavations in African American Dance,* ed. Thomas DeFrantz (Madison: University of Wisconsin Press, 2002), 3–35.

41. This method of establishing a traceable tradition of African American dance by first positing African roots was later duplicated in published histories of African American dance by Marshall and Jean Stearns, Lynn Fauley Emery, and Jacqui Malone. See Marshall and Jean Stearns, *Jazz Dance: The Story of American Vernacular Dance* (New York: Schirmer Books, 1968); Emery, *Black Dance from 1619 to Today;* and Jacqui Malone, *Steppin' on the Blues: The Visible Rhythms of African American Dance* (Urbana: University of Illinois Press, 1996).

42. Significantly, Joe Nash's delineation of the "Pioneers in Negro Concert Dance" places Hall Johnson's 1933 Broadway success *Run, Little Chillun!* on the map of black concert dance's early years. Although the dances in this production were officially, as Nash records, staged by white modern dance choreographer Doris Humphrey, it was, by all indications, Hurston's choreographic treatment of the Fire Dance and members of her assembled troupe of dancers that were featured in Johnson's program. See chapters 5 and 6 for discussion of the Hurston-Johnson-Humphrey connection. In *Modern Bodies: Dance and American Modernism from Martha Graham to Alvin Ailey* (Chapel Hill: University of North Carolina Press, 2002), Julia Foulkes simultaneously grants and withholds credit from Hurston for her contributions to Johnson's musical: "In the fall of 1932, the noted African American musician and choir director Hall Johnson solicited choreographic help from Doris Humphrey for *Run, Li'l Chillun!,* a folk drama that utilized the work of the anthropologist and writer Zora Neale Hurston" (51). The continued identification of Hurston as anthropologist and writer elides her choreographic work even while acknowledging her influence. On the other hand, two dissertations written in the 1990s, Leah Creque-Harris's "The Representation of African Dance on the Concert Stage: From the Early Black Musicals to Pearl Primus" (PhD diss., Emory University, 1991) and Elgie

Gaynell Sherrod's "The Dance Griots: An Examination of the Dance Pedagogy of Katherine Dunham and Black Pioneering Dancers in Chicago and New York City, from 1931–1946" (EdD diss., Temple University, 1998), reclaim Hurston as a key figure in the evolution of a black concert dance tradition. Gaynell Sherrod designates *The Great Day* "the first musical to present authentic African-based dance materials on a concert stage in America" (267).

43. Hurston, *Dust Tracks*, 172–73.

44. In 1903, for example, Bert Williams and George Walker featured interpretations of African song and dance in their musical production *In Dahomey*. See Thomas Riis, ed., *The Music and Scripts of "In Dahomey"* (Madison, Wis.: American Musicological Society, 1996). According to Errol Hill, "The earliest known [theatrical productions] showing Caribbean influence were a score of revues and musical comedies featuring the multitalented composer, lyricist, playwright, and bandleader Donald Heywood," who was born in Trinidad. From 1923 to 1941, Heywood "was involved in nineteen full-scale musical stage productions and an original one-act sketch." Errol G. Hill, "The Caribbean Connection," in *A History of African American Theatre*, ed. Errol G. Hill and James V. Hatch (Cambridge: Cambridge University Press, 2003), 276. And as Irma Watkins-Owens notes, in 1926, Amy Ashwood Garvey, the first wife of Marcus Garvey, collaborated with Caribbean-born theatrical performer Sam Manning on a musical comedy titled *Hey, Hey*. Staged at the Lafayette Theatre, the play was "performed in Caribbean English" and featured dancing done to a calypso beat. In 1927, again at the Lafayette, Garvey produced a second musical comedy, *Brown Sugar*, which also featured Caribbean actors and eventually toured Panama and the West Indies. Irma Watkins-Owens, *Blood Relations: Caribbean Immigrants and the Harlem Community, 1900–1930* (Bloomington: Indiana University Press, 1996), 155.

45. Manning, *Modern Dance, Negro Dance*, xxi.

46. See Manning, *Modern Dance, Negro Dance*; Dixon Gottschild, *Digging the Africanist Presence* and *Waltzing in the Dark*; Foulkes, *Modern Bodies*; Perpener, *African-American Concert Dance*; and Mark Franko, *The Work of Dance: Labor, Movement, and Identity in the 1930s* (Middletown, Conn.: Wesleyan University Press, 2002). See also Jacqueline Shea Murphy, *The People Have Never Stopped Dancing: Native American Modern Dance Histories* (Minneapolis: University of Minnesota Press, 2007); Priya Srinivasan, "The Bodies Beneath the Smoke or What's Behind the Cigarette Poster: Unearthing Kinesthetic Connections in American Dance History," *Discourses in Dance* 4, no. 1 (2007): 7–47; and Yutian Wong, "Towards a New Asian American Dance Theory: Locating the Dancing Asian American Body," *Discourses in Dance* 1, no. 1 (2002): 69–90.

47. Locke to Mason, 31 December 1931, Alain Locke Papers, Manuscript Division, Moorland Spingarn Research Center, Howard University [hereafter MSRC].

48. Saidiya V. Hartman, *Scenes of Subjection: Terror, Slavery, and Self-Making in Nineteenth-Century America* (New York: Oxford University Press, 1997), 11.

49. Richards, "Writing the Absent Potential."

50. Foster, "Choreographing History," 4.

51. Jane Desmond, "Introduction," *Meaning in Motion: New Cultural Studies of Dance,* ed. Jane Desmond (Durham, N.C.: Duke University Press, 1997), 2.

52. Rose, "Black Texts/Black Contexts," in *Black Popular Culture,* ed. Gina Dent (Seattle: Bay Press, 1992), 223. Rose's call resonates with Linda Tomko's espousal of a "triangulated approach" to the analysis of dance, one that heeds the "at least three-way intersections among the ongoing practice itself; the individual biographies of practitioners and innovators; and the complex of social, political, and economic struggles to make meaning and wield power at particular historical moments." Linda J. Tomko, *Dancing Class: Gender, Ethnicity, and Social Divides in American Dance, 1890–1920* (Bloomington: Indiana University Press, 1999), xv.

53. Foster, "Choreographing History," 6.

54. James Wilkinson, "A Choice of Fictions: Historians, Memory, and Evidence," *PMLA* 111, no. 1 (January 1996): 86.

55. Houston A. Baker Jr., *Blues, Ideology, and Afro-American Literature: A Vernacular Theory* (Chicago: University of Chicago Press, 1984); Henry Louis Gates Jr., *The Signifying Monkey: A Theory of Afro-American Literary Criticism* (New York: Oxford University Press, 1988). As David Nicholls points out, other major studies of African American literary production, such as Robert Bone's *The Negro Novel in America* (New Haven, Conn.: Yale University Press, 1958) and Bernard W. Bell's *The Afro-American Novel and Its Tradition* (Amherst: University of Massachusetts Press, 1987), also employ the folk as an organizing trope (*Conjuring the Folk,* 4).

56. Diana Fuss, *Essentially Speaking: Feminism, Nature and Difference* (New York: Routledge, 1989); Barbara Johnson, "Response" to Gates's "Canon-Formation, Literary History, and the Afro-American Tradition: From the Seen to the Told," in *Afro-American Literary Study in the 1990s,* ed. Houston A. Baker Jr. and Patricia Redmond (Chicago: University of Chicago Press, 1989), 39–44; Kenneth Warren, *Black and White Strangers: Race and American Literary Realism* (Chicago: University of Chicago Press, 1993); duCille, *The Coupling Convention;* Carby, "The Politics of Fiction"; Madhu Dubey, "Narration and Migration: *Jazz* and Vernacular Theories of Black Women's Fiction," *American Literary History* 10, no. 2 (1998): 291–316; J. Martin Favor, *Authentic Blackness: The Folk in the New Negro Renaissance* (Durham, N.C.: Duke University Press, 1999).

57. Favor, *Authentic Blackness,* 5. The construction of a vernacular tradition, while celebrating writers like Hurston, has indeed entailed a corresponding derogation of African American writers who did not draw on vernacular modes. In *Workings of the Spirit,* for example, Houston Baker accuses novelists Jessie Fauset and Nella Larsen of turning their backs on a southern vernacular domain; their novels are thus deemed as less than authentically black.

Houston A Baker Jr., *Workings of the Spirit: The Poetics of Afro-American Women's Writing* (Chicago: University of Chicago Press, 1991).

58. DuCille, *The Coupling Convention,* 71. See Evelyn Brooks Higginbotham, "Rethinking Vernacular Culture: Black Religion and Race Records in the 1920s and 1930s," in *The House That Race Built: Black Americans, U.S. Terrain,* ed. Wahneema Lubiano (New York: Pantheon Books, 1997). Higginbotham observes that "blues culture, working-class culture, and 'blackness' have become virtually synonymous" (157).

59. Nicholls, *Conjuring the Folk,* 7.

60. Stearns, *Jazz Dance,* xvi, 32.

61. Katrina Hazzard-Gordon's *Jookin': The Rise of Social Dance Formations in African-American Culture* (Philadelphia: Temple University Press, 1990) examines African American "secular social dancing" without applying the terms "folk" or "vernacular." Her primary concern is not to identify the distinguishing stylistic qualities of this dancing but to shed light on the institutions in which it developed. Still, much like the Stearnses and Malone, Hazzard-Gordon begins her study with the Middle Passage and argues that "social dancing links African-Americans to their African past more strongly than any other aspect of their culture" (3).

62. McKayle, "The Negro Dancer in Our Time," in *The Dance Has Many Faces,* ed. Walter Sorell (New York: Columbia University Press, 1966), 187–92. As Susan Manning elucidates in *Modern Dance, Negro Dance,* the emergence of a white modern dance tradition in America rested on the assumption that Euro-American bodies could embrace black dance styles as source material.

63. See Dixon Gottschild, "Black Dance and Dancers and the White Public," Allen, "What Is Black Dance?," and Brenda Dixon Gottschild, *The Black Dancing Body: A Geography from Coon to Cool* (New York: Palgrave Macmillan, 2003).

64. John W. Roberts, "African American Diversity and the Study of Folklore," *Western Folklore* 52, nos. 2–4 (April–October 1993): 159.

65. See Regina Bendix, *In Search of Authenticity: The Formation of Folklore Studies* (Madison: University of Wisconsin Press, 1997), for an extremely useful comparison of the emergence of folklore studies in Germany and the United States. See also Simon J. Bronner, *Folk Nation: Folklore in the Creation of American Tradition* (Wilmington, Del.: Scholarly Resources, 2002).

66. While the terms "vernacular" and "folk" each carry their own complex history of usage, the two are often used interchangeably. In "African American Diversity and the Study of Folklore," for example, Roberts explains that the folk are generally considered to be those individuals in society who participate in processes of vernacular creativity.

67. Robin D. G. Kelley, "Notes on Deconstructing 'The Folk,'" *American Historical Review* 97, no. 5 (December 1992): 1403.

68. Robert Cantwell, *When We Were Good: The Folk Revival* (Cambridge, Mass.: Harvard University Press, 1996), 38.

69. Roberts, "African American Diversity," 158–59; Henry Glassie quoted in David Brody, "The Building of a Label: The New American Folk Art Museum," *American Quarterly* 55, no. 2 (June 2003): 258.

70. Fuss, *Essentially Speaking,* 90.

71. Bendix, *In Search of Authenticity,* 144.

72. In *Time and the Other: How Anthropology Makes Its Object* (New York: Columbia University Press, 1983), Johannes Fabian addresses the "persistent and systematic tendency to place the referent(s) of anthropology in a Time other than the present of the producer of anthropological discourse," a phenomenon he terms the "denial of coevalness" (31).

73. See Dubey, "Narration and Migration," and Nicholls, *Conjuring the Folk.* See also Renato Rosaldo, "Imperialist Nostalgia," *Representations* 26 (Spring 1989): 107–22, on the colonialist tendency of people to "mourn the passing of what they themselves have transformed" (108).

74. Dubey, "Narration and Migration," 295.

75. Steven Feld, "From Schizophonia to Schismogenesis: On the Discourses and Commodification Practices of 'World Music' and 'World Beat,'" in *Music Grooves,* ed. Charles Keil and Steven Feld (Chicago: University of Chicago Press, 1994), 284.

76. John Roberts's "African American Diversity" describes the difficulties American folklorists have had addressing the influence of diversity on vernacular creativity.

77. The folk are also frequently aligned with orality and opposed to the literary. See Susan Stewart's *Crimes of Writing: Problems in the Containment of Representation* (New York: Oxford University Press, 1991) on the constructedness of this opposition.

78. Zora Neale Hurston, "Go Gator and Muddy the Water," in *Go Gator and Muddy the Water: Writings by Zora Neale Hurston from the Federal Writers' Project,* ed. Pamela Bordelon (New York: W. W. Norton, 1999), 69. With its white protagonists, Hurston's 1948 novel *Seraph on the Suwanee* (New York: Scribner's, 1948; repr., New York: HarperCollins, 1991) further demonstrates her interest in exploring dimensions of folk life outside of African American communities.

79. Hurston, "Characteristics of Negro Expression," 56.

80. Hurston, "Proposed Recording Expedition into the Floridas," in *Go Gator,* 66.

81. Cantwell, *When We Were Good,* 38.

82. While the United States' fascination with African American folk expression dates back to well before the 1930s, evidenced in the nineteenth-century minstrel show's mimicry and mockery of slave culture, for example, scholars agree that "an array of efforts to embrace vernacular American culture . . . coalesce[d] powerfully during the Depression." Benjamin Filene, "O Brother, What Next? Making Sense of the Folk Fad," *Southern Cultures* 10, no. 2 (Summer

2004): 51. Growing acceptance for the anthropologist Franz Boas's notion of cultural relativism and a more inclusive concept of culture played a large role in propelling this trend. Often figured as the father of American anthropology, Boas presented a serious challenge to evolutionary beliefs in a fixed hierarchy of human stages of civilization, and in the 1930s, the work of many of his students—including Margaret Mead, Ruth Benedict, Melville Herskovits, and Hurston—increasingly reached mainstream audiences. See, among others, George W. Stocking Jr., "Franz Boas and the Culture Concept in Historical Perspective," in *Race, Culture and Evolution: Essays in the History of Anthropology* (Chicago: University of Chicago Press, 1982), 195–233.

83. See Carl Sandburg, *The People, Yes* (New York: Harcourt, Brace, 1936); Constance Rourke, *American Humor: A Study of the National Character* (1931; repr., New York: New York Review Classic Books, 2004); Langston Hughes, *The Weary Blues* (New York: Knopf, 1926) and *Fine Clothes to the Jew* (New York: Knopf, 1927); Sterling Brown, *Southern Road* (New York: Harcourt, Brace, 1932); Benjamin Filene, *Romancing the Folk: Public Memory and American Roots Music* (Chapel Hill: University of North Carolina Press, 2000); Cantwell, *When We Were Good*; Michael Denning, *The Cultural Front: The Laboring of American Culture* (New York: Verso, 1997); DuBose and Dorothy Heyward, *Porgy: A Play in Four Acts* (Garden City, N.Y.: Doubleday, 1927); Frederick H. Koch, *American Folk Plays* (New York: Appleton-Century, 1939); Marc Connelly, *The Green Pastures: A Fable* (New York: Farrar and Rinehart, 1929); Paul Green, *The Field God and In Abraham's Bosom* (New York: McBride, 1927); Carol Easton, *No Interruptions: The Life of Agnes de Mille* (New York: Da Capa Press, 2000); Foulkes, *Modern Bodies*; Ellen Graff, *Stepping Left: Dance and Politics in New York City, 1928–1942* (Durham, N.C.: Duke University Press, 1997); Perpener, *African-American Concert Dance*; Joyce Ashenbrenner, *Katherine Dunham: Dancing a Life* (Urbana: University of Illinois Press, 2002).

84. Cantwell, *When We Were Good*, 31.

85. Denning defines the Cultural Front as "the encounter between a powerful democratic social movement—the Popular Front—and the modern cultural apparatuses of mass entertainment and education" (*The Cultural Front*, xviii). The "left's discovery of American vernacular culture" arose not only from the general "proletarianization" of American culture at this time but also, as Robert Cantwell has argued, "from the failure of Soviet communism in the 1920s, with its sense of imminent worldwide economic collapse and its politicialization of all aesthetic expression, to create a workable native proletarian art" (*When We Were Good*, 91).

86. In 1930, for instance, Marc Connelly's Pulitzer Prize–winning play *The Green Pastures*, a dramatization of heavily stereotyped African American religious beliefs that featured an all-black cast speaking in southern dialect, became "one of the biggest hits of the decade." Allen Woll, *Black Musical Theatre* (Baton Rouge: Louisiana State University Press, 1989), 137.

87. Ray Allen, "An American Folk Opera? Triangulating Folkness, Blackness, and Americanness in Gerswhin and Heyward's *Porgy and Bess*," *Journal of American Folklore* 117, no. 465 (2004): 244. Additional scholarship on the place of the folk in the 1930s includes Warren I. Susman, "The Culture of the Thirties," in *Culture as History: The Transformation of American Society in the Twentieth Century* (New York: Pantheon, 1984), 150–83; Terry Cooney, *Balancing Acts: American Thought and Culture in the 1930s* (New York: Twayne, 1995); Filene, "O Brother, What Next?"; Denning, *The Cultural Front*; Cantwell, *When We Were Good*; David E. Whisnant, *All That Is Native and Fine: The Politics of Culture in an American Region* (Chapel Hill: University of North Carolina Press, 1983).

## 1. Commercialization and the Folk

1. Hurston to Hughes, 12 April 1928, Beinecke.

2. Hurston to Mason, 15 October 1931, MSRC; Hurston to Edwin Grover, 8 June 1932, Department of Special Collections, George A. Smathers Libraries, University of Florida [hereafter UFL].

3. Arthur Ruhl, "Second Nights," review of *The Great Day*, *New York Herald Tribune*, 17 January 1932, 11. Although, as suggested here, Hurston tended to use terms like "real," "genuine," "natural," and "original" more often than "authentic" to promote her concert and to signal its distance from other stage representations of black folk culture, I use "authenticity" throughout this chapter as an umbrella term encompassing all of these variants. These terms are not identical and carry slightly different connotations, but I find "authenticity" useful in that it brings together a host of Hurston's concerns about treatments of the folk. In particular, the sense that "authenticity" conveys of being uncommodified and uncontaminated by the commercial mainstream helps keep the focus on the paradoxes of Hurston's stage project.

4. Rena Fraden, *Blueprints for a Black Federal Theatre 1935–1939* (Cambridge: Cambridge University Press, 1994), 16.

5. E. Patrick Johnson refers to the "fallibility" of authenticity in *Appropriating Blackness: Performance and the Politics of Authenticity* (Durham, N.C.: Duke University Press, 2003), 16. The anthropologist James Clifford has contended that authenticity has "no essence except as a political, cultural invention, a local tactic." James Clifford, *The Predicament of Culture: Twentieth-Century Ethnography, Literature, and Art* (Cambridge, Mass.: Harvard University Press, 1988), 12. Regina Bendix's history of folklore studies contains the similar assertion that authenticity is "constructed and contingent, if not deceptive." Bendix, *In Search of Authenticity*, 8. See also Richard A. Peterson's study, *Creating Country Music: Fabricating Authenticity* (Chicago: University of Chicago Press, 1997), and David Grazian's *Blue Chicago: The Search for Authenticity in Urban Blues Clubs* (Chicago: University of Chicago Press, 2003).

6. Fraden, *Blueprints for a Black Federal Theatre 1935–1939*, 16.

7. Carby, "The Politics of Fiction, Anthropology, and the Folk," 31. Other scholars have situated Hurston's work in contrast to more specific commercial forms. In *The Hammers of Creation*, Eric J. Sundquist identifies the advent of recorded African American sermons in the 1920s and 1930s, part of the general rise of "race records" in that era, as a prime motivating factor for Hurston's inclusion of a sermon in her 1934 novel *Jonah's Gourd Vine* (79). John Trombold, meanwhile, writes that "the adaptation of minstrel routines for radio constituted the most extreme expression of the culture industry against which Hurston reacted as she sought out, perhaps paradoxically, genuine folkloric traditions." Trombold, "The Minstrel Show Goes to the Great War," 85–86.

8. Brian Carr and Tova Cooper, "Zora Neale Hurston and Modernism at the Critical Limit," *Modern Fiction Studies* 48, no. 2 (Summer 2002): 288.

9. Here I take issue with Carr and Cooper's contentions that Hurston stopped short of "claiming the authority to represent [folk forms like] spirituals authentically" and "resist[ed] the notion of authenticity altogether," for they fail to take into account the claims that undergirded and enveloped her revues ("Zora Neale Hurston and Modernism," 291, 300–301).

10. In *The Real Thing: Imitation and Authenticity in American Culture, 1880–1940* (Chapel Hill: University of North Carolina Press, 1989), Miles Orvell documents a shift in American culture at large from a nineteenth-century privileging of art that merely imitated familiar experiences to a valorization of "more 'authentic' works that were themselves real things" (xv). See also Walter Benjamin's famous 1936 essay, "The Work of Art in the Age of Mechanical Reproduction," in *Illuminations: Essays and Reflections,* ed. Hannah Arendt (New York: Schocken Books, 1968), and Susan Stewart, *Crimes of Writing: Problems in the Containment of Representation* (New York: Oxford University Press, 1991).

11. As literary scholar J. Martin Favor writes in *Authentic Blackness*, "African American social and intellectual history is replete with examples of the struggle over the definition of black identity and its corollary of authenticity" (2–3).

12. Saidiya Hartman's *Scenes of Subjection* provides a compelling discussion of the difficulty—if not impossibility—of disentangling the authentic and the counterfeit in slave performance. See also Jon Cruz, *Culture on the Margins: The Black Spiritual and the Rise of American Cultural Interpretation* (Princeton, N.J.: Princeton University Press, 1999), which connects white "discovery" of black music and the emergence of the concept of cultural authenticity with the abolitionist movement of the mid-nineteenth century.

13. See Robert Toll, *Blacking Up: The Minstrel Show in Nineteenth-Century America* (New York: Oxford University Press, 1974); Eric Lott, *Love and Theft: Blackface Minstrelsy and the American Working Class* (New York: Oxford University Press, 1993); and Brenda Dixon Gottschild, *Digging the Africanist Presence in American Performance.*

14. Quoted in Lott, *Love and Theft*, 115.

15. Not only did whites continue to "black up" on stage well into the 1930s,

and in film into the 1940s, but the actual minstrel show format remained in circulation for many years. See Michael Rogin, *Blackface, White Noise: Jewish Immigrants in the Hollywood Melting Pot* (Berkeley and Los Angeles: University of California Press, 1996). The persistence of the form is perhaps best demonstrated by the fact that, just five days before Hurston staged a version of her folk concert in Orlando in April 1933, an "Old Time Minstrel" show was given in the very same auditorium. Presented by the Orlando Male Chorus and sponsored by the Orlando Lions Club to raise money for the blind, the minstrel show included a "stately interlocutor," two end men who exchanged rapid-fire talk and jokes, tap dancing, and choral singing. According to the *Orlando Morning Sentinel*, a "large and appreciative audience" attended. "Minstrel Show Huge Success," *Orlando Morning Sentinel*, 4 April 1933, 2. The proximity between the two evidently led a journalist to misreport Hurston's revue as a minstrel show, suggesting the extent to which her project was haunted by the legacy of minstrelsy. Underneath the headline announcing Hurston's imminent "Negro Folk-Lore Concert" read the statement "Minstrel Show at Municipal Auditorium Will Feature Songs, Jokes and Dances of Real Negro Life." Most likely, the misidentification was the product of carelessness, for in the article that follows, the journalist makes a point of contrasting minstrelsy—which dealt in the "superficial and artificial"—with Hurston's "actual negro drama." "Negro Folk-Lore Concert to Be Saturday Attraction of Greater Orlando Movement," *Orlando Sunday Sentinel* and *Reporter Star*, 2 April 1933, 4B.

16. For a discussion of many of these changes and their effects on black musical culture in particular, see Kathy J. Ogren, *The Jazz Revolution: Twenties America and the Meaning of Jazz* (New York: Oxford University Press, 1989); William Barlow, *"Looking Up at Down": The Emergence of Blues Culture* (Philadelphia: Temple University Press, 1989); and Burton W. Peretti, *The Creation of Jazz: Music, Race, and Culture in Urban America* (Urbana: University of Illinois Press, 1992). See also Ann Douglas, *Terrible Honesty: Mongrel Manhattan in the 1920s* (New York: Farrar, Straus and Giroux, 1995).

17. David Krasner, *A Beautiful Pageant*, 223; Fraden, *Blueprints for a Black Federal Theatre 1935–1939*, 16.

18. Scholarship on the Harlem Renaissance includes Nathan Huggins, *Harlem Renaissance*; Arna W. Bontemps, ed., *The Harlem Renaissance Remembered* (New York: Dodd, Mead, 1972); David Levering Lewis, *When Harlem Was in Vogue* (New York: Knopf, 1981); Houston A. Baker Jr., *Modernism and the Harlem Renaissance* (Chicago: University of Chicago Press, 1987); and Favor, *Authentic Blackness*.

19. Speisman, "From 'Spears' to *The Great Day*."

20. Hurston, *Dust Tracks on a Road*, 104.

21. Hurston to Connie Sheen, 2 February 1926, UFL. Speisman also calls attention to Hurston's exposure to the Baltimore theatre scene, where she lived between 1916 and 1919 ("From 'Spears' to *The Great Day*," 15).

22. Many of these plays were only recently rediscovered thanks to the efforts of manuscript collector Wyatt Hourston Day and Library of Congress historian Alice Birney (Speisman, ibid.).

23. It appears that *Color Struck* was at least scheduled for production at one time. As Hurston proudly announced to the author Annie Nathan Meyer in late 1925, "The Negro Art Theatre of Harlem is fairly launched now and the first program will include my 'Color Struck.' I am hoping that you will find time to come. It will be near the end of the year, the presentation." Hurston to Annie Nathan Meyer, 10 November 1925, Hurston-Annie Nathan Meyer Correspondence, American Jewish Archives. Hurston may have been referring to the New Negro Art Theatre, a New York little theatre group organized and led by the African American choreographer and theatre artist Hemsley Winfield. I have uncovered no further evidence of plans for this production, nor have I found any documentation as to why it was canceled.

24. Zora Neale Hurston, *Spears, Zeta Phi Beta Ex-Ray* 1, no. 3 (December 1926): 9–12, Department of College Archives and Special Collections, Rollins College [hereafter Rollins]; Zora Neale Hurston, *Meet the Mamma: A Musical Play in Three Acts,* Music Division, Library of Congress [hereafter LOC]; Speisman, "From 'Spears' to *The Great Day,*" 36.

25. Eugene O'Neill, *The Emperor Jones,* in *The Emperor Jones, Anna Christie, The Hairy Ape* (New York: Vintage Books, 1972).

26. Zora Neale Hurston, *Cold Keener, a revue,* Manuscript Division, LOC, 62–63. Although portions of the play script are scratched out, Hurston clearly intended her Jones character as a satire of Marcus Garvey and his "Africa for the Africans" program. While the popular and ambitious Jamaican-born leader may have inspired O'Neill's depiction, Hurston's version made this correlation unequivocal. See Joel Pfister's description of Garvey as "the most publicized black 'emperor' in uniform in 1920" in *Staging Depth: Eugene O'Neill and the Politics of Psychological Discourse* (Chapel Hill: University of North Carolina Press, 1995), 129. In an unpublished 1928 essay titled "The Emperor Effaces Himself," Hurston derided Garvey for profiting from the money collected for his back-to-Africa movement. Robert Hemenway, *Zora Neale Hurston,* 37.

27. I use the term "signifying" in the sense that Gates outlines in *The Signifying Monkey*—through a process of repetition and revision with a critical difference.

28. Hurston to Hughes, 12 April 1928, Beinecke.

29. Zora Neale Hurston, *Mules and Men* (Philadelphia: J.B. Lippincott, 1935; repr., New York: HarperPerennial, 1990), 1.

30. See Zora Neale Hurston, "Dance Songs and Tales from the Bahamas," *Journal of American Folklore* 43, no. 169 (July–October 1930): 294–312.

31. Hurston to Thomas Jones, 12 October 1934, Thomas Elsa Jones Collection, Special Collections, Fisk University Library [hereafter Fisk].

32. Hurston, *Dust Tracks,* 279, 280.

33. See Rawn Spearman, "Vocal Concert Music in the Harlem Renaissance," in *Black Music in the Harlem Renaissance: A Collection of Essays,* ed. Samuel A. Floyd Jr. (Westport, Conn.: Greenwood Press, 1990), 41–54.

34. Mellonee V. Burnim, "Religious Music," in *African American Music: An Introduction,* ed. Mellonee V. Burnim and Portia K. Maultsby (New York: Routledge, 2006), 53, 61–63. My thanks to Eileen Hayes for bringing this essay to my attention.

35. Gilroy, *The Black Atlantic,* 89, 90.

36. Ibid., 91. For a survey of the concert spiritual during the Harlem Renaissance, see Eileen Southern, *The Music of Black Americans* (New York: W. W. Norton, 1997), 408–24. See also Paul Allen Anderson, *Deep River: Music and Memory in Harlem Renaissance Thought* (Durham, N.C.: Duke University Press, 2001), on Harlem Renaissance debates about the proper role and presentation of African American folk spirituals.

37. Hurston, "Characteristics of Negro Expression," 67.

38. Hurston, "Spirituals and Neo-Spirituals," 80. In "Religious Music," Burnim makes a similar—although less partisan—distinction between the "folk spiritual" that developed out of slavery in the late eighteenth century and the "arranged spiritual" that emerged following the Civil War (52).

39. Hurston, "Spirituals and Neo-Spirituals," 80. Lawrence Brown was a concert accompanist to Roland Hayes and Paul Robeson. Nathaniel Dett led Hampton Institute's touring choral group and edited a volume of spirituals: *Religious Folk-Songs of the Negro as Sung at Hampton Institute* (Hampton, Va.: Hampton Institute Press, 1927). John Work headed the music department at Fisk University and directed the Fisk Jubilee Singers.

40. See chapter 4 for further discussion of the vocal breathiness that Hurston identified as key to "Negro song," in contradistinction to the polish of white vocal art, and that she incorporated into her own concert.

41. Hurston, "Spirituals and Neo-Spirituals," 80. Emphasis in the original.

42. Johnson, *Appropriating Blackness,* 3.

43. Langston Hughes, "The Negro Artist and the Racial Mountain," *Nation,* 23 June 1926, 692–94. See Anderson, *Deep River,* for a discussion of the challenge Hughes and Hurston mounted to W. E. B. Du Bois's and Alain Locke's progress narratives about the development of black folk music (167–217).

44. David Krasner, *Resistance, Parody, and Double Consciousness in African American Theatre, 1895–1910* (New York: St. Martin's Press, 1997), 15.

45. On early black musical theatre, see Krasner, *Resistance, Parody, and Double Consciousness;* James Weldon Johnson, *Black Manhattan* (New York: Knopf, 1930; repr., New York: Da Capo Press, 1991); Thomas L. Riis, *Just Before Jazz: Black Musical Theater in New York, 1890 to 1915* (Washington, D.C.: Smithsonian Institution Press, 1989); and Allen Woll, *Black Musical Theatre.*

46. Stearns, *Jazz Dance,* 139.

47. Theophilus Lewis, "Survey of the Negro Theatre—III," *Messenger* 8, no. 10 (October 1926): 301.

48. Hurston, "You Don't Know Us Negroes," Lawrence E. Spivak Papers, Manuscript Division, LOC. A handwritten note on the manuscript, written for *American Mercury* magazine, indicates that this article was "killed" in 1934 for unspecified reasons.

49. Hurston, "Characteristics of Negro Expression," 63.

50. Woll, *Black Musical Theatre,* 110–12.

51. Hurston, "Characteristics of Negro Expression," 63–64. See John Perpener's work on Edna Guy for a vivid example of the hiring obstacles darker-complected performers faced in New York in the early decades of the twentieth century. Perpener, *African-American Concert Dance.* See also Dixon Gottschild, *Waltzing in the Dark,* especially 132–38.

52. See Zora Neale Hurston, *Color Struck,* in Perkins, *Black Female Playwrights,* 89–102. See also H. Lin Classon, "Re-evaluating *Color Struck:* Zora Neale Hurston and the Issue of Colorism," *Theatre Studies* 42 (1997): 5–18.

53. Hurston, "Characteristics of Negro Expression," 66.

54. The white producer George White, for example, claimed to have originated the Charleston. See Lynn Fauley Emery, *Black Dance from 1619 to Today,* 226. Chapters 2 and 6 give further consideration to what counted as choreography and the racial politics of artistic credit in dance.

55. Hurston, "Spirituals and Neo-Spirituals," 79.

56. Hurston to Charlotte Osgood Mason, 23 July 1931, MSRC.

57. Although Hurston reports to Mason in her letter of 23 July that the *Jungle Scandals* show "seems definitely settled," I have not been able to discover any additional information about the production. Hemenway indicates that Hurston's work on *Jungle Scandals* began after *Fast and Furious* closed and promptly "died a mercifully early death" itself, but I have found no corroborating primary documentation (*Zora Neale Hurston,* 176).

58. Hurston to Mason, 23 July 1931, MSRC. The production Hurston had in mind at the time of the letter was *Spunk,* a three-act bearing no apparent relation to her short story by the same name, which she eventually copyrighted in 1935. As the typescript housed in the Library of Congress's Manuscript Division reveals, *Spunk* contained several musical and dance numbers that were featured in *The Great Day* and *From Sun to Sun.*

59. Extant records indicate that Hurston first entered into a contract with the Fast and Furious Company, managed by Forbes Randolph, on 6 July 1931, in the capacity of "Actor." Compensation is listed as seventy-five dollars per week for each week of performance; no payment was made for the obligatory five weeks of rehearsal leading up to the musical's opening. Agreement between Fast and Furious Company, Inc., and Zora Hurston, 6 July 1931, MSRC. A second surviving contract between Randolph and Hurston is dated 28 August; here Hurston's services are listed as that of "author," which is defined as "Author

and/or Proprietor of a certain play or dramatic composition." The contract also indicates that Hurston was to be paid twenty-five dollars per week for each of four sketches she was to contribute to the play. Dramatic contract between Forbes Randolph and Hurston, 28 August 1931, MSRC.

60. Playbill, *Fast and Furious*, 7 September 1931, Brandt's Flatbush Theatre; playbill, *Fast and Furious*, 15 September 1931, New Yorker Theatre, Programs and Playbills, Manuscript, Archives, and Rare Books Division, Schomburg Center for Research in Black Culture, New York Public Library [hereafter Schomburg]; Arthur Pollock, "The Theaters," review of *Fast and Furious, Brooklyn Daily Eagle*, 16 September 1931, 23.

61. Pollock, "The Theaters."

62. Richard Lockridge, "Negro Revue Offered," review of *Fast and Furious, New York Sun*, 16 September 1931, 32, clipping, MSRC. See also John Mason Brown, "The Play," review of *Fast and Furious, New York Evening Post*, 16 September 1931, 10; Thelma Herod, "'Fast and Furious' A Review," *New York Amsterdam News*, 23 September 1931, 10.

63. Pollock, "The Theaters"; Wilella Walsorf, "Forecasts and Postscripts," *New York Evening Post*, 1 September 1931, 10; "Theatre News," *New York Age*, 3 October 1931, 6; 10 October 1931, 6. At the Lafayette, the show's two acts apparently ran independently, with the first act presented one week, the second act the following week.

64. Hurston, "Lawing and Jawing, a sketch," typescript; "Forty Yards, a skit," typescript, Manuscript Division, LOC.

65. Hurston, "Woofing, a sketch," typescript, Manuscript Division, LOC. Robert Hemenway also identifies "At Home in Georgia" as Hurston's (*Zora Neale Hurston*, 176).

66. Hurston to Mason, 14 August 1931, MSRC.

67. In the end, Hurston's compensation amounted to only $75, a far cry from the $525 she initially expected to receive. This too Hurston chalked up to "show business." Hurston to Mason, 25 September 1931, MSRC.

68. The behind-the-scenes talent was not exclusively black; at least one of the contributing authors, Allie Wrubel, was white. Hurston to Mason, 25 September 1931, MSRC.

69. "Theatre News," *New York Age*, 3 October 1931, 6. A major contributor to early black musical theatre, Johnson became renowned in the 1920s for conducting the *Shuffle Along* orchestra, for *The Book of American Negro Spirituals*, the collection of spiritual arrangements he compiled with his brother, James Weldon Johnson, and for his concert tours of traditional African American music.

70. Hurston to Mason, 23 July 1931, MSRC.

71. Hurston to Mason, 25 September 1931, MSRC.

72. Herod, "'Fast and Furious' A Review."

73. Ibid.

74. Ibid. However, the bigoted remark by *Evening Post* critic John Mason Brown that the "brown-skinned maidens" of the chorus line "have obviously been chosen for their disposition and not for their beauty" suggests that Forbes Randolph may have shunned the demand for what Hurston termed the "bleached chorus" ("The Play," 10). *Fast and Furious* also featured the work of Hemsley Winfield and Edna Guy, who had organized and performed in the "First Negro Dance Recital in America" just six months earlier. Their involvement in *Fast and Furious* attests to the limited opportunities for African American dancers at that time, for despite their eagerness to develop their work for the high art concert hall, financial exigencies made eschewing Broadway impractical. Both Winfield and Guy performed as actors in several vignettes in *Fast and Furious,* in addition to presenting solo dances that were part of their general choreographic repertories: *Madrassi Nautch,* in Guy's case, and *Dance of the Moods* in Winfield's. Hurston left no record of her estimation of their involvement in the musical. For more on the careers of Winfield and Guy, see Perpener, *African-American Concert Dance.*

75. Hurston to Mason, 25 September 1931, MSRC.

76. Ibid.

77. "Announcing 'Great Day,'" program announcement, Beinecke.

78. See chapter 3 for a more extensive discussion of Locke's role in *The Great Day.*

79. Program, *The Great Day.*

80. James Scott, *Domination and the Arts of Resistance: Hidden Transcripts* (New Haven, Conn.: Yale University Press, 1990), xii.

81. Ticket prices from *New York Evening Post,* 9 January 1932, 5.

82. "'Singing Steel' Plays Women's Club Fri.-Sat."; "'Singin' Steel' on Club Program"; "Zora Hurston in Show Friday"; clippings, UFL.

83. Frank L. Hayes, "Campaigns Here for Negro Art in Natural State," *Chicago Daily News,* 16 November 1934, 27.

84. "Wunsch's Class Hears Hurston," *Rollins Sandspur,* 16 November 1932, 1, Rollins.

85. "Negro Folk-Lore Concert to Be Saturday Attraction of Greater Orlando Movement." Although this statement is not directly attributed to Hurston, the reporter was no doubt responding to the advance publicity she provided.

86. Andrew Ross, "Hip, and the Long Front of Color," in *No Respect: Intellectuals and Popular Culture* (New York: Routledge, 1989), 70.

87. Ibid., 69.

88. The phrase "regime of value" is Arjun Appadurai's. See his "Introduction: Commodities and the Politics of Value," in Arjun Appadurai, ed., *The Social Life of Things: Commodities in Cultural Perspective* (Cambridge: Cambridge University Press, 1986), 3–63, for a discussion of the varying conditions under which economic objects are exchanged and circulated.

89. "Announcing 'Great Day.'"

90. Program, *The Great Day.*

91. "'Singing Steel' to Be Given at 11th St. Theater," clipping, UFL.

92. My thanks to Sandra Richards for first alerting me to this parallel. Toll, *Blacking Up,* 45, 50.

93. Roger D. Abrahams, *Singing the Master: The Emergence of African-American Culture in the Plantation South* (New York: Penguin Books, 1992), 143.

94. See Toll, *Blacking Up,* 198, 201.

95. Ray Allen, "An American Folk Opera? Triangulating Folkness, Blackness, and Americanness in Gershwin and Heyward's *Porgy and Bess,*" *Journal of American Folklore* 117, no. 465 (2004): 250.

96. As Regina Bendix succinctly puts it, "Once a cultural good has been declared authentic, the demand for it rises, and it acquires a market value" (*In Search of Authenticity,* 8).

97. Whipper appeared in numerous Broadway productions in 1932, and later helped Noble Sissle organize the Negro Actors' Guild of America. Bernard L. Peterson Jr., *The African American Theatre Directory, 1816–1960: A Comprehensive Guide to Early Black Theatre Organizations, Companies, Theatres, and Performing Groups* (Westport, Conn.: Greenwood Press, 1997), 145.

98. Lucien H. White, "The Great Day," *New York Age,* 16 January 1932, 7.

99. Review of *The Great Day, New York Sun,* 11 January 1932, 37; Oscar Thompson, "Music," review of *The Great Day, New York Evening Post,* 11 January 1932, 11; White, *"The Great Day."*

100. Cora Gary Illidge, "'The Great Day' Heartily Received," *New York Amsterdam News,* 13 January 1932, 7; "Rare Negro Songs Given," review of *The Great Day, New York Times,* 11 January 1932, 29.

101. *American Heritage Dictionary,* 4th ed., s.v. "interlocutor."

102. Toll, *Blacking Up,* 53.

103. Illidge, "'The Great Day' Heartily Received."

104. The master of ceremonies or emcee continued to be a common performance convention in productions throughout the 1930s. The Cotton Club revues, for example, relied on a master of ceremonies, as did the Apollo Theatre. See Constance Valis Hill's work on the Cotton Club in *Brotherhood in Rhythm: The Jazz Tap Dancing of the Nicholas Brothers* (New York: Oxford University Press, 2000). In addition, I am grateful for Kim Ellis's suggestion, made at the 1999 Black Theatre Network Conference in Winston-Salem, North Carolina, that Hurston possibly envisioned Leigh Whipper's role as that of a griot in the West African tradition of the performer-storyteller. The tension between these two interpretations—interlocutor and griot—is suggestive of the broader tension that exists between the stage conventions of minstrelsy and African diasporic practices.

105. "The Fiery Chariot" filled the spot where a "Conjure Ceremony" appeared on *The Great Day* program. As I will discuss in chapter 3, Hurston pulled the ceremony at the last minute.

106. Hurston, "The Fiery Chariot," typescript, Playscripts, Schomburg. Robert Hemenway mistakenly states that Hurston first wrote the play in 1933 (*Zora Neale Hurston,* 224). A second, apparently later script of the same skit is housed in the Department of Special Collections at the University of Florida's George A. Smathers Libraries. This version, which was included in Hurston's 1933 staging of *From Sun to Sun* at Rollins College, was evidently the one Hemenway examined. The tale also surfaces in Hurston's 1935 volume *Mules and Men.* And as both Hemenway and Adele Newson have pointed out, Hurston was probably already familiar with the story before formally collecting it. Hemenway, *Zora Neale Hurston,* 223–25; Newson, "'The Fiery Chariot': A One-Act Play by Zora Neale Hurston," *The Zora Neale Hurston Forum,* no. 1 (Fall 1986): 32–37.

107. In the 1931 iteration, the characters' names are John and Liza.

108. As the tale is told in Hurston's folklore volume *Mules and Men,* it is a part of the everyday activities of southern black workers. Instructed by their white foreman to head over to the sawmill, the men share stories of John as they slowly make their way to the next work site (69–72).

109. The content of "The Fiery Chariot" also picked up on the antagonism between the white boss and the black workers that Hurston introduced in the work section of her concert, to be addressed in chapter 4. As both Hemenway and Newson point out in their discussions of "The Fiery Chariot," enacted onstage, the presence of a figure covered in a white sheet surely evoked the Ku Klux Klan, a formidable presence in the 1930s. Thus, while the skit conformed to many white expectations about black behavior, it simultaneously featured the imagery of racism, extending Hurston's subtle yet undeniable critique of the white power structure that governed the workaday lives of the folk.

110. According to the surviving archival evidence, the only time Hurston omitted "The Fiery Chariot" from her program was in early 1934, when she produced a follow-up to *From Sun to Sun* at Rollins College in Winter Park, Florida. This version, *All De Live Long Day,* featured a one-act folk play called "De Possum's Tail Hairs" following the work section in the first act. Program, *Singing Steel,* 23 November 1934, Chicago Woman's Club Theatre, Archives and Manuscripts, Chicago Historical Society; program, *All De Live Long Day,* 5 January 1934, Recreation Hall, Rollins College, Rollins.

111. Hurston, "Spirituals and Neo-Spirituals," 80.

112. Press release, Rollins College News Service, January 1934, Rollins.

113. Program, *Singing Steel.*

114. On the Buck and Wing, see Stearns, *Jazz Dance,* 50; and Dixon Gottschild, *Digging the Africanist Presence,* 121. On the Shim Sham, see Stearns, *Jazz Dance,* 195–96. Constance Valis Hill provides the following description of the Shim Sham: "Created in the 1920s by Leonard Reed and Willie Bryant and also called 'goofus,' a one-chorus routine to a thirty-two-bar tune, with eight bars each of the Double Shuffle, Crossover, Tack-Annie, and Falling Off a Log" (*Brotherhood in Rhythm,* 299). Hurston had first tried incorporating Buck and

Wing dancing in her Orlando presentation of *From Sun to Sun*, where it appeared as "Happy Feet." Program, *From Sun to Sun*, 8 April 1933.

115. "Announcing 'Great Day,'" Beinecke.

116. As Hurston writes in *Mules and Men*, when she declares that she has "come to collect some old stories and tales," one of her subjects replies, "What do you mean, Zora, them big old lies we tell when we're jus' sittin' around here on the store porch doin' nothin'?" (Hurston, *Mules and Men*, 8).

117. Ronald Radano, *Lying Up a Nation: Race and Black Music* (Chicago: University of Chicago Press, 2003), 47–48. The title of Radano's book takes its inspiration from Hurston. Thanks to Eileen Hayes for suggesting the relevance of Radano's work here.

118. Chapter 4 provides an in-depth discussion of the distinctive features of Hurston's stage presentation of black folk idioms.

119. Ruhl, "Second Nights."

120. "Zora Hurston Gives Program," *Rollins Sandspur*, 19 January 1934, Rollins; Charles Collins, "'Singing Steel' Is Folklore of Negro Toilers," *Chicago Daily Tribune* 24 November 1934, 17. The *New York Age*'s Lucien White alone took issue with the self-proclaimed authenticity of Hurston's revue. He deemed the first-act sermon "too long drawn out to be authentic" and raised questions about Hurston's stated authority on the planned conjure ritual, remarking that "some of the native southerners present would probably like to know just where the 'conjure field' in which Miss Hurston spent so much time is located." He conceded, however, that the Crow Dance "had the earmarks of authenticity." White, "The Great Day."

## 2. Choreography and the Folk

1. Program, *The Fire Dance*, 25 January 1939, New Auditorium, Orlando, Florida, UFL.

2. Susan Leigh Foster, *Choreography and Narrative: Ballet's Staging of Story and Desire* (Bloomington: Indiana University Press, 1996), 295 n. 57.

3. Michael Huxley, "Some Historical Origins of the Choreographed Body as a Modernist Statement" (paper given at the Thirty-second International Congress on Research in Dance, 2–4 December 1999, Pomona College, Claremont, California, U.S.A., and published in the Congress Proceedings). As Martha Graham recalls in her autobiography, *Blood Memory* (New York: Doubleday, 1991), "I had never heard the word 'choreographer' used to describe a maker of dances until I left Denishawn," the early modern dance school and company in New York run by Ruth St. Denis and Ted Shawn from 1915 to 1932. "There," Graham goes on to say, "you didn't choreograph, you made up dances" (236).

4. Cynthia J. Novack, *Sharing the Dance: Contact Improvisation and American Culture* (Madison: University of Wisconsin Press, 1990), 23. See Amy Koritz's *Gendering Bodies/Performing Art: Dance and Literature in Early Twentieth-Century British Culture* (Ann Arbor: University of Michigan Press,

1995) for an illuminating discussion of the shifts in aesthetic ideology in England around the turn of the twentieth century and the gendered implications of those shifts in both ballet and early modern dance.

5. Susan Leigh Foster, *Dances That Describe Themselves: The Improvised Choreography of Richard Bull* (Middletown, Conn.: Wesleyan University Press, 2002); Ann Cooper Albright and David Gere, eds., *Taken by Surprise: A Dance Improvisation Reader* (Middletown, Conn.: Wesleyan University Press, 2003).

6. As Brenda Dixon Gottschild has noted, in the early-twentieth-century world of entertainment, where choreographers were known as "dance-directors," African Americans who performed that function "were not credited for their work but were looked upon as dispensable assistants to the white dance director." Dixon Gottschild, *Waltzing in the Dark*, 102. For additional examples of racialized allocations of credit in dance, see Constance Valis Hill, "Cabin in the Sky: Dunham's and Balanchine's Ballet (Afro)Americana," *Discourses in Dance* 3, no. 1 (2005): 59–71; Dixon Gottschild, *Digging the Africanist Presence in American Performance*; and Stearns, *Jazz Dance.*

7. Arthur Ruhl, "Second Nights," review of *The Great Day, New York Herald Tribune* 17 January 1932, 11.

8. As Kariamu Welsh-Asante argues in "Commonalties in African Dance: An Aesthetic Foundation" (in *Moving History/Dancing Cultures,* ed. Ann Cooper Albright and Ann Dils [Middletown, Conn.: Wesleyan University Press, 2001]), "There are no permanent stamps of the creators" in the oral tradition of African dance, "only the changing designs, rhythms, movements that change with the performers" (145).

9. Hurston, *Dust Tracks on a Road,* 279.

10. Mary Helen Washington, "Zora Neale Hurston: A Woman Half in Shadow," in *I Love Myself When I Am Laughing . . . And Then Again When I Am Looking Mean and Impressive: A Zora Neale Hurston Reader,* ed. Alice Walker (New York: Feminist Press, 1979), 20. Like Washington, a number of scholars have commented on the inconsistencies, reversals, and avoidance of self-disclosure in Hurston's autobiography. Among them are Nellie Y. McKay, "Race, Gender, and Cultural Context in Zora Neale Hurston's *Dust Tracks on a Road," Life/Lines: Theorizing Women's Autobiography,* ed. Bella Brodzki and Celeste Schenck (Ithaca, N.Y.: Cornell University Press, 1988), 175–88; Claudine Raynaud, "Autobiography as 'Lying' Session: Zora Neale Hurston's *Dust Tracks on a Road," Black Feminist Criticism and Critical Theory,* ed. Joe Weixlmann and Houston A. Baker Jr. (Greenwood, Fla.: Penkevill, 1988), 111–38; Françoise Lionnet, "Autoethnography: The An-Archic Style of *Dust Tracks on a Road,"* in *Autobiographical Voices: Race, Gender, Self-Portraiture* (Ithaca, N.Y.: Cornell University Press, 1989); James Krasner, "The Life of Women: Zora Neale Hurston and Female Autobiography," *Black American Literature Forum* 23, no. 1 (Spring 1989): 113–24; and Pierre A. Walker, "Zora Neale Hurston and the Post-Modern Self in *Dust Tracks on a Road," African American Review* 32, no. 3

(1998): 387–99. As Hurston's biographers have pointed out, *Dust Tracks* also suffered from editorial censorship. Hemenway, *Zora Neale Hurston,* 286–88; Boyd, *Wrapped in Rainbows,* 356–61.

11. Charlotte Mason made reference to disobedience on the part of Hurston's cast, and Hurston herself cited "back stage arguments, eternal demands for money, [and] a disturbance in my dance group" as contributing to her desire to leave New York after producing *The Great Day* and *From Sun to Sun* in the winter of 1932. Mason's notes on Hurston, 8 April 1932, MSRC; Hurston, *Dust Tracks,* 284.

12. While Katherine Dunham and Pearl Primus have typically been figured as the foremothers to a black concert dance tradition, John Perpener's *African-American Concert Dance* paints a more complex picture of the various artists who labored to forge a "high art" tradition of African American stage dance in the early twentieth century.

13. Michel Foucault, "What Is an Author?" in *Language, Counter-Memory, Practice,* ed. Donald F. Bouchard (1969; Ithaca, N.Y.: Cornell University Press, 1977), 115.

14. Ibid., 123, 125, 127.

15. Peggy Kamuf, *Signature Pieces: On the Institution of Authorship* (Ithaca, N.Y.: Cornell University Press, 1988), x. See also Martha Woodmansee, *The Author, Art, and the Market: Rereading the History of Aesthetics* (New York: Columbia University Press, 1994); and Rosemary J. Coombe, *The Cultural Life of Intellectual Properties: Authorship, Appropriation, and the Law* (Durham, N.C.: Duke University Press, 1998).

16. See, for example, Stearns, *Jazz Dance;* Paul Berliner, *Thinking in Jazz: The Infinite Art of Improvisation* (Chicago: University of Chicago Press, 1994); Malone, *Steppin' on the Blues;* and Valis Hill, *Brotherhood in Rhythm.*

17. Susan Foster, "Taken by Surprise: Improvisation in Dance and Mind," in Albright and Gere, *Taken by Surprise,* 3–4.

18. Hurston, *Dust Tracks,* 172.

19. Rosalind Krauss, *The Originality of the Avant-Garde and Other Modernist Myths* (Cambridge, Mass.: MIT Press, 1985).

20. Martha Woodmansee and Peter Jaszi, "Introduction," in Woodmansee and Jaszi, eds., *The Construction of Authorship: Textual Appropriation in Law and Literature* (Durham, N.C.: Duke University Press, 1994), 3. Emphasis in the original.

21. Hurston, "Characteristics of Negro Expression," 58.

22. Krauss, *The Originality of the Avant-Garde,* 160.

23. Doris Humphrey, *The Art of Making Dances* (New York: Grove Press, 1959), 46.

24. Randy Martin, *Critical Moves: Dance Studies in Theory and Politics* (Durham, N.C.: Duke University Press, 1998), 214.

25. Ibid.

26. Cora Gary Illidge, "'The Great Day' Heartily Received," *New York Amsterdam News*, 13 January 1932, 7; program, *The Great Day*, 10 January 1932, John Golden Theatre, Prentiss Taylor Papers, Archives of American Art, Smithsonian Institution.

27. Hurston to Annie Nathan Meyer, 10 November 1925, Zora Neale Hurston-Annie Nathan Meyer Correspondence, American Jewish Archives.

28. Hurston to Locke, 10 May 1928, MSRC.

29. Hurston to Hughes, 20 September 1928, Beinecke.

30. Rachel Rosenberg, "Looking for Zora's *Mule Bone:* The Battle for Artistic Authority in the Hurston-Hughes Collaboration," *Modernism/Modernity* 6 no. 2 (1999): 79–105

31. Ibid., 80.

32. Ibid., 82.

33. Hurston, "Go Gator and Muddy the Water," in Bordelon, *Go Gator and Muddy the Water*, 154.

34. I refer here to Gerald Davis's concept of an aesthetic community as a group of performers and audience members who share knowledge of the aesthetic codes governing a particular expressive form. Gerald Davis, *I Got the Word in Me and I Can Sing It, You Know: A Study of the Performed African-American Sermon* (Philadelphia: University of Pennsylvania Press, 1985), 30–31.

35. Charlotte Mason's legal control over much of Hurston's folk material, to be addressed in the following chapter, likewise must have fueled Hurston's appetite for authorial credit.

36. Hurston, *Dust Tracks*, 285. Although Hurston offers no details as to how the studio exchange came about, in a 2002 interview, Dunham recalled meeting Hurston at a cultural gathering for artists in Chicago. Katherine Dunham, personal telephone interview, 21 August 2002. In her biography of Hurston, Valerie Boyd reports that it was Dunham who threw a party in Hurston's honor (*Wrapped in Rainbows*, 261–62).

37. Hurston, *Dust Tracks*, 284–85, 173.

38. Hurston to Melville Herskovits, 30 July 1936, Northwestern University Archives.

39. Ruthe T. Sheffey, "Behold the Dreamers: Katherine Dunham and Zora Neale Hurston among the Maroons," *Trajectory: Fueling the Future and Preserving the African-American Literary Past, Essays in Criticism (1962–1986)* (Baltimore: Morgan State University Press, 1989), 186–87; Perpener, *African-American Concert Dance*, 136–37.

40. Herskovits to Hurston, 28 September 1936, Northwestern University Archives. For a fuller account of the Hurston-Dunham-Rosenwald connection, see my dissertation, "Re-framing the Vernacular: The Dance Praxis of Zora Neale Hurston" (Northwestern University, 2002).

41. Hurston to Herskovits, 6 April 1937, Northwestern University Archives.

42. Hurston to Herskovits, 30 July 1936, Northwestern University Archives.

43. Zora Neale Hurston, *Tell My Horse* (Philadelphia: J. B. Lippincott, 1938; repr., HarperCollins, HarperPerennial, 1990), 22–23.

44. Ibid., 23.

45. Hurston, "Thirty Days among Maroons," *New York Herald Tribune Weekly Book Report*, 12 January 1947, reprinted in *Kaiso! Writings by and about Katherine Dunham*, ed. VéVé A. Clark and Sara E. Johnson (Madison: University of Wisconsin Press, 2005), 272–73.

46. Herskovits to Hurston, 10 April 1937, Northwestern University Archives. Katherine Dunham also recalled feeling slightly competitive with Hurston, noting that she considered Hurston to be working in essentially the same field. The two crossed paths on numerous occasions, and according to Dunham, she periodically came across publicity for Hurston's theatrical productions while on tour with her own company. Katherine Dunham, personal telephone interview, 21 August 2002.

47. Herskovits to Hurston, 28 September 1937, Northwestern University Archives.

48. Hurston to Henry Allen Moe, 24 September 1936, Robert Hemenway personal files. Despite Hurston's assertion here, and a write-up in the *Rollins Sandspur* dated 10 October 1934, announcing "Zora Hurston to Join Chicago Civic Opera Company" (Rollins College Clippings), I have found no evidence that Hurston staged her concert in Chicago anywhere but at the Chicago Woman's Club Theatre.

49. VéVé Clark, "Performing the Memory of Difference in Afro-Caribbean Dance: Katherine Dunham's Choreography, 1938–87," in *History and Memory in African-American Culture,* ed. Geneviève Fabre and Robert O'Meally (New York: Oxford University Press, 1994), 188–204. See also Sheffey, "Behold the Dreamers," 193.

50. "Enthusiastic Response Is Given 'From Sun to Sun,'" *Rollins Sandspur,* 8 February 1933, 2, Rollins.

51. "Announcing 'Great Day,'" program announcement, Beinecke.

52. Hurston, *Dust Tracks,* 281.

53. Ibid. As Hurston reported to Hughes, she "collected 20 marvelous Bahamian songs and learned the two native folk dances" and "got 3 reels of the dancing too." Hurston to Hughes, 15 October 1929, Beinecke.

54. While several films taken by Hurston are currently held in the Motion Picture Division of the Library of Congress, I have been unable to locate the dance footage Hurston made while in the Bahamas. For a discussion of Hurston's extant research films, see Fatimah Tobing Rony, *The Third Eye: Race, Cinema, and Ethnographic Spectacle* (Durham, N.C.: Duke University Press, 1996), 203–11; and Elaine Charnov, "The Performative Visual Anthropology Films of Zora Neale Hurston," *Film Criticism* 23, no. 1 (Fall 1998): 38–47.

55. Zora Neale Hurston, "Dance Songs and Tales from the Bahamas," *Journal of American Folklore* 43, no. 169 (July–October 1930): 295; Hurston, WPA

interview by Carita Doggett Corse, Jacksonville, Fla., June 1939, sound recording, Archive of Folk Culture, LOC (transcribed in Bordelon, ed., *Go Gator*, 177);
Hurston, "The Fire Dance," in *Go Gator*, 153; program, *The Fire Dance*.

56. Hurston, "The Passing of a Day," typescript, MSRC. Believed to have
African antecedents, Jonkonnu was widely practiced in North America during
slavery. As Geneviève Fabre has pointed out, its many different spellings attest
to the indeterminacy of its origins as well as to its plurality of incarnations.
Geneviève Fabre, "Festive Moments in Antebellum African American Culture,"
in *The Black Columbiad: Defining Moments in African American Literature and
Culture*, ed. Werner Sollors and Maria Dietrich (Cambridge, Mass.: Harvard
University Press, 1994), 52–63.

57. For an image of the house headdress most frequently seen in relation
to Jonkonnu, see http://hitchcock.itc.virginia.edu/SlaveTrade/collection/large/
Belisario05.jpg. In her dissertation, "The Representation of African Dance on
the Concert Stage," Leah Creque-Harris also notes the resemblance between
*The Great Day* performers' attire and traditional Jonkonnu Carnival costumes
(47). During her 1943 interview with radio personality Mary Margaret McBride,
Hurston spoke of the "wonderful costumes" the Bahamians wore "when they
have their ceremonies, the Jonkonnu ceremony." Hurston, radio interview by
Mary Margaret McBride, WEAF radio, 25 January 1943, Motion Picture, Broadcasting, and Recorded Sound Division, LOC; rerecorded on the accompanying
audio CD to Lucy Anne Hurston and the Estate of Zora Neale Hurston, *Speak,
So You Can Speak Again: The Life of Zora Neale Hurston* (New York: Doubleday,
2004). A 1936 article in a Jamaican newspaper reported that during her earlier
visit to the Bahamas, Hurston had taken motion pictures "of the annual John-
nie Canoe Parade at Christmas time." "U.S. Woman Anthropologist on Hoodoo
Hunt in Jamaica," *Daily Gleaner* 24 April 1936, Hemenway files.

58. Hurston, "Dance Songs and Tales from the Bahamas," 294; Hurston,
"The Fire Dance," 153; program, *The Fire Dance*. In her autobiography, Hurston
cited the Congo as the third section of the Fire Dance (*Dust Tracks*, 281).

59. Nicolette Bethel, "Quadrilles, Polkas, and Fire Dances: Ring Games
and Round Dances in the Bahamas," liner notes, *Bahamas 1935: Ring Games
and Round Dances*, Deep River of Song, Alan Lomax Collection (Cambridge,
Mass.: Rounder Records, 2002).

60. At times Hurston also seemed to use the term "Fire Dance" and "Jumping Dance" interchangeably. Other sources on and descriptions of the Bahamian
Fire Dance include L. D. Powles, *Land of the Pink Pearl, or Recollections of Life
in the Bahamas* (London: Sampson Low, Marston, Searle, & Rivington, 1888),
148–49; E. Clement Bethel, *Music in the Bahamas: Its Roots, Development and
Personality* (master's thesis, University of California, Los Angeles, 1978); John
A. Lomax and Alan Lomax, *Our Singing Country* (New York: Macmillan, 1941),
79–93. Not surprisingly, the term "Fire Dance" applies to a number of African-
derived and Caribbean folk dances. Today, a Fire Dance is in the repertoire of

Najwa Dance Corps, a Chicago-based company that presents dances from West Africa, the Caribbean, and contemporary African American culture. See http://malcolmx.ccc.edu/najwa/default.asp.

61. Program, *The Fire Dance.*

62. Hurston, "The Fire Dance," 154.

63. Ibid.

64. Ibid., 155.

65. Ibid.

66. See Bethel, "Quadrilles, Polkas, and Fire Dances."

67. Hurston, "Dance Songs and Tales from the Bahamas," 295, 294.

68. Hurston, "The Fire Dance," 155. As Hurston explained in an interview, while the crow may have been sacred in Africa, the dance referred to "what we know in the United States as the buzzard." Hurston, in *Go Gator,* 174.

69. Hurston, "The Fire Dance," 156.

70. Hurston performed the Crow Dance song for Herbert Halpert during a 1939 WPA interview, singing both the solo and chorus parts and clapping her hands to accompany herself. Sound recording, Archive of Folk Culture, LOC; rerecorded on audio CD, *Speak, So You Can Speak Again.*

71. Hurston, "The Fire Dance," 156.

72. Hurston, "Characteristics of Negro Expression," 59–60.

73. Hurston, radio interview by Mary Margaret McBride; rerecorded on the accompanying audio CD to *Speak, So You Can Speak Again.*

74. Hurston, WPA interview by Herbert Halpert, Jacksonville, Fla., June 1939, sound recording, Archive of Folk Culture, LOC; also transcribed (with slight variations) in Bordelon, *Go Gator,* 171.

75. Hurston, *Dust Tracks,* 281.

76. "Mr. Motorboat's Last Stand: One of Ten Best of 1933," *Movie Makers* (December 1933), Composition Notebook, Theodore Huff Papers, Stills, Posters and Paper Collections, Motion Picture Department, George Eastman House. In 1933, Motor Boat appeared in a short film by John A. Flory and Theodore Huff, titled *Mr. Motorboat's Last Stand: A Comedy of the Depression.* A satire of the Depression, the film followed "Mr. Motorboat" as he went through the business of his day, attempting to find a livelihood. See Chuck Kleinhans, "Theodore Huff: Historian and Filmmaker," in *Lovers of Cinema: The First American Film Avant-Garde, 1910–1945,* ed. Jan-Christopher Horak (Madison: University of Wisconsin Press, 1995), 180–204. My thanks to Chuck Kleinhans for calling my attention to this film, and to Anthony L'Abbate, the stills archivist at the Eastman House, for searching through the Theodore Huff papers for references to Motor Boat. In addition to this intimation of Motor Boat's prior dance history, the late tap dancer and "vocal choreographer" Cholly Atkins cites Motor Boat as a "Hoofers Club character," suggesting his renown at what the Stearnses refer to as the "Harlem headquarters for tap dance." Cholly Atkins and Jacqui Malone, *Class Act: The Jazz Life of*

*Choreographer Cholly Atkins* (New York: Columbia University Press, 2001), 140; Stearns, *Jazz Dance,* 337.

77. Although historian Richard Long states that the group was from an island of Bimini and "had already acquired some reputation as performers," I have found no evidence that they performed as an ensemble before Hurston recruited them. Richard Long, *The Black Tradition in American Dance,* 40. Beyond supplying this statement, Long has likewise been unable to discover any particulars on the Bahamian dancers. Personal e-mail correspondence, 7 November 2000. Before his untimely death, historian and collector of African American dance materials Joe Nash also remarked on the paucity of information on the group. Personal telephone conversation, June 2000.

78. "Lias Strawn," like "Motor Boat" and "Stew Beef," may have been a nickname, for that name does not appear on the cast list of *The Great Day.*

79. As Nancy Foner documents in the introduction to her volume *Islands in the City: West Indian Migration to New York* (Berkeley and Los Angeles: University of California Press, 2001), the first mass influx of Caribbean-born blacks to the United States began around 1900 and peaked in the early 1920s, with New York City as the main port of entry (4).

80. John Lovell Jr., "Democracy in a Hit Revue," *Crisis* 54, no. 3 (March 1947): 76. It was far from uncommon for productions around this time to promote their African American performers as native Africans. As John Perpener notes in *African-American Concert Dance,* the female performers in Asadata Dafora's 1934 *Kykunkor* were African Americans with no prior training in African dance (108).

81. Hurston to Mason, 15 October 1931, MSRC.

82. Hurston, "Dance Songs and Tales from the Bahamas," 295.

83. Zora Neale Hurston, "Drenched in Light," in Hurston, *The Complete Stories* (New York: HarperCollins, 1995), 17–25.

84. A 1935 *New York Amsterdam News* article reported that Hurston "just thrills over doing the Lindy Hop." Thelma Berlack-Boozer, "Zora Neale Hurston as Author and Scientist," *New York Amsterdam News,* 6 April 1935, 9. On Hurston's love of dancing, see Boyd, *Wrapped in Rainbows,* 95, 193. Carita Doggett Corse, the director of the Florida Writers' Project, who hired Hurston in 1938, recalled in a 1971 interview with Robert Hemenway that Hurston was a "supurb [sic] dancer" and "had a wonderful sense of rhythm." Hemenway notes, interview with Corse, 25 February 1971, Hemenway files.

85. See Susan Leigh Foster's "Dancing Bodies," in *Meaning in Motion: New Cultural Studies of Dance,* ed. Jane Desmond (Durham, N.C.: Duke University Press, 1997), 235–57, on how bodily consciousness in several Western dance idioms is formed through the various methods and techniques that are used to construct the dancing body.

86. Thanks to Constance Valis Hill for helping me identify body-to-body transmission of movement material as a key constituent of choreographic labor.

87. Kate Ramsey, "Vodou, Nationalism, and Performance: The Staging of Folklore in Mid-Twentieth-Century Haiti," in Desmond, *Meaning in Motion*, 363. See also Joan H. Burroughs, "Haitian Ceremonial Dance on the Concert Stage: The Contextual Transference and Transformation of Yanvalou" (PhD diss., New York University, 1995); and Anthony Shay, *Choreographic Politics: State Folk Dance Companies, Representation and Power* (Middletown, Conn.: Wesleyan University Press, 2002).

88. Quoted in Anthony Shay, "Parallel Traditions: State Folk Dance Ensembles and Folk Dance in 'The Field,'" *Dance Research Journal* 31, no. 1 (Spring 1999): 43.

89. Hurston, "The Fire Dance," 153.

90. Hurston to Mason, 15 October 1931.

91. Hurston, "Characteristics of Negro Expression," 63–64.

92. Hurston to Mason, 15 October 1931.

93. Hurston, *Dust Tracks*, 284.

94. Hurston to Mason, 25 September 1931, MSRC; "Announcing 'Great Day,'" program announcement.

95. Hamilton Holt to Robert Wunsch, 29 January 1933, Rollins.

96. See Hurston's "Characteristics of Negro Expression" for her delineation of these black aesthetic principles.

97. Hurston to Mason, 6 January 1933 [misdated as 1932], MSRC.

98. Hurston to Edwin Grover, 1 February 1933, UFL.

99. "Wunsch's Class Hears Hurston," *Rollins Sandspur*, 16 November 1932, 1, Rollins.

100. Hurston to Thomas Jones, 12 October 1934, Fisk.

101. Hurston, *Dust Tracks*, 285.

102. Lloyd Lewis, "Worried 'De Lawd,'" *Chicago Daily News*, 26 November 1934, 27.

103. As Hurston scholar Pamela Bordelon reports, Hurston's niece, Winifred Hurston Clark, recalled "a number of young people coming to Eatonville and staying in local homes, and her aunt teaching them dances." Bordelon, *Go Gator and Muddy the Water*, 36. Hurston may have had additional reasons for casting young people for the Fire Dance performance. As Hurston's WPA supervisor, Carita Doggett Corse, told Bordelon, "Zora was smart enough to get young, slender fourteen-year-olds, tall and graceful, for her dances. So while they were true, the true motions of the spring rites, they were graceful and only slightly suggestive. In older people they would have been quite shocking" (*Go Gator*, 37).

104. According to newspaper accounts, Dobson was famous for his on-air performance as "Ol' Uncle Joe." "'Singing Steel' Plays Women's Club Fri.-Sat.," clipping, UFL; program, *Singing Steel*, 23 November 1934, Chicago Woman's Club Theatre, Archives and Manuscripts, Chicago Historical Society.

105. "Announcing 'Great Day,'" program announcement; program, *The Great Day*.

106. Program, *From Sun to Sun,* 29 March 1932, New School Auditorium, UFL.

107. Program, *All De Live Long Day,* 5 January 1934, Recreation Hall, Rollins College, Rollins. See also program, *From Sun to Sun,* 27 January 1933, UFL; program, *Singing Steel.*

108. Illidge, "'The Great Day' Heartily Received."

109. Ruhl, "Second Nights."

110. Hurston, *Dust Tracks,* 283.

111. See, for example, Wallace Thurman's fictionalization of Hurston as the consummate performer Sweetie May Carr in his novel *Infants of the Spring* (Hemenway, *Zora Neale Hurston,* 64).

112. Susan Meisenhelder, *Hitting a Straight Lick with a Crooked Stick: Race and Gender in the Work of Zora Neale Hurston* (Tuscaloosa: University of Alabama Press, 1999).

113. Mason's notes to Hurston, 8 April 1932, MSRC.

114. Program, *From Sun to Sun,* 27 January 1933.

115. By April 1933, when she staged *From Sun to Sun* in Orlando, reports establish that she had found "[a] group from the Bahama Islands" to appear in the Bahamian dance numbers." "All Florida Negro Cast to Sing and Dance in Famous Folklore Concert on Apr. 8," *Orlando Morning Sentinel and Reporter Star,* 26 March 1933, 3A.

116. Clipping, Luces Press Clipping Bureau, Thomas Jones Collection, Fisk.

117. Hurston, *Dust Tracks,* 284.

118. See, for example, Gordon, "The Politics of Ethnographic Authority"; Boxwell, "'Sis Cat' as Ethnographer"; and Hernández, "Multiple Subjectivities and Strategic Positionality."

119. "'Singing Steel' to Be Given at 11th St. Theater," clipping, UFL.

120. In her combined use of theatrical and anthropological methods, Hurston should be considered an important pioneer of performance ethnography as espoused and promoted by performance studies scholars like Victor Turner. See Victor and Edith Turner, "Performing Ethnography," *Drama Review: TDR* 26, no. 2 (Summer 1982): 33–50.

121. Gwendolyn Mikell, "Feminism and Black Culture in the Ethnography of Zora Neale Hurston," in *African-American Pioneers in Anthropology,* ed. Ira E. Harrison and Faye V. Harrison (Urbana: University of Illinois Press, 1999), 61.

122. Gordon, "The Politics of Ethnographic Authority," 162.

### 3. *Producing* The Great Day

1. Janet Wolff, *The Social Production of Art* (New York: St. Martin's Press, 1981), 137.

2. The original contract between Mason and Hurston, signed in December 1927, furnished Hurston with a motion picture camera, a car, and $200 a month to conduct research in the South for one year, with the possibility of extension.

It also stipulated that Hurston was Mason's "independent agent," hired to collect "music, folklore, poetry, hoodoo, conjure, manifestations of art, and kindred matters existing among the American negroes" on Mason's behalf, and barred Hurston from sharing this collection with anyone else without Mason's express written approval. Contract between Zora Neale Hurston and Charlotte Osgood Mason, 8 December 1927, MSRC. After the official contract expired at the end of 1929, Hurston secured another fifteen months of support, which lasted until March 1931. Although Mason then tried to terminate the arrangement, Hurston managed to obtain irregular payments until at least September 1932. See Hemenway, *Zora Neale Hurston*, 109–11, 175–84.

3. Hurston to Mason, 15 October 1931, MSRC.

4. The volume Mason helped finance was Natalie Curtis's *The Indians Book*. See Boyd, *Wrapped in Rainbows*, 157.

5. Hemenway, *Zora Neale Hurston*, 105.

6. As Langston Hughes wrote of Mason in *The Big Sea: An Autobiography* (New York: Hill and Wang, 1940), "She possessed the power to control people's lives—pick them up and put them down when and where she wished" (324). Hurston complained privately about Mason's tight hold, telling Hughes after several years under Mason's thumb, "I just feel she ought not to exert herself to supervise every little detail. It destroys my self-respect and utterly demoralizes me for weeks." Hurston to Hughes, n.d. [1929–30], Beinecke.

7. Hurston to Locke, 16 December 1928, MSRC.

8. James C. Scott, *Domination and the Arts of Resistance*, xii.

9. Kaplan, *Zora Neale Hurston*, 20.

10. Ibid. Emphasis in the original.

11. As Diana Taylor writes in *The Archive and the Repertoire: Performing Cultural Memory in the Americas* (Durham, N.C.: Duke University Press, 2003), performance constitutes both the "object/process of analysis in performance studies" and "the methodological lens that enables scholars to analyze events *as* performance" (3). She attributes the as/is distinction to Richard Schechner, *Performance Studies: An Introduction* (London: Routledge, 2002), 30–32.

12. I draw here on Diana Taylor's distinction between "the *archive* of supposedly enduring materials (i.e., texts, documents, buildings, bones) and the so-called ephemeral *repertoire* of embodied practice/knowledge (i.e., spoken language, dance, sports, ritual)" (*The Archive and the Repertoire*, 19). Taylor maintains that while the two modes do not exist in a binary relationship, it is essential to "take seriously the repertoire of embodied practices as an important system of knowing and transmitting knowledge" (26). See Richards's "Writing the Absent Potential," on the need to "write the absent potential into criticism; that is, in addition to analysis of the written text, one must offer informed accounts of the latent intertexts likely to be produced in performance, increasing and complicating meaning" (65).

13. Mason to Hurston, 20 January 1932; draft of letter from Mason to

Hurston, 8 April 1932, MSRC. Mason openly worried that *The Great Day* would develop a "jazzy quality" should it become commercially successful, and she abhorred Hurston's involvement in a dinner cabaret at the Vanderbilt Hotel. Mason, notes on "Zora," 17 January 1932; Mason to Locke, 17 April 1932, MSRC. Chapter 6 discusses Hurston's involvement in the Vanderbilt Hotel event, produced by the white theatre artist Irene Lewisohn.

14. See Jonas Barish, *The Antitheatrical Prejudice* (Berkeley and Los Angeles: University of California Press, 1981), on the history of moral prejudices against the theatre.

15. Thanks to Priya Srinivasan for pushing me to think through the implications of Mason's and Hurston's divergent stances on performance.

16. Ann Cooper Albright, *Choreographing Difference: The Body and Identity in Contemporary Dance* (Middletown, Conn.: Wesleyan University Press, 1997), 5; Jill Dolan, *Geographies of Learning: Theory and Practice, Activism and Performance* (Middletown, Conn.: Wesleyan University Press, 2001), 72; Diana Taylor, "Scenes of Cognition: Performance and Conquest," *Theatre Journal* 56, no. 3 (2004): 365.

17. Here I refer to what Peggy Phelan calls performance's "distinctive oppositional edge." "Without a copy," she writes in *Unmarked: The Politics of Performance* (New York: Routledge, 1996), "live performance plunges into visibility—in a maniacally charged present—and disappears into memory, into the realm of invisibility and the unconscious where it eludes regulation and control" (148).

18. See Philip Auslander's *Liveness: Performance in a Mediatized Culture* (New York: Routledge, 1999), which "problematizes the claim that performance's continued existence in spectatorial memory places it outside the reach of regulation by showing that memory is both policed by law and pressed into service as a mechanism for the enforcement of law" (113).

19. Later chapters examine how the Fire Dance that Hurston staged as the finale to *The Great Day* continued to circulate across the dance landscape and to influence performances (Diana Taylor's "repertoire") by other American artists.

20. Here I paraphrase Diana Taylor, who points out the converse—that "performance belongs to the strong as well as the weak" (*The Archive and the Repertoire*, 22). Accordingly, it is important to bear in mind that, while my focus is on Hurston's situation, Locke and Mason were also embodied subjects, and they, too, sought to use performative means to advance their respective agendas.

21. Hurston, *Dust Tracks on a Road*, 281, 283.

22. Hurston to Mason, 26 October 1931, MSRC.

23. Locke to Mason, 18 November 1931, MSRC.

24. Hurston to Mason, 24 November 1931, MSRC.

25. Wen Talbert's Choir had earlier appeared in the 1931 Broadway drama *Singin' the Blues* and later performed for the Federal Theatre Project's 1936 African dance drama *Bassa Moona*.

26. Hurston, *Dust Tracks*, 281.

27. Ibid., 281–82.

28. See chapter 4 for an exploration of how Hurston used performance to address the relationship between African Americans and Bahamian migrants. The transcript from a September 1974 interview with Ivy Jackman for the "Voices from the Harlem Renaissance" project, housed in the David Levering Lewis Collection at the Schomburg Center for Research in Black Culture at the New York Public Library, provides another example of tensions between West Indians and African Americans in Harlem in the early decades of the twentieth century. The transcript reveals that Jackman recalled "theatres with their anti–West Indian vaudeville acts—Franklin, Lincoln, and later the Lafayette." "The ones that got the greatest laugh," she comments, "were the ones with the West Indian jokes. I remember that distinctly. And it seemed to have made many of the West Indians bitter because they were not accepted."

29. Hurston, *Dust Tracks*, 282.

30. Hurston to Mason, 24 November 1931, MSRC.

31. See Rogin, *Blackface, White Noise*, and Harley Erdman, *Staging the Jew: The Performance of an American Ethnicity* (New Brunswick, N.J.: Rutgers University Press, 1997), for accounts of the Jewish presence in the early-twentieth-century American entertainment industry.

32. Hurston, *Dust Tracks*, 282.

33. Hurston to Mason, 15 October 1931; Hurston to Mason, 24 November 1931; Hurston to Mason, 16 December 1931, MSRC. It is not clear whether this last audition consisted of the attendance of Golden's secretary at a rehearsal as described by Hurston in *Dust Tracks* or a separate, more formal audition. Hurston's first contact with the producer John Golden came sometime in early October when he contacted her about serving as "Negro adviser" to a play he was scheduled to produce. As Hurston explained to Mason, "It was written by white people and they want to be sure of the atmosphere. I shall insist on program credit along with salary. If the play he is producing at present clicks, it will be about January before he does the Negro play. If it flops he will do the Negro play at once." Hurston to Mason, 15 October 1931, MSRC. This "Negro play" was *Savage Rhythm*, written by Norman Foster and Harry Hamilton. It opened on January 1 at the John Golden Theatre and ran for ten days, closing just prior to *The Great Day*. The connection to Golden eventually translated into the break Hurston needed to mount her production.

34. Locke to Mason, 16 December 1931, MSRC.

35. Arnold Rampersad, "Introduction," *The New Negro*, ed. Alain Locke (New York: Atheneum, 1992), xii.

36. Hurston, "The Chick with One Hen," typescript, Beinecke. Hurston intended the piece for publication in *Opportunity*, but the periodical refused to run it. See Hemenway, *Zora Neale Hurston*, 241–42. The term "abstifically" is Hurston's invention and also appears in her 1935 volume *Mules and Men*.

37. Lewis, *When Harlem Was in Vogue*, 154. For biographical information

on Locke, see also Michael R. Winston, "Locke, Alain Leroy," in *Dictionary of American Negro Biography*, ed. Rayford W. Logan and Michael R. Winston (New York: W.W. Norton, 1982), 398–404; and Jeffrey C. Stewart, "Introduction," in *Race Contacts and Interracial Relations: Lectures on the Theory and Practice of Race*, ed. Jeffrey C. Stewart (Washington, D.C.: Howard University Press, 1992), xix–lix.

38. Hurston, *Dust Tracks*, 282.

39. Locke to Mason, 12 November 1931; Hurston to Locke, n.d., MSRC.

40. Boyd, *Wrapped in Rainbows*, 229.

41. Mason's notes to Locke, 22 November 1931, MSRC.

42. Mason's notes to Locke, 29 November 1931, MSRC.

43. Locke to Mason, 18 November 1931, MSRC.

44. Locke to Mason, 16 December 1931, MSRC.

45. In a letter to Mason in late December, Hurston spoke of tardiness and no-shows among her cast members. Hurston to Mason, 21 December 1931, MSRC. Mason later held this against Hurston, contemptibly telling her, "I saw that you did not have leadership and that your people did not obey you." Mason's notes on Hurston, 8 April 1932, MSRC.

46. Mason's notes on Hurston, 17 January 1932, MSRC.

47. Only forty-two names appear on the cast list in the *Great Day* program. It is possible that some dropped out between the date of this letter and the program printing, or that not all cast members were identified on the program.

48. Hurston to Mason, 16 December 1931, MSRC.

49. Ibid.

50. Locke to Mason, 16 December 1931, MSRC.

51. Locke to Mason, 31 December 1931, MSRC.

52. Hurston, "In the Beginning: a concert of Negro Secular music," typescript; Hurston, "From Sun to Sun," typescript; Hurston, "The Passing of a Day," typescript, MSRC.

53. Hurston was later compelled to replace "The Great Day" with "From Sun to Sun" because of the white composer and producer Vincent Youmans's 1929 musical *Great Day*, which was set on a plantation in New Orleans and featured blackface comedy routines by Flournoy Miller and Aubrey Lyles. A note dictated by Mason in January 1932 includes the instruction to "show Paul [Chapin] . . . the letter enclosure from Vincent Youmans about use of name 'Great Day.'" Mason, notes on Hurston, "Agreement with Zora," 17 January 1932, MSRC.

54. Locke to Mason, 16 December 1931, MSRC.

55. Hurston to Mason, 21 December 1931, MSRC.

56. As Hurston presciently complained to Langston Hughes in 1929, Locke "wants to autograph all successes." Hurston to Hughes, n.d. [1929], Beinecke.

57. Locke to Mason, 5 January 1932 [misdated as 1931], MSRC.

58. Mason's notes to Locke, 8 January 1932, MSRC.

59. As Hurston writes in *Mules and Men*, "The Negro, in spite of his open-

faced laughter, his seeming acquiescence, is particularly evasive. You see we are a polite people and we do not say to our questioner, 'Get out of here!' We smile and tell him or her something that satisfies the white person because, knowing so little about us, he doesn't know what he is missing. The Indian resists curiosity by a stony silence. The Negro offers a feather-bed resistance. That is, we let the probe enter, but it never comes out. It gets smothered under a lot of laughter and pleasantries." Zora Neale Hurston, *Mules and Men*, 2–3. Carla Kaplan describes "feather-bed resistance" as "deception necessitated by social inequality" (*A Life in Letters*, 21).

60. Locke to Mason, 10 January 1932, MSRC.

61. Mason's notes to Locke, 10 January 1932, MSRC.

62. Zora Neale Hurston, "From Sun to Sun," typescript; Zora Neale Hurston, "The Passing of a Day," typescript, MSRC. The program announcement for *The Great Day* promoted the "CONJURE RITUAL" as one of the principal attractions of the concert, declaring it "authentic in every detail, and filled with weird, impressive rites." "Announcing 'Great Day,'" program announcement, Beinecke.

63. See, for example, Hurston's 1928 letter to Langston Hughes, in which she declares, "Oh, honey, I have the most marvellous ceremony. The dance of the nine snakes! Just you wait till you see that." Hurston to Hughes, 22 November 1928, Beinecke. Hurston incorporated just such a ceremony into *Mules and Men*, her written volume of folklore (215–17). On Hurston's intensive conjure study, see Boyd, *Wrapped in Rainbows*, 175–84.

64. Mason's notes to Locke, 10 January 1932, MSRC.

65. Ruhl, "Second Nights." *Savage Rhythm* told the story of a Harlem singer who returns to the South and discovers she has inherited her family's conjuring powers. The set for *Savage Rhythm*, which included moss-hung trees, doubled as the backdrop for *The Great Day*—a money-saving concession on Hurston's part.

66. Mason's notes to Hurston, 17 January 1932, MSRC.

67. Mason to Hurston, 20 January 1932, MSRC.

68. Archival evidence suggests that Hurston contemplated staging the Conjure Ceremony for a later performance at the National Folk Festival in St. Louis, although she may ultimately have decided against it. M. W. Childs, "Native America—In Song, Dance and Drama," *St. Louis Post-Dispatch*, Sunday magazine, 25 March 1934, 4.

69. Mason's notes to Locke, 10 January 1932, MSRC.

70. Chapter 6 recounts the use others made of Hurston's folk material subsequent to *The Great Day*.

71. Ruhl, "Second Nights."

72. A review in the *New York Evening Post* confirms that Whipper introduced Hurston to the audience. Oscar Thompson, "Music."

73. Hurston, *Dust Tracks*, 283.

74. Locke to Mason, 10 January 1932, MSRC.

75. Mason's notes, 10 January 1932, MSRC. A note in the *Great Day* program

officially acknowledged the "spiritual and material support from Mrs. R. Osgood Mason of New York" for the collecting that made the concert possible.

76. Hurston to Mason, 14 January 1932, MSRC.

77. Boyd, *Wrapped in Rainbows*, 232.

78. Hemenway, *Zora Neale Hurston*, 181.

79. Contract between Mason and Hurston, 20 January 1932, MSRC.

80. Ibid.

81. Hurston, *Dust Tracks*, 158.

82. Hurston to Mason, 19 March 1932, MSRC.

83. Locke to Mason, Easter Monday [28 March 1932], MSRC; Mason to Hurston, 8 April 1932, MSRC.

84. Hurston to Mason, 4 April 1932, MSRC.

85. Mason to Hurston, 8 April 1932, MSRC.

86. Hurston to Mason, 4 April 1932, MSRC.

87. See Meisenhelder, *Hitting a Straight Lick with a Crooked Stick*, 17.

88. Draft of letter from Mason to Hurston, 8 April 1932, MSRC.

89. See, for example, Meisenhelder, *Hitting a Straight Lick with a Crooked Stick;* Deborah G. Plant, *Every Tub Must Sit on Its Own Bottom: The Philosophy and Politics of Zora Neale Hurston* (Urbana: University of Illinois Press, 1995); Lowe, *Jump at the Sun.*

### 4. Hurston's Embodied Theory of the Folk

1. Hurston, *Dust Tracks on a Road*, 172.

2. Barbara Christian, "The Race for Theory," in *Within the Circle: An Anthology of African American Literary Criticism from the Harlem Renaissance to the Present*, ed. Angela Mitchell (Durham, N.C.: Duke University Press, 1994), 349.

3. The following reconstruction is based on *The Great Day* program and surviving typescripts for the concert, as well as information garnered from some of Hurston's interviews and published writings. Hurston's subsequent concerts, including *From Sun to Sun, All De Live Long Day,* and *Singing Steel,* adhered to a nearly identical narrative structure.

4. Hurston, "From Sun to Sun," typescript, MSRC. As Valerie Boyd discloses in her biography, Hurston had an intense love affair with Percival McGuire Punter, a graduate student at Columbia University who possessed some musical talent. He eventually became the model for Tea Cake in *Their Eyes Were Watching God.* See Boyd, *Wrapped in Rainbows*, 271–75, 303.

5. Hurston, "From Sun to Sun," typescript; Hurston, "The Passing of a Day," typescript, MSRC.

6. Although one review described this section as "a quaint bit done by black children and their mother," it is unclear whether *The Great Day* cast included actual children or whether adult cast members played the parts of children. Ruhl, "Second Nights."

7. The "Conjure Ceremony" that precedes "In the Palm Woods" on the *Great Day* program was never actually performed (see chapter 3).

8. Hurston, "The Fire Dance," in *Go Gator and Muddy the Water*, 154, 155; Hurston, "Dance Songs and Tales from the Bahamas," *Journal of American Folklore* 43 (1930): 295; Hurston, "Other Negro Folklore Influences," in *Go Gator*, 90–91.

9. Although only the "Deep River" spiritual appears under the Group Finale heading on *The Great Day* program, Robert Hemenway's interviews with performers and audience members establish that the blues song was performed in counterpoint. Robert Hemenway, *Zora Neale Hurston*, 180; Hemenway Files.

10. Thompson, "Music"; John Martin, "Rare Negro Songs Given," *New York Times*, 11 January 1932, 29; Illidge, "'The Great Day' Heartily Received"; Ruhl, "Second Nights."

11. Hans Robert Jauss, *Toward an Aesthetic of Reception*, trans. Timothy Bahti (Minneapolis: University of Minnesota Press, 1982), 41.

12. As Allen Woll notes, eleven black musicals appeared between 1930 and 1932, though not all could be considered successful. Woll, *Black Musical Theatre*, 135–36.

13. Ibid., 110. See also Krasner, *A Beautiful Pageant*, 260–61.

14. Woll, *Black Musical Theatre*, 156; Bernard L. Peterson Jr., *A Century of Musicals in Black and White: An Encyclopedia of Musical Stage Works By, About, or Involving African Americans* (Westport, Conn.: Greenwood Press, 1993), 154. *The Green Pastures* was also made into a film in 1936.

15. Brown, *Negro Poetry and Drama*, 122.

16. Hurston, *Dust Tracks*, 283.

17. Hurston, *Mules and Men*, 1.

18. Patterson, *Zora Neale Hurston*, 11.

19. Hurston, "From Sun to Sun," typescript.

20. Hurston, *Mules and Men*, 67.

21. Hurston, WPA interview by Herbert Halpert, Jacksonville, Fla., June 1939, sound recording, Archive of Folk Culture, LOC. Also transcribed in Bordelon, *Go Gator*, 160.

22. The version of "Oh, Lulu!" recorded here is taken from Hurston's 1934 novel *Jonah's Gourd Vine*, 172. The song also appears in her 1935 folklore volume, *Mules and Men* (262–63), and in *Go Gator* (159). While the title of the song given in these other sources is "Goin' to See My Long-haired Babe" rather than "Oh, Lulu!," the lyrics make clear that the two were one and the same.

23. See Hurston, *Jonah's Gourd Vine*, 171–72; Hurston, *Mules and Men*, 265–66; and Bordelon, *Go Gator*, 161–62.

24. Hurston, "The Passing of a Day," typescript.

25. Hurston performed this role herself in a later production of the concert. Program, *Singing Steel*, 23 November 1934, Chicago Woman's Club Theatre, Archives and Manuscripts, Chicago Historical Society.

26. Earlier stage directions stated that three of the men grabbed their guitars as they left their shacks for the rail in the morning. Hurston, "The Passing of a Day," typescript.

27. Ibid.

28. Hurston, *Mules and Men*, 55.

29. David G. Nicholls, "Migrant Labor, Folklore, and Resistance in Hurston's Polk County: Reframing *Mules and Men*," *African American Review* 33, no. 3 (Fall 1999): 471. Nicholls also provides a useful discussion of how work stoppage functions as a mode of resistance for the African American workers in Hurston's *Mules and Men.*

30. Hurston, *Mules and Men*, 248.

31. Hurston, "The Passing of a Day," typescript.

32. Robin D. G. Kelley, *Race Rebels: Culture, Politics, and the Black Working Class* (New York: Free Press, 1994), 45.

33. Among the many scholars who have addressed the correspondence between work and black expressive practices are James Weldon Johnson, "Preface" to *The Books of American Negro Spirituals* (New York: Viking Press, 1925); Lawrence Levine, *Black Culture and Black Consciousness: Afro-American Folk Thought from Slavery to Freedom* (New York: Oxford University Press, 1977), especially 208–17; Abrahams, *Singing the Master;* Sterling Stuckey, *Slave Culture: Nationalist Theory and the Foundations of Black America* (New York: Oxford University Press, 1987), 64–66; and Kelley, *Race Rebels.* On the relationship between labor and expression in Africa, see John Miller Chernoff, *African Rhythm and African Sensibility: Aesthetics and Social Action in African Musical Idioms* (Chicago: University of Chicago Press, 1981).

34. Hurston's awareness of labor's centrality to her folk stagings is evident in her adoption of the title "Singing Steel" when she staged the revue in Chicago in 1934. Whereas titles like "The Great Day," "From Sun to Sun," and "All De Live Long Day" (the latter two of which she used between 1932 and 1933) all denoted the temporal framework of the concert's narrative, "Singing Steel" subtly shifted the focus from the passing of a day to the interplay between work and utterance. Hurston no doubt made the adjustment to appeal to spectators in the northern urban working-class center who were more sensitized to labor issues. Indeed, more so than in any other location, Chicago reviewers depicted the railroad worker as the protagonist of the entire production, declaring the revue to be "a remarkable revelation of the laborer's heart and mind" and running headlines such as "'Singing Steel' Is Folklore of Negro Toilers." "Zora Hurston's 'Singing Steel' for Chicago," clipping, UFL; Charles Collins, "'Singing Steel' Is Folklore of Negro Toilers."

35. Hurston, *Mules and Men*, 141.

36. Hurston, "Spirituals and Neo-Spirituals," 82.

37. Hurston, *Mules and Men*, 249.

38. Sundquist, *The Hammers of Creation*, 72, 74.

39. Hurston, "Spirituals and Neo-Spirituals," 81–82.

40. Hurston, *Mules and Men,* 146; Hurston, in *Go Gator,* 170–71.

41. Hurston, in *Go Gator,* 165.

42. Malone, *Steppin' on the Blues,* 27.

43. In what appears to be Hurston's earliest draft of the concert, the children's games opened the revue, suggesting that she originally intended to stage the progression of these rhythmic skills from their earliest incarnation to their adult manifestation. Hurston, "In the Beginning," typescript.

44. Hurston, "Characteristics of Negro Expression," 56.

45. Hurston, "From Sun to Sun," typescript.

46. Hurston, in *Go Gator,* 175–76.

47. Hurston, *Mules and Men,* 269; Hurston, "From Sun to Sun," typescript; Hurston, in *Go Gator,* 163.

48. See Nathaniel Mackey, "From Noun to Verb," *Representations* 39 (Summer 1992): 51–70, for an insightful discussion of what he terms "othering," the privileging of variation in Hurston's work.

49. Hurston, "Spirituals and Neo-Spirituals," 83.

50. Hurston, "The Sanctified Church," repr. in *The Sanctified Church* (Berkeley, Calif.: Turtle Island, 1981), 103–4.

51. Davis, *I Got the Word in Me,* 30–31. Davis cites Hurston's discussion of religious worship to support his contention that a unified aesthetics underlies African American expressive practices (36).

52. Hurston, "Spirituals and Neo-Spirituals," 81.

53. See Amiri Baraka [formerly LeRoi Jones], *Black Music* (New York: Quill, 1967), 180–211.

54. *New York Sun,* 8 January 1932, 36.

55. Carby, "The Politics of Fiction, Anthropology, and the Folk," 31. Emphasis in the original.

56. Hurston, *Mules and Men,* 264.

57. "Announcing 'Great Day,'" program announcement, Beinecke.

58. Hurston, "Characteristics of Negro Expression," 62–63.

59. Richards, "Writing the Absent Potential," 76–77.

60. Interestingly, Hurston's autobiographical account of *The Great Day* gives the impression that the Fire Dance rather than the "Deep River" spiritual terminated the concert. Speaking of the Caribbean cycle, she writes, "It was good it was the last thing, for nothing could have followed it" (*Dust Tracks,* 284). In all of Hurston's subsequent stagings of the revue, nothing did follow the Fire Dance.

61. Although Hurston's initial trip to the Bahamas was made without the approval of her white patron, Charlotte Osgood Mason, Alain Locke did encourage Hurston to scope out African survivals as she gathered material in the South (Hurston, *Dust Tracks,* 157). As Locke advised Hurston in a 1928 letter, "The more I think of it the more important the work becomes, especially from the point of view of the possible survivals of African traits in the pantomime

and action side of the games and stories. Do not let this side of the matter escape your attention." Locke to Hurston, 24 February 1928, MSRC.

62. Hurston, "Other Negro Folklore Influences," in *Go Gator,* 91.

63. Hurston, "Proposed Recording Expedition into the Floridas," in *Go Gator,* 66.

64. Hurston, *Dust Tracks,* 283–84.

65. Illidge, "'The Great Day' Heartily Received."

66. "Bahaman Dance," photo, *Theatre Arts Monthly* 16, no. 4 (1932): 263.

67. Hurston, *Their Eyes Were Watching God,* 133; "Announcing 'Great Day,'" program announcement, Beinecke.

68. The pantomimic bird gestures of Chick-mah-chick and the Crow Dance must have resonated with popular dance steps that derived their names and features from birds, such as the Buzzard Lope, the Turkey Trot, and the Pigeon Wing. It is worth noting, too, that another children's game that Hurston documented and at one time planned to include in her revue, called "There Stands a Bluebird," not only employed a ring formation like the Fire Dance but also required children to take turns performing solo steps in the center of the circle. Hurston, "In the Beginning," typescript; Hurston, *Mules and Men,* 267.

69. Hurston to Hughes, 15 October 1929, Beinecke.

70. See Gilroy, *The Black Atlantic;* James Clifford, "Traveling Cultures," in *Cultural Studies,* ed. Laurence Grossberg, Cary Nelson, and Paula Treichler (London: Routledge, 1992), 96–116; James Clifford, "Diasporas," in *Routes: Travel and Translation in the Late Twentieth Century* (Cambridge, Mass.: Harvard University Press, 1997), 244–77.

71. Gilroy, *The Black Atlantic,* 9.

72. Sandra Gunning, "Nancy Prince and the Politics of Mobility, Home and Diasporic (Mis)Identification," *American Quarterly* 53, no. 1 (March 2001): 33. See also Barnor Hesse's discussion of the simultaneous "cartographic" and "dispositional" vectors of diaspora formations. Barnor Hesse, "Introduction: Un/Settled Multiculturalisms," in *Un/Settled Multiculturalisms: Diasporas, Entanglements, Transruptions,* ed. Barnor Hesse (London: Zed Books, 2000), 20.

73. Gunning, "Nancy Prince," 39.

74. Hurston, "The Passing of a Day," typescript.

75. Hurston, "From Sun to Sun," typescript.

76. Hurston, "The Passing of a Day," typescript.

77. I borrow this term from Katrina Hazzard-Donald, who along with Sterling Stuckey, describes how the counterclockwise circle formation united disparate African ethnic groups transported to the Americas as slaves. Katrina Hazzard-Donald, "The Circle and the Line: Speculations on the Development of African American Vernacular Dancing," *Western Journal of Black Studies* 20, no. 1 (Spring 1996): 29; Stuckey, *Slave Culture,* especially 12. My thanks to Cheryl Wall for suggesting the importance of the circle as an enactment of diasporic harmony.

78. The Fire Dance functions as a similar marker of cultural difference in Hurston's 1937 novel *Their Eyes Were Watching God*. In the novel, the West Indians' performance provokes scorn on the part of African Americans. It is only when Janie and Tea Cake befriend the Bahamians (one of whom is named Stew Beef) in the Everglades "muck" and express an interest in their expressive practices that they hold their dances openly and without fear of ridicule. Eventually, as in *The Great Day*, "Many of the Americans learned to jump and liked it as much as the 'Saws'" (146).

79. Wall, *Women of the Harlem Renaissance*, 163. See also Cheryl A. Wall, "Response to Kimberly W. Benston's 'Performing Blackness,'" in *Afro-American Literary Studies in the 1990s*, ed. Houston A. Baker Jr. and Patricia Redmond (Chicago: University of Chicago Press, 1989), 188. In *Authentic Blackness*, J. Martin Favor questions the accuracy of Wall's contention that women have been denied participation in black folk cultural traditions (18).

80. Hurston, "From Sun to Sun," typescript. A "Pea Vine Candle Drill" also appears in Hurston's *Mules and Men*, though here it is a male, Father Watson, who leads the drill (216).

81. See, among others, Wall, *Women of the Harlem Renaissance*, 172–73; Pryse, "Zora Neale Hurston, Alice Walker and the Ancient Power of Black Women"; Houston A. Baker Jr., "Workings of the Spirit: Conjure and the Space of Black Women's Creativity," in *Workings of the Spirit: The Poetics of Afro-American Women's Writing*, 69–101; and Daphne Lamothe, "Vodou Imagery, African-American Tradition and Cultural Transformation in Zora Neale Hurston's *Their Eyes Were Watching God*," *Callaloo* 22, no. 1 (1999): 157–75. In *Women Intellectuals, Modernism, and Difference: Transatlantic Culture, 1919–1945* (Cambridge: Cambridge University Press, 1997), Alice Gambrell argues that conjure is a more ambivalent site in Hurston's writings, one that nonetheless "enables her continually to consider and reconsider the problematical status of the female 'medium'" (122–23).

82. Program, *All De Live Long Day*, 5 January 1934, Recreation Hall, Rollins College, Rollins.

83. Hurston, *Mules and Men*, 141.

84. Cheryl A. Wall, "Zora Neale Hurston: Changing Her Own Words," in *American Novelists Revisited: Essays in Feminist Criticism*, ed. Fritz Fleischmann (Boston: G. K. Hall, 1982), 378. See also Cheryl A. Wall, "*Mules and Men* and Women: Zora Neale Hurston's Strategies of Narration and Visions of Female Empowerment," *Black American Literature Forum* 23, no. 4. (Winter 1989): 661–80.

85. Interestingly, that powerful woman, Big Sweet, does appear as a character in an early draft version of the revue. See Hurston, "From Sun to Sun," typescript.

86. Deborah Plant argues that Hurston frequently "appropriated the folk preacher's voice" and sermonic form in her written work "as a vehicle to inspire spiritual rebirth as well as to incite resistance to European cultural hegemony."

See Plant, "The Folk Preacher and the Folk Sermon Form," in *Every Tub Must Sit on Its Own Bottom*, 93.

87. In *Women Intellectuals, Modernism, and Difference*, Alice Gambrell argues that for Hurston, the "vision of coalition remained the material of folkloric possibility, of shared revisionary imagining; her own position was far too isolated to allow for the actual formation of these kinds of coalitional bonds" (123). In a related vein, Leigh Anne Duck's "'Go there tuh know there'" asserts that Hurston's *Mules and Men* offers "a model of subjectivity that allows for the interaction of multiple cultural forms" and thus "provides an understanding of southern African-American culture that could enable readers to imagine transregional interaction and, accordingly, transregional political activism" (277). I am arguing that the embodied medium of theatre allowed Hurston to enact the possibility of an interactive diasporic coalition in the flesh, thereby increasing the potency of the vision. For other takes on Hurston's engagement with the black Caribbean in her written anthropological work, see John Carlos Rowe, "Opening the Gate to the Other America: The Afro-Caribbean Politics of Hurston's *Mules and Men* and *Tell My Horse*," in *Literary Culture and U.S. Imperialism: From the Revolution to World War II* (Oxford: Oxford University Press, 2000), 254–55; and Ifeoma C. K. Nwankwo, "Insider and Outsider, Black and American: Rethinking Hurston's Caribbean Ethnography," *Radical History Review* 87, no. 1 (Fall 2003): 49–77.

88. Kimberly Jaye Banks, "Representations of Vernacular Culture: Women as Culture Bearers in the Works of Claude McKay, Langston Hughes, Zora Neale Hurston, and Katherine Dunham" (PhD diss., Rutgers University, 2001), 151.

89. It is worth noting, in this regard, how much the foregoing analysis of *The Great Day* owes to a variety of recent scholarly approaches to black culture. In particular, this chapter has benefited from cultural materialist approaches, critical studies of the black vernacular, theorizations of the black diaspora, and feminist treatments of Hurston's literature. To the extent that the work of contemporary scholars helps illuminate some of the major principles animating Hurston's concert—and attests to the farsightedness and continuing relevance of Hurston's theoretical insights—it is also true that these insights were not necessarily discernible to audiences in the 1930s. Among the exemplary works of cultural materialism in black studies are Stuart Hall, "What Is This 'Black' in Black Popular Culture?" in *Black Popular Culture*, ed. Gina Dent (Seattle: Bay Press), 21–36; Kelley, *Race Rebels*; Tricia Rose, *Black Noise: Rap Music and Black Culture in Contemporary America* (Hanover, N.H.: Wesleyan University Press, 1994); and Tera Hunter, "'Dancing and Carousing the Night Away,'" in *To 'Joy My Freedom: Southern Black Women's Lives and Labors after the Civil War* (Cambridge, Mass.: Harvard University Press, 1997), 168–86. For analyses of black vernacular culture, see Baker, *Blues, Ideology, and Afro-American Literature*; Gates, *The Signifying Monkey*; Ralph Ellison, *Shadow and Act* (New York: Random House, 1964); Albert Murray, *Stomping the Blues* (New York: Da Capo

Press, 1976); Levine, *Black Culture and Black Consciousness*; Barlow, *"Looking Up at Down"*; Ogren, *The Jazz Revolution*; Peretti, *The Creation of Jazz*; Berliner, *Thinking in Jazz*; Davis, *I Got the Word in Me*; and Malone, *Steppin' on the Blues*. Influential scholarship on the black diaspora includes Gilroy, *The Black Atlantic*; Clifford, "Diasporas" and "Traveling Cultures"; Stuart Hall, "Subjects in History: Making Diasporic Identities," in *The House That Race Built: Black Americans, U.S. Terrain*, ed. Wahneema Lubiano (New York: Pantheon Books, 1997), 289–99; and Brent Hayes Edwards, *The Practice of Diaspora: Literature, Translation, and the Rise of Black Internationalism* (Cambridge, Mass.: Harvard University Press, 2003). Feminist analyses of Hurston's work are too numerous to mention, but I profited especially from Wall's *Women of the Harlem Renaissance* and *"Mules and Men* and Women," as well as from Meisenhelder's *Hitting a Straight Lick with a Crooked Stick*.

### 5. Interpreting the Fire Dance

1. Marianna Torgovnick, *Gone Primitive: Savage Intellects, Modern Lives* (Chicago: University of Chicago Press, 1990), 10.

2. Susan Hiller, ed., *The Myth of Primitivism: Perspectives on Art* (London: Routledge, 1991), 11.

3. For discussions of primitivism in a variety of early-twentieth-century milieus, see Clifford, *The Predicament of Culture*; Sieglende Lemke, *Primitivist Modernism: Black Culture and the Origins of Transatlantic Modernism* (Oxford: Oxford University Press, 1998); Torgovnick, *Gone Primitive*; Hiller, *The Myth of Primitivism*; Douglas, *Terrible Honesty*; Huggins, *Harlem Renaissance*.

4. Brent Hayes Edwards, "The Uses of Diaspora," *Social Text* 19, no. 1 (2001): 45.

5. Gilroy, *The Black Atlantic*; see also Clifford, "Diasporas." As Sandra Gunning points out in her article "Nancy Prince and the Politics of Mobility, Home and Diasporic (Mis)Identification," Gilroy was by no means the first to emphasize the transatlantic connections that shape black identity. See, for example, Édouard Glissant's *Caribbean Discourse: Selected Essays,* translated with an introduction by J. Michael Dash (Charlottesville: University Press of Virginia, 1989); Eric Sundquist's "Melville, Delany, and New World Slavery," in *To Wake the Nations: Race in the Making of American Literature* (Cambridge, Mass.: The Belknap Press of Harvard University Press, 1993); Joseph Roach, *Cities of the Dead: Circum-Atlantic Performance* (New York: Columbia University Press, 1996).

6. Harry J. Elam Jr., "The Device of Race: An Introduction," in *African American Performance and Theater History: A Critical Reader,* ed. Harry J. Elam Jr. and David Krasner (New York: Oxford University Press, 2001), 5–6.

7. I take the terms "emergent" and "residual" from Raymond Williams, whose 1977 book *Marxism and Literature* (New York: Oxford University Press) argues that at any given moment, cultures contain not only ideological elements

and forms that are dominant but also those from the past that continue to exert an influence on the present, as well as those that are newly emerging.

8. "Announcing 'Great Day,'" program announcement, Beinecke. A notice in the *New York Sun* likewise advertised that "a group from the Bahama Islands will make its first stage appearance in several primitive tribal dances." *New York Sun*, 9 January 1932, 8.

9. White, "The Great Day."

10. Ruhl, "Second Nights."

11. Illidge, "'The Great Day' Heartily Received."

12. Ruhl, "Second Nights."

13. Review of *The Great Day*, *New York Sun*, 11 January 1932, 37.

14. White, "The Great Day."

15. Hemenway, *Zora Neale Hurston*, 205–6.

16. Zora Neale Hurston, "Race Cannot Become Great Until It Recognizes Its Talent," *Washington Tribune*, 29 December 1934.

17. The National Folk Festival was the brainchild of Sarah Gertrude Knott, director of St. Louis's Dramatic League. Her goal was "to bring a cross section of the most representative folk treasures together on one festival program, to see what the story would tell of our people and our country." Sarah Gertrude Knott, "The National Folk Festival After Twelve Years," *California Folklore Quarterly* 5, no. 1 (January 1946): 84. On the folk festival movement in the United States, see Archie Green, "The National Folk Festival Association," *John Edwards Memorial Foundation Quarterly* 11 (1975): 23–32; Cantwell, *When We Were Good*; and Whisnant, *All That Is Native and Fine.*

18. Clipping, *St. Louis Globe Democrat*, 3 May 1934, Thomas Jones Collection, Fisk.

19. Ibid.

20. While the publicity announcement for *The Great Day* characterized the Crow Dance as a "primitive and exciting folk dance," Locke's program notes referred to Hurston's "three years of intimate living among the common folk in the primitive privacy of their own Negro way of life." "Announcing 'Great Day'"; program, *The Great Day.*

21. Hurston, *Dust Tracks on a Road*, 145.

22. See chapter 4 for Hurston's precise comments to Hughes.

23. Hurston to Mason, 6 January 1933 [misdated as 1932], MSRC.

24. Failing to find any way around the interdiction at Rollins College, Hurston decided to offer a subsequent, smaller-scale performance at the all-black Hungerford School in Eatonville "so that our own people may hear us." Hurston to Mason, 6 January 1933 [misdated as 1932], MSRC. If Hurston did stage portions of the revue at Hungerford, I have not been able to discover any record of the event.

25. Will Traer, "The Listening Place," *Winter Park Herald*, 26 January 1933, 5.

26. "Enthusiastic Response Is Given 'From Sun to Sun,'" *Rollins Sandspur*, 8 February 1933, 2, Rollins.

27. Program, *All De Live Long Day,* 5 January 1934, Recreation Hall, Rollins College, Rollins.

28. "Zora Hurston Gives Program," *Rollins Sandspur,* 19 January 1934, Rollins.

29. Press release, Rollins College News Service, January 1934, Rollins. Emphasis added. This description also appeared in "Folklore Revue," *Orlando Morning Sentinel,* 5 January 1934, 8.

30. Press release, Rollins College News Service, 2 January 1934, Rollins.

31. A full account of Hurston's work for the Florida Federal Writers' Project can be found in Bordelon, *Go Gator and Muddy the Water.*

32. Although there is no record of how large the audience for "The Fire Dance" was, the *Orlando Morning Sentinel* reported that "more than 2,000 people visited the National Exhibit of Skills of the Unemployed" on January 25. "WPA Display Attracts 2,000," *Orlando Morning Sentinel,* 26 January 1939, 12.

33. "WPA Writers to Present Dance," *Orlando Morning Sentinel,* 25 January 1939, 12; "WPA Display Attracts 2,000."

34. Program, *The Fire Dance,* 25 January 1939, New Auditorium, Orlando, Florida, UFL.

35. The *Sentinel* announced that "Dr. Corita Doggett Corse, State Federal Writers' director, will introduce the program," making it likely that she also served as narrator, though it is possible that Hurston performed this task herself. "WPA Writers to Present Dance."

36. Hurston, "The Fire Dance," in *Go Gator,* 153.

37. "WPA Writers to Present Dance."

38. Walter White to Hurston, 31 May 1932, NAACP Papers, Manuscript Division, LOC.

39. See René Maran, *Batouala* (1921; repr., Washington, D.C.: Black Orpheus Press, 1972).

40. White to Hurston, 31 May 1932, LOC.

41. Hurston to White, telegram, n.d., LOC.

42. Hurston to White and "Folks," n.d., LOC.

43. Both White and Hurston biographer Robert Hemenway interpreted Hurston's proposed loan as disingenuous. Certainly, White seems to have gotten an earful of grievances from Dawson in the course of retrieving Hurston's things, including claims that barefoot dancing had induced illness and allegations of insufficient payment. White to Hurston, 9 August 1932; White to Hurston, 14 March 1934, LOC. See also Hemenway, *Zora Neale Hurston,* 183–84.

44. Hurston to White and "Folks," n.d., LOC.

45. Hurston to Mason, 19 March 1932, MSRC.

46. Hurston to White and "Folks," n.d., LOC.

47. Hurston to White, 8 March 1934, LOC.

48. White to Hurston, 14 March 1934, LOC.

49. The title of Johnson's musical appears variously as *Run, Little Chillun, Run Little Chillun!,* and *Run, Little Chillun!* For consistency's sake, I will use the syntax of the original program for the production: *Run, Little Chillun!*

50. Program, *Run, Little Chillun!*, 1 March 1933, Lyric Theatre, Programs and Playbills, Schomburg.

51. Hall Johnson, *Run Little Chillun,* in *Lost Plays of the Harlem Renaissance, 1920–1940,* ed. James V. Hatch and Leo Hamilton (Detroit: Wayne State University Press, 1996), 235.

52. Ibid., 254.

53. Carl Carmer, "'Run, Little Chillun!' A Critical Review," *Opportunity* 11, no. 4 (April 1933): 13; clipping, *New York World Telegram,* 2 March 1933, Humphrey-Weidman Collection, New York Public Library [hereafter NYPL].

54. Johnson, *Run Little Chillun,* 251.

55. Ibid.

56. Fraden, *Blueprints for a Black Federal Theatre,* 169–70.

57. Two exceptions are John Martin, who recognized the Bahamian troupe from their previous performances with Hurston, and Doris Humphrey, who learned about the group's background when she was brought on to work with them. Martin, "The Dance: A Negro Play," review of *Run, Little Chillun!, New York Times,* 12 March 1933, sec. 10, p. 7; Doris Humphrey, "Bahama Fire Dance," manuscript, Doris Humphrey Collection, NYPL.

58. Vere E. Johns, "'Run, Little Chillun,'" *New York Age,* 11 March 1933, 6.

59. Hurston, "You Don't Know Us Negroes," Lawrence E. Spivak Papers, Manuscript Division, LOC.

60. Hurston, *Mules and Men,* 185.

61. L. N., "Whimper of the Jungle," *New York Times,* 27 November 1934, 26; cast information from the Internet Broadway Database, http://www.ibdb.com/production.asp?ID=9384, July 7, 2005 (Donald Heywood misidentified as Donald Heyward).

62. Arthur Ruhl, review of *Africana, New York Herald Tribune,* 28 November 1934, clipping, Harvard Theatre Collection.

63. The premature closing was due in no small part to a public disturbance on opening night that generated more press than the onstage content. Shortly after *Africana* got under way, a man named Almamy Camaro approached the orchestra pit and swung a chair at Heywood, who was conducting. Camaro claimed that he had contributed to the operetta and that Heywood had failed to credit him. Stephen Rathbun, "'Africana' Opens,' *New York Sun,* 27 November 1934, clipping, Harvard Theatre Collection; "Row Disrupts Premiere of Operetta," *New York Times,* 27 November 1934, 23.

64. Program, Dan Healy's *Cotton Club Parade,* n.d., Cotton Club, Programs and Playbills, Schomburg. The date May 1938 is handwritten on the cover of the program, but to all indications, this is inaccurate. Newspaper accounts establish that this particular program corresponds to the September 1936 production.

65. The uptown Cotton Club closed on February 16, 1936, in the face of the deepening Depression and the 1935 Harlem race riot. The downtown location, it was hoped, would provide a more amenable environment for the club. See

James Haskins, *The Cotton Club* (New York: Random House, 1977; repr., New York: New American Library, 1984).

66. As Burton Peretti has noted in regard to this whites-only customer policy, "The black players at the second Cotton Club . . . received a subtler reminder of their neominstrel status: among the only black customers ever allowed in to hear the band were the film actors Clarence Muse and Stepin Fetchit, the greatest (and wealthiest) exponents of the servile stereotypes." Peretti, *The Creation of Jazz*, 187.

67. Haskins, *The Cotton Club;* "Night Club Notes," *New York Times,* 5 September 1936, 7; "Night Club Notes," *New York Times,* 26 September 1936, 11.

68. Program, Dan Healy's *Cotton Club Parade.*

69. Marshall and Jean Stearns, *Jazz Dance,* 232.

70. Stearns, *Jazz Dance,* 277, 235; Haskins, *The Cotton Club,* 116; "Night Club Notes," *New York Times,* 5 September 1936, 7.

71. "Night Club Reviews," *Variety,* 20 September 1936, 51.

72. Haskins, *The Cotton Club,* 53.

73. "Harlem Goes Broadway—Broadway Goes Harlem," in program, Dan Healy's *Cotton Club Parade.*

74. Program, Dan Healy's *Cotton Club Parade.* Kriegsmann's name is misprinted as "Kriegsman" in the program.

75. The female dancer's costume appears to be an exact match of that seen in the *New York Amsterdam News*'s cartoon rendering of the Bahamian dancers at Lewisohn Stadium three years earlier. (See Figure 10.)

76. Leonard Reed, interview by Fred Strickler, 11 February–27 March 1997, transcript of sound recording, Dance Collection, NYPL.

77. "Harlem Goes Broadway—Broadway Goes Harlem."

78. Norma Miller, *Swingin' at the Savoy: The Memoir of a Jazz Dancer* (Philadelphia: Temple University Press, 1996), 136. I am deeply grateful to Terry Monaghan for alerting me to Motor Boat and Stew Beef's involvement in the fair.

79. In a 2007 interview, Norma Miller identified the female dancer on the far left as Tanya, the "African princess," but could not recall the name of the male dancer with her, although she maintained he was neither Motor Boat nor Stew Beef. Miller also identified the cakewalkers in the center as LeRoy and Little Bea, and the Lindy Hoppers at right as Tiny Bunch and two dwarf dancers. Personal interview with Norma Miller, 16 July 2007.

80. "New York Opens the Gates to the World of Tomorrow," *Life,* 15 May 1939, 20. An article in the *New York Amsterdam News* refers to "two lads who insist on being known only by the names of 'Motorboat' and 'Stew Beef.'" This article provides a slightly different account of the stage action. Following a swing overture, the paper reports, "the African group appears, one lad beating a tom tom while two others offer a shuffling prelude to the appearance of a scantily-clad lass whose bodily contortions are something to be remembered." "Savoy Theatre on Fair Site Is Gala Spot," *New York Amsterdam*

*News*, 3 June 1939, 3. It is unclear which lad was the drummer and who the shufflers were.

81. Miller, *Swingin' at the Savoy*, 140.

82. For a more in-depth account of the Savoy exhibit and the politics surrounding African Americans' cultural contributions to the 1939 World's Fair, see Joel Dinerstein, "Swinging the Machine: White Technology and Black Culture between the World Wars" (PhD diss., University of Texas at Austin, 2000), especially 468–83; published as Joel Dinerstein, *Swinging the Machine: Modernity, Technology, and African American Culture between the World Wars* (Amherst: University of Massachusetts Press, 2003). My sincere thanks to Joel for sharing portions of his research with me.

83. George Walker, "The Real Coon on the American Stage," *Theatre Magazine* supplement (August 1906), i–ii; quoted in Riis, ed., *The Music and Scripts of "In Dahomey,"* xx.

84. Publicity flyer, "Negro Dance Evening"; program, "Negro Dance Evening," 7 March 1937, Theresa L. Kaufmann Auditorium, Young Men's Hebrew Association, Dance Collection, NYPL.

85. Hurston, *Dust Tracks*, 172–73.

## 6. Black Authenticity, White Artistry

1. Charlotte Mason's notes to Alain Locke, 10 January 1932, MSRC.

2. Dixon Gottschild, *Digging the Africanist Presence in American Performance*.

3. Dixon Gottschild points to the visual art of Picasso and the modern dance writings of Louis Horst as instances in which Africanist influences were cast as "primitive" raw materials turned into "high art" by white artists (*Digging the Africanist Presence*, 40–41, 48).

4. Pierre Bourdieu, *The Field of Cultural Production: Essays on Art and Literature*, ed. Randal Johnson (Cambridge: Polity Press, 1993).

5. Ibid., 30.

6. Hurston to Mason, 19 March 1932, MSRC.

7. Hurston to Mason, 4 April 1932, MSRC. In her letter, Hurston refers only to a "Miss Burchenal." On the career of Elizabeth Burchenal and the significance of her work with the Girls' Branch of New York City's Public Schools Athletic League during the Progressive Era, see Linda J. Tomko, *Dancing Class*, 180–211. Given that Burchenal's notion of folk dance typically encompassed only traditional Anglo dances, her fascination with Hurston's material is especially remarkable. Burchenal also later appeared on the National Dance Congress and Festival program, in which Hurston and the Bahamian dancers were involved.

8. Program, *Mura Dehn*, 10 April 1932, Guild Theatre, Dance Collection, NYPL.

9. Shortly after the 1932 Guild recital, Dehn founded the Academy of Swing with the African choreographer Asadata Dafora to train dancers in the jazz

idiom and trace the origins of the practice. Dehn clippings, NYPL. See also Kimberly Chandler, "Moved by the Spirit: Illuminating the Voice of Mura Dehn and Her Efforts to Promote and Document Jazz Dance" (PhD diss., Temple University, 1997).

10. Announcement, *The Wise and Foolish Virgins*, Dehn clippings, NYPL.

11. John Martin, "2 Dance Recitals Full of Contrasts," *New York Times*, 11 April 1932, 18. Six years later, Hurston again used the term "chanters" to describe the group of performers she brought to the Fifth National Folk Festival in Washington, D.C. "Zora Hurston's Chanters Offer Concert Sponsored by Rollins Folk-Lore Group," *Orlando Sentinel-Star*, 1 May 1938, 4B.

12. Manning, *Modern Dance, Negro Dance*, 10, 108. In contrast to Dehn's concert, the black choir in at least one production of *How Long Brethren?* was visible to spectators (Manning, *Modern Dance, Negro Dance*, 103).

13. Clipping, *New York Herald Tribune*, 20 March 1932, NYPL.

14. "Mura Dehn Gives Dance Recital," *New York Sun*, 11 April 1932, 19.

15. Hurston to Mason, 16 April 1932, MSRC.

16. There is some discrepancy on the question of the chorus's directorship. While the recital announcement includes the statement "Speaking Chorus arranged and directed by Donald B. Brayshaw," the actual program lists Hurston alone as chorus director, with no mention of Brayshaw. Notwithstanding this disparity, Hurston's custodianship of the black performers seemed to be the salient point. Clipping, *World Telegram*, 11 April 1932, NYPL; *New York Sun*, 11 April 1932, 19; program, *Mura Dehn*, 10 April 1932, Guild Theatre, NYPL.

17. Martin, "2 Dance Recitals Full of Contrasts."

18. Mary F. Watkins, "Paul Haakon Seen at Cort in Dance Recital, Mura Dehn at the Guild," *New York Herald Tribune*, 11 April 1932, Dehn clippings, NYPL.

19. Mary F. Watkins, "The Dance," *Arts Weekly*, n.d., Dehn clippings, NYPL.

20. Clipping, *World Telegram*, 11 April 1932, NYPL. Generally understood to be dancing performed to jazz rhythms, jazz dance developed in tandem with jazz music in the early twentieth century. Like its musical counterpart, jazz dance was for the most part "popular in design and commercial in intent" and therefore not regarded as "high art." See Hill, *Brotherhood in Rhythm*, 19. The *World Telegram* invoked the Jazz Era in direct reference to the *Wise and Foolish Virgins* "ballet."

21. Adolf Dehn, letter to editor, *Arts Weekly*, May 1932, Dehn clippings, NYPL. Mr. Dehn also casts doubt on whether Watkins even saw Mura's recital, pointing out that she reviewed a concert performed concurrently with Mura Dehn's on April 10. While Watkins did review Paul Haakon's performance at the Cort Theater that same night, it is possible that she, like John Martin, attended the first half of Haakon's concert and the second half of Dehn's—in which case she may have missed *The Wise and Foolish Virgins*, which took place at the end of the first half.

22. Martin, "2 Dance Recitals Full of Contrasts."

23. In contrast to Isadora Duncan, who, as Ann Daly has argued, associated her dancing with Greek classicism to distinguish it from the "debased" practices of "African primitives," Mura Dehn did not consider the two to be antithetical and drew equally on Greek antiquity and "Negro" primitive styles as choreographic source material. Ann Daly, *Done into Dance: Isadora Duncan in America* (Bloomington: Indiana University Press, 1995), especially 217–19.

24. Dehn clippings, NYPL.

25. Karen Backstein's essay "Keeping the Spirit Alive: The Jazz Dance Testament of Mura Dehn," in *Representing Jazz*, ed. Krin Gabbard (Durham, N.C.: Duke University Press, 1995), 229–43, provides a useful discussion of the relationship between Dehn and the African American subjects of her film *The Spirit Moves*. Backstein points out that even as Dehn was attracted to the "almost utopian image of physical liberation" associated with black diasporic dance, she assumed that African Americans lacked knowledge about the cultural history of their vernacular dance forms (236, 237).

26. "A Latin-American Cabaret," *New York Times*, 17 April 1932, sec. 10, p. 8; Zora Neale Hurston, *Dust Tracks on a Road*, 159.

27. See Melanie Blood, "The Neighborhood Playhouse 1915–1927: A History and Analysis" (PhD diss., Northwestern University, 1994), and Tomko, *Dancing Class*, especially 79–136.

28. John Martin, "Dinner-Cabaret Musical Novelty," *New York Times*, 23 April 1932, 10.

29. *New York Times*, 17 April 1932, sec. 10, p. 11.

30. Locke to Mason, 14 March 1932, MSRC.

31. Hurston to Mason, 19 March 1932, MSRC.

32. Draft of letter from Mason to Hurston, 8 April 1932; Hurston to Mason, 16 April 1932, MSRC.

33. *New York Times*, 17 April 1932, sec. 10, p. 11. The reunion of Hurston and Hall Johnson for the Vanderbilt production is certainly interesting. The archive's only hint of any discord between the two (arising from their failed collaboration, discussed in chapter 3) is John Martin's mention that Johnson's singers performed earlier than originally programmed ("Dinner-Cabaret Musical Novelty").

34. The Neighborhood Playhouse served not only Russian Jews but also Italians and other turn-of-the-century European immigrants. See Blood, "The Neighborhood Playhouse."

35. "The Dancers," *New York Evening Post*, 16 April 1932, 5.

36. Tomko, *Dancing Class*, 119; Blood, "The Neighborhood Playhouse," 256–64.

37. As Melanie Blood points out, "Of a total twenty-four lyric offerings between 1915 and 1927, all but three drew on either Oriental or premodern European sources" ("The Neighborhood Playhouse," 282).

38. Ibid., 145; Tomko, *Dancing Class*, 131.

39. Martin, "The Dance: A Folk Art Trend," *New York Times*, 8 May 1932, clipping enclosed in letter from Locke to Mason, 7 May 1932, MSRC.

40. Martin distinguishes between folk dance groups like the English Folk Dance Society, whose spectacular annual festivals do not compromise its goal of attracting new members, and the "more literal folk arts," by which he presumably means non-Anglo folk idioms. The implication seems to be that non-white folk dancing is somehow more removed from and therefore more threatened by Western theatrical conventions.

41. Martin, "The Dance: A Folk Art Trend."

42. Ibid.

43. Hurston, "Spirituals and Neo-Spirituals," 80.

44. Mason to Locke, 17 April 1932, MSRC.

45. Lewis Erenberg, *Steppin' Out: New York Nightlife and the Transformation of American Culture, 1890–1920* (Westport, Conn.: Greenwood Press, 1981).

46. Mason to Locke, 7 May 1932, MSRC.

47. The review in the *Times* of *The Great Day* is unsigned but appeared alongside other music reviews. "Rare Negro Songs Given," review of *The Great Day, New York Times*, 11 January 1932, 29.

48. Program, *Run, Little Chillun!*, 1 March 1933, Lyric Theatre, Programs and Playbills, Schomburg.

49. Hatch and Hamalian, *Lost Plays of the Harlem Renaissance, 1920–1940*, 227.

50. In March of that year, Alain Locke reported to Charlotte Mason that Hurston's "singers and dancers are back under control after their escapade with Hall." Locke to Mason, 14 March 1932, MSRC.

51. See Walter White to Hurston, 14 March 1934, NAACP Papers, Manuscript Division, LOC.

52. Hurston to Mason, 11 August 1932, MSRC.

53. Hurston to White, 8 March 1934, NAACP Papers, Manuscript Division, LOC.

54. Clipping, enclosed in letter from Locke to Mason, 23 February 1933, MSRC.

55. Locke to Mason, 18 April 1933, MSRC.

56. Hurston, *Dust Tracks*, 284.

57. Doris Humphrey, "Bahama Fire Dance," manuscript, Doris Humphrey Collection, NYPL.

58. Doris Humphrey, "Dance, Little Chillun!" *American Dancer* 6, no. 10 (July 1933): 8. Much of the language in Humphrey's handwritten piece corresponds to that of the longer article.

59. See Marcia Siegel, "Modern Dance before Bennington: Sorting It All Out," *Dance Research Journal* 19, no. 1 (Summer 1987): 3–9.

60. Humphrey to family, January–February 1933, Doris Humphrey Collection, NYPL. Why Johnson did not seek out an African American choreographer for the job remains a mystery. Humphrey was evidently the only white person involved in the *Run, Little Chillun!* production. Selma Jeanne Cohen, interview

with Charles Francis Woodford, 14, 15 November 1970, sound recording, NYPL. In a telephone interview in 2002, renowned African American artist Katherine Dunham, who choreographed a later Chicago production of *Run, Little Chillun!*, related her frustration at having been passed over by Johnson for the Broadway run. Personal interview with Katherine Dunham, 21 August 2002.

61. Humphrey to family, 1931, Doris Humphrey Collection, NYPL.

62. Hurston, "The Fire Dance," in *Go Gator and Muddy the Water*, 155.

63. John Martin, "The Dance: A Negro Play," review of *Run, Little Chillun!*, *New York Times*, 12 March 1933, sec. 10, p. 7. Martin's association of Hurston's material with a dance audience as opposed to a dramatic audience suggests that he was thinking of the production at the Vanderbilt, rather than *The Great Day*.

64. Martin, "The Dance: A Negro Play."

65. Ibid. On Winfield, Guy, and Sawyer, see Perpener, *African-American Concert Dance*.

66. Humphrey, "Dance, Little Chillun!" In fact, Humphrey expressed frustration with the time limits imposed by Johnson. As she wrote to her parents, while she found the Bahamian dancers "superb" and "the most interesting feature of the whole show," Johnson insisted that they be "cut down to nothing almost so his rather heavy and sanctimonious drama may proceed." Humphrey to family, February 1933, Doris Humphrey Collection, NYPL.

67. In an interesting counterpoint to John Martin's account, Carl Carmer's review in the black monthly *Opportunity* deemed the "aesthetic" procession that led into the Fire Dance finale utterly ineffectual. He maintained that it was only when the Bahamians finally "'let go' in primitive and savage abandon" of the instruction provided by Humphrey that the dancing became "irresistibly stirring." Carl Carmer, "'Run, Little Chillun!' A Critical Review," *Opportunity* 11, no. 4 (April 1933): 13.

68. The chronology provided at the end of Marcia Siegel's biography of Humphrey, for example, reports that she choreographed *Run, Little Chillun!* Marcia Siegel, *Days on Earth: The Dance of Doris Humphrey* (New Haven, Conn.: Yale University Press, 1987), 294. Joe Nash, too, states that Humphrey "created" the dances in Johnson's musical. See his "Pioneers in Negro Concert Dance: 1931 to 1937," 12; and his essay "Talley Beatty," in *African American Genius in Modern Dance*, ed. Gerald Myers (Durham, N.C.: American Dance Festival, 1993), 12. The chronology that Richard Long provides in *The Black Tradition in American Dance*, which is singular for its inclusion of Hurston's *Great Day* concert, also lists Humphrey as choreographer of *Run, Little Chillun!*, although Long makes the crucial addition "with Bahama Dancers" (181). Woll's *Black Musical Theatre*, however, notes that Johnson's *Run, Little Chillun!* was "indebted to the works of Zora Neale Hurston" (157).

69. "Zora Hurston Dances for Ruth St. Denis," *Rollins Sandspur*, 8 March 1933, 2, Rollins.

70. For more on Ruth St. Denis's career and early modern dance, see

Suzanne Shelton, *Divine Dancer: A Biography of Ruth St. Denis* (Garden City, N.Y.: Doubleday, 1981); Jane Desmond, "Dancing Out the Difference: Cultural Imperialism and Ruth St. Denis's *Radha* of 1906," *Signs* 17, no. 1 (Autumn 1991): 28–49; Susan Manning, "The Female Dancer and the Male Gaze: Feminist Critiques of Early Modern Dance," in *Meaning in Motion: New Cultural Studies of Dance,* ed. Jane Desmond (Durham, N.C.: Duke University Press, 1997), 153–66; Deborah Jowitt, *Time and the Dancing Image* (Berkeley and Los Angeles: University of California Press, 1988); Marcia Siegel, *The Shapes of Change: Images of American Dance* (Boston: Houghton Mifflin, 1979).

71. "Zora Hurston Dances for Ruth St. Denis."

72. Ibid.

73. Ibid.

74. Hurston to Locke, 20 March 1933, MSRC.

75. St. Denis, *Ruth St. Denis: An Unfinished Life* (New York: Harper & Brothers, 1939), 331.

76. Despite the imbalance of power that allowed St. Denis to approach Hurston but would not have allowed Hurston to solicit St. Denis, this incident marks an interesting reversal of the scene in which the young African American dancer Edna Guy waited backstage for St. Denis to offer her services to the celebrated performer over a decade earlier. See Perpener, *African-American Concert Dance,* 57.

77. These consisted of the "Crow Dance," "Dance of the Coconut Grove" (whose lyrics matched those of the "Evalina" number in *The Great Day*), "Congo" (whose lyrics matched those of "Mamma Don't Want No Peas," which Hurston presented in *From Sun to Sun* in March 1932), and "The Jumpin' Dance and the Fire Dance." Program, "Tamiris and Bahama Negro Dancers," 18 and 19 August 1933, Lewisohn Stadium, Stadium Concerts Review, Helen Tamiris Collection, NYPL.

78. As the *Evening Post* reported, "The former [Motor Boat] was born in the Bahamas twenty three years ago and was a waiter in a hotel at Nassau when he danced at a dinner given by a New Yorker who said, 'That black boy's too fast to be human; he runs as fast as a motorboat,' and he has been known as Motorboat ever since. Pearl of Nassau was born in Panama but went to the Bahamas as a baby and got her name from tourists who said, 'She moves like a black nymph in the moonlight.'" Clipping, *New York Evening Post,* 9 August 1933, Tamiris Clippings, NYPL.

79. John Martin, "Appearance of Tamiris," *New York Times,* 27 August 1933, 5, Tamiris Collection, NYPL.

80. Manning, *Modern Dance, Negro Dance,* 2, 12.

81. John Perpener notes that Tamiris's teaching may have brought her into contact with Hemsley Winfield, one of the first African Americans to push for the development of black modern dance (*African-American Concert Dance,* 41). On Tamiris's career and choreography, see Christena Schlundt, *Tamiris:*

*A Chronicle of Her Dance Career* (New York: New York Public Library, 1972); Manning, *Modern Dance, Negro Dance*, 1–2, 11–20, 101–13.

82. "Dark Wiggling," *Time*, 28 August 1933, 47, Tamiris Clippings, NYPL.

83. In her autobiography, Hurston writes, "Hall Johnson took my group to appear with his singers at the Lewisohn Stadium" during the summer following her *Great Day* concert, but while Johnson and his choir did appear at the stadium in the summer of 1932, I have discovered no evidence that the Bahamian dancers performed with him. More than likely, Hurston was thinking of the dancers' 1933 appearance with Tamiris. Hurston, *Dust Tracks*, 158.

84. "Tamiris Tonight at the Stadium," *New York Times*, 18 August 1933, Tamiris Clippings, NYPL; "Ballet at the Stadium," Lewisohn Stadium Programs, NYPL.

85. "Dark Wiggling"; program, "Stadium Concerts Review," Tamiris Collection, NYPL.

86. "Tamiris Offers Dance Program at the Stadium," unidentified clipping, Tamiris Collection, NYPL.

87. Ibid.

88. Pitts Sanborn, "Bahama Negro Dancers Delight Crowd in Stadium," *New York World Telegram*, 19 August 1933, Tamiris Clippings, NYPL.

89. Bill Chase, "Cartoonist's Conception of Bahama Dancers at Stadium," *New York Amsterdam News*, 23 August 1933, 7.

90. Interestingly, as Susan Manning has documented, in 1938, two other black newspapers, the *Pittsburgh Courier* and the *Baltimore Afro-American*, used photo essays to provide visual critiques of Tamiris's all-white casting of *How Long Brethren?* See Manning, *Modern Dance, Negro Dance*, 110–13.

91. "Tamiris and Her Group Seen in Dance Recital," 18 December 1932, unidentified clipping; John Martin, "The Dance: A Musical Experiment," *New York Times*, 19 November 1931, Tamiris Collection, NYPL.

92. Henry Beckett, "Tamiris and Negro Dancers," *New York Evening Post*, 19 August 1933, Tamiris Collection, NYPL. The archive contains no indication that reviewers detected any sexual tension in the joint appearance of a white woman and eight black men.

93. "Dancers at Stadium," unidentified clipping, Tamiris Collection, NYPL.

94. Martin, "Appearance of Tamiris."

95. Martin, "Art of Tamiris Wins Plaudits at Stadium"; Martin, "Appearance of Tamiris."

96. Martin, "Art of Tamiris Wins Plaudits at Stadium."

97. Martin, "Appearance of Tamiris."

98. See, for example, "Dark Wiggling"; "A New Low for Art," unidentified clipping, Tamiris Collection, NYPL.

99. Beckett, "Tamiris and Negro Dancers."

100. Martin, "Art of Tamiris Wins Plaudits at Stadium."

101. Susan Manning cites Martin's comments as evidence of how accepted

the convention of metaphorical minstrelsy was in 1933 (*Modern Dance, Negro Dance*, 15).

102. Although the details surrounding their representation are unknown, according to the stadium concert program, "Both Tamiris and the Bahama Negro Dancers are under the management of William C. Gassner, Steinway Hall, New York City." Program, "Tamiris and Bahama Negro Dancers."

103. Unidentified clipping, 10 December 1933, Tamiris Collection, NYPL.

104. "Irene Castle Learns New Dance," *Chicago Daily News*, 23 November 1934, 23.

105. On the popularity of the Castles, see Stearns, *Jazz Dance*, 97–98; Erenberg, *Steppin' Out*; and Susan C. Cook, "Passionless Dancing and Passionate Reform: Respectability, Modernism, and the Social Dancing of Irene and Vernon Castle," in *The Passion of Music and Dance: Body, Gender, and Sexuality*, ed. William Washabaugh (Oxford: Berg, 1998), 133–50.

106. Just a month before she chanced upon Hurston's performers, Castle attracted notice for dancing at the "Pooch Ball," a fund-raising event for the pet shelter she ran in suburban Chicago. "Time Turns Back as Irene Castle Dances Again," *Chicago Daily News*, 15 October 1934, 10; June Provines, "Front Views and Profiles," *Chicago Daily Tribune*, 11 October 1934, 17; "Irene Castle McLaughlin to Dance at 'Pooch Ball,'" *Chicago Daily News*, 12 October 1934, 16; Donna Gianell, "Irene and Vernon Castle," *Dance Pages* 2 (Fall 1992): 44–45.

107. Stearns, *Jazz Dance*, 128.

108. In an interesting counterpoint to the *Daily News*'s seeming ignorance of Castle's relationship to black vernacular dance, a cartoon that appeared in the black *Chicago Defender* several months earlier portrayed her as unable to keep up with the stylistic variations carried out by African American dancers. "Irene Castle's colored students put so many racial twists into the famous castle dances," it reads, "that Irene hardly recognized them!" Jay Jackson, "As Others See Us," *Chicago Defender*, 8 September 1934, 12.

109. "Constitution," The National Dance Congress, National Dance Congress and Festival Clippings, NYPL.

110. Program, "First National Dance Congress and Festival," 18–25 May 1936, Theresa L. Kaufmann Theatre, National Dance Congress and Festival Clippings, NYPL.

111. On the relationship between leftist culture and black theatre dancers, see Susan Manning's chapter "Dancing Left" in *Modern Dance, Negro Dance*, 57–113.

112. Hurston frequently expressed her distaste for communism, most explicitly in her June 1951 essay "Why the Negro Won't Buy Communism," published in the *American Legion Magazine*, in which she rejected what she regarded as the Communist Party's pitying attitude toward black Americans. Her much-publicized disagreement with the black communist writer Richard Wright—the two exchanged biting critiques of each other's work in 1937 and

1938—has contributed to the impression that a wide gulf stood between Hurston and those with leftist sympathies. See Richard Wright, "Between Laughter and Tears," review of *Their Eyes Were Watching God* by Zora Neale Hurston, *New Masses,* 5 October 1937, 22, 25; and Zora Neale Hurston, "Stories of Conflict," review of *Uncle Tom's Children* by Richard Wright, *Saturday Review of Literature,* 2 April 1938, 32. Yet Hurston's embrace of the folk occasionally overlapped with left-wing culture in the 1930s. In addition to her planned participation in the National Dance Congress and Festival, Hurston contributed several essays to Nancy Cunard's *Negro: An Anthology,* which supported communism as a solution to international race- and class-based oppression. For a revisionary take on the Hurston-Wright rift, see William J. Maxwell, "Black Belt/Black Folk: The End(s) of the Richard Wright-Zora Neale Hurston Debate," in *New Negro, Old Left: African-American Writing and Communism between the Wars* (New York: Columbia University Press, 1999), 153–78. On the role of the folk in Popular Front culture, see Michael Denning, *The Cultural Front,* as well as Robbie Lieberman, *"My Song Is My Weapon": People's Songs, American Communism, and the Politics of Culture, 1930–1950* (Urbana: University of Illinois Press, 1989); Robert Cantwell, *When We Were Good;* and Steven Garabedian, "Reds, Whites, and the Blues: Lawrence Gellert, 'Negro Songs of Protest,' and the Left-Wing Folk-Song Revival of the 1930s and 1940s," *American Quarterly* 57, no. 1 (2005): 179–206. Thanks to Susan Manning for calling my attention to the issue of Hurston's affiliation—and lack thereof—with leftist culture.

113. The Bahamian dancers also elicited mention during the conference session titled "Dance in a Changing World." Two separate talks, one by Mura Dehn and one by the African American dancer Lenore Cox, cited the Bahamian group's dancing as a model of "authentic" movement. Mura Dehn, "A Few Words about Jazz Dancing," and Lenore Cox, "On a Few Aspects of Negro Dancing," in *The Proceedings of the First National Dance Congress and Festival* (New York: n.p., 1936), 43–46 and 52–55, respectively. While Dehn's project was in large part to promote jazz dance as a legitimate American art form, suitable for white choreographers, Cox expressed concern with jazz's perpetuation of minstrel-era stereotypes and urged African American dancers to push beyond its confines. The fact that the Bahamian ensemble merited praise from both speakers is again suggestive of the ability of their dancing to support multiple and competing agendas.

114. "Call for Dance Congress," National Dance Congress and Festival Clippings, NYPL.

115. "Dance Congress Festival," National Dance Congress and Festival Clippings, NYPL. By all indications, the flyer did not represent a final or definitive version of the festival program, for the information it provided proved erroneous on several counts. For example, in place of the "Experimental" and "Theatre and Ballet" performance sessions listed on the flyer, the actual festival featured "Demonstration Groups" and "Theatre and Variety" evenings.

116. "The Dance," unidentified clipping (possibly *New York Sun,* 9 May 1936), National Dance Congress and Festival Clippings, NYPL.

117. Hemenway, *Zora Neale Hurston,* 218, 223, 227; Hurston to Edwin Grover, 29 December 1935, UFL. See Rena Fraden, *Blueprints for a Black Federal Theatre,* on the Negro Units of the Federal Theatre Project.

118. Hemenway, *Zora Neale Hurston,* 227.

119. John Martin, "Folk Dances Given by Five Groups," *New York Times,* 20 May 1936, 24.

120. The dances that bore the label "American" on the festival's folk program, presented by the American Folk Group, were "country" dances of European origin: square dances, contra dances, and quadrilles found in New England and the southern Appalachian mountains. Program, "First National Dance Congress and Festival." The designation "American" in the National Dance Congress and Festival's formulation thus meant *white* American. This division between Bahamian and American was a marked departure from Hurston's insistence on the presence of the Fire Dance in Florida.

121. Martin, "Folk Dances Given by Five Groups."

122. "Who's Who in the First National Dance Congress and Festival," National Dance Congress and Festival Clippings, NYPL. Dehn's time at the Savoy laid the foundation for her work with the Lindy Hoppers, but it is less apparent how she came to establish a connection with the Bahamian dancers. The archive does establish that her involvement in the National Dance Congress and Festival began very early on, for like Hurston, she signed the preliminary call to action to become a member of the Congress Joint Committee. If the two former collaborators interacted with one another before Hurston left New York, they left no record of their communication. Although Dehn never established a "Negro Ballet," she did go on to form a jazz dance company—alternately known as the Jazz Dance Theatre and Traditional Jazz Dance Company—with the African American tap artist James Berry. Dehn clippings, NYPL.

123. "Who's Who in the First National Dance Congress and Festival."

124. Program, "First National Dance Congress and Festival." This may have been the same Gabriel Brown whom Hurston recruited in Eatonville, Florida, to play guitar in her 1934 production of *All De Live Long Day.* See Coda, note 5.

125. Program, "First National Dance Congress and Festival."

126. The Congress and Festival's treatment of black dancers thus confirms Susan Manning's finding that "the patronage and critical advocacy of the leftist dance network always coexisted with assumptions that limited the participation of Negro dancers" (*Modern Dance, Negro Dance,* 59).

127. Kelley, "Notes on Deconstructing 'The Folk,'" 1402.

## Coda

1. In 1940, Hurston briefly pursued a collaboration with the renowned white playwright Paul Green on a play titled *John de Conqueror.* And in 1944,

working with a white woman named Dorothy Waring, Hurston wrote and copyrighted a script for a musical comedy called *Polk County*, which incorporated some of her *Great Day* material.

2. Hemenway, *Zora Neale Hurston*, 254–55; Boyd, *Wrapped in Rainbows*, 327, 339–41.

3. Hurston to Jean Parker Waterbury, 6 March 1952, UFL.

4. Hurston, *Dust Tracks on a Road*, 284–85.

5. Program, "First National Dance Congress and Festival"; program, *Haiti*, n.d., Lafayette Theatre, NYPL Theatre Collection; program, *Turpentine*, n.d., Lafayette Theatre, NYPL Theatre Collection. A Gabriel Brown also appears on the cast list for Orson Welles's version of *Macbeth*, which was set in Haiti and became known as the "Voodoo" *Macbeth* (http://ibdb.com/). Because the National Dance Congress and Festival occurred in the middle of *Macbeth*'s run (April through June 1936), it is by no means certain that the Bahaman dancer was the same one performing in the FTP productions. The archive yields additional information about Hurston's connections to a Gabriel Brown who appeared in her 1934 production *All De Live Long Day*. While on a research expedition with Hurston in Eatonville, Florida, Alan Lomax wrote a letter to his family reporting that "Zora had found about here a young giant of a Negro, named Gabriel Brown, whom I judge to be the most accomplished guitar player I have so far heard, especially with a knife. He doesn't have the fire or the passion of Lead Belly, but his tricks and turns and titillations on the guitar are something marvellous. He is a sweet person and quite young." Lomax to family, 22 June 1935, Hemenway files. It is distinctly possible, therefore, that Hurston was partly responsible for Brown's joining the Bahaman Dancers in New York in 1936. A 1947 letter from Hurston to her editor, Burroughs Mitchell, reveals that Hurston still had contact with Brown at that point. "If you want to hear a really good guitarist in the Negro manner," she writes, "contact Gabriel Brown, 1254½ Washington St., Asbury Park, NJ. Also ask him about picking up rattlesnakes." Hurston to Mitchell, 5 December 1947, Hemenway files.

6. Griffith evidently joined the Bahamian ensemble sometime after the 1933 *Run, Little Chillun!* engagement and therefore never performed for Hurston. Notably, *Bassa Moona* also featured Wen Talbert's choir, who had appeared in Hurston's *Great Day* concert four years earlier; Talbert then went on to direct "the first all-Negro Symphony Orchestra" for the German-born Eugene von Grona's American Negro Ballet, which debuted in New York in November 1937. "First American Negro Ballet to Make Debut Tonight," *Daily Worker*, 21 November 1937.

7. "No Native Africans Cast in New York 'Bassa Moona,'" *Afro-American Washington Final*, 2 January 1937, 11. Another *Great Day* cast member, Bruce (Mabel) Howard went on to perform in Gertrude Stein's all-black opera *Four Saints in Three Acts* in 1934, and in such Broadway productions as *Virginia* in 1937, *The Hot Mikado* (as a Singing Girl) in 1939, *The Pirate* in 1942, and *Call Me*

*Mister,* which ran from 1946 to 1948 (http://ibdb.com). Although Howard was predominantly a singer, a 1947 *Crisis* article reported that she "did folk dancing with Zora Hurston's group and had an audition with Hall Johnson." Lovell, "Democracy in a Hit Revue."

8. Hill, "The Caribbean Connection."

9. Hurston, *Dust Tracks on a Road,* 284–85.

10. Although Dafora may have choreographed *The Ostrich* in 1932—the same year as Hurston's *The Great Day*—the dance evidently had its New York premiere in 1934 (http://www.pbs.org/wnet/freetodance/timeline/timeline4. html). Charles Moore's version of the dance is available on the videorecording *Dance Black America* (State University of New York and Pennebaker Associates Inc., imprint U.S.: Pennebaker Associates, 1984; Pennington, N.J.: distributed by Dance Horizons Video, 1990).

11. The Cleo Parker Robinson Dance Ensemble reconstructs "Barrelhouse Blues" on *Free to Dance* ([videorecording] produced and directed by Madison Davis Lacy; a coproduction of the American Dance Festival and the John F. Kennedy Center for the Performing Arts in association with Thirteen/WNET New York. New York: National Black Programming Consortium, 2000).

12. See, for example, Anna Beatrice Scott's description of how her own black body served as a "regulator" of "authenticity" and the "real" in an Afro-Brazilian dance class in San Francisco in "Spectacle and Dancing Bodies that Matter: OR If it don't fit, don't force it," in *Meaning in Motion: New Cultural Studies in Dance,* ed. Jane Desmond (Durham, N.C.: Duke University Press, 1997), 266.

13. Dixon Gottschild, *The Black Dancing Body,* 7.

# Index

with authenticity, 83–86, 88, 192; in tension with patronage, 91, 112, 117, 254n35. *See also* authenticity: in tension with authorship; choreographer
Avila, Anita, 209

Backstein, Karen, 280n25
Bahamian dancers, 2–3, 216, 223–25, 227; in *Africana*, 161–62; as choreographers, 58, 89, 282n68; at the Cotton Club, 162–67, 225; dissolution of, 87, 253n11; ethnic bias against, 97–98, 137–40; at First National Dance Congress and Festival, 205–10, 225, 286n113; Hurston's recruitment of, 77, 86, 260n115; interface with modern dance, 210; at Lewisohn Stadium, 194–201, 224, 285n102; national origins of, 70, 78, 147–48, 274n8; at the New York World's Fair, 168–69, 277n80; paucity of information about, 78, 174, 195, 215, 258n77; in *Run, Little Chillun!*, 157–61, 167; "theft" of, 65, 186–188
Bahamian Fire Dance. *See* Fire Dance
Bailey, Pearl, 216
Baker, Houston, 17–18, 237n57
Baker, Josephine, 175
ballet, 56, 58, 62, 193, 195, 198, 206, 209, 210, 252n4, 288n6
*Bal Nègre* (Dunham), 170
Banks, Kimberly Jaye, 144
Baraka, Amiri, 133
Barnard College, 32
*Barrelhouse Blues* (Dunham), 217, 289n11
Barthe, Richmond, 92
*Bassa Moona* (Johnson), 216, 262n25, 288n6
*Batouala* (Maran), 155–57, 162
Beckett, Henry, 199, 200

Bendix, Regina, 20, 238n65, 241n5, 249n96
Bethel, Nicolette, 71–72
Bethune-Cookman College, 82, 224
Black Atlantic, 10, 137, 153, 171, 234n37. *See also* Gilroy, Paul
Black Bottom, 79, 134, 214
black concert dance, 7, 11, 12, 170, 217, 235n42, 253n12. *See also* modern dance: African American; Negro dance
black musical theater, 32, 35–37, 50, 123–24, 213, 247n69, 267n12. *See also* Broadway; *Fast and Furious*
Blake, Eubie, 35
Blood, Melanie, 182, 280n37
blues, 1, 18, 32, 39, 121, 122, 123, 127, 129, 134, 141, 209, 238n58, 267n9
*Blues Suite* (Ailey), 217
Boas, Franz, 32, 146, 240n82
Bordelon, Pamela, 259n103
Boulevard Theatre, 38
Bourdieu, Pierre, 174–75, 206
Boyd, Valerie, 4, 254n36
Braithwith (Braithwaite), Ruby, 207, 227. *See also* Bahamian dancers
Brayshaw, Donald B., 289n16
Broadway, 3, 23, 29, 35, 56, 66, 78, 101, 115, 162, 170, 174, 189, 213, 216, 217, 248n74; Hurston's complicity with, 27, 38, 49, 81, 82, 123; Hurston's opposition to, 7, 37, 40, 43, 45, 80, 133. *See also Africana*; black musical theater; commercialism; *Fast and Furious*; *Great Day, The*; *Run, Little Chillun!*
Brown, Gabriel, 208, 215, 227, 287n124, 288n5. *See also* Bahamian dancers
Brown, John Mason, 248n74
Brown, Lawrence, 34, 245n39
Brown, Sterling, 2, 23, 124, 229n5
Bryant, Edna, 202
Buck and Wing, 36, 50, 153, 250n114

Harlem Renaissance, 3, 6–7, 21, 30, 34, 94, 99, 185, 245n36. *See also* New Negro movement

Harrison, Julian, 164

Hartman, Saidiya, 15, 242n12

Harvey, Georgette, 81

Haskins, James, 164

Hayes, Roland, 7, 33

Hazzard-Donald, Katrina, 270n77

Hazzard-Gordon, Katrina, 238n61

Healy, Dan, 162, 163

Hemenway, Robert, 4, 6, 92, 113, 149, 230n7, 246n57, 250n106, 267n9, 275n43

Hernández, Amalia, 79

Herskovits, Melville, 67, 68, 69, 146

Hesse, Barnor, 270n72

Heyward, Dorothy and DuBose, 23, 81

Heywood, Donald, 161, 225, 236n44, 276n63

Hicks, A. B., 50

Higginbotham, Evelyn Brooks, 238n58

Hill, Errol, 236n44

Hill, Lynda, 6, 231n15

Holt, Hamilton, 81, 83

Homer, Louise, 2, 230n7

*House of Flowers* (Capote), 216

Howard, Bruce (Mabel), 77, 227, 288n7. *See also* Bahamian dancers

Howard University, 30, 99, 100, 229n5

*How Long Brethren?* (Tamiris), 176, 279n12, 284n90

Huggins, Nathan, 231n17

Hughes, Langston: correspondence with Hurston, 25, 63, 136, 150, 255n53, 264n56, 265n63; and the folk, 23, 34, 245n43; and Harlem Renaissance, 6; *Mule Bone*, 4, 31, 64, 82, 232n20; and patronage of Charlotte Osgood Mason, 92, 93, 187, 261n6; and view of Hurston, 231n15

Humphrey, Doris, 3, 174, 182, 196, 210; *The Art of Making Dances,* 61; and the folk, 23; and *Run, Little Chillun!,* 158, 185, 188–92, 224, 235n42, 276n57, 281n60, 282nn66–68

Hurston, Zora Neale: *All De Live Long Day,* 2, 50, 84, 142, 152–53, 224, 250n110, 266n3, 268n34, 287n124, 288n5; as anthropologist, 32, 88, 260n120; anticommunist views of, 206, 285n112; association with the folk, 9, 86, 88–89; background in commercial theater, 30–31, 38–42; biography, 3–4; "Campaigns Here for Negro Art in Natural State," 44; "Characteristics of Negro Expression," 10, 26, 33, 36, 61, 76, 128, 134, 143; "The Chick with One Hen," 100, 263n36; as choreographer, 53–55, 57–59, 60–62, 77–83, 89; choreographic legacy of, 216–17; *Cold Keener,* 31, 244n26; collaboration with Mura Dehn, 175–77, 179–80; collaboration with Irene Lewisohn, 180–85; collaboration with Ruth St. Denis, 192–94, 283n76; *Color Struck,* 30, 36–37, 134, 244n23; contracts with Charlotte Osgood Mason, 92, 112–13, 115, 260n2; correspondence with Alain Locke, 63, 93, 193–94, 269n61; correspondence with Mason, 38, 40, 41, 42, 78, 80, 82, 96, 97, 98, 151, 176, 186, 246n57, 253n11, 263n33, 264n45; "Dance Songs and Tales from the Bahamas," 71; descriptions of Fire Dance by, 70–76; *De Turkey and De Law,* 31; *Dust Tracks on a Road,* 5–6, 30, 58, 65–66, 85, 97, 99, 111, 138, 170, 188, 231n13,

**Anthea Kraut** is assistant professor of dance at the University of California, Riverside, where she teaches courses in dance history and theory.